Get more out of your GMAT® Official Guides!

ONLINE

Visit gmat.wiley.com to get free online access to the same questions in this guide

- Build your own practice sets based on difficulty and question type
- View performance metrics to help you focus your study
- Practice pacing and time management in exam mode

Go to gmat.wiley.com

Create an account and enter the access code on the inside front cover of this book

For customer support, please visit http://wileyactual.com/gmat/help

GMAT™

M

de

8

ne ONLY
rce of real
® questions
om past
exams

Graduate Management Admission Council®

mba.com

GMAT® OFFICIAL GUIDE 2018 VERBAL REVIEW

Published by John Wiley & Sons, Inc., Hoboken, New Jersey.

For general information on our other products and services or to obtain technical support please contact our Customer Care Department within the U.S. at (877) 762-2974, outside the U.S. at (317) 572-3993 or fax (317) 572-4002.

Wiley also publishes its books in a variety of electronic formats. Some content that appears in print may not be available in electronic books. For more information about Wiley products, please visit our Web site at www.wiley.com.

ISBN: 978-81-265-6706-5

Printed by: Sanat Printers.

10 9 8 7 6 5 4 3 2 1

Table of Contents

Dear GMAT Test-Taker,

Thank you for your interest in graduate management education. Taking the GMAT® exam lets schools know that you're serious about your graduate business education. By using the *Official Guide* to prepare for the GMAT, you're taking a very important step toward achieving your goals and pursuing admission to a high-quality business school or master's program.

This book, *GMAT® Official Guide 2018 Verbal Review*, is designed to help you prepare for and build confidence to do your best on the GMAT exam. It's the only guide of its kind on the market that includes real GMAT exam questions published by the Graduate Management Admission Council (GMAC), the makers of the exam.

GMAC was founded by the world's leading business schools in 1953. The GMAT exam was developed to help people who aspire to careers in management demonstrate their command of the skills needed for success in the classroom. Schools use and trust the GMAT exam as part of their admissions process because it's an excellent predictor of classroom success and your ability to excel in your chosen program.

Today more than 6,500 graduate programs around the world use the GMAT exam to establish their MBA, graduate-level management degrees and specialized programs as hallmarks of excellence. Nine out of 10 new MBA enrollments at Top 50 US full-time MBA programs are made using a GMAT score.

These facts make us proud and drive us to keep improving the GMAT as well as play a role in helping you find and gain admission to the best school or program for you. We're committed to ensuring that no talent goes undiscovered, and that more people around the world can pursue opportunities in graduate management education.

I applaud your commitment to educational success, and I know that this book and the other Official GMAT preparation materials available at mba.com will give you the confidence to achieve your personal best on the GMAT exam and launch or reinvigorate a rewarding career.

I wish you the best success on all your educational and professional endeavors in the future.

Sincerely,

Sangeet Chowfla
CEO of the Graduate Management Admission Council

GMAT® Official Guide 2018
Verbal Review

1.0 What Is the GMAT® Exam?

1.0 What Is the GMAT® Exam?

The Graduate Management Admission Test® (GMAT®) exam is a standardized exam used in admissions decisions by more than 6,500 graduate management programs worldwide. It helps you gauge, and demonstrate to schools, your academic potential for success in graduate-level management studies.

The four-part exam measures your Analytical Writing, Verbal, Quantitative, and Integrated Reasoning skills—higher-order reasoning skills that management faculty worldwide have identified as important for incoming students to have. "Higher-order" reasoning skills involve complex judgments, and include critical thinking, analysis, and problem solving. Unlike undergraduate grades and curricula, which vary in their meaning across regions and institutions, your GMAT scores provide a standardized, statistically valid and reliable measure of how you are likely to perform academically in the core curriculum of a graduate management program. The GMAT exam's validity, fairness, and value in admissions have been well-established through numerous academic studies.

The GMAT exam is delivered entirely in English and solely on computer. It is not a test of business knowledge, subject matter mastery, English vocabulary, or advanced computational skills. The GMAT exam also does not measure other factors related to success in graduate management study, such as job experience, leadership ability, motivation, and interpersonal skills. Your GMAT score is intended to be used as one admissions criterion among other, more subjective, criteria, such as admissions essays and interviews.

1.1 Why Take the GMAT® Exam?

Launched in 1954 by a group of nine business schools to provide a uniform measure of the academic skills needed to succeed in their programs, the GMAT exam is now used by more than 6,500 graduate management programs at approximately 2,100 institutions worldwide.

Taking the GMAT exam helps you stand out in the admissions process and demonstrate your readiness and commitment to pursuing graduate management education. Schools use GMAT scores to help them select the most qualified applicants—because they know that candidates who take the GMAT exam are serious about earning a graduate business degree, and it's a proven predictor of a student's ability to succeed in his or her chosen program. When you consider which programs to apply to, you can look at a school's use of the GMAT exam as one indicator of quality. Schools that use the GMAT exam typically list score ranges or average scores in their class profiles, so you may also find these profiles helpful in gauging the academic competitiveness of a program you are considering and how well your performance on the exam compares with that of the students enrolled in the program.

No matter how you perform on the GMAT exam, you should contact the schools that interest you to learn more and to ask how they use GMAT scores and other criteria (such as your undergraduate grades, essays, and letters of recommendation) in their admissions processes. School

Myth -vs- FACT

M – **If I don't achieve a high score on the GMAT, I won't get into my top choice schools.**

F – There are great schools available for candidates at any GMAT score range.

Fewer than 50 of the more than 250,000 people taking the GMAT exam each year get a perfect score of 800; and many more get into top business school programs around the world each year. Admissions officers use GMAT scores as one component in their admissions decisions, in conjunction with undergraduate records, application essays, interviews, letters of recommendation, and other information when deciding whom to accept into their programs. Visit School Finder on mba.com to learn about schools that are the best fit for you.

admissions offices, web sites, and materials published by schools are the key sources of information when you are doing research about where you might want to go to business school.

For more information on the GMAT, test preparation materials, registration, how to use and send your GMAT scores to schools, and applying to business school, please visit mba.com.

1.2 GMAT® Exam Format

The GMAT exam consists of four separately timed sections (see the table on the next page). For the Analytical Writing Assessment (AWA) essay prompt, you will have 30 minutes to type your essay on a computer keyboard. The 30-minute Integrated Reasoning section features 12 question prompts in four different formats. There are two 75-minute, multiple-choice sections: the Quantitative section, with 37 questions, and the Verbal section, with 41 questions.

The Verbal and Quantitative sections of the GMAT exam are computer adaptive, which means that the test draws from a large bank of questions to tailor itself to your ability level, and you won't get many questions that are too hard or too easy for you. The first question will be of medium difficulty. As you answer each question, the computer scores your answer and uses it—as well as your responses to any preceding questions—to select the next question.

Computer-adaptive tests become more difficult the more questions you answer correctly, but if you get a question that seems easier than the last one, it does not necessarily mean you answered the last question incorrectly. The test has to cover a range of content, both in the type of question asked and the subject matter presented.

Because the computer uses your answers to select your next questions, you may not skip questions or go back and change your answer to a previous question. If you don't know the answer to a question, try to eliminate as many choices as possible, then select the answer you think is best.

Myth -vs- FACT

M – **Getting an easier question means I answered the last one wrong.**

F – **You should not become distracted by the difficulty level of a question.**

Most people are not skilled at estimating question difficulty, so don't worry when taking the test or waste valuable time trying to determine the difficulty of the question you are answering.

To ensure that everyone receives the same content, the test selects a specific number of questions of each type. The test may call for your next problem to be a relatively hard data sufficiency question involving arithmetic operations. But, if there are no more relatively difficult data sufficiency questions involving arithmetic, you might be given an easier question.

Though the individual questions are different, the content mixture is the same for every GMAT exam. Your score is determined by the difficulty and statistical characteristics of the questions you answer as well as the number of questions you answer correctly. By adapting to each test-taker, the GMAT exam is able to accurately and efficiently gauge skill levels over a full range of abilities, from very high to very low.

The test includes the types of questions found in this book and in the online Integrated Reasoning component, but the format and presentation of the questions are different on the computer. When you take the test:

- Only one question or question prompt at a time is presented on the computer screen.
- The answer choices for the multiple-choice questions will be preceded by circles, rather than by letters.
- Different question types appear in random order in the multiple choice and Integrated Reasoning sections.
- You must select your answer using the computer.
- You must choose an answer and confirm your choice before moving on to the next question.
- You may not go back to previous screens to change answers to previous questions.

Format of the GMAT® Exam

	Questions	Timing
Analytical Writing Analysis of an Argument	1	30 min.
Integrated Reasoning Multi-Source Reasoning Table Analysis Graphics Interpretation Two-Part Analysis	12	30 min.
Optional break		up to 8 min.
Quantitative Problem Solving Data Sufficiency	37	75 min.
Optional break		up to 8 min.
Verbal Reading Comprehension Critical Reasoning Sentence Correction	41	75 min.
	Total Time:	210 min.

1.3 What Is the Content of the Exam Like?

The GMAT exam measures higher-order analytical skills encompassing several types of reasoning. The Analytical Writing Assessment asks you to analyze the reasoning behind an argument and respond in writing; the Integrated Reasoning section asks you to interpret and synthesize information from multiple sources and in different formats to make reasoned conclusions; the Quantitative section asks you to reason quantitatively using basic arithmetic, algebra, and geometry; and the Verbal section asks you to read and comprehend written material and to reason and evaluate arguments.

Test questions may address a variety of subjects, but all of the information you need to answer the questions will be included on the exam, with no outside knowledge of the subject matter necessary. The GMAT exam is not a test of business knowledge, English vocabulary, or advanced computational skills. You will need to read and write in English and have basic math and English skills to perform well on the test, but its difficulty comes from the English analytical and critical thinking abilities.

The questions in this book are organized by question type and from easiest to most difficult, but keep in mind that when you take the test, you may see different types of questions in any order within each section.

1.4 Integrated Reasoning

The Integrated Reasoning section highlights the relevant skills that business managers in today's data-driven world need in order to analyze sophisticated streams of data and solve complex problems. It measures your ability to understand and evaluate multiple sources and types of information—graphic, numeric, and verbal—as they relate to one another; use both quantitative and verbal reasoning to solve complex problems; and solve multiple problems in relation to one another.

Four types of questions are used in the Integrated Reasoning section:

- Multi-Source Reasoning
- Table Analysis
- Graphics Interpretation
- Two-Part Analysis

Integrated Reasoning questions may be quantitative, verbal, or a combination of both. You will have to interpret graphics and sort tables to extract meaning from data, but advanced statistical knowledge and spreadsheet manipulation skills are not necessary. You will have access to an online calculator with basic functions for the Integrated Reasoning section, but note that the calculator is not available on the Quantitative section.

1.5 Quantitative Section

The GMAT Quantitative section measures your ability to reason quantitatively, solve quantitative problems, and interpret graphic data.

Two types of multiple-choice questions are used in the Quantitative section:

- Problem Solving
- Data Sufficiency

Both are intermingled throughout the Quantitative section, and require basic knowledge of arithmetic, elementary algebra, and commonly known concepts of geometry.

To review the basic mathematical concepts that will be tested in the GMAT Quantitative questions and for test-taking tips specific to the question types in the Quantitative section of the GMAT exam, sample questions, and answer explanations, see *GMAT® Official Guide 2018* or *GMAT® Official Guide 2018 Quantitative Review*; both are available for purchase at mba.com.

1.6 Verbal Section

The GMAT Verbal section measures your ability to read and comprehend written material, to reason and evaluate arguments, and to correct written material to conform to standard written English. Because the Verbal section includes reading sections from several different content areas, you may be generally familiar with some of the material; however, neither the reading passages nor the questions assume detailed knowledge of the topics discussed.

Three types of multiple-choice questions are used in the Verbal section:

- Reading Comprehension
- Critical Reasoning
- Sentence Correction

All three require basic knowledge of the English language, but the Verbal section is not a test of advanced vocabulary.

For test-taking tips specific to each question type in the Verbal section, sample questions, and answer explanations, see chapters 3 through 5.

1.7 Analytical Writing Assessment

The Analytical Writing Assessment (AWA) consists of one 30-minute writing task: Analysis of an Argument. The AWA measures your ability to think critically, communicate your ideas, and formulate an appropriate and constructive critique. You will type your essay on a computer keyboard.

1.8 What Computer Skills Will I Need?

The GMAT exam requires only computer skills. You will type your AWA essay on the computer keyboard using standard word-processing keystrokes. In the Integrated Reasoning and multiple-choice sections, you will select your responses using either your computer mouse or the keyboard. The Integrated Reasoning section includes basic computer navigation and functions, such as clicking on tabs and using drop-down menus to sort tables and select answers.

1.9 What Are the Test Centers Like?

The GMAT exam is administered under standardized conditions at test centers worldwide. Each test center has a proctored testing room with individual computer workstations that allow you to sit for the exam under quiet conditions and with some privacy. You will be able to take two optional 8-minute breaks during the course of the exam. You may not take notes or scratch paper with you into the testing room, but an erasable notepad and marker will be provided for you to use during the test.

1.10 How Are Scores Calculated?

Verbal and Quantitative sections are scored on a scale of 0 to 60, with scores below 6 or above 51 extremely rare. The Total GMAT score ranges from 200 to 800 and is based on your performance in these two sections. Your score is determined by:

- The number of questions you answer
- The number of questions you answer correctly or incorrectly
- The level of difficulty and other statistical characteristics of each question

Your Verbal, Quantitative, and Total GMAT scores are determined by a complex mathematical procedure that takes into account the difficulty of the questions that were presented to you and how you answered them. When you answer the easier questions correctly, you get a chance to answer harder questions, making it possible to earn a higher score. After you have completed all the questions on the test, or when your time is expired, the computer will calculate your scores. Your scores on the Verbal and Quantitative sections are combined to produce your Total score which ranges from 200 to 800 in 10 point increments.

The Analytical Writing Assessment consists of one writing task, Analysis of an Argument, and your essay will be scored two times independently. Essays are evaluated by college and university faculty members from a variety of disciplines, including management education, who rate the overall quality of your critical thinking and writing. (For details on how readers are qualified, visit mba.com.) In addition, your response may be scored by an automated scoring program designed to reflect the judgment of expert readers.

Your essay is scored on a scale of 0 to 6, in half point increments, with 6 being the highest score and 0 the lowest. A score of zero is given for responses that are off topic, are in a foreign language, merely attempt to copy the topic, consist only of keystroke characters, or are blank. Your AWA score is typically the average of two independent ratings. If the independent scores vary by more than one point, a third reader adjudicates, but because of ongoing training and monitoring, discrepancies are rare.

Your Integrated Reasoning score is calculated on a scale of 1 to 8, in one-point increments. You must answer all parts of a single question correctly in order to receive credit. No partial credit is given. Like your AWA score, your Integrated Reasoning score will not count toward your Total score.

Your Analytical Writing Assessment and Integrated Reasoning scores are computed and reported separately from the other sections of the test and have no effect on your Verbal, Quantitative, or Total scores. The schools that you have designated to receive your scores may receive a copy of your Analytical Writing Assessment essay with your score report. Your own copy of your score report will not include your essay.

Your GMAT score includes a percentile ranking that compares your skill level with other test-takers from the past three years. The percentile rank of your score shows the percentage of tests taken with scores lower than your score. Every July, percentile ranking tables are updated. Visit mba.com to view the most recent percentile rankings tables.

1.11 Test Development Process

The GMAT exam is developed by experts who use standardized procedures to ensure high-quality, widely-appropriate test material. All questions are subjected to independent reviews and are revised or discarded as necessary. Multiple-choice questions are tested during GMAT test administrations. Analytical Writing Assessment tasks are tested on mba.com registrants and then assessed for their fairness and reliability. For more information on test development, visit mba.com.

2.0 How to Prepare

2.0 How to Prepare

2.1 How Can I Best Prepare to Take the Test?

The GMAT® exam is designed specifically to measure reasoning skills needed for management education, and the test contains several question formats unique to the GMAT exam. At a minimum, you should be familiar with the test format and the question formats before you sit for the test. Because the GMAT exam is a timed exam, you should practice answering test questions not only to better understand the question formats and the skills they require, but also to help you learn to pace yourself so you can finish each section when you sit for the exam.

Because the exam measures reasoning rather than subject matter knowledge, you most likely will not find it helpful to memorize facts. You do not need to study advanced mathematical concepts, but you should be sure your grasp of basic arithmetic, algebra, and geometry is sound enough that you can use these skills in quantitative problem solving. Likewise, you do not need to study advanced vocabulary words, but you should have a firm understanding of basic English vocabulary and grammar for reading, writing, and reasoning.

This book and other study materials released by the Graduate Management Admission Council (GMAC) are the ONLY source of questions that have been retired from the GMAT exam. All questions that appear or have appeared on the GMAT exam are copyrighted and owned by GMAC, which does not license them to be reprinted elsewhere. Accessing live Integrated Reasoning, Quantitative, or Verbal test questions in advance or sharing test content during or after you take the test is a serious violation, which could cause your scores to be canceled and schools to be notified. In cases of a serious violation, you may be banned from future testing and other legal remedies may be pursued.

Myth -vs- FACT

M – **You need very advanced math skills to get a high GMAT score.**

F – **The GMAT measures your reasoning and critical thinking abilities, rather than your advanced math skills.**

The GMAT exam only requires basic quantitative analytic skills. You should review the math skills (algebra, geometry, basic arithmetic) presented in the *GMAT® Official Guide 2018* and the *GMAT® Official Guide Quantitative Review 2018*, but the required skill level is low. The difficulty of GMAT Quantitative questions stems from the logic and analysis used to solve the problems and not the underlying math skills.

2.2 What About Practice Tests?

The Quantitative and Verbal sections of the GMAT exam are computer-adaptive, and the Integrated Reasoning section includes questions that require you to use the computer to sort tables and navigate to different sources of information. Our official practice materials will help you get comfortable with the format of the test and better prepare for exam day. Two full-length GMAT practice exams are available at no charge for those who have created an account on mba.com. The practice exams include computer-adaptive Quantitative and Verbal sections, plus additional practice questions, information about the test, and tutorials to help you become familiar with how the GMAT exam will appear on the computer screen at the test center.

To maximize your studying efforts with the free practice exams, you should leverage official practice materials as you start to prepare for the test. Take one practice test to familiarize yourself with the exam and to get a baseline score. After you have studied using this book and other study materials, take the second practice test to determine whether you need to shift your focus to other areas you need to strengthen. Note that the free practice tests may include questions that are also published in this book. As your test day approaches, consider taking more official practice tests to help measure your progress and give you a better idea of how you might score on exam day.

2.3 Where Can I Get Additional Practice?

If you complete all the questions in this guide and think you would like additional practice, you may want to purchase the *GMAT® Official Guide 2018* and/or *GMAT® Official Guide 2018 Quantitative Review*. You can find these guides as well as even more Quantitative, Verbal, and Integrated Reasoning practice questions, full-length, computer-adaptive practice exams, and other helpful study materials at mba.com.

2.4 General Test-Taking Suggestions

Specific test-taking strategies for individual question types are presented later in this book. The following are general suggestions to help you perform your best on the test.

1. Use your time wisely

Although the GMAT exam stresses accuracy more than speed, it is important to use your time wisely. On average, you will have about 1¾ minutes for each Verbal question, about 2 minutes for each Quantitative question, and about 2½ minutes for each Integrated Reasoning question, some of which have multiple questions. Once you start the test, an onscreen clock will continuously count the time you have left. You can hide this display if you want, but it is a good idea to check the clock periodically to monitor your progress. The clock will automatically alert you when 5 minutes remain in the allotted time for the section you are working on.

2. Answer practice questions ahead of time

After you become generally familiar with all question types, use the sample questions in this book to prepare for the actual test. It may be useful to time yourself as you answer the practice questions to get an idea of how long you will have for each question during the actual GMAT exam as well as to determine whether you are answering quickly enough to complete the test in the time allotted.

3. Read all test directions carefully

The directions explain exactly what is required to answer each question type. If you read hastily, you may miss important instructions and impact your ability to answer correctly. To review directions during the test, click on the Help icon. But be aware that the time you spend reviewing directions will count against the time allotted for that section of the test.

4. Read each question carefully and thoroughly

Before you answer a multiple-choice question, determine exactly what is being asked, then eliminate the wrong answers and select the best choice. Never skim a question or the possible answers; skimming may cause you to miss important information or nuances.

5. Do not spend too much time on any one question

If you do not know the correct answer, or if the question is too time consuming, try to eliminate choices you know are wrong, select the best of the remaining answer choices, and move on to the next question. Not completing sections and randomly guessing answers to questions at the end of each test section can significantly lower your score. As long as you have worked on each section, you will receive a score even if you do not finish one or more sections in the allotted time. But you will not earn points for questions you never get to see.

6. Confirm your answers ONLY when you are ready to move on

On the Quantitative and Verbal sections, once you have selected your answer to a multiple-choice question, you will be asked to confirm it. Once you confirm your response, you cannot go back and change it. You may not skip questions. In the Integrated Reasoning section, there may be several questions based on information provided in the same question prompt. When there is more than one response on a single screen, you can change your response to any of the questions on the screen before moving on to the next screen. However, you may not navigate back to a previous screen to change any responses.

7. Plan your essay answers before you begin to write

The best way to approach the Analysis of an Argument section is to read the directions carefully, take a few minutes to think about the question, and plan a response before you begin writing. Take time to organize your ideas and develop them fully, but leave time to reread your response and make any revisions that you think would improve it.

Myth -vs- FACT

M – It is more important to respond correctly to the test questions than it is to finish the test.

F – There is a significant penalty for not completing the GMAT exam.

Pacing is important. If you are stumped by a question, give it your best guess and move on. If you guess incorrectly, the computer program will likely give you an easier question, which you are likely to answer correctly, and the computer will rapidly return to giving you questions matched to your ability. If you don't finish the test, your score will be reduced. Failing to answer five verbal questions, for example, could reduce your score from the 91st percentile to the 77th percentile.

Myth -vs- FACT

M – The first 10 questions are critical and you should invest the most time on those.

F – All questions count.

The computer-adaptive testing algorithm uses each answered question to obtain an *initial* estimate. However, as you continue to answer questions, the algorithm self-corrects by computing an updated estimate on the basis of all the questions you have answered, and then administers items that are closely matched to this new estimate of your ability. Your final score is based on all your responses and considers the difficulty of all the questions you answered. Taking additional time on the first 10 questions will not game the system and can hurt your ability to finish the test.

3.0 Reading Comprehension

3.0 Reading Comprehension

Reading comprehension questions appear in the Verbal section of the GMAT® exam. The Verbal section uses multiple-choice questions to measure your ability to read and comprehend written material, to reason and evaluate arguments, and to correct written material to conform to standard written English. Because the Verbal section includes content from a variety of topics, you may be generally familiar with some of the material; however, neither the passages nor the questions assume knowledge of the topics discussed. Reading comprehension questions are intermingled with critical reasoning and sentence correction questions throughout the Verbal section of the test.

You will have 75 minutes to complete the Verbal section, or an average of about 1¾ minutes to answer each question. Keep in mind you will need time to read the written passages—and that time is not factored into the 1¾ minute average. Therefore, you should plan to proceed more quickly through the reading comprehension questions in order to give yourself enough time to read the passages thoroughly.

Reading comprehension questions begin with written passages up to 350 words long. The passages discuss topics from the social sciences, humanities, the physical or biological sciences, and such business-related fields as marketing, economics, and human resource management. The passages are accompanied by questions that will ask you to interpret the passage, apply the information you gather from the reading, and make inferences (or informed assumptions) based on the reading. For these questions, you will see a split computer screen. The written passage will remain visible on the left side as each question associated with that passage appears, in turn, on the right side. You will see only one question at a time. However, the number of questions associated with each passage may vary.

As you move through the reading comprehension sample questions, try to determine a process that works best for you. You might begin by reading a passage carefully and thoroughly. Some test-takers prefer to skim the passages the first time through, or even to read the first question before reading the passage. You may want to reread any sentences that present complicated ideas or introduce terms that are new to you. Read each question and series of answers carefully. Make sure you understand exactly what the question is asking and what the answer choices are.

If you need to, you may go back to the passage and read any parts that are relevant to answering the question. Specific portions of the passages may be indicated in the related questions.

The following pages describe what reading comprehension questions are designed to measure, present the directions that will precede questions of this type, and describe the various question types. This chapter also provides test-taking strategies, sample questions, and detailed explanations of all the questions. The explanations further illustrate the ways in which reading comprehension questions evaluate basic reading skills.

3.1 What Is Measured

Reading comprehension questions measure your ability to understand, analyze, and apply information and concepts presented in written form. All questions are to be answered on the basis of what is stated or implied in the reading material, and no specific prior knowledge of the material is required.

The GMAT reading comprehension questions evaluate your ability to do the following:

- **Understand words and statements.**
  Although the questions do not test your vocabulary (they will not ask you to define terms), they do test your ability to interpret special meanings of terms as they are used in the reading passages. The questions will also test your understanding of the English language. These questions may ask about the overall meaning of a passage.
- **Understand logical relationships between points and concepts.**
  This type of question may ask you to determine the strong and weak points of an argument or evaluate the relative importance of arguments and ideas in a passage.
- **Draw inferences from facts and statements.**
  The inference questions will ask you to consider factual statements or information presented in a reading passage and reach conclusions on the basis of that information.
- **Understand and follow the development of quantitative concepts as they are presented in written material.**
  This may involve the interpretation of numerical data or the use of simple arithmetic to reach conclusions about material in a passage.

There are six kinds of reading comprehension questions, each of which tests a different skill. The reading comprehension questions ask about the following areas:

Main idea

Each passage is a unified whole—that is, the individual sentences and paragraphs support and develop one main idea or central point. Sometimes you will be told the central point in the passage itself, and sometimes it will be necessary for you to determine the central point from the overall organization or development of the passage. You may be asked in this kind of question to

- recognize a correct restatement, or paraphrasing, of the main idea of a passage
- identify the author's primary purpose or objective in writing the passage
- assign a title that summarizes, briefly and pointedly, the main idea developed in the passage

Supporting ideas

These questions measure your ability to comprehend the supporting ideas in a passage and differentiate them from the main idea. The questions also measure your ability to differentiate ideas that are *explicitly stated* in a passage from ideas that are *implied* by the author but are not explicitly stated. You may be asked about

- facts cited in a passage
- the specific content of arguments presented by the author in support of his or her views
- descriptive details used to support or elaborate on the main idea

Whereas questions about the main idea ask you to determine the meaning of a passage *as a whole*, questions about supporting ideas ask you to determine the meanings of individual sentences and paragraphs that *contribute* to the meaning of the passage as a whole. In other words, these questions ask for the main point of *one small part* of the passage.

Inferences

These questions ask about ideas that are not explicitly stated in a passage but are *implied* by the author. Unlike questions about supporting details, which ask about information that is directly stated in a passage, inference questions ask about ideas or meanings that must be inferred from information that is directly stated. Authors can make their points in indirect ways, suggesting ideas without actually stating them. Inference questions measure your ability to understand an author's intended meaning in parts of a passage where the meaning is only suggested. These questions do not ask about meanings or implications that are remote from the passage; rather, they ask about meanings that are developed indirectly or implications that are specifically suggested by the author.

To answer these questions, you may have to

- logically take statements made by the author one step beyond their literal meanings
- recognize an alternative interpretation of a statement made by the author
- identify the intended meaning of a word used figuratively in a passage

If a passage explicitly states an effect, for example, you may be asked to infer its cause. If the author compares two phenomena, you may be asked to infer the basis for the comparison. You may be asked to infer the characteristics of an old policy from an explicit description of a new one. When you read a passage, you should concentrate not only on the explicit meaning of the author's words, but also on the more subtle meaning implied by those words.

Applying information to a context outside the passage itself

These questions measure your ability to discern the relationships between situations or ideas presented by the author and other situations or ideas that might parallel those in the passage. In this kind of question, you may be asked to

- identify a hypothetical situation that is comparable to a situation presented in the passage
- select an example that is similar to an example provided in the passage
- apply ideas given in the passage to a situation not mentioned by the author
- recognize ideas that the author would probably agree or disagree with on the basis of statements made in the passage

Unlike inference questions, application questions use ideas or situations *not* taken from the passage. Ideas and situations given in a question are *like* those given in the passage, and they parallel ideas and situations in the passage; therefore, to answer the question, you must do more than recall what you read. You must recognize the essential attributes of ideas and situations presented in the passage when they appear in different words and in an entirely new context.

Logical structure

These questions require you to analyze and evaluate the organization and logic of a passage. They may ask you

- how a passage is constructed—for instance, does it define, compare or contrast, present a new idea, or refute an idea?
- how the author persuades readers to accept his or her assertions
- the reason behind the author's use of any particular supporting detail
- to identify assumptions that the author is making
- to assess the strengths and weaknesses of the author's arguments
- to recognize appropriate counterarguments

These questions measure your ability not only to comprehend a passage but also to evaluate it critically. However, it is important for you to realize that logical structure questions do not rely on any kind of formal logic, nor do they require you to be familiar with specific terms of logic or argumentation. You can answer these questions using only the information in the passage and careful reasoning.

About the style and tone

Style and tone questions ask about the expression of a passage and about the ideas in a passage that may be expressed through its diction—the author's choice of words. You may be asked to deduce the author's attitude to an idea, a fact, or a situation from the words that he or she uses to describe it. You may also be asked to select a word that accurately describes the tone of a passage—for instance, "critical," "questioning," "objective," or "enthusiastic."

To answer this type of question, you will have to consider the language of the passage as a whole. It takes more than one pointed, critical word to make the tone of an entire passage "critical." Sometimes, style and tone questions ask what audience the passage was probably intended for or what type of publication it probably appeared in. Style and tone questions may apply to one small part of the passage or to the passage as a whole. To answer them, you must ask yourself what meanings are contained in the words of a passage beyond the literal meanings. Did the author use certain words because of their emotional content, or because a particular audience would expect to hear them? Remember, these questions measure your ability to discern meaning expressed by the author through his or her choice of words.

3.2 Test-Taking Strategies

1. **Do not expect to be completely familiar with any of the material presented in reading comprehension passages.**
   You may find some passages easier to understand than others, but all passages are designed to present a challenge. If you have some familiarity with the material presented in a passage, do not let this knowledge influence your choice of answers to the questions. Answer all questions on the basis of what is *stated or implied* in the passage itself.

2. **Analyze each passage carefully, because the questions require you to have a specific and detailed understanding of the material.**
   You may find it easier to do the analysis first before moving to the questions. You may find that you prefer to skim the passage the first time and read more carefully once you understand what a question asks. You may even want to read the question before reading the passage. You should choose the method most suitable for you.

3. **Focus on key words and phrases, and make every effort to avoid losing the sense of what is discussed in the passage.**

   Keep the following in mind:

   - Note how each fact relates to an idea or an argument.
   - Note where the passage moves from one idea to the next.
   - Separate main ideas from supporting ideas.
   - Determine what conclusions are reached and why.

4. **Read the questions carefully, making certain that you understand what is asked.**
   An answer choice that accurately restates information in the passage may be incorrect if it does not answer the question. If you need to, refer back to the passage for clarification.

5. **Read all the choices carefully.**
   Never assume that you have selected the best answer without first reading all the choices.

6. **Select the choice that answers the question best in terms of the information given in the passage.**
   Do not rely on outside knowledge of the material to help you answer the questions.

7. **Remember that comprehension—not speed—is the critical success factor when it comes to reading comprehension questions.**

3.3 The Directions

These are the directions that you will see for reading comprehension questions when you take the GMAT exam. If you read them carefully and understand them clearly before going to sit for the test, you will not need to spend too much time reviewing them once you are at the test center and the test is under way.

The questions in this group are based on the content of a passage. After reading the passage, choose the best answer to each question. Answer all questions following the passage on the basis of what is *stated or implied in the passage.*

3.4 Sample Questions

Each of the reading comprehension questions is based on the content of a passage. After reading the passage, answer all questions pertaining to it on the basis of what is stated or implied in the passage. For each question, select the best answer of the choices given.

Human beings, born with a drive to explore and experiment, thrive on learning. Unfortunately, corporations are oriented predominantly toward controlling employees, not fostering their learning. Ironically, this orientation creates the very conditions that predestine employees to mediocre performances. Over time, superior performance requires superior learning, because long-term corporate survival depends on continually exploring new business and organizational opportunities that can create new sources of growth.

To survive in the future, corporations must become "learning organizations," enterprises that are constantly able to adapt and expand their capabilities. To accomplish this, corporations must change how they view employees. The traditional view that a single charismatic leader should set the corporation's direction and make key decisions is rooted in an individualistic worldview. In an increasingly interdependent world, such a view is no longer viable. In learning organizations, thinking and acting are integrated at all job levels. Corporate leadership is shared, and leaders become designers, teachers, and stewards, roles requiring new skills: the ability to build shared vision, to reveal and challenge prevailing mental models, and to foster broader, more integrated patterns of thinking. In short, leaders in learning organizations are responsible for building organizations in which employees are continually learning new skills and expanding their capabilities to shape their future.

Questions 1–4 refer to the passage.

1. According to the passage, traditional corporate leaders differ from leaders in learning organizations in that the former

   (A) encourage employees to concentrate on developing a wide range of skills
   (B) enable employees to recognize and confront dominant corporate models and to develop alternative models
   (C) make important policy decisions alone and then require employees in the corporation to abide by those decisions
   (D) instill confidence in employees because of their willingness to make risky decisions and accept their consequences
   (E) are concerned with offering employees frequent advice and career guidance

2. Which of the following best describes employee behavior encouraged within learning organizations, as such organizations are described in the passage?

   (A) Carefully defining one's job description and taking care to avoid deviations from it
   (B) Designing mentoring programs that train new employees to follow procedures that have been used for many years
   (C) Concentrating one's efforts on mastering one aspect of a complicated task
   (D) Studying an organizational problem, preparing a report, and submitting it to a corporate leader for approval
   (E) Analyzing a problem related to productivity, making a decision about a solution, and implementing that solution

3. According to the author of the passage, corporate leaders of the future should do which of the following?

   (A) They should encourage employees to put long-term goals ahead of short-term profits.
   (B) They should exercise more control over employees in order to constrain production costs.
   (C) They should redefine incentives for employees' performance improvement.
   (D) They should provide employees with opportunities to gain new skills and expand their capabilities.
   (E) They should promote individual managers who are committed to established company policies.

4. The primary purpose of the passage is to

   (A) endorse a traditional corporate structure
   (B) introduce a new approach to corporate leadership and evaluate criticisms of it
   (C) explain competing theories about management practices and reconcile them
   (D) contrast two typical corporate organizational structures
   (E) propose an alternative to a common corporate approach

Structural unemployment—the unemployment that remains even at the peak of the economy's upswings—is caused by an imbalance between the types and locations of available employment on the one hand and the qualifications and locations of workers on the other hand. When such an imbalance exists, both labor shortages and unemployment may occur, despite a balance between supply and demand for labor in the economy as a whole.

Because technological change is likely to displace some workers, it is a major factor in producing structural unemployment. While technological advance almost invariably results in shifts in demands for different types of workers, it does not necessarily result in unemployment. Relatively small or gradual changes in demand are likely to cause little unemployment. In the individual firm or even in the labor market as a whole, normal attrition may be sufficient to reduce the size of the work force in the affected occupations. Relatively large or rapid changes, however, can cause serious problems. Workers may lose their jobs and find themselves without the skills necessary to obtain new jobs. Whether this displacement leads to structural unemployment depends on the amount of public and private sector resources devoted to retraining and placing those workers. Workers can be encouraged to move where there are jobs, to reeducate or retrain themselves, or to retire. In addition, other factors affecting structural unemployment, such as capital movement, can be controlled.

Increased structural unemployment, should it occur, makes it difficult for the economy to achieve desired low rates of unemployment along with low rates of inflation. If there is a growing pool of workers who lack the necessary skills for the available jobs, increases in total labor demand will rapidly generate shortages of qualified workers. As the wages of those workers are bid up, labor costs, and thus prices, rise. This phenomenon may be an important factor in the rising trend, observed for the past two decades, of unemployment combined with inflation. Government policy has placed a priority on reducing inflation, but these efforts have nevertheless caused unemployment to increase.

Questions 5–10 refer to the passage.

5. All of the following are mentioned as ways of controlling the magnitude of structural unemployment EXCEPT

   (A) using public funds to create jobs
   (B) teaching new skills to displaced workers
   (C) allowing displaced workers to retire
   (D) controlling the movement of capital
   (E) encouraging workers to move to where jobs are available

6. The passage suggests that a potential outcome of higher structural unemployment is

   (A) increased public spending for social services
   (B) placement of workers in jobs for which they are not qualified
   (C) higher wages for those workers who have skills that are in demand
   (D) an increase in the length of time jobs remain unfilled
   (E) a shift in the government's economic policy priorities

7. It can be inferred from the passage that even when there are unemployed workers, labor shortages are still likely to occur if

(A) the inflation rate is unusually high
(B) there is insufficient technological innovation
(C) the level of structural unemployment is exceptionally low
(D) the jobs available in certain places require skills that the labor force in those areas lacks
(E) the workers in some industries are dissatisfied with the pay offered in those industries

8. The passage suggests that the phenomenon of combined unemployment and inflation is

(A) a socioeconomic problem that can only be addressed by government intervention
(B) a socioeconomic problem that can be characteristic of periods of structural unemployment
(C) an economic problem that results from government intervention in management-labor relations
(D) an economic problem that results from imperfect applications of technology
(E) an economic problem that can be eliminated by relatively small changes in the labor force

9. The passage is primarily concerned with

(A) clarifying the definition of a concept
(B) proposing a way to eliminate an undesirable condition
(C) discussing the sources and consequences of a problem
(D) suggesting ways to alleviate the effects of a particular social policy
(E) evaluating the steps that have been taken to correct an imbalance

10. According to the passage, small downward shifts in the demand for labor will not usually cause unemployment because

(A) such shifts are frequently accompanied by upswings in the economy
(B) such shifts usually occur slowly
(C) workers can be encouraged to move to where there are jobs
(D) normal attrition is often sufficient to reduce the size of the work force
(E) workers are usually flexible enough to learn new skills and switch to new jobs

The Gross Domestic Product (GDP), which measures the dollar value of finished goods and services produced by an economy during a given period, serves as the chief indicator of the economic well-being of the United States. The GDP assumes that the economic significance of goods and services lies solely in their price, and that these goods and services add to the national well-being, not because of any intrinsic value they may possess, but simply because they were produced and bought. Additionally, only those goods and services involved in monetary transactions are included in the GDP. Thus, the GDP ignores the economic utility of such things as a clean environment and cohesive families and communities. It is therefore not merely coincidental, since national policies in capitalist and noncapitalist countries alike are dependent on indicators such as the GDP, that both the environment and the social structure have been eroded in recent decades. Not only does the GDP mask this erosion, it can actually portray it as an economic gain: an oil spill off a coastal region "adds" to the GDP because it generates commercial activity. In short, the nation's central measure of economic well-being works like a calculating machine that adds but cannot subtract.

Questions 11–16 refer to the passage.

11. The primary purpose of the passage is to

    (A) identify ways in which the GDP could be modified so that it would serve as a more accurate indicator of the economic well-being of the United States

    (B) suggest that the GDP, in spite of certain shortcomings, is still the most reliable indicator of the economic well-being of the United States

    (C) examine crucial shortcomings of the GDP as an indicator of the economic well-being of the United States

    (D) argue that the growth of the United States economy in recent decades has diminished the effectiveness of the GDP as an indicator of the nation's economic well-being

    (E) discuss how the GDP came to be used as the primary indicator of the economic well-being of the United States

12. Which of the following best describes the function of the second sentence of the passage in the context of the passage as a whole?

    (A) It describes an assumption about the GDP that is defended in the course of the passage.

    (B) It contributes to a discussion of the origins of the GDP.

    (C) It clarifies a common misconception about the use of the GDP.

    (D) It identifies a major flaw in the GDP.

    (E) It suggests a revision to the method of calculating the GDP.

13. It can be inferred that the author of the passage would agree with which of the following about the "economic significance" of those goods and services that are included in the GDP?

(A) It is a comprehensive indicator of a nation's economic well-being.
(B) It is not accurately captured by the price of those goods and services.
(C) It is usually less than the intrinsic value of those goods and services.
(D) It is more difficult to calculate than the economic significance of those goods and services that are not included in the GDP.
(E) It is calculated differently in capitalist countries than in noncapitalist countries.

14. The comparison of the GDP to a calculating machine serves to do which of the following?

(A) Refute an assertion that the calculations involved in the GDP are relatively complex in nature
(B) Indicate that the GDP is better suited to record certain types of monetary transactions than others
(C) Suggest that it is likely that the GDP will be supplanted by other, more sophisticated economic indicators
(D) Illustrate the point that the GDP has no way of measuring the destructive impact of such things as oil spills on the nation's economic well-being
(E) Exemplify an assertion that the GDP tends to exaggerate the amount of commercial activity generated by such things as oil spills

15. The passage implies that national policies that rely heavily on economic indicators such as the GDP tend to

(A) become increasingly capitalistic in nature
(B) disregard the economic importance of environmental and social factors that do not involve monetary transactions
(C) overestimate the amount of commercial activity generated by environmental disasters
(D) overestimate the economic significance of cohesive families and communities
(E) assume that the economic significance of goods and services does not lie solely in the price of those goods and services

16. It can be inferred that the author of the passage would agree with which of the following assessments of the GDP as an indicator of the economic well-being of the United States?

(A) It masks social and environmental erosion more fully than the chief economic indicators of other nations.
(B) It is based on inaccurate estimations of the prices of many goods and services.
(C) It overestimates the amount of commercial activity that is generated in the United States.
(D) It is conducive to error because it conflates distinct types of economic activity.
(E) It does not take into account the economic utility of certain environmental and social conditions.

In 1971 researchers hoping to predict earthquakes in the short term by identifying precursory phenomena (those that occur a few days before large quakes but not otherwise) turned their attention to changes in seismic waves that had been detected prior to earthquakes. An explanation for such changes was offered by "dilatancy theory," based on a well-known phenomenon observed in rocks in the laboratory: as stress builds, microfractures in rock close, decreasing the rock's volume. But as stress continues to increase, the rock begins to crack and expand in volume, allowing groundwater to seep in, weakening the rock. According to this theory, such effects could lead to several precursory phenomena in the field, including a change in the velocity of seismic waves, and an increase in small, nearby tremors.

Researchers initially reported success in identifying these possible precursors, but subsequent analyses of their data proved disheartening. Seismic waves with unusual velocities were recorded before some earthquakes, but while the historical record confirms that most large earthquakes are preceded by minor tremors, these foreshocks indicate nothing about the magnitude of an impending quake and are indistinguishable from other minor tremors that occur without large earthquakes.

In the 1980s, some researchers turned their efforts from short-term to long-term prediction. Noting that earthquakes tend to occur repeatedly in certain regions, Lindh and Baker attempted to identify patterns of recurrence, or earthquake cycles, on which to base predictions. In a study of earthquake-prone sites along the San Andreas Fault, they determined that quakes occurred at intervals of approximately 22 years near one site and concluded that there was a 95 percent probability of an earthquake in that area by 1992. The earthquake did not occur within the time frame predicted, however.

Evidence against the kind of regular earthquake cycles that Lindh and Baker tried to establish has come from a relatively new field, paleoseismology. Paleoseismologists have unearthed and dated geological features such as fault scarps that were caused by earthquakes thousands of years ago. They have determined that the average interval between ten earthquakes that took place at one site along the San Andreas Fault in the past two millennia was 132 years, but individual intervals ranged greatly, from 44 to 332 years.

Questions 17–22 refer to the passage.

17. The passage is primarily concerned with

(A) explaining why one method of earthquake prediction has proven more practicable than an alternative method

(B) suggesting that accurate earthquake forecasting must combine elements of long-term and short-term prediction

(C) challenging the usefulness of dilatancy theory for explaining the occurrence of precursory phenomena

(D) discussing the deficiency of two methods by which researchers have attempted to predict the occurrence of earthquakes

(E) describing the development of methods for establishing patterns in the occurrence of past earthquakes

18. According to the passage, laboratory evidence concerning the effects of stress on rocks might help account for

(A) differences in magnitude among earthquakes
(B) certain phenomena that occur prior to earthquakes
(C) variations in the intervals between earthquakes in a particular area
(D) differences in the frequency with which earthquakes occur in various areas
(E) the unreliability of short-term earthquake predictions

19. It can be inferred from the passage that one problem with using precursory phenomena to predict earthquakes is that minor tremors

(A) typically occur some distance from the sites of the large earthquakes that follow them
(B) are directly linked to the mechanisms that cause earthquakes
(C) are difficult to distinguish from major tremors
(D) have proven difficult to measure accurately
(E) are not always followed by large earthquakes

20. According to the passage, some researchers based their research about long-term earthquake prediction on which of the following facts?

(A) The historical record confirms that most earthquakes have been preceded by minor tremors.
(B) The average interval between earthquakes in one region of the San Andreas Fault is 132 years.
(C) Some regions tend to be the site of numerous earthquakes over the course of many years.
(D) Changes in the volume of rock can occur as a result of building stress and can lead to the weakening of rock.
(E) Paleoseismologists have been able to unearth and date geological features caused by past earthquakes.

21. The passage suggests which of the following about the paleoseismologists' findings described in lines 42–50?

(A) They suggest that the frequency with which earthquakes occurred at a particular site decreased significantly over the past two millennia.
(B) They suggest that paleoseismologists may someday be able to make reasonably accurate long-term earthquake predictions.
(C) They suggest that researchers may someday be able to determine which past occurrences of minor tremors were actually followed by large earthquakes.
(D) They suggest that the recurrence of earthquakes in earthquake-prone sites is too irregular to serve as a basis for earthquake prediction.
(E) They indicate that researchers attempting to develop long-term methods of earthquake prediction have overlooked important evidence concerning the causes of earthquakes.

22. The author implies which of the following about the ability of the researchers mentioned in line 18 to predict earthquakes?

(A) They can identify when an earthquake is likely to occur but not how large it will be.
(B) They can identify the regions where earthquakes are likely to occur but not when they will occur.
(C) They are unable to determine either the time or the place that earthquakes are likely to occur.
(D) They are likely to be more accurate at short-term earthquake prediction than at long-term earthquake prediction.
(E) They can determine the regions where earthquakes have occurred in the past but not the regions where they are likely to occur in the future.

A key decision required of advertising managers is whether a "hard-sell" or "soft-sell" strategy is appropriate for a specific target market. The hard-sell approach involves the use of direct, forceful claims regarding the benefits of the advertised brand over competitors' offerings. In contrast, the soft-sell approach involves the use of advertising claims that imply superiority more subtly.

One positive aspect of the hard-sell approach is its use of very simple and straightforward product claims presented as explicit conclusions, with little room for confusion regarding the advertiser's message. However, some consumers may resent being told what to believe and some may distrust the message. Resentment and distrust often lead to counterargumentation and to boomerang effects where consumers come to believe conclusions diametrically opposed to conclusions endorsed in advertising claims. By contrast, the risk of boomerang effects is greatly reduced with soft-sell approaches. One way to implement the soft-sell approach is to provide information that implies the main conclusions the advertiser wants the consumer to draw, but leave the conclusions themselves unstated. Because consumers are invited to make up their own minds, implicit conclusions reduce the risk of resentment, distrust, and counterargumentation.

Recent research on consumer memory and judgment suggests another advantage of implicit conclusions. Beliefs or conclusions that are self-generated are more accessible from memory than beliefs from conclusions provided explicitly by other individuals, and thus have a greater impact on judgment and decision making. Moreover, self-generated beliefs are often perceived as more accurate and valid than the beliefs of others, because other individuals may be perceived as less knowledgeable, or may be perceived as manipulative or deliberately misleading.

Despite these advantages, implicit conclusions may not always be more effective than explicit conclusions. One risk is that some consumers may fail to draw their own conclusions and thus miss the point of the message. Inferential activity is likely only when consumers are motivated and able to engage in effortful cognitive processes. Another risk is that some consumers may draw conclusions other than the one intended. Even if inferential activity is likely there is no guarantee that consumers will follow the path provided by the advertiser. Finally, a third risk is that consumers may infer the intended conclusion but question the validity of their inference.

Questions 23–29 refer to the passage.

23. It can be inferred from the passage that one reason an advertiser might prefer a hard-sell approach to a soft-sell approach is that

(A) the risks of boomerang effects are minimized when the conclusions an advertiser wants the consumer to draw are themselves left unstated

(B) counterargumentation is likely from consumers who fail to draw their own conclusions regarding an advertising claim

(C) inferential activity is likely to occur even if consumers perceive themselves to be more knowledgeable than the individuals presenting product claims

(D) research on consumer memory suggests that the explicit conclusions provided by an advertiser using the hard-sell approach have a significant impact on decision making

(E) the information presented by an advertiser using the soft-sell approach may imply different conclusions to different consumers

24. Each of the following is mentioned in the passage as a characteristic of the hard-sell approach EXCEPT:

(A) Its overall message is readily grasped.
(B) It appeals to consumers' knowledge about the product.
(C) It makes explicit claims that the advertised brand is superior to other brands.
(D) It uses statements that are expressed very clearly.
(E) It makes claims in the form of direct conclusions.

25. It can be inferred from the passage that advertisers could reduce one of the risks discussed in the last paragraph if they were able to provide

(A) motivation for consumers to think about the advertisement's message
(B) information that implies the advertiser's intended conclusion but leaves that conclusion unstated
(C) subtle evidence that the advertised product is superior to that of competitors
(D) information comparing the advertised product with its competitors
(E) opportunity for consumers to generate their own beliefs or conclusions

26. The primary purpose of the passage is to

(A) point out the risks involved in the use of a particular advertising strategy
(B) make a case for the superiority of one advertising strategy over another
(C) illustrate the ways in which two advertising strategies may be implemented
(D) present the advantages and disadvantages of two advertising strategies
(E) contrast the types of target markets for which two advertising strategies are appropriate

27. Which of the following best describes the function of the sentence in lines 25–28 in the context of the passage as a whole?

(A) It reiterates a distinction between two advertising strategies that is made in the first paragraph.
(B) It explains how a particular strategy avoids a drawback described earlier in the paragraph.
(C) It suggests that a risk described earlier in the paragraph is less serious than some researchers believe it to be.
(D) It outlines why the strategy described in the previous sentence involves certain risks for an advertiser.
(E) It introduces an argument that will be refuted in the following paragraph.

28. It can be inferred from the passage that one situation in which the boomerang effect often occurs is when consumers

(A) have been exposed to forceful claims that are diametrically opposed to those in an advertiser's message
(B) have previous self-generated beliefs or conclusions that are readily accessible from memory
(C) are subjected to advertising messages that are targeted at specific markets to which those consumers do not belong
(D) are confused regarding the point of the advertiser's message
(E) come to view the advertiser's message with suspicion

29. It can be inferred from the passage that the research mentioned in line 29 supports which of the following statements?

(A) Implicit conclusions are more likely to capture accurately the point of the advertiser's message than are explicit conclusions.
(B) Counterargumentation is less likely to occur if an individual's beliefs or conclusions are readily accessible from memory.
(C) The hard-sell approach results in conclusions that are more difficult for the consumer to recall than are conclusions resulting from the soft-sell approach.
(D) When the beliefs of others are presented as definite and forceful claims, they are perceived to be as accurate as self-generated beliefs.
(E) Despite the advantages of implicit conclusions, the hard-sell approach involves fewer risks for the advertiser than does the soft-sell approach.

Coral reefs are one of the most fragile, biologically complex, and diverse marine ecosystems on Earth. This ecosystem is one of the fascinating paradoxes of the biosphere: how do clear, and thus nutrient-poor, waters support such prolific and productive communities? Part of the answer lies within the tissues of the corals themselves. Symbiotic cells of algae known as zooxanthellae carry out photosynthesis using the metabolic wastes of the corals, thereby producing food for themselves, for their coral hosts, and even for other members of the reef community. This symbiotic process allows organisms in the reef community to use sparse nutrient resources efficiently.

Unfortunately for coral reefs, however, a variety of human activities are causing worldwide degradation of shallow marine habitats by adding nutrients to the water. Agriculture, slash-and-burn land clearing, sewage disposal, and manufacturing that creates waste by-products all increase nutrient loads in these waters. Typical symptoms of reef decline are destabilized herbivore populations and an increasing abundance of algae and filter-feeding animals. Declines in reef communities are consistent with observations that nutrient input is increasing in direct proportion to growing human populations, thereby threatening reef communities sensitive to subtle changes in nutrient input to their waters.

Questions 30–34 refer to the passage.

30. The passage is primarily concerned with

(A) describing the effects of human activities on algae in coral reefs

(B) explaining how human activities are posing a threat to coral reef communities

(C) discussing the process by which coral reefs deteriorate in nutrient-poor waters

(D) explaining how coral reefs produce food for themselves

(E) describing the abundance of algae and filter-feeding animals in coral reef areas

31. The passage suggests which of the following about coral reef communities?

(A) Coral reef communities may actually be more likely to thrive in waters that are relatively low in nutrients.

(B) The nutrients on which coral reef communities thrive are only found in shallow waters.

(C) Human population growth has led to changing ocean temperatures, which threatens coral reef communities.

(D) The growth of coral reef communities tends to destabilize underwater herbivore populations.

(E) Coral reef communities are more complex and diverse than most ecosystems located on dry land.

32. The author refers to "filter-feeding animals" (lines 23–24) in order to

(A) provide an example of a characteristic sign of reef deterioration

(B) explain how reef communities acquire sustenance for survival

(C) identify a factor that helps herbivore populations thrive

(D) indicate a cause of decreasing nutrient input in waters that reefs inhabit

(E) identify members of coral reef communities that rely on coral reefs for nutrients

33. According to the passage, which of the following is a factor that is threatening the survival of coral reef communities?

    (A) The waters they inhabit contain few nutrient resources.
    (B) A decline in nutrient input is disrupting their symbiotic relationship with zooxanthellae.
    (C) The degraded waters of their marine habitats have reduced their ability to carry out photosynthesis.
    (D) They are too biologically complex to survive in habitats with minimal nutrient input.
    (E) Waste by-products result in an increase in nutrient input to reef communities.

34. It can be inferred from the passage that the author describes coral reef communities as paradoxical most likely for which of the following reasons?

    (A) They are thriving even though human activities have depleted the nutrients in their environment.
    (B) They are able to survive in spite of an overabundance of algae inhabiting their waters.
    (C) They are able to survive in an environment with limited food resources.
    (D) Their metabolic wastes contribute to the degradation of the waters that they inhabit.
    (E) They are declining even when the water surrounding them remains clear.

Suppose we were in a spaceship in free fall, where objects are weightless, and wanted to know a small solid object's mass. We could not simply balance that object against another of known weight, as we would on Earth. The unknown mass could be determined, however, by placing the object on a spring scale and swinging the scale in a circle at the end of a string. The scale would measure the tension in the string, which would depend on both the speed of revolution and the mass of the object. The tension would be greater, the greater the mass or the greater the speed of revolution. From the measured tension and speed of whirling, we could determine the object's mass.

Astronomers use an analogous procedure to "weigh" double-star systems. The speed with which the two stars in a double-star system circle one another depends on the gravitational force between them, which holds the system together. This attractive force, analogous to the tension in the string, is proportional to the stars' combined mass, according to Newton's law of gravitation. By observing the time required for the stars to circle each other (the period) and measuring the distance between them, we can deduce the restraining force, and hence the masses.

Questions 35–38 refer to the passage.

35. It can be inferred from the passage that the two procedures described in the passage have which of the following in common?

    (A) They have been applied in practice.
    (B) They rely on the use of a device that measures tension.
    (C) Their purpose is to determine an unknown mass.
    (D) They can only be applied to small solid objects.
    (E) They involve attraction between objects of similar mass.

36. According to the passage, the tension in the string mentioned in lines 8–9 is analogous to which of the following aspects of a double-star system?

    (A) The speed with which one star orbits the other
    (B) The gravitational attraction between the stars
    (C) The amount of time it takes for the stars to circle one another
    (D) The distance between the two stars
    (E) The combined mass of the two stars

37. Which of the following best describes the relationship between the first and the second paragraph of the passage?

    (A) The first paragraph provides an illustration useful for understanding a procedure described in the second paragraph.
    (B) The first paragraph describes a hypothetical situation whose plausibility is tested in the second paragraph.
    (C) The first paragraph evaluates the usefulness of a procedure whose application is described further in the second paragraph.
    (D) The second paragraph provides evidence to support a claim made in the first paragraph.
    (E) The second paragraph analyzes the practical implications of a methodology proposed in the first paragraph.

38. The author of the passage mentions observations regarding the period of a double-star system as being useful for determining

(A) the distance between the two stars in the system

(B) the time it takes for each star to rotate on its axis

(C) the size of the orbit the system's two stars occupy

(D) the degree of gravitational attraction between the system's stars

(E) the speed at which the star system moves through space

In 1994, a team of scientists led by David McKay began studying the meteorite ALH84001, which had been discovered in Antarctica in 1984. Two years later, the McKay team announced that ALH84001, which scientists generally agree originated on Mars, contained compelling evidence that life once existed on Mars. This evidence includes the discovery of organic molecules in ALH84001, the first ever found in Martian rock. Organic molecules—complex, carbon-based compounds—form the basis for terrestrial life. The organic molecules found in ALH84001 are polycyclic aromatic hydrocarbons, or PAHs. When microbes die, their organic material often decays into PAHs.

Skepticism about the McKay team's claim remains, however. For example, ALH84001 has been on Earth for 13,000 years, suggesting to some scientists that its PAHs might have resulted from terrestrial contamination. However, McKay's team has demonstrated that the concentration of PAHs increases as one looks deeper into ALH84001, contrary to what one would expect from terrestrial contamination. The skeptics' strongest argument, however, is that processes unrelated to organic life can easily produce all the evidence found by McKay's team, including PAHs. For example, star formation produces PAHs. Moreover, PAHs frequently appear in other meteorites, and no one attributes their presence to life processes. Yet McKay's team notes that the particular combination of PAHs in ALH84001 is more similar to the combinations produced by decaying organisms than to those originating from nonbiological processes.

Questions 39–44 refer to the passage.

39. The primary purpose of the passage is to

(A) describe new ways of studying the possibility that life once existed on Mars

(B) revise a theory regarding the existence of life on Mars in light of new evidence

(C) reconcile conflicting viewpoints regarding the possibility that life once existed on Mars

(D) evaluate a recently proposed argument concerning the origin of ALH84001

(E) describe a controversy concerning the significance of evidence from ALH84001

40. The passage asserts which of the following about the claim that ALH84001 originated on Mars?

(A) It was initially proposed by the McKay team of scientists.

(B) It is not a matter of widespread scientific dispute.

(C) It has been questioned by some skeptics of the McKay team's work.

(D) It has been undermined by recent work on PAHs.

(E) It is incompatible with the fact that ALH84001 has been on Earth for 13,000 years.

41. The passage suggests that the fact that ALH84001 has been on Earth for 13,000 years has been used by some scientists to support which of the following claims about ALH84001?

(A) ALH84001 may not have originated on Mars.

(B) ALH84001 contains PAHs that are the result of nonbiological processes.

(C) ALH84001 may not have contained PAHs when it landed on Earth.

(D) The organic molecules found in ALH84001 are not PAHs.

(E) The organic molecules found in ALH84001 could not be the result of terrestrial contamination.

42. The passage suggests that if a meteorite contained PAHs that were the result of terrestrial contamination, then one would expect which of the following to be true?

(A) The meteorite would have been on Earth for more than 13,000 years.

(B) The meteorite would have originated from a source other than Mars.

(C) The PAHs contained in the meteorite would have originated from nonbiological processes.

(D) The meteorite would contain fewer PAHs than most other meteorites contain.

(E) The PAHs contained in the meteorite would be concentrated toward the meteorite's surface.

43. Which of the following best describes the function of the last sentence of the first paragraph?

(A) It identifies a possible organic source for the PAHs found in ALH84001.

(B) It describes a feature of PAHs that is not shared by other types of organic molecules.

(C) It explains how a characteristic common to most meteorites originates.

(D) It suggests how the terrestrial contamination of ALH84001 might have taken place.

(E) It presents evidence that undermines the claim that life once existed on Mars.

44. The passage suggests that McKay's team would agree with which of the following regarding the PAHs produced by nonorganic processes?

(A) These PAHs are not likely to be found in any meteorite that has been on Earth for 13,000 years or more.

(B) These PAHs are not likely to be found in any meteorite that originated from Mars.

(C) These PAHs are not likely to be produced by star formation.

(D) These PAHs are likely to be found in combinations that distinguish them from the PAHs produced by organic processes.

(E) These PAHs are likely to be found in fewer meteorites than the PAHs produced by organic processes.

Exactly when in the early modern era Native Americans began exchanging animal furs with Europeans for European-made goods is uncertain. What is fairly certain, even though they left no written evidence of having done so, is that the first Europeans to conduct such trade during the modern period were fishing crews working the waters around Newfoundland. Archaeologists had noticed that sixteenth-century Native American sites were strewn with iron bolts and metal pins. Only later, upon reading Nicolas Denys's 1672 account of seventeenth-century European settlements in North America, did archaeologists realize that sixteenth-century European fishing crews had dismantled and exchanged parts of their ships for furs.

By the time Europeans sailing the Atlantic coast of North America first documented the fur trade, it was apparently well underway. The first to record such trade—the captain of a Portuguese vessel sailing from Newfoundland in 1501—observed that a Native American aboard the ship wore Venetian silver earrings. Another early chronicler noted in 1524 that Native Americans living along the coast of what is now New England had become selective about European trade goods: they accepted only knives, fishhooks, and sharp metal. By the time Cartier sailed the Saint Lawrence River ten years later, Native Americans had traded with Europeans for more than thirty years, perhaps half a century.

Questions 45–53 refer to the passage.

45. The author of the passage draws conclusions about the fur trade in North America from all of the following sources EXCEPT

(A) Cartier's accounts of trading with Native Americans

(B) a seventeenth-century account of European settlements

(C) a sixteenth-century account written by a sailing vessel captain

(D) archaeological observations of sixteenth-century Native American sites

(E) a sixteenth-century account of Native Americans in what is now New England

46. The passage suggests that which of the following is partially responsible for the difficulty in establishing the precise date when the fur trade in North America began?

(A) A lack of written accounts before that of Nicolas Denys in 1672

(B) A lack of written documentation before 1501

(C) Ambiguities in the evidence from Native American sources

(D) Uncertainty about Native American trade networks

(E) Uncertainty about the origin of artifacts supposedly traded by European fishing crews for furs

47. Which of the following, if true, most strengthens the author's assertion in the first sentence of the second paragraph?

(A) When Europeans retraced Cartier's voyage in the first years of the seventeenth century, they frequently traded with Native Americans.

(B) Furs from beavers, which were plentiful in North America but nearly extinct in Europe, became extremely fashionable in Europe in the final decades of the sixteenth century.

(C) Firing arms were rarely found on sixteenth-century Native American sites or on European lists of trading goods since such arms required frequent maintenance and repair.

(D) Europeans and Native Americans had established trade protocols, such as body language assuring one another of their peaceful intentions, that antedate the earliest records of trade.

(E) During the first quarter of the sixteenth century, an Italian explorer recorded seeing many Native Americans with what appeared to be copper beads, though they may have been made of indigenous copper.

48. Which of the following best describes the primary function of lines 11–16?

(A) It offers a reconsideration of a claim made in the preceding sentence.
(B) It reveals how archaeologists arrived at an interpretation of the evidence mentioned in the preceding sentence.
(C) It shows how scholars misinterpreted the significance of certain evidence mentioned in the preceding sentence.
(D) It identifies one of the first significant accounts of seventeenth-century European settlements in North America.
(E) It explains why Denys's account of seventeenth-century European settlements is thought to be significant.

49. It can be inferred from the passage that the author would agree with which of the following statements about the fur trade between Native Americans and Europeans in the early modern era?

(A) This trade may have begun as early as the 1480s.
(B) This trade probably did not continue much beyond the 1530s.
(C) This trade was most likely at its peak in the mid-1520s.
(D) This trade probably did not begin prior to 1500.
(E) There is no written evidence of this trade prior to the seventeenth century.

50. Which of the following can be inferred from the passage about the Native Americans mentioned in line 24?

(A) They had little use for decorative objects such as earrings.
(B) They became increasingly dependent on fishing between 1501 and 1524.
(C) By 1524, only certain groups of Europeans were willing to trade with them.
(D) The selectivity of their trading choices made it difficult for them to engage in widespread trade with Europeans.
(E) The selectivity of their trading choices indicates that they had been trading with Europeans for a significant period of time prior to 1524.

51. The passage supports which of the following statements about sixteenth-century European fishing crews working the waters off Newfoundland?

(A) They wrote no accounts of their fishing voyages.
(B) They primarily sailed under the flag of Portugal.
(C) They exchanged ship parts with Native Americans for furs.
(D) They commonly traded jewelry with Native Americans for furs.
(E) They carried surplus metal implements to trade with Native Americans for furs.

52. Which of the following can be inferred from the passage about evidence pertaining to the fur trade between Native Americans and Europeans in the early modern era?

(A) A lack of written evidence has made it difficult to establish which Europeans first participated in this trade.
(B) In general, the physical evidence pertaining to this trade has been more useful than the written evidence has been.
(C) There is more written evidence pertaining to this trade from the early part of the sixteenth century than from later in that century.
(D) The earliest written evidence pertaining to this trade dates from a time when the trade was already well established.
(E) Some important pieces of evidence pertaining to this trade, such as Denys's 1672 account, were long overlooked by archaeologists.

53. The passage suggests which of the following about the sixteenth-century Native Americans who traded with Europeans on the coast of what is now called New England?

(A) By 1524 they had become accustomed to exchanging goods with Europeans.
(B) They were unfamiliar with metals before encountering Europeans.
(C) They had no practical uses for European goods other than metals and metal implements.
(D) By 1524 they had become disdainful of European traders because such traders had treated them unfairly in the past.
(E) By 1524 they demanded only the most prized European goods because they had come to realize how valuable furs were on European markets.

Determining whether a given population of animals constitutes a distinct species can be difficult because no single accepted definition of the term exists. One approach, called the biological species concept, bases the definition on reproductive compatibility. According to this view, a species is a group of animals that can mate with one another to produce fertile offspring but cannot mate successfully with members of a different group. Yet this idea can be too restrictive. First, mating between groups labeled as different species (hybridization), as often occurs in the canine family, is quite common in nature. Second, sometimes the differences between two populations might not prevent them from interbreeding, even though they are dissimilar in traits unrelated to reproduction; some biologists question whether such disparate groups should be considered a single species. A third problem with the biological species concept is that investigators cannot always determine whether two groups that live in different places are capable of interbreeding.

When the biological species concept is difficult to apply, some investigators use phenotype, an organism's observable characteristics, instead. Two groups that have evolved separately are likely to display measurable differences in many of their traits, such as skull size or width of teeth. If the distribution of measurements from one group does not overlap with those of another, the two groups might reasonably be considered distinct species.

Questions 54–57 refer to the passage.

54. The passage is primarily concerned with

(A) describing the development of the biological species concept

(B) responding to a critique of reproductive compatibility as a criterion for defining a species

(C) considering two different approaches to identifying biological species

(D) pointing out the advantage of one method of distinguishing related species

(E) identifying an obstacle to the classification of biological species

55. The author of the passage mentions "groups that live in different places" (line 21) most probably in order to

(A) point out a theoretical inconsistency in the biological species concept

(B) offer evidence in support of the biological species concept

(C) identify an obstacle to the application of the biological species concept

(D) note an instance in which phenotype classification is customarily used

(E) describe an alternative to the biological species concept

56. With which of the following statements regarding the classification of individual species would the author most likely agree?

    (A) Phenotype comparison may help to classify species when application of the biological species concept proves inconclusive.
    (B) Because no standard definition exists for what constitutes a species, the classification of animal populations is inevitably an arbitrary process.
    (C) The criteria used by biologists to classify species have not been based on adequate research.
    (D) The existence of hybrids in wild animal species is the chief factor casting doubt on the usefulness of research into reproductive compatibility as a way of classifying species.
    (E) Phenotype overlap should be used as the basic criterion for standardizing species classification.

57. Which of the following best describes the function of lines 10–13?

    (A) It elaborates the definition of the biological species concept given in a previous sentence.
    (B) It develops a point about the biological species concept made in the previous sentence.
    (C) It states the author's central point about the biological species concept.
    (D) It identifies a central assumption underlying the biological species concept.
    (E) It demonstrates why the biological species concept is invalid.

The new school of political history that emerged in the 1960's and 1970's sought to go beyond the traditional focus of political historians on leaders and government institutions by examining directly the political practices of ordinary citizens. Like the old approach, however, this new approach excluded women. The very techniques these historians used to uncover mass political behavior in the nineteenth century United States—quantitative analyses of election returns, for example—were useless in analyzing the political activities of women, who were denied the vote until 1920.

By redefining "political activity," historian Paula Baker has developed a political history that includes women. She concludes that among ordinary citizens, political activism by women in the nineteenth century prefigured trends in twentieth century politics. Defining "politics" as "any action taken to affect the course of behavior of government or of the community," Baker concludes that, while voting and holding office were restricted to men, women in the nineteenth century organized themselves into societies committed to social issues such as temperance and poverty. In other words, Baker contends, women activists were early practitioners of nonpartisan, issue-oriented politics and thus were more interested in enlisting lawmakers, regardless of their party affiliation, on behalf of certain issues than in ensuring that one party or another won an election. In the twentieth century, more men drew closer to women's ideas about politics and took up modes of issue-oriented politics that Baker sees women as having pioneered.

Questions 58–63 refer to the passage

58. The primary purpose of the passage is to

(A) enumerate reasons why both traditional scholarly methods and newer scholarly methods have limitations

(B) identify a shortcoming in a scholarly approach and describe an alternative approach

(C) provide empirical data to support a long-held scholarly assumption

(D) compare two scholarly publications on the basis of their authors' backgrounds

(E) attempt to provide a partial answer to a long-standing scholarly dilemma

59. The passage suggests which of the following concerning the techniques used by the new political historians described in the first paragraph of the passage?

(A) They involved the extensive use of the biographies of political party leaders and political theoreticians.

(B) They were conceived by political historians who were reacting against the political climates of the 1960's and 1970's.

(C) They were of more use in analyzing the positions of United States political parties in the nineteenth century than in analyzing the positions of those in the twentieth century.

(D) They were of more use in analyzing the political behavior of nineteenth-century voters than in analyzing the political activities of those who could not vote during that period.

(E) They were devised as a means of tracing the influence of nineteenth-century political trends on twentieth-century political trends.

60. It can be inferred that the author of the passage quotes Baker directly in the second paragraph primarily in order to

    (A) clarify a position before providing an alternative to that position
    (B) differentiate between a novel definition and traditional definitions
    (C) provide an example of a point agreed on by different generations of scholars
    (D) provide an example of the prose style of an important historian
    (E) amplify a definition given in the first paragraph

61. According to the passage, Paula Baker and the new political historians of the 1960's and 1970's shared which of the following?

    (A) A commitment to interest group politics
    (B) A disregard for political theory and ideology
    (C) An interest in the ways in which nineteenth-century politics prefigured contemporary politics
    (D) A reliance on such quantitative techniques as the analysis of election returns
    (E) An emphasis on the political involvement of ordinary citizens

62. Which of the following best describes the structure of the first paragraph of the passage?

    (A) Two scholarly approaches are compared, and a shortcoming common to both is identified.
    (B) Two rival schools of thought are contrasted, and a third is alluded to.
    (C) An outmoded scholarly approach is described, and a corrective approach is called for.
    (D) An argument is outlined, and counterarguments are mentioned.
    (E) A historical era is described in terms of its political trends.

63. The information in the passage suggests that a pre-1960s political historian would have been most likely to undertake which of the following studies?

    (A) An analysis of voting trends among women voters of the 1920's
    (B) A study of male voters' gradual ideological shift from party politics to issue-oriented politics
    (C) A biography of an influential nineteenth-century minister of foreign affairs
    (D) An analysis of narratives written by previously unrecognized women activists
    (E) A study of voting trends among naturalized immigrant laborers in a nineteenth-century logging camp

In a 1918 editorial, W. E. B. Du Bois advised African Americans to stop agitating for equality and to proclaim their solidarity with White Americans for the duration of the First World War. The editorial surprised many African Americans who viewed Du Bois as an uncompromising African American leader and a chief opponent of the accommodationist tactics urged by Booker T. Washington. In fact, however, Du Bois often shifted positions along the continuum between Washington and confrontationists such as William Trotter. In 1895, when Washington called on African Americans to concentrate on improving their communities instead of opposing discrimination and agitating for political rights, Du Bois praised Washington's speech. In 1903, however, Du Bois aligned himself with Trotter, Washington's militant opponent, less for ideological reasons than because Trotter had described to him Washington's efforts to silence those in the African American press who opposed Washington's positions.

Du Bois's wartime position thus reflected not a change in his long-term goals but rather a pragmatic response in the face of social pressures: government officials had threatened African American journalists with censorship if they continued to voice grievances. Furthermore, Du Bois believed that African Americans' contributions to past war efforts had brought them some legal and political advances. Du Bois's accommodationism did not last, however. Upon learning of systematic discrimination experienced by African Americans in the military, he called on them to "return fighting" from the war.

Questions 64–68 refer to the passage

64. The passage is primarily concerned with

(A) identifying historical circumstances that led Du Bois to alter his long-term goals

(B) defining "accommodationism" and showing how Du Bois used this strategy to achieve certain goals

(C) accounting for a particular position adopted by Du Bois during the First World War

(D) contesting the view that Du Bois was significantly influenced by either Washington or Trotter

(E) assessing the effectiveness of a strategy that Du Bois urged African Americans to adopt

65. The passage indicates which of the following about Du Bois's attitude toward Washington?

(A) It underwent a shift during the First World War as Du Bois became more sympathetic with Trotter's views.

(B) It underwent a shift in 1903 for reasons other than Du Bois's disagreement with Washington's accommodationist views.

(C) It underwent a shift as Du Bois made a long-term commitment to the strategy of accommodation.

(D) It remained consistently positive even though Du Bois disagreed with Washington's efforts to control the African American press.

(E) It was shaped primarily by Du Bois's appreciation of Washington's pragmatic approach to the advancement of the interests of African Americans.

66. The passage suggests which of the following about the contributions of African Americans to the United States war effort during the First World War?

    (A) The contributions were made largely in response to Du Bois's 1918 editorial.
    (B) The contributions had much the same effect as African Americans' contributions to previous wars.
    (C) The contributions did not end discrimination against African Americans in the military.
    (D) The contributions were made in protest against Trotter's confrontationist tactics.
    (E) The contributions were made primarily by civil rights activists who returned to activism after the war.

67. The author of the passage refers to Washington's call to African Americans in 1895 primarily in order to

    (A) identify Du Bois's characteristic position on the continuum between accommodationism and confrontationism
    (B) explain why Du Bois was sympathetic with Washington's views in 1895
    (C) clarify how Trotter's views differed from those of Washington in 1895
    (D) support an assertion about Du Bois's tendency to shift his political positions
    (E) dismiss the claim that Du Bois's position in his 1918 editorial was consistent with his previous views

68. According to the passage, which of the following is true of the strategy that Du Bois's 1918 editorial urged African Americans to adopt during the First World War?

    (A) It was a strategy that Du Bois had consistently rejected in the past.
    (B) It represented a compromise between Du Bois's own views and those of Trotter.
    (C) It represented a significant redefinition of the long-term goals Du Bois held prior to the war.
    (D) It was advocated by Du Bois in response to his recognition of the discrimination faced by African Americans during the war.
    (E) It was advocated by Du Bois in part because of his historical knowledge of gains African Americans had made during past wars.

The fact that superior service can generate a competitive advantage for a company does not mean that every attempt at improving service will create such an advantage. Investments in service, like those in production and distribution, must be balanced against other types of investments on the basis of direct, tangible benefits such as cost reduction and increased revenues. If a company is already effectively on a par with its competitors because it provides service that avoids a damaging reputation and keeps customers from leaving at an unacceptable rate, then investment in higher service levels may be wasted, since service is a deciding factor for customers only in extreme situations.

This truth was not apparent to managers of one regional bank, which failed to improve its competitive position despite its investment in reducing the time a customer had to wait for a teller. The bank managers did not recognize the level of customer inertia in the consumer banking industry that arises from the inconvenience of switching banks. Nor did they analyze their service improvement to determine whether it would attract new customers by producing a new standard of service that would excite customers or by proving difficult for competitors to copy. The only merit of the improvement was that it could easily be described to customers.

Questions 69–74 refer to the passage.

69. The primary purpose of the passage is to

(A) contrast possible outcomes of a type of business investment

(B) suggest more careful evaluation of a type of business investment

(C) illustrate various ways in which a type of business investment could fail to enhance revenues

(D) trace the general problems of a company to a certain type of business investment

(E) criticize the way in which managers tend to analyze the costs and benefits of business investments

70. According to the passage, investments in service are comparable to investments in production and distribution in terms of the

(A) tangibility of the benefits that they tend to confer

(B) increased revenues that they ultimately produce

(C) basis on which they need to be weighed

(D) insufficient analysis that managers devote to them

(E) degree of competitive advantage that they are likely to provide

71. The passage suggests which of the following about service provided by the regional bank prior to its investment in enhancing that service?

(A) It enabled the bank to retain customers at an acceptable rate.

(B) It threatened to weaken the bank's competitive position with respect to other regional banks.

(C) It had already been improved after having caused damage to the bank's reputation in the past.

(D) It was slightly superior to that of the bank's regional competitors.

(E) It needed to be improved to attain parity with the service provided by competing banks.

72. The passage suggests that bank managers failed to consider whether or not the service improvement mentioned in lines 18–20

(A) was too complicated to be easily described to prospective customers

(B) made a measurable change in the experiences of customers in the bank's offices

(C) could be sustained if the number of customers increased significantly

(D) was an innovation that competing banks could have imitated

(E) was adequate to bring the bank's general level of service to a level that was comparable with that of its competitors

73. The discussion of the regional bank in the second paragraph serves which of the following functions within the passage as a whole?

(A) It describes an exceptional case in which investment in service actually failed to produce a competitive advantage.

(B) It illustrates the pitfalls of choosing to invest in service at a time when investment is needed more urgently in another area.

(C) It demonstrates the kind of analysis that managers apply when they choose one kind of service investment over another.

(D) It supports the argument that investments in certain aspects of service are more advantageous than investments in other aspects of service.

(E) It provides an example of the point about investment in service made in the first paragraph.

74. The author uses the word "only" in line 27 most likely in order to

(A) highlight the oddity of the service improvement

(B) emphasize the relatively low value of the investment in service improvement

(C) distinguish the primary attribute of the service improvement from secondary attributes

(D) single out a certain merit of the service improvement from other merits

(E) point out the limited duration of the actual service improvement

Findings from several studies on corporate mergers and acquisitions during the 1970's and 1980's raise questions about why firms initiate and consummate such transactions. One study showed, for example, that acquiring firms were on average unable to maintain acquired firms' pre-merger levels of profitability. A second study concluded that post-acquisition gains to most acquiring firms were not adequate to cover the premiums paid to obtain acquired firms. A third demonstrated that, following the announcement of a prospective merger, the stock of the prospective acquiring firm tends to increase in value much less than does that of the firm for which it bids. Yet mergers and acquisitions remain common, and bidders continue to assert that their objectives are economic ones. Acquisitions may well have the desirable effect of channeling a nation's resources efficiently from less to more efficient sectors of its economy, but the individual acquisitions executives arranging these deals must see them as advancing either their own or their companies' private economic interests. It seems that factors having little to do with corporate economic interests explain acquisitions. These factors may include the incentive compensation of executives, lack of monitoring by boards of directors, and managerial error in estimating the value of firms targeted for acquisition. Alternatively, the acquisition acts of bidders may derive from modeling: a manager does what other managers do.

Questions 75–81 refer to the passage.

75. The primary purpose of the passage is to

(A) review research demonstrating the benefits of corporate mergers and acquisitions and examine some of the drawbacks that acquisition behavior entails

(B) contrast the effects of corporate mergers and acquisitions on acquiring firms and on firms that are acquired

(C) report findings that raise questions about a reason for corporate mergers and acquisitions and suggest possible alternative reasons

(D) explain changes in attitude on the part of acquiring firms toward corporate mergers and acquisitions

(E) account for a recent decline in the rate of corporate mergers and acquisitions

76. The findings cited in the passage suggest which of the following about the outcomes of corporate mergers and acquisitions with respect to acquiring firms?

(A) They include a decrease in value of many acquiring firms' stocks.

(B) They tend to be more beneficial for small firms than for large firms.

(C) They do not fulfill the professed goals of most acquiring firms.

(D) They tend to be beneficial to such firms in the long term even though apparently detrimental in the short term.

(E) They discourage many such firms from attempting to make subsequent bids and acquisitions.

77. It can be inferred from the passage that the author would be most likely to agree with which of the following statements about corporate acquisitions?

(A) Their known benefits to national economies explain their appeal to individual firms during the 1970's and 1980's.
(B) Despite their adverse impact on some firms, they are the best way to channel resources from less to more productive sectors of a nation's economy.
(C) They are as likely to occur because of poor monitoring by boards of directors as to be caused by incentive compensation for managers.
(D) They will be less prevalent in the future, since their actual effects will gain wider recognition.
(E) Factors other than economic benefit to the acquiring firm help to explain the frequency with which they occur.

78. The author of the passage mentions the effect of acquisitions on national economies most probably in order to

(A) provide an explanation for the mergers and acquisitions of the 1970's and 1980's overlooked by the findings discussed in the passage
(B) suggest that national economic interests played an important role in the mergers and acquisitions of the 1970's and 1980's
(C) support a noneconomic explanation for the mergers and acquisitions of the 1970's and 1980's that was cited earlier in the passage
(D) cite and point out the inadequacy of one possible explanation for the prevalence of mergers and acquisitions during the 1970's and 1980's
(E) explain how modeling affected the decisions made by managers involved in mergers and acquisitions during the 1970's and 1980's

79. According to the passage, during the 1970's and 1980's bidding firms differed from the firms for which they bid in that bidding firms

(A) tended to be more profitable before a merger than after a merger
(B) were more often concerned about the impact of acquisitions on national economies
(C) were run by managers whose actions were modeled on those of other managers
(D) anticipated greater economic advantages from prospective mergers
(E) experienced less of an increase in stock value when a prospective merger was announced

80. According to the passage, which of the following was true of corporate acquisitions that occurred during the 1970's and 1980's?

(A) Few of the acquisitions that firms made were subsequently divested.
(B) Most such acquisitions produced only small increases in acquired firms' levels of profitability.
(C) Most such acquisitions were based on an overestimation of the value of target firms.
(D) The gains realized by most acquiring firms did not equal the amounts expended in acquiring target firms.
(E) About half of such acquisitions led to long-term increases in the value of acquiring firms' stocks.

81. The author of the passage implies that which of the following is a possible partial explanation for acquisition behavior during the 1970's and 1980's?

(A) Managers wished to imitate other managers primarily because they saw how financially beneficial other firms' acquisitions were.
(B) Managers miscalculated the value of firms that were to be acquired.
(C) Lack of consensus within boards of directors resulted in their imposing conflicting goals on managers.
(D) Total compensation packages for managers increased during that period.
(E) The value of bidding firms' stock increased significantly when prospective mergers were announced.

In addition to conventional galaxies, the universe contains very dim galaxies that until recently went unnoticed by astronomers. Possibly as numerous as conventional galaxies, these galaxies have the same general shape and even the same approximate number of stars as a common type of conventional galaxy, the spiral, but tend to be much larger. Because these galaxies' mass is spread out over larger areas, they have far fewer stars per unit volume than do conventional galaxies. Apparently these low-surface-brightness galaxies, as they are called, take much longer than conventional galaxies to condense their primordial gas and convert it to stars—that is, they evolve much more slowly.

These galaxies may constitute an answer to the long-standing puzzle of the missing baryonic mass in the universe. Baryons—subatomic particles that are generally protons or neutrons—are the source of stellar, and therefore galactic, luminosity, and so their numbers can be estimated based on how luminous galaxies are. However, the amount of helium in the universe, as measured by spectroscopy, suggests that there are far more baryons in the universe than estimates based on galactic luminosity indicate. Astronomers have long speculated that the missing baryonic mass might eventually be discovered in intergalactic space or as some large population of galaxies that are difficult to detect.

Questions 82–88 refer to the passage.

82. According to the passage, conventional spiral galaxies differ from low-surface-brightness galaxies in which of the following ways?

(A) They have fewer stars than do low-surface-brightness galaxies.

(B) They evolve more quickly than low-surface-brightness galaxies.

(C) They are more diffuse than low-surface-brightness galaxies.

(D) They contain less helium than do low-surface-brightness galaxies.

(E) They are larger than low-surface-brightness galaxies.

83. It can be inferred from the passage that which of the following is an accurate physical description of typical low-surface-brightness galaxies?

(A) They are large spiral galaxies containing fewer stars than conventional galaxies.

(B) They are compact but very dim spiral galaxies.

(C) They are diffuse spiral galaxies that occupy a large volume of space.

(D) They are small, young spiral galaxies that contain a high proportion of primordial gas.

(E) They are large, dense spirals with low luminosity.

84. It can be inferred from the passage that the "long-standing puzzle" refers to which of the following?

(A) The difference between the rate at which conventional galaxies evolve and the rate at which low-surface-brightness galaxies evolve

(B) The discrepancy between estimates of total baryonic mass derived from measuring helium and estimates based on measuring galactic luminosity

(C) The inconsistency between the observed amount of helium in the universe and the number of stars in typical low-surface-brightness galaxies

(D) Uncertainties regarding what proportion of baryonic mass is contained in intergalactic space and what proportion in conventional galaxies

(E) Difficulties involved in detecting very distant galaxies and in investigating their luminosity

85. The author implies that low-surface-brightness galaxies could constitute an answer to the puzzle discussed in the second paragraph primarily because

(A) they contain baryonic mass that was not taken into account by researchers using galactic luminosity to estimate the number of baryons in the universe
(B) they, like conventional galaxies that contain many baryons, have evolved from massive, primordial gas clouds
(C) they may contain relatively more helium, and hence more baryons, than do galaxies whose helium content has been studied using spectroscopy
(D) they have recently been discovered to contain more baryonic mass than scientists had thought when low-surface-brightness galaxies were first observed
(E) they contain stars that are significantly more luminous than would have been predicted on the basis of initial studies of luminosity in low-surface-brightness galaxies

86. The author mentions the fact that baryons are the source of stars' luminosity primarily in order to explain

(A) how astronomers determine that some galaxies contain fewer stars per unit volume than do others
(B) how astronomers are able to calculate the total luminosity of a galaxy
(C) why astronomers can use galactic luminosity to estimate baryonic mass
(D) why astronomers' estimates of baryonic mass based on galactic luminosity are more reliable than those based on spectroscopic studies of helium
(E) how astronomers know bright galaxies contain more baryons than do dim galaxies

87. The author of the passage would be most likely to disagree with which of the following statements?

(A) Low-surface-brightness galaxies are more difficult to detect than are conventional galaxies.
(B) Low-surface-brightness galaxies are often spiral in shape.
(C) Astronomers have advanced plausible ideas about where missing baryonic mass might be found.
(D) Astronomers have devised a useful way of estimating the total baryonic mass in the universe.
(E) Astronomers have discovered a substantial amount of baryonic mass in intergalactic space.

88. The primary purpose of the passage is to

(A) describe a phenomenon and consider its scientific significance
(B) contrast two phenomena and discuss a puzzling difference between them
(C) identify a newly discovered phenomenon and explain its origins
(D) compare two classes of objects and discuss the physical properties of each
(E) discuss a discovery and point out its inconsistency with existing theory

Antonia Castañeda has utilized scholarship from women's studies and Mexican-American history to examine nineteenth-century literary portrayals of Mexican women. As Castañeda notes, scholars of women's history observe that in the United States, male novelists of the period—during which, according to these scholars, women's traditional economic role in home-based agriculture was threatened by the transition to a factory-based industrial economy—define women solely in their domestic roles of wife and mother. Castañeda finds that during the same period that saw non-Hispanic women being economically displaced by industrialization, Hispanic law in territorial California protected the economic position of "Californianas" (the Mexican women of the territory) by ensuring them property rights and inheritance rights equal to those of males.

For Castañeda, the laws explain a stereotypical plot created primarily by male, non-Hispanic novelists: the story of an ambitious non-Hispanic merchant or trader desirous of marrying an elite Californiana. These novels' favorable portrayal of such women is noteworthy, since Mexican-American historians have concluded that unflattering literary depictions of Mexicans were vital in rallying the United States public's support for the Mexican-American War (1846–1848). The importance of economic alliances forged through marriages with Californianas explains this apparent contradiction. Because of their real-life economic significance, the Californianas were portrayed more favorably than were others of the same nationality.

Questions 89–91 refer to the passage.

89. The "apparent contradiction" mentioned in line 29 refers to the discrepancy between the

(A) legal status of Mexican women in territorial California and their status in the United States

(B) unflattering depiction of Mexicans in novels and the actual public sentiment about the Mexican-American War

(C) existence of many marriages between Californianas and non-Hispanic merchants and the strictures against them expressed in novels

(D) literary depiction of elite Californianas and the literary depiction of other Mexican individuals

(E) novelistic portrayals of elite Californianas' privileged lives and the actual circumstances of those lives

90. Which of the following could best serve as an example of the kind of fictional plot discussed by Antonia Castañeda?

(A) A land speculator of English ancestry weds the daughter of a Mexican vineyard owner after the speculator has migrated to California to seek his fortune.

(B) A Californian woman of Hispanic ancestry finds that her agricultural livelihood is threatened when her husband is forced to seek work in a textile mill.

(C) A Mexican rancher who loses his land as a result of the Mexican-American War migrates to the northern United States and marries an immigrant schoolteacher.

(D) A wealthy Californiana whose father has bequeathed her all his property contends with avaricious relatives for her inheritance.

(E) A poor married couple emigrate from French Canada and gradually become wealthy as merchants in territorial California.

91. Which of the following, if true, would provide the most support for Castañeda's explanation of the "stereotypical plot" mentioned in the lines 18–19?

(A) Non-Hispanic traders found business more profitable in California while it was a territory than when it became a state.

(B) Very few marriages between Hispanic women and non-Hispanic men in nineteenth-century territorial California have actually been documented.

(C) Records from the nineteenth century indicate that some large and valuable properties were owned by elite Californianas in their own right.

(D) Unmarried non-Hispanic women in the nineteenth-century United States were sometimes able to control property in their own right.

(E) Most of the property in nineteenth-century territorial California was controlled by Hispanic men.

This passage is excerpted from material published in 1997.

Scientists have been puzzled by the seeming disparity between models of global warming based on greenhouse gas emissions and actual climatological data. In short, the world is not warming up as much as these models have predicted. In the early 1990s, Pat Michaels sought to explain this disparity, suggesting that sulfate emissions in industrial areas had a cooling effect, thus temporarily retarding global warming. Michaels later came to doubt this idea, however, pointing out that since most sulfate is emitted in the Northern Hemisphere, its cooling influence should be largely limited to that hemisphere. Yet, since 1987, warming in the Southern Hemisphere, which had been relatively intense, has virtually ceased, while warming in the north has accelerated. Thus, Michaels not only doubted the idea of sulfate cooling, but came to feel that global warming models themselves may be flawed.

Ben Santer disagrees. Santer contends that, in general, global warming occurs more slowly in the south because this hemisphere is dominated by oceans, which warm more slowly than the landmasses that dominate the Northern Hemisphere. But, according to Santer, the situation remains complicated by sulfate cooling, which peaked in the north in the mid-twentieth century. It drastically slowed warming in the Northern Hemisphere, and warming in the Southern Hemisphere raced ahead. Since 1987, Santer argues, the greenhouse effect has reasserted itself, and the north has taken the lead. Thus, Santer disputes Michaels's claim that model predictions and observed data differ fundamentally.

Questions 92–94 refer to the passage.

92. The passage suggests that, in the early 1990s, Michaels would have been most likely to agree with which of the following statements about the disparity mentioned in the lines 3–4?

(A) This disparity is relatively less extreme in the Northern Hemisphere because of sulfate cooling.

(B) This disparity is only a short-term phenomenon brought about by sulfate cooling.

(C) This disparity is most significant in those parts of the world dominated by oceans.

(D) The extent of this disparity is being masked by the temporary effect of sulfate cooling.

(E) The disparity confirms that current models of global warming are correct.

93. According to the passage, Santer asserts which of the following about global warming?

(A) It will become a more serious problem in the Southern Hemisphere than in the Northern Hemisphere in spite of the cooling influence of oceans in the south.

(B) It is unlikely to be a serious problem in the future because of the pervasive effect of sulfate cooling.

(C) It will proceed at the same general rate in the Northern and Southern Hemispheres once the temporary influence of sulfate cooling comes to an end.

(D) Until the late 1980s, it was moderated in the Northern Hemisphere by the effect of sulfate cooling.

(E) Largely because of the cooling influence of oceans, it has had no discernible impact on the Southern Hemisphere.

94. The passage suggests that Santer and Michaels would be most likely to DISAGREE over which of the following issues?

(A) Whether climatological data invalidates global warming models

(B) Whether warming in the Northern Hemisphere has intensified since 1987

(C) Whether disparities between global warming models and climatological data can be detected

(D) Whether landmasses warm more rapidly than oceans

(E) Whether oceans have a significant effect on global climate patterns

Micro-wear patterns found on the teeth of long-extinct specimens of the primate species australopithecine may provide evidence about their diets. For example, on the basis of tooth micro-wear patterns, Walker dismisses Jolly's hypothesis that australopithecines ate hard seeds. He also disputes Szalay's suggestion that the heavy enamel of australopithecine teeth is an adaptation to bone crunching, since both seed cracking and bone crunching produce distinctive micro-wear characteristics on teeth. His conclusion that australopithecines were frugivores (fruit eaters) is based upon his observation that the tooth micro-wear characteristics of east African australopithecine specimens are indistinguishable from those of chimpanzees and orangutans, which are commonly assumed to be frugivorous primates.

However, research on the diets of contemporary primates suggests that micro-wear studies may have limited utility in determining the foods that are actually eaten. For example, insect eating, which can cause distinct micro-wear patterns, would not cause much tooth abrasion in modern baboons, who eat only soft-bodied insects rather than hard-bodied insects. In addition, the diets of current omnivorous primates vary considerably depending on the environments that different groups within a primate species inhabit; if australopithecines were omnivores too, we might expect to find considerable population variation in their tooth micro-wear patterns. Thus, Walker's description of possible australopithecine diets may need to be expanded to include a much more diverse diet.

Questions 95–101 refer to the passage.

95. According to the passage, Walker and Szalay disagree on which of the following points?

(A) The structure and composition of australopithecine teeth

(B) The kinds of conclusions that can be drawn from the micro-wear patterns on australopithecine teeth

(C) The idea that fruit was a part of the australopithecine diet

(D) The extent to which seed cracking and bone crunching produce similar micro-wear patterns on teeth

(E) The function of the heavy enamel on australopithecine teeth

96. The passage suggests that Walker's research indicated which of the following about australopithecine teeth?

(A) They had micro-wear characteristics indicating that fruit constituted only a small part of their diet.

(B) They lacked micro-wear characteristics associated with seed eating and bone crunching.

(C) They had micro-wear characteristics that differed in certain ways from the micro-wear patterns of chimpanzees and orangutans.

(D) They had micro-wear characteristics suggesting that the diet of australopithecines varied from one region to another.

(E) They lacked the micro-wear characteristics distinctive of modern frugivores.

97. The passage suggests that which of the following would be true of studies of tooth micro-wear patterns conducted on modern baboons?

(A) They would inaccurately suggest that some baboons eat more soft-bodied than hard-bodied insects.
(B) They would suggest that insects constitute the largest part of some baboons' diets.
(C) They would reveal that there are no significant differences in tooth micro-wear patterns among baboon populations.
(D) They would inadequately reflect the extent to which some baboons consume certain types of insects.
(E) They would indicate that baboons in certain regions eat only soft-bodied insects, whereas baboons in other regions eat hard-bodied insects.

98. The passage suggests which of the following about the micro-wear patterns found on the teeth of omnivorous primates?

(A) The patterns provide information about what kinds of foods are not eaten by the particular species of primate, but not about the foods actually eaten.
(B) The patterns of various primate species living in the same environment resemble one another.
(C) The patterns may not provide information about the extent to which a particular species' diet includes seeds.
(D) The patterns provide more information about these primates' diet than do the tooth micro-wear patterns of primates who are frugivores.
(E) The patterns may differ among groups within a species depending on the environment within which a particular group lives.

99. It can be inferred from the passage that if studies of tooth micro-wear patterns were conducted on modern baboons, which of the following would most likely be true of the results obtained?

(A) There would be enough abrasion to allow a determination of whether baboons are frugivorous or insectivorous.
(B) The results would suggest that insects constitute the largest part of the baboons' diet.
(C) The results would reveal that there are no significant differences in tooth micro-wear patterns from one regional baboon population to another.
(D) The results would provide an accurate indication of the absence of some kinds of insects from the baboons' diet.
(E) The results would be unlikely to provide any indication of what inferences about the australopithecine diet can or cannot be drawn from micro-wear studies.

100. It can be inferred from the passage that Walker's conclusion about the australopithecine diet would be called into question under which of the following circumstances?

(A) The tooth enamel of australopithecines is found to be much heavier than that of modern frugivorous primates.
(B) The micro-wear patterns of australopithecine teeth from regions other than east Africa are analyzed.
(C) Orangutans are found to have a much broader diet than is currently recognized.
(D) The environment of east Africa at the time australopithecines lived there is found to have been far more varied than is currently thought.
(E) The area in which the australopithecine specimens were found is discovered to have been very rich in soft-bodied insects during the period when australopithecines lived there.

101. The author of the passage mentions the diets of baboons and other living primates most likely in order to

(A) provide evidence that refutes Walker's conclusions about the foods making up the diets of australopithecines

(B) suggest that studies of tooth micro-wear patterns are primarily useful for determining the diets of living primates

(C) suggest that australopithecines were probably omnivores rather than frugivores

(D) illustrate some of the limitations of using tooth micro-wear patterns to draw definitive conclusions about a group's diet

(E) suggest that tooth micro-wear patterns are caused by persistent, as opposed to occasional, consumption of particular foods

In current historiography, the picture of a consistent, unequivocal decline in women's status with the advent of capitalism and industrialization is giving way to an analysis that not only emphasizes both change (whether improvement or decline) and continuity but also accounts for geographical and occupational variation. The history of women's work in English farmhouse cheese making between 1800 and 1930 is a case in point. In her influential *Women Workers and the Industrial Revolution* (1930), Pinchbeck argued that the agricultural revolution of the eighteenth and early nineteenth centuries, with its attendant specialization and enlarged scale of operation, curtailed women's participation in the business of cheese production. Earlier, she maintained, women had concerned themselves with feeding cows, rearing calves, and even selling the cheese in local markets and fairs. Pinchbeck thought that the advent of specialization meant that women's work in cheese dairying was reduced simply to processing the milk. "Dairymen" (a new social category) raised and fed cows and sold the cheese through factors, who were also men. With this narrowing of the scope of work, Pinchbeck believed, women lost business ability, independence, and initiative.

Though Pinchbeck portrayed precapitalist, preindustrial conditions as superior to what followed, recent scholarship has seriously questioned the notion of a golden age for women in precapitalist society. For example, scholars note that women's control seldom extended to the disposal of the proceeds of their work. In the case of cheese, the rise of factors may have compromised women's ability to market cheese at fairs. But merely selling the cheese did not necessarily imply access to the money: Davidoff cites the case of an Essex man who appropriated all but a fraction of the money from his wife's cheese sales.

By focusing on somewhat peripheral operations, moreover, Pinchbeck missed a substantial element of continuity in women's participation: throughout the period women did the central work of actually making cheese. Their persistence in English cheese dairying contrasts with women's early disappearance from arable agriculture in southeast England and from American cheese dairying. Comparing these three divergent developments yields some reasons for the differences among them. English cheese-making women worked in a setting in which cultural values, agricultural conditions, and the nature of their work combined to support their continued participation. In the other cases, one or more of these elements was lacking.

Questions 102–105 refer to the passage.

102. The primary purpose of the passage is to

(A) present recently discovered evidence that supports a conventional interpretation of a historical period

(B) describe how reinterpretations of available evidence have reinvigorated a once-discredited scholarly position

(C) explain why some historians have tended to emphasize change rather than continuity in discussing a particular period

(D) explore how changes in a particular occupation serve to counter the prevailing view of a historical period

(E) examine a particular area of historical research in order to exemplify a general scholarly trend

103. Regarding English local markets and fairs, which of the following can be inferred from the passage?

(A) Both before and after the agricultural revolution, the sellers of agricultural products at these venues were men.

(B) Knowing who the active sellers were at these venues may not give a reliable indication of who controlled the revenue from the sales.

(C) There were no parallel institutions at which American cheese makers could sell their own products.

(D) Prior to the agricultural revolution, the sellers of agricultural products at these venues were generally the producers themselves.

(E) Prior to the agricultural revolution, women sold not only cheese but also products of arable agriculture at these venues.

104. The passage describes the work of Pinchbeck primarily in order to

(A) demonstrate that some of the conclusions reached by recent historians were anticipated in earlier scholarship

(B) provide an instance of the viewpoint that, according to the passage's author, is being superseded

(C) illustrate the ways in which recent historians have built on the work of their predecessors

(D) provide a point of reference for subsequent scholarship on women's work during the agricultural revolution

(E) show the effect that the specialization introduced in the agricultural and industrial revolutions had on women's work

105. It can be inferred from the passage that women did work in

(A) American cheesemaking at some point prior to industrialization

(B) arable agriculture in northern England both before and after the agricultural revolution

(C) arable agriculture in southeast England after the agricultural revolution, in those locales in which cultural values supported their participation

(D) the sale of cheese at local markets in England even after the agricultural revolution

(E) some areas of American cheese dairying after industrialization

3.5 Answer Key

1. C
2. E
3. D
4. E
5. A
6. C
7. D
8. B
9. C
10. D
11. C
12. D
13. B
14. D
15. B
16. E
17. D
18. B
19. E
20. C
21. D
22. C
23. E
24. B
25. A
26. D
27. B
28. E
29. C
30. B
31. A
32. A
33. E
34. C
35. C
36. B
37. A
38. D
39. E
40. B
41. C
42. E
43. A
44. D
45. A
46. B
47. D
48. B
49. A
50. E
51. C
52. D
53. A
54. C
55. C
56. A
57. B
58. B
59. D
60. B
61. E
62. A
63. C
64. C
65. B
66. C
67. D
68. E
69. B
70. C
71. A
72. D
73. E
74. B
75. C
76. C
77. E
78. D
79. E
80. D
81. B
82. B
83. C
84. B
85. A
86. C
87. E
88. A
89. D
90. A
91. C
92. B
93. D
94. A
95. E
96. B
97. D
98. E
99. D
100. C
101. D
102. E
103. B
104. B
105. A

3.6 Answer Explanations

The following discussion of reading comprehension is intended to familiarize you with the most efficient and effective approaches to the kinds of problems common to reading comprehension. The particular questions in this chapter are generally representative of the kinds of reading comprehension questions you will encounter on the GMAT. Remember that it is the problem solving strategy that is important, not the specific details of a particular question.

Questions 1–4 refer to the passage on page 20.

1. According to the passage, traditional corporate leaders differ from leaders in learning organizations in that the former

   (A) encourage employees to concentrate on developing a wide range of skills
   (B) enable employees to recognize and confront dominant corporate models and to develop alternative models
   (C) make important policy decisions alone and then require employees in the corporation to abide by those decisions
   (D) instill confidence in employees because of their willingness to make risky decisions and accept their consequences
   (E) are concerned with offering employees frequent advice and career guidance

Supporting idea

This question requires understanding of the contrast the passage draws between leaders of traditional corporations and leaders of learning organizations. According to the second paragraph, the former are traditionally charismatic leaders who set policy and make decisions, while the latter foster integrated thinking at all levels of the organization.

A According to the passage, it is leaders in learning organizations, not traditional corporate leaders, who encourage the development of a wide range of skills.

B Leaders in learning organizations are those who want their employees to challenge dominant models.

C **Correct.** The second paragraph states that traditional corporate leaders are individualistic; they alone *set the corporation's direction and make key decisions.*

D The passage does not address the question of whether traditional corporate leaders instill confidence in employees. In fact, the first paragraph suggests that they may not; rather, they might come across as objectionably controlling.

E The passage suggests that advice and guidance are more likely to be offered by leaders of learning organizations than by leaders of traditional corporations.

The correct answer is C.

2. Which of the following best describes employee behavior encouraged within learning organizations, as such organizations are described in the passage?

   (A) Carefully defining one's job description and taking care to avoid deviations from it
   (B) Designing mentoring programs that train new employees to follow procedures that have been used for many years
   (C) Concentrating one's efforts on mastering one aspect of a complicated task
   (D) Studying an organizational problem, preparing a report, and submitting it to a corporate leader for approval
   (E) Analyzing a problem related to productivity, making a decision about a solution, and implementing that solution

Application

The second paragraph of the passage indicates that employees of learning organizations are encouraged to think and act for themselves; they learn new skills and expand their capabilities.

A Avoiding deviations from one's carefully defined job description would more likely be encouraged in a traditional corporation, as described in the first paragraph, than in a learning organization.

B Any employee training that involves following long-standing procedures would more likely be encouraged in a traditional corporation than a learning organization.

C According to the passage, mastering only one aspect of a task, no matter how complicated, would be insufficient in a learning organization, in which broad patterns of thinking are encouraged.

D As described in the passage, the role of corporate leaders in learning organizations is not, characteristically, to approve employees' solutions to problems, but rather to enable and empower employees to implement solutions on their own.

E **Correct.** Employees in learning organizations are expected to act on their own initiative; thus, they would be encouraged to analyze and solve problems on their own, implementing whatever solutions they devised.

The correct answer is E.

3. According to the author of the passage, corporate leaders of the future should do which of the following?

(A) They should encourage employees to put long-term goals ahead of short-term profits.

(B) They should exercise more control over employees in order to constrain production costs.

(C) They should redefine incentives for employees' performance improvement.

(D) They should provide employees with opportunities to gain new skills and expand their capabilities.

(E) They should promote individual managers who are committed to established company policies.

Supporting idea

This question focuses on what the author recommends in the passage for future corporate leaders. In the second paragraph, the author states that, among other things, corporate leaders need to be teachers to provide challenges to their employees and create an atmosphere where *employees are continually learning new skills and expanding their capabilities to shape their future.*

A The passage does not directly discuss the issue of corporate goals and profitability in the long or short term.

B The passage does not address the topic of production costs, and it suggests that its author would favor reducing, rather than increasing, corporate leaders' control over employees. The first paragraph states that leaders who attempt to control employees lead those employees to perform in mediocre fashion.

C The passage does not discuss incentivizing employees' performance; rather, employees' performance will improve, the passage suggests, under different corporate leadership.

D **Correct.** The final sentence of the passage states directly that leaders must build organizations in which employees can learn new skills and expand their capabilities.

E The first paragraph indicates that clinging to established company policies is a strategy for the future that is likely to be unproductive.

The correct answer is D.

4. The primary purpose of the passage is to

(A) endorse a traditional corporate structure

(B) introduce a new approach to corporate leadership and evaluate criticisms of it

(C) explain competing theories about management practices and reconcile them

(D) contrast two typical corporate organizational structures

(E) propose an alternative to a common corporate approach

Main idea

This question depends on understanding the passage as a whole. The first paragraph explains the way in which corporations fail to facilitate how humans learn. The second paragraph suggests that corporations should change the way they view employees in order to promote learning, and it explains the positive outcomes that would result from that shift in thinking.

A The first paragraph explains that the traditional corporate structure leads to mediocre performance; it does not endorse that structure.

B The second paragraph introduces the concept of a *learning organization* and its attendant approach to corporate leadership. Rather than identifying any criticisms of that approach, the passage endorses it wholeheartedly.

C The passage discusses the difference between the idea of a single charismatic leader and that of a shared corporate leadership, but it does not attempt to reconcile these two ideas.

D The passage's main focus is on advocating a particular approach, not on merely contrasting it with another. Furthermore, it portrays only one of the approaches as typical. It suggests that the organizational structure that relies on a single charismatic leader is typical but that another approach, that in which leadership is shared, should instead become typical.

E Correct. The passage identifies a common corporate approach, one based on controlling employees, and proposes that corporations should instead become *learning organizations.*

The correct answer is E.

Questions 5–10 refer to the passage on page 22.

5. All of the following are mentioned as ways of controlling the magnitude of structural unemployment EXCEPT

(A) using public funds to create jobs
(B) teaching new skills to displaced workers
(C) allowing displaced workers to retire
(D) controlling the movement of capital
(E) encouraging workers to move to where jobs are available

Supporting idea

This question addresses what the passage states directly about how the magnitude of structural unemployment can be controlled. The last few sentences of the second paragraph state several ways in which this control may be exerted.

A Correct. The passage mentions using public sector resources, but it does not say that those resources could be used to create jobs.

B The passage states that workers can be reeducated or retrained as a way of addressing structural unemployment.

C Encouraging workers to retire is one of the options mentioned in the passage for controlling structural unemployment.

D Capital movement is one of the factors affecting structural unemployment, and the passage states that controlling this movement can be used as a way of controlling structural unemployment.

E The passage indicates that encouraging displaced workers to move where there are jobs is a way to help control structural unemployment.

The correct answer is A.

6. The passage suggests that a potential outcome of higher structural unemployment is

(A) increased public spending for social services
(B) placement of workers in jobs for which they are not qualified
(C) higher wages for those workers who have skills that are in demand
(D) an increase in the length of time jobs remain unfilled
(E) a shift in the government's economic policy priorities

Supporting idea

The third paragraph discusses a potential result of higher structural unemployment: if more workers lack skills that are in demand, there will be shortages of qualified workers. The wages of workers who do have the desired skills will thus rise.

A While higher structural unemployment might result in an increased demand for social services, such as job training and the like, the passage does not suggest that the government would in fact respond by spending more on such services.

B Nothing in the passage indicates that employers would hire workers who lack necessary skills—indeed, the lack of qualified workers is itself a cause of increased structural unemployment.

C **Correct.** The passage indicates that when growth in demand for workers with certain skills outpaces the growth in the number of workers who possess those skills, the wages of those workers are bid up, resulting in increased pay for the skilled workers.

D The passage does not discuss the length of time that jobs are likely to remain unfilled as structural unemployment increases. The amount of time jobs remain unfilled could remain the same, but the number or type of jobs that go unfilled may change.

E The passage suggests that certain types of public sector spending (presumably spending as a result of government policy) can help control the magnitude of structural unemployment, but the passage does not indicate whether the government is in fact likely to change policy so as to try to control this magnitude. Furthermore, the passage states that government policy has placed a priority on reducing inflation. Yet there is no suggestion that the government is likely to shift away from this priority in the face of higher structural unemployment.

The correct answer is C.

7. It can be inferred from the passage that even when there are unemployed workers, labor shortages are still likely to occur if

(A) the inflation rate is unusually high
(B) there is insufficient technological innovation
(C) the level of structural unemployment is exceptionally low
(D) the jobs available in certain places require skills that the labor force in those areas lacks
(E) the workers in some industries are dissatisfied with the pay offered in those industries

Inference

This question relies on the passage's characterization of structural unemployment—that there is a mismatch between the number of jobs available in a certain location and the number of workers in that location who possess the skills required for those jobs. Even if there is a sufficient number of workers in the area to fill the positions, if those workers had the requisite skills, labor shortages will occur if an insufficient number of those workers lack the required skills.

A The passage in the third paragraph explains that structural unemployment and inflation can coexist, but it does not suggest that a high rate of inflation will make labor shortages likely; rather, the passage indicates that structural unemployment may lead to inflation by pushing wages, and thus prices, higher.

B The passage indicates that greater technological innovation can produce structural unemployment, not that insufficient technological innovation can.

C When there are unemployed workers, labor shortages would be unlikely to occur if the level of structural unemployment is low, because low structural unemployment would mean that no imbalance exists between available employment and workers with requisite skills. Thus, unemployed workers would likely be able to find jobs.

D **Correct.** The labor shortages associated with structural unemployment can, according to the passage, be caused by a mismatch in a certain location between available jobs requiring particular skills and the number of workers possessing those skills.

E The passage does not discuss what would happen if some industries' workers are dissatisfied with their pay. Presumably, though, even if those workers were to quit their jobs due to that dissatisfaction, unemployed workers may very well be happy to take those jobs (assuming they are not lacking the requisite skills). So the passage gives us no reason to think that labor shortages would be likely to occur—at least without a situation like that described in answer choice D.

The correct answer is D.

8. The passage suggests that the phenomenon of combined unemployment and inflation is

(A) a socioeconomic problem that can only be addressed by government intervention

(B) a socioeconomic problem that can be characteristic of periods of structural unemployment

(C) an economic problem that results from government intervention in management-labor relations

(D) an economic problem that results from imperfect applications of technology

(E) an economic problem that can be eliminated by relatively small changes in the labor force

Supporting idea

This question depends on understanding the phenomenon of combined unemployment and inflation, which is addressed in the third paragraph. That paragraph states that a trend associated with structural unemployment—that of rising labor costs and prices—is responsible for the phenomenon.

A The third paragraph indicates that government policy has been unable, thus far, to remedy the problem of combined unemployment and inflation, and it gives no indication whether a nongovernmental solution is available.

B **Correct.** Periods of structural unemployment have, according to the passage, featured both inflation and unemployment.

C The passage does not discuss government intervention into management-labor relations.

D Certain applications of technology may be responsible for increasing structural unemployment, but the passage provides no way to distinguish between imperfect and other such applications.

E The passage discusses the phenomenon of combined unemployment and inflation only in relation to structural unemployment, which the passage suggests is likely to arise only in relation to large or rapid changes in demand for labor. Therefore, it seems unlikely that relatively small changes in the labor force can eliminate the phenomenon of combined unemployment and inflation.

The correct answer is B.

9. The passage is primarily concerned with

(A) clarifying the definition of a concept

(B) proposing a way to eliminate an undesirable condition

(C) discussing the sources and consequences of a problem

(D) suggesting ways to alleviate the effects of a particular social policy

(E) evaluating the steps that have been taken to correct an imbalance

Main idea

This question depends on understanding the passage as a whole in order to identify its primary concern. The first paragraph defines structural unemployment (which the passage, in its second paragraph, indicates is a *serious problem*). The second paragraph describes a major factor that can cause structural unemployment, as well as some steps that might be taken to alleviate it. Finally, the third paragraph identifies possible effects of structural unemployment, including wage and price inflation.

A The first paragraph clarifies the definition of structural unemployment, but this definition is not the passage's primary concern.

B The passage's second paragraph indicates some ways that an increase in structural unemployment can be mitigated, but nowhere does the passage suggest that the condition can be eliminated entirely.

C **Correct.** The passage discusses the problem of structural unemployment, explaining how it can arise and what some of its consequences may be.

D The passage does suggest some ways in which structural unemployment might be alleviated, but this kind of unemployment is not characterized as an effect of a social policy. Rather, it is a state of economic affairs.

E The second paragraph identifies some steps that could be taken to correct a particular situation of worker displacement. It does not, however, evaluate those steps.

The correct answer is C.

10. According to the passage, small downward shifts in the demand for labor will not usually cause unemployment because

(A) such shifts are frequently accompanied by upswings in the economy

(B) such shifts usually occur slowly

(C) workers can be encouraged to move to where there are jobs

(D) normal attrition is often sufficient to reduce the size of the work force

(E) workers are usually flexible enough to learn new skills and switch to new jobs

Supporting idea

This question requires noting that the second paragraph of the passage discusses small changes in demand for labor: their effect on unemployment is likely to be small because normal attrition can reduce the size of the work force accordingly.

A The passage does not mention upswings in the economy in relation to small shifts in demand for labor. Furthermore, the passage indicates that structural unemployment can occur even at peaks of economic upswings, so presumably even if small downward shifts in the demand for labor are frequently accompanied by economic upswings, structural unemployment could still result.

B The passage suggests that shifts in demand for workers that do not result in unemployment may be small *or* gradual. Nothing indicates that small changes are also necessarily gradual.

C The second paragraph indicates that workers being encouraged to move to where there are jobs would be a reasonable response to large or rapid changes in demand for workers; it does not discuss such encouragement in relation to small shifts in demand.

D **Correct.** The passage identifies normal attrition as a factor that can reduce the work force sufficiently to accommodate small reductions in the demand for labor in particular occupations.

E Workers' ability to learn new skills is identified in the passage as a factor affecting whether structural unemployment will grow in response to large or rapid changes, not small changes, in the demand for workers in particular occupations.

The correct answer is D.

Questions 11–16 refer to the passage on page 24.

11. The primary purpose of the passage is to

(A) identify ways in which the GDP could be modified so that it would serve as a more accurate indicator of the economic well-being of the United States

(B) suggest that the GDP, in spite of certain shortcomings, is still the most reliable indicator of the economic well-being of the United States

(C) examine crucial shortcomings of the GDP as an indicator of the economic well-being of the United States

(D) argue that the growth of the United States economy in recent decades has diminished the effectiveness of the GDP as an indicator of the nation's economic well-being

(E) discuss how the GDP came to be used as the primary indicator of the economic well-being of the United States

Main idea

This question requires determining the main purpose of the passage as a whole. The passage begins by broadly defining GDP and describing how it is used as an indicator of the economic well-being of the United States. The passage then describes in more detail what is and is not taken into account by the GDP and then draws a causal connection between the limitations of what the GDP measures and disturbing trends within the U.S. in recent decades.

A There is no discussion in the passage about modifying how the GDP is calculated.

B The passage makes no judgment about the merits of using the GDP in relation to other economic indicators.

C Correct. The passage portrays the GDP as having limitations that make it a problematic indicator of real economic well-being.

D The passage does not portray the GDP as being any less useful as an economic indicator than it ever was.

E There is no discussion in the passage of the history of how the GDP came to be used as an economic indicator.

The correct answer is C.

12. Which of the following best describes the function of the second sentence of the passage in the context of the passage as a whole?

(A) It describes an assumption about the GDP that is defended in the course of the passage.

(B) It contributes to a discussion of the origins of the GDP.

(C) It clarifies a common misconception about the use of the GDP.

(D) It identifies a major flaw in the GDP.

(E) It suggests a revision to the method of calculating the GDP.

Evaluation

Answering this question requires understanding how a particular part of the passage functions in the passage as a whole. The second sentence describes the GDP as being solely concerned with the prices of goods and services produced in the United States, aside from any other kind of value. The passage then goes on to imply that by ignoring value other than price, the GDP may actually mask problems present in the nation's overall economy.

A The passage is concerned with calling into question the use of the GDP, not defending it.

B The passage does not mention how the GDP came to be used as a primary economic indicator.

C The passage does not describe the function of the GDP as being commonly misunderstood.

D **Correct.** The limitations of the GDP as described in the second sentence are then, in the rest of the passage, tied to problems in the United States.

E The passage makes no explicit recommendations about revising how the GDP is measured.

The correct answer is D.

13. It can be inferred that the author of the passage would agree with which of the following about the "economic significance" of those goods and services that are included in the GDP?

(A) It is a comprehensive indicator of a nation's economic well-being.

(B) It is not accurately captured by the price of those goods and services.

(C) It is usually less than the intrinsic value of those goods and services.

(D) It is more difficult to calculate than the economic significance of those goods and services that are not included in the GDP.

(E) It is calculated differently in capitalist countries than in noncapitalist countries.

Inference

This question asks what the author implies about a piece of information given in the passage. The passage states that *the GDP assumes that the economic significance of goods and services lies solely in their price* (lines 5–7) and that *the GDP ignores the economic utility* (lines 13–14) of things such as a healthy environment and a cohesive social structure. The passage then implies that the worsening problems with the environment and social structure in recent decades are due to the way the GDP is calculated.

A In describing the GDP as limited in what it measures, the author would not agree that the GDP is a comprehensive indicator.

B **Correct.** The author implies that because the GDP ignores the economic utility of certain things, it is an inaccurate indicator of economic well-being.

C The author makes no comparison between the economic value and the intrinsic value of goods and services.

D The author makes no judgment about the difficulty of measuring the value of goods and services not measured by the GDP.

E The author does not indicate how noncapitalist countries calculate GDP.

The correct answer is B.

14. The comparison of the GDP to a calculating machine serves to do which of the following?

(A) Refute an assertion that the calculations involved in the GDP are relatively complex in nature

(B) Indicate that the GDP is better suited to record certain types of monetary transactions than others

(C) Suggest that it is likely that the GDP will be supplanted by other, more sophisticated economic indicators

(D) Illustrate the point that the GDP has no way of measuring the destructive impact of such things as oil spills on the nation's economic well-being

(E) Exemplify an assertion that the GDP tends to exaggerate the amount of commercial activity generated by such things as oil spills

Evaluation

This question asks how a certain statement in the passage functions in the passage as a whole. In lines 13–16 and 20–24, respectively, the passage indicates that the GDP not only ignores problems affecting a nation's economy but that it actually can portray these problems as economic gains, and it subsequently uses the example of an oil spill adding to the GDP to illustrate this. The passage then closes by describing the GDP as a calculating machine that can add but not subtract.

A The passage does not discuss the complexities of calculating the GDP.

B The passage makes no judgment about the relative successes of the GDP in recording different types of monetary transactions.

C The passage makes no mention of other economic indicators aside from the GDP.

D **Correct.** By characterizing the GDP as a calculating machine that cannot subtract, the passage helps illustrate why something like an oil spill is misrepresented by the GDP.

E While the passage does mention that the GDP measures commercial activity generated by an oil spill, it does not suggest that the GDP exaggerates the amount of that activity.

The correct answer is D.

15. The passage implies that national policies that rely heavily on economic indicators such as the GDP tend to

(A) become increasingly capitalistic in nature

(B) disregard the economic importance of environmental and social factors that do not involve monetary transactions

(C) overestimate the amount of commercial activity generated by environmental disasters

(D) overestimate the economic significance of cohesive families and communities

(E) assume that the economic significance of goods and services does not lie solely in the price of those goods and services

Inference

This question requires understanding what the passage implies about the main issue it discusses. In lines 13–14, the passage states that *the GDP ignores the economic utility* of things such as a clean environment and social cohesiveness. It then indicates that in countries that are dependent on economic indicators such as the GDP, *the environment and the social structure have been eroded in recent decades* (lines 19–20).

A The passage does not mention how or if the GDP affects the capitalist nature of national policies.

B **Correct.** In indicating that the GDP ignores environmental and social factors, the passage implies that policies dependent on the GDP will also ignore these issues.

C The passage indicates that the GDP takes into account the commercial activity generated by environmental disasters but does not suggest that the amount of that activity is overestimated.

D The passage indicates that the GDP ignores the value of social cohesion.

E The passage indicates that *the GDP assumes that the economic significance of goods and services lies solely in their price* (lines 5–7).

The correct answer is B.

16. It can be inferred that the author of the passage would agree with which of the following assessments of the GDP as an indicator of the economic well-being of the United States?

(A) It masks social and environmental erosion more fully than the chief economic indicators of other nations.

(B) It is based on inaccurate estimations of the prices of many goods and services.

(C) It overestimates the amount of commercial activity that is generated in the United States.

(D) It is conducive to error because it conflates distinct types of economic activity.

(E) It does not take into account the economic utility of certain environmental and social conditions.

Inference

This question requires understanding what the author implies about information in the passage. The passage states that the GDP is *the chief indicator of the economic well-being of the United States* (lines 4–5). It also states that *the GDP ignores the economic utility* (lines 13–16) of things such as a clean environment and social cohesiveness. Therefore, the GDP does not take into account the economic utility of certain environmental and social conditions.

A The passage makes no comparisons among different nations' economic indicators.

B The passage does not describe the GDP as being inaccurate in its estimates of the prices of goods and services.

C The passage does not describe the GDP as overestimating amounts of commercial activity.

D The passage does not describe the GDP as confusing different types of economic activity.

E **Correct.** The passage states that the GDP ignores the economic utility of a clean environment and social cohesiveness.

The correct answer is E.

Questions 17–22 refer to the passage on page 26.

17. The passage is primarily concerned with

(A) explaining why one method of earthquake prediction has proven more practicable than an alternative method

(B) suggesting that accurate earthquake forecasting must combine elements of long-term and short-term prediction

(C) challenging the usefulness of dilatancy theory for explaining the occurrence of precursory phenomena

(D) discussing the deficiency of two methods by which researchers have attempted to predict the occurrence of earthquakes

(E) describing the development of methods for establishing patterns in the occurrence of past earthquakes

Main idea

To answer this question, focus on what the passage as a whole is trying to do. The first paragraph describes a method for predicting the occurrence of earthquakes, and the second paragraph explains problems with that method. The third paragraph describes a second method for predicting the occurrence of earthquakes, and the fourth paragraph explains problems with that method. Thus, the passage as a whole is primarily concerned with explaining the deficiencies of two methods for predicting the occurrence of earthquakes.

A The passage does not compare the practicability of the two methods.

B The passage does not discuss combining long-term and short-term methods.

C Only the first half of the passage discusses dilatancy theory; the second half discusses a different method for predicting the occurrence of earthquakes.

D **Correct.** The passage describes two methods for predicting the occurrence of earthquakes and explains the shortcomings of each method.

E Only the second half of the passage discusses patterns in the occurrence of past earthquakes; the first half discusses a different method for predicting the occurrence of earthquakes.

The correct answer is D.

18. According to the passage, laboratory evidence concerning the effects of stress on rocks might help account for

(A) differences in magnitude among earthquakes

(B) certain phenomena that occur prior to earthquakes

(C) variations in the intervals between earthquakes in a particular area

(D) differences in the frequency with which earthquakes occur in various areas

(E) the unreliability of short-term earthquake predictions

Supporting ideas

This question asks for information explicitly stated in the passage. The first paragraph explains that rocks subjected to stress in the laboratory undergo multiple changes. According to *dilatancy theory*, such changes happening to rocks in the field could lead to earthquake precursors—phenomena that occur before large earthquakes.

A The passage explains how laboratory evidence might be used to predict the occurrence of large earthquakes, not to differentiate between earthquakes' magnitudes.

B **Correct.** According to dilatancy theory, the sort of changes that have been observed in laboratories to occur in rocks might lead to earthquake precursors in the field.

C Although the passage discusses variation in earthquake intervals, that evidence is based on historical records, not laboratory evidence.

D The passage does not refer in any way to differences in the frequency of earthquakes in various regions.

E The unreliability of one method for making short-term earthquake predictions is implied by information gathered in the field, not by laboratory evidence.

The correct answer is B.

19. It can be inferred from the passage that one problem with using precursory phenomena to predict earthquakes is that minor tremors

(A) typically occur some distance from the sites of the large earthquakes that follow them

(B) are directly linked to the mechanisms that cause earthquakes

(C) are difficult to distinguish from major tremors

(D) have proven difficult to measure accurately

(E) are not always followed by large earthquakes

Inference

This question asks what can be inferred from certain information in the passage. The second paragraph explains two problems with using minor tremors to predict earthquakes. First, minor tremors provide no information about how large an impending earthquake will be. Second, the minor tremors that occur prior to a large earthquake are indistinguishable from other minor tremors. Thus, it can be inferred that minor tremors sometimes occur when no large earthquake follows.

A The passage does not mention the distance between minor tremors and ensuing earthquakes.

B The passage implies that minor tremors sometimes occur without an ensuing earthquake, so the phenomena are most likely not directly linked.

C The passage suggests no difficulty in distinguishing between minor tremors and major tremors.

D The passage does not mention any difficulties in the measurement of minor tremors.

E **Correct.** The passage indicates that minor tremors occurring prior to a large earthquake are indistinguishable from minor tremors that are not followed by large earthquakes. So the fact that minor tremors are not always followed by large earthquakes, together with the inability to distinguish between those that are and those that are not, poses a problem for any attempt to predict large earthquakes on the basis of this type of precursory phenomena.

The correct answer is E.

20. According to the passage, some researchers based their research about long-term earthquake prediction on which of the following facts?

(A) The historical record confirms that most earthquakes have been preceded by minor tremors.

(B) The average interval between earthquakes in one region of the San Andreas Fault is 132 years.

(C) Some regions tend to be the site of numerous earthquakes over the course of many years.

(D) Changes in the volume of rock can occur as a result of building stress and can lead to the weakening of rock.

(E) Paleoseismologists have been able to unearth and date geological features caused by past earthquakes.

Supporting idea

This question asks for information explicitly provided in the passage. The question asks what the basis is for the research into long-term earthquake prediction described in the third paragraph. Based on the fact that numerous earthquakes occur in some regions over the course of many years, the researchers tried to identify regular earthquake intervals that would assist in making long-term predictions. Thus, the basis of their research is the occurrence of numerous earthquakes at particular sites.

A The passage indicates that minor tremors are used by some scientists to make short-term earthquake predictions, not that they were the basis for research about long-term predictions.

B This fact about the San Andreas Fault was used by paleoseismologists to show the inadequacy of the long-term prediction research, since actual earthquake intervals varied greatly from the average.

C Correct. Since earthquakes occur repeatedly in certain regions, researchers tried to identify regular cycles in earthquake intervals.

D The passage indicates that changes in rock volume have been used by some scientists to make short-term earthquake predictions, not that they were the basis for research about long-term predictions.

E Paleoseismologists' research provided evidence against the existence of regular earthquake cycles used in making long-term predictions.

The correct answer is C.

21. The passage suggests which of the following about the paleoseismologists' findings described in lines 42–50?

(A) They suggest that the frequency with which earthquakes occurred at a particular site decreased significantly over the past two millennia.

(B) They suggest that paleoseismologists may someday be able to make reasonably accurate long-term earthquake predictions.

(C) They suggest that researchers may someday be able to determine which past occurrences of minor tremors were actually followed by large earthquakes.

(D) They suggest that the recurrence of earthquakes in earthquake-prone sites is too irregular to serve as a basis for earthquake prediction.

(E) They indicate that researchers attempting to develop long-term methods of earthquake prediction have overlooked important evidence concerning the causes of earthquakes.

Inference

This question asks about what can be inferred from a particular portion of the passage (lines 42–50). The third paragraph describes research that attempted to identify regular patterns of recurrence in earthquake-prone regions, to aid in long-term earthquake prediction. The fourth paragraph describes evidence discovered by paleoseismologists that undermines this idea that regular earthquake cycles exist. The paragraph indicates that in one region along the San Andreas Fault, the average interval between earthquakes was 132 years, but individual intervals varied widely—from 44 to 332 years. This information implies that earthquake intervals are too irregular to be used for accurate long-term earthquake prediction.

A The evidence suggests that the earthquake intervals are irregular, not that they have become shorter over time.

B The findings provide evidence against the use of regular earthquake cycles in long-term earthquake prediction.

C The findings do not clearly pertain to minor tremors.

D Correct. The great variation in intervals between earthquakes suggests that recurrence is too irregular to serve as the basis for long-term earthquake prediction.

E The paleoseismologists studied evidence showing when earthquakes occurred. The passage does not suggest that the evidence has any implications regarding the causes of earthquakes.

The correct answer is D.

22. The author implies which of the following about the ability of the researchers mentioned in line 18 to predict earthquakes?

(A) They can identify when an earthquake is likely to occur but not how large it will be.

(B) They can identify the regions where earthquakes are likely to occur but not when they will occur.

(C) They are unable to determine either the time or the place that earthquakes are likely to occur.

(D) They are likely to be more accurate at short-term earthquake prediction than at long-term earthquake prediction.

(E) They can determine the regions where earthquakes have occurred in the past but not the regions where they are likely to occur in the future.

Supporting idea

The question asks for information explicitly provided in the passage. The second paragraph indicates that researchers at first reported success in identifying earthquake precursors, but further analysis of the data undermined their theory. The passage then explains that atypical seismic waves were recorded before some earthquakes; this evidence at first seemed to support the researchers' theory, before further analysis proved the evidence inadequate.

A Although earthquakes are caused by stress on rock, the passage does not indicate that this fact encouraged researchers to believe that precursors could be used to predict earthquakes.

B This fact would undermine the theory that changes in seismic waves are precursory phenomena that can be used to predict earthquakes.

C **Correct.** Seismic waves with unusual velocities occurring before earthquakes at first seemed to provide support for researchers' theory that earthquakes could be predicted by precursory phenomena.

D Though earthquakes' recurrence in certain regions is mentioned as being important to researchers seeking to make long-term earthquake predictions, it is not mentioned as being relevant to researchers' theory that earthquakes can be predicted by precursory phenomena.

E This is not mentioned as being relevant to scientists' belief that earthquakes could be predicted on the basis of precursory phenomena.

The correct answer is C.

Questions 23–29 refer to the passage on page 28.

23. It can be inferred from the passage that one reason an advertiser might prefer a hard-sell approach to a soft-sell approach is that

(A) the risks of boomerang effects are minimized when the conclusions an advertiser wants the consumer to draw are themselves left unstated

(B) counterargumentation is likely from consumers who fail to draw their own conclusions regarding an advertising claim

(C) inferential activity is likely to occur even if consumers perceive themselves to be more knowledgeable than the individuals presenting product claims

(D) research on consumer memory suggests that the explicit conclusions provided by an advertiser using the hard-sell approach have a significant impact on decision making

(E) the information presented by an advertiser using the soft-sell approach may imply different conclusions to different consumers

Inference

This question relies on what the passage suggests about the difference between the hard-sell and soft-sell approaches—and why the hard-sell approach might be preferred. The hard-sell approach, according to the second paragraph, presents explicit conclusions. The soft-sell approach, on the other hand, does not explicitly state conclusions about products; instead, consumers make up their own minds.

A While the passage makes clear that boomerang effects are minimized when conclusions are left unstated, this is an advantage of the soft-sell approach over the hard-sell approach.

B According to the second paragraph, counterargumentation is a disadvantage, not an advantage, of the hard-sell approach. This is a reason not to prefer the hard sell.

C The third paragraph suggests that in cases in which consumers may perceive themselves as more knowledgeable than individuals presenting product claims, the soft-sell approach offers an advantage over the hard-sell approach.

D According to the third paragraph, self-generated conclusions that are associated with the soft-sell approach have a greater impact on decision making than explicit conclusions. The passage does not allude to any research on memory that would favor the hard-sell approach.

E **Correct.** The fourth paragraph suggests that one problem with the soft-sell approach is that consumers could miss the point; they may not come to the conclusions that the advertiser would prefer. Thus an advertiser might prefer a hard-sell approach.

The correct answer is E.

24. Each of the following is mentioned in the passage as a characteristic of the hard-sell approach EXCEPT:

(A) Its overall message is readily grasped.

(B) It appeals to consumers' knowledge about the product.

(C) It makes explicit claims that the advertised brand is superior to other brands.

(D) It uses statements that are expressed very clearly.

(E) It makes claims in the form of direct conclusions.

Supporting idea

This question asks about what is directly stated in the passage about the hard-sell approach. The first and second paragraphs provide the details about this approach, including that it uses *direct, forceful claims* about benefits of a brand over competitors' brands; its claims are simple and straightforward, in the form of explicit conclusions; and consumers are generally left with little room for confusion about the message.

A The second paragraph states that there is little room for confusion about the message.

B Correct. The extent of consumers' knowledge about the product is not mentioned in the passage.

C The first paragraph indicates that in the hard-sell approach advertisers make direct claims regarding the benefits of the advertised brand over other offerings.

D The first and second paragraphs say that hard-sell claims are direct, simple, and straightforward.

E The second paragraph emphasizes that the hard-sell approach presents it claims in the form of explicit conclusions.

The correct answer is B.

25. It can be inferred from the passage that advertisers could reduce one of the risks discussed in the last paragraph if they were able to provide

(A) motivation for consumers to think about the advertisement's message

(B) information that implies the advertiser's intended conclusion but leaves that conclusion unstated

(C) subtle evidence that the advertised product is superior to that of competitors

(D) information comparing the advertised product with its competitors

(E) opportunity for consumers to generate their own beliefs or conclusions

Inference

This question requires understanding the risks discussed in the last paragraph of the passage. Those risks are, first, that consumers would not be motivated to think about the advertisement and thus would miss the message's point; second, that consumers may draw conclusions that the advertiser did not intend; and finally, that consumers could question the validity of the conclusions they reach, even if those conclusions are what advertisers intend.

A Correct. Providing motivation for consumers to think about an advertisement's message would reduce the first risk discussed in the last paragraph: that consumers would fail to draw any conclusions because they would lack motivation to engage with advertisements.

B Providing *information that implies a conclusion but leaves it unstated* is the very definition of the soft-sell approach, and it is this approach that gives rise to the risks discussed in the last paragraph.

C Providing subtle evidence that a product is superior is most likely to give rise to all three of the risks identified in the last paragraph, in that its subtlety would leave consumers free to draw their own conclusions, to fail to draw those conclusions, or to question the validity of their own conclusions.

D A direct comparison of the advertised product with its competitors would run all the risks identified in the last paragraph: consumers might not find the comparison motivating; they could draw conclusions that the advertiser did not intend (e.g., that the competing products are superior); or they could question whatever conclusions they do draw.

E Giving consumers the opportunity *to generate their own beliefs or conclusions* is an intrinsic part of the soft-sell approach, which produces the risks discussed in the last paragraph.

The correct answer is A.

26. The primary purpose of the passage is to

(A) point out the risks involved in the use of a particular advertising strategy

(B) make a case for the superiority of one advertising strategy over another

(C) illustrate the ways in which two advertising strategies may be implemented

(D) present the advantages and disadvantages of two advertising strategies

(E) contrast the types of target markets for which two advertising strategies are appropriate

Inference

Overall, the passage is concerned with two advertising strategies. The first paragraph introduces the strategies. The second paragraph explains how a particular aspect of one approach may be both positive and negative and how the second approach mitigates these problems. The third paragraph continues this discussion of mitigation, while the fourth paragraph points out that there are drawbacks to this approach, too. Thus, according to the passage, both strategies have positive and negative aspects.

A The passage is concerned not with one particular advertising strategy but with two, and it discusses benefits, as well as risks, involved with both strategies.

B The passage does not suggest that one strategy is superior to the other but rather that each has positive and negative aspects.

C The passage does not discuss how to implement either of the strategies it is concerned with; instead, it deals with how consumers are likely to respond once the implementation has already taken place.

D **Correct.** The passage is primarily concerned with showing that both of the strategies described have advantages and disadvantages.

E The passage provides some indirect grounds for inferring the target markets for which each advertising strategy might be appropriate, but it is not primarily concerned with contrasting those markets.

The correct answer is D.

27. Which of the following best describes the function of the sentence in lines 25–28 in the context of the passage as a whole?

(A) It reiterates a distinction between two advertising strategies that is made in the first paragraph.

(B) It explains how a particular strategy avoids a drawback described earlier in the paragraph.

(C) It suggests that a risk described earlier in the paragraph is less serious than some researchers believe it to be.

(D) It outlines why the strategy described in the previous sentence involves certain risks for an advertiser.

(E) It introduces an argument that will be refuted in the following paragraph.

Evaluation

The sentence in lines 25–28 explains how the kinds of conclusions consumers are invited to draw based on the soft-sell approach reduce the risk that consumers will respond with *resentment, distrust, and counterargumentation*—that is, the possible *boomerang effect* identified earlier in the paragraph as a drawback of the hard-sell approach.

A The sentence does not reiterate the distinction between the hard- and soft-sell approaches; rather, it explains an advantage of the soft-sell approach.

B **Correct.** The sentence explains how the soft-sell approach avoids the problems that can arise from the hard-sell approach's explicitly stated conclusions.

C The sentence suggests that the risk of boomerang effects described earlier in the paragraph is serious but that a different approach can mitigate it.

D The sentence outlines why the strategy described in the previous sentence reduces advertisers' risks, not why it involves risks.

E At no point does the passage refute the idea that implicit conclusions reduce the risk of boomerang effects. It does say that there could be drawbacks to the soft-sell approach, but those drawbacks are related to the problem with implicit conclusions themselves and how people reach them. In addition, the *following paragraph* does not mention the drawbacks, only the advantages of implicit conclusions.

The correct answer is B.

28. It can be inferred from the passage that one situation in which the boomerang effect often occurs is when consumers

(A) have been exposed to forceful claims that are diametrically opposed to those in an advertiser's message

(B) have previous self-generated beliefs or conclusions that are readily accessible from memory

(C) are subjected to advertising messages that are targeted at specific markets to which those consumers do not belong

(D) are confused regarding the point of the advertiser's message

(E) come to view the advertiser's message with suspicion

Inference

The passage discusses the boomerang effect in the second paragraph. This effect is defined as consumers deriving conclusions from advertising that are the opposite of those that advertisers intended to present, and it occurs when consumers resent and/or distrust what they are being told.

A The passage provides no grounds for inferring that consumers need to be exposed to opposing claims in order to believe such claims; they may reach opposing claims on their own.

B The passage indicates that the boomerang effect can be reduced by using a soft-sell approach, which can result in self-generated conclusions, but it provides no evidence about any possible effects of preexisting self-generated beliefs or conclusions on the boomerang effect.

C The passage does not address how consumers who are subjected to advertising messages not intended for them might respond.

D Confusion regarding the point of the advertiser's message is more likely to occur, the passage suggests, when advertisers use a soft-sell approach—but it is the hard-sell approach, not the soft-sell, that is likely to result in the boomerang effect.

E **Correct.** The second paragraph indicates that consumers who resent being told what to believe and come to distrust the advertiser's message—that is, those who view the message with suspicion—may experience a boomerang effect, believing the opposite of the conclusions offered.

The correct answer is E.

29. It can be inferred from the passage that the research mentioned in line 29 supports which of the following statements?

(A) Implicit conclusions are more likely to capture accurately the point of the advertiser's message than are explicit conclusions.

(B) Counterargumentation is less likely to occur if an individual's beliefs or conclusions are readily accessible from memory.

(C) The hard-sell approach results in conclusions that are more difficult for the consumer to recall than are conclusions resulting from the soft-sell approach.

(D) When the beliefs of others are presented as definite and forceful claims, they are perceived to be as accurate as self-generated beliefs.

(E) Despite the advantages of implicit conclusions, the hard-sell approach involves fewer risks for the advertiser than does the soft-sell approach.

Inference

The research this item refers to—research on consumer memory and judgment—indicates that beliefs are more memorable when they are self-generated and so matter when making judgments and decisions. Further, self-generated beliefs seem more believable to those who have them than beliefs that come from elsewhere.

A The fourth paragraph indicates that implicit conclusions are more likely to fail to replicate the advertiser's message than explicit conclusions are.

B The research discussed in the passage does not address when counterargumentation is more or less likely to occur. Even though counterargumentation is a risk when consumers distrust the advertiser's message—as they may do when harder-to-recall explicit conclusions are given—it may be as much of a risk when consumers reach an implicit conclusion that is readily accessible from memory.

C **Correct.** The research indicates that it is easier for consumers to recall conclusions they have reached on their own—that is, the sorts of conclusions that are encouraged by the soft-sell approach—than conclusions that have been provided explicitly, as happens in the hard-sell approach.

D The research does not show that the forcefulness with which claims are presented increases perceptions of the accuracy of those claims. Indeed, it is most likely the opposite, as the forcefulness of others' claims may make them seem even less related to any conclusions the consumer might generate for him- or herself.

E The research suggests that it is the soft-sell, not the hard-sell, approach that has fewer risks. The fourth paragraph indicates that there could be some risks to the implicit conclusions that consumers draw, but this is not part of the research in question.

The correct answer is C.

Questions 30–34 refer to the passage on page 30.

30. The passage is primarily concerned with

(A) describing the effects of human activities on algae in coral reefs

(B) explaining how human activities are posing a threat to coral reef communities

(C) discussing the process by which coral reefs deteriorate in nutrient-poor waters

(D) explaining how coral reefs produce food for themselves

(E) describing the abundance of algae and filter-feeding animals in coral reef areas

Main idea

This question concerns the author's main point, the focus of the passage as a whole. The first paragraph describes the symbiotic process of coral reefs so that readers will understand how human activities are degrading this fragile ecosystem, as explained in the second paragraph. The author focuses on how harmful these human activities are to coral reefs.

A The increased abundance of algae (line 23) is a detail supporting the main point.

B Correct. Human activities are threatening complex coral reef communities.

C The first paragraph explains how coral reefs thrive in nutrient-poor waters.

D The zooxanthellae cells of algae feed the coral reefs (lines 7–12); this point is a detail that supports the main idea.

E This abundance is a detail supporting the main idea, not the main idea itself.

The correct answer is B.

31. The passage suggests which of the following about coral reef communities?

(A) Coral reef communities may actually be more likely to thrive in waters that are relatively low in nutrients.

(B) The nutrients on which coral reef communities thrive are only found in shallow waters.

(C) Human population growth has led to changing ocean temperatures, which threatens coral reef communities.

(D) The growth of coral reef communities tends to destabilize underwater herbivore populations.

(E) Coral reef communities are more complex and diverse than most ecosystems located on dry land.

Inference

The word *suggests* in the question indicates that the answer will be an inference based on what the passage says about coral reef communities. The beginning of the passage states that *nutrient-poor* waters (lines 4–5) sustain the thriving life of a coral reef. Lines 25–27 show that *nutrient input is increasing* because of human activities, with consequent *declines in reef communities* (line 24). Given this information, it is reasonable to conclude that coral reefs thrive in nutrient-poor, rather than nutrient-rich, waters.

A Correct. Coral reefs flourish in clear, nutrient-poor waters.

B Shallow waters are mentioned only in the context of deteriorating marine habitats (line 17), not as a source of nutrients; the passage does not indicate that the nutrients are unique to shallow waters.

C Ocean temperatures are not mentioned in the passage.

D Reef decline, not reef growth, leads to destabilized herbivore populations (lines 21–22).

E No comparisons are made between ecosystems in water and on land.

The correct answer is A.

32. The author refers to "filter-feeding animals" (lines 23–24) in order to

(A) provide an example of a characteristic sign of reef deterioration

(B) explain how reef communities acquire sustenance for survival

(C) identify a factor that helps herbivore populations thrive

(D) indicate a cause of decreasing nutrient input in waters that reefs inhabit

(E) identify members of coral reef communities that rely on coral reefs for nutrients

Logical structure

This question concerns why the author has included a particular detail. Look at the context for the phrase *filter-feeding animals*. The complete sentence (lines 21–24) shows that a higher population of filter-feeding animals is a symptom of reef decline.

A **Correct.** An *increasing abundance* of these animals is a *typical* sign of reef decline.

B Zooxanthellae cells of algae, not filter-feeding animals, provide sustenance for reef communities (lines 7–12).

C An increase in filter-feeding animals is associated with *destabilized*, not thriving, herbivore populations.

D An increase in nutrients, rather than a decrease, causes reef decline, when the population of filter-feeding animals then grows.

E The author includes filter-feeding animals in the context of the decline of coral reefs, not the symbiotic process of coral reefs.

The correct answer is A.

33. According to the passage, which of the following is a factor that is threatening the survival of coral reef communities?

(A) The waters they inhabit contain few nutrient resources.

(B) A decline in nutrient input is disrupting their symbiotic relationship with zooxanthellae.

(C) The degraded waters of their marine habitats have reduced their ability to carry out photosynthesis.

(D) They are too biologically complex to survive in habitats with minimal nutrient input.

(E) Waste by-products result in an increase in nutrient input to reef communities.

Supporting ideas

The phrase *according to the passage* indicates that the necessary information is explicitly stated in the passage. Look at the threats to coral reefs listed in lines 18–21 and match them against the possible answers. Waste by-products increase nutrients in the water, and reefs decline as nutrients grow more plentiful (lines 21–24).

A Coral reefs thrive in nutrient-poor waters, as the first paragraph explains.

B Nutrient input is increasing, not decreasing (lines 20–21).

C The passage does not say that the degraded waters inhibit photosynthesis.

D The complex ecosystem of coral reefs thrives in nutrient-poor waters.

E **Correct.** Waste by-products contribute to increased nutrient input, which causes reef decline.

The correct answer is E.

34. It can be inferred from the passage that the author describes coral reef communities as paradoxical most likely for which of the following reasons?

(A) They are thriving even though human activities have depleted the nutrients in their environment.

(B) They are able to survive in spite of an overabundance of algae inhabiting their waters.

(C) They are able to survive in an environment with limited food resources.

(D) Their metabolic wastes contribute to the degradation of the waters that they inhabit.

(E) They are declining even when the water surrounding them remains clear.

Inference

A paradox is a puzzling statement that seems to contradict itself. To answer this question, look for information that appears puzzling. The author calls coral reefs *one of the fascinating paradoxes of the biosphere* because the reefs are *prolific and productive* despite inhabiting clear waters with few nutrients. The paradox is that the reefs seem to flourish with little food.

A Human activities have harmed coral reefs by increasing nutrient input (lines 24–29).

B An increase in algae is a sign of reef decline, not reef survival (lines 21–23).

C **Correct.** Coral reefs thrive in waters that provide little food.

D Algae cells use the metabolic wastes of the corals to carry out photosynthesis; the result is sustenance for the reef community, not a degradation of waters (lines 9–12).

E Coral reefs thrive in clear, nutrient-poor water and decline in nutrient-rich water.

The correct answer is C.

Questions 35–38 refer to the passage on page 32.

35. It can be inferred from the passage that the two procedures described in the passage have which of the following in common?

(A) They have been applied in practice.
(B) They rely on the use of a device that measures tension.
(C) Their purpose is to determine an unknown mass.
(D) They can only be applied to small solid objects.
(E) They involve attraction between objects of similar mass.

Inference

The procedures described in the passage are introduced by the suggestion in the first paragraph that someone in a spaceship who wanted to determine a solid object's mass could do so in a particular way. The second paragraph uses the word *weigh* in quotes to refer to a similar procedure for determining the mass of a double-star system.

A The language of the first paragraph is hypothetical: we *could* do particular things. Thus, there is no way to determine from the passage whether that procedure has been applied in practice.

B The first procedure relies on a spring scale, which measures tension, but the second procedure measures time and distance to determine restraining force.

C **Correct.** Both procedures determine mass: the first procedure can determine the mass of a small solid object on a spaceship in free fall, and the second can determine the mass of a double-star system.

D The first procedure would, according to the passage, be applied to a small solid object, but the second *weighs* double-star systems, which are clearly not small objects.

E The second procedure involves attraction between two stars, which could be of similar mass, in the same system, but the first procedure involves measuring tension in a string and speed of whirling, not attraction between objects.

The correct answer is C.

36. According to the passage, the tension in the string mentioned in lines 8–9 is analogous to which of the following aspects of a double-star system?

(A) The speed with which one star orbits the other
(B) The gravitational attraction between the stars
(C) The amount of time it takes for the stars to circle one another
(D) The distance between the two stars
(E) The combined mass of the two stars

Supporting idea

The second paragraph states that an *attractive force* is analogous to the tension in the string. This attractive force is identified in the previous sentence as the gravitational force between the two stars in a double-star system.

A The second paragraph states that the speed with which the stars circle each other depends on the gravitational force between them, but it is that force that is analogous to the tension in the string.

B **Correct.** The second paragraph clearly identifies the gravitational force between the two stars as the attractive force that is analogous to the tension in the spring scale's string.

C The amount of time it takes for the stars to circle one another is necessary for calculating the force that holds them together, but it is the force itself that is analogous to the string's tension.

D The distance between the stars must be measured if the attraction between them is to be determined, but the attraction, not the distance, is analogous to the string's tension.

E The combined mass of the two stars is what the procedure is designed to determine; it is analogous to the mass of the small solid object, as described in the first paragraph.

The correct answer is B.

37. Which of the following best describes the relationship between the first and the second paragraph of the passage?

(A) The first paragraph provides an illustration useful for understanding a procedure described in the second paragraph.

(B) The first paragraph describes a hypothetical situation whose plausibility is tested in the second paragraph.

(C) The first paragraph evaluates the usefulness of a procedure whose application is described further in the second paragraph.

(D) The second paragraph provides evidence to support a claim made in the first paragraph.

(E) The second paragraph analyzes the practical implications of a methodology proposed in the first paragraph.

Evaluation

This question requires understanding that the second paragraph describes a somewhat difficult-to-understand procedure that the first paragraph illustrates in smaller, and simpler, terms.

A **Correct.** The first paragraph illustrates, hypothetically, a simple procedure for determining mass, and this illustration provides the grounds on which the passage explains the procedure of the second paragraph.

B The first paragraph describes a situation in hypothetical terms, but the second paragraph does not test that situation's plausibility. Instead, the second paragraph draws an analogy between the initial situation and another procedure.

C The first paragraph does not evaluate the usefulness of the procedure for determining a small solid object's mass while in a spaceship in freefall; it simply describes how that procedure would work.

D The second paragraph provides no evidence; it describes a procedure analogous to what is described in the first paragraph.

E The second paragraph does not discuss the practical implications of the first paragraph's methodology but rather a procedure that is analogous to the hypothetical situation of the first paragraph.

The correct answer is A.

38. The author of the passage mentions observations regarding the period of a double-star system as being useful for determining

(A) the distance between the two stars in the system

(B) the time it takes for each star to rotate on its axis

(C) the size of the orbit the system's two stars occupy

(D) the degree of gravitational attraction between the system's stars

(E) the speed at which the star system moves through space

Supporting idea

The author mentions the period of a double-star system in the final sentence of the second paragraph, defining it as the time required for stars to circle each other. Knowing this time, in combination with the distance between the stars, enables the determination of the restraining force between the stars.

A The final sentence of the second paragraph indicates that the period of a double-star system is measured independently of the distance between the two stars in the system.

B The passage is not concerned with how long it takes each star to rotate on its axis.

C The passage does not mention anyone's trying to determine the size of the orbit of a system's two stars. It does mention the related topic of distance between the stars but indicates that knowing such distance is required for measuring the stars' mass, not that it can be inferred from the period of the system.

D Correct. According to the passage, the restraining force, or gravitational attraction, between the two stars can be deduced based on the period and the distance between them.

E The passage does not mention the speed at which the star system moves through space.

The correct answer is D.

Questions 39–44 refer to the passage on page 34.

39. The primary purpose of the passage is to

(A) describe new ways of studying the possibility that life once existed on Mars

(B) revise a theory regarding the existence of life on Mars in light of new evidence

(C) reconcile conflicting viewpoints regarding the possibility that life once existed on Mars

(D) evaluate a recently proposed argument concerning the origin of ALH84001

(E) describe a controversy concerning the significance of evidence from ALH84001

Main idea

Answering this question requires determining the purpose of the passage as a whole. In the first paragraph, the passage indicates that a research team found that a Martian meteorite in Antarctica contains compelling evidence that life existed on Mars. The rest of the passage then describes arguments by skeptics against the research team's conclusion together with the research team's rebuttals to the skeptics' arguments.

A While the passage discusses one type of evidence that life might have existed on Mars, it does not describe multiple ways of studying the possibility of Martian life, nor characterize any method of study as *new*.

B The passage merely reports and does not make any attempt at revising existing theories.

C The passage describes but does not try to reconcile conflicting viewpoints concerning life on Mars.

D The origin of ALH84001 is generally agreed upon (line 5), not a recently proposed hypothesis evaluated by the passage.

E Correct. The passage describes opposing arguments about whether ALH84001 suggests life ever existed on Mars.

The correct answer is E.

40. The passage asserts which of the following about the claim that ALH84001 originated on Mars?

(A) It was initially proposed by the McKay team of scientists.

(B) It is not a matter of widespread scientific dispute.

(C) It has been questioned by some skeptics of the McKay team's work.

(D) It has been undermined by recent work on PAHs.

(E) It is incompatible with the fact that ALH84001 has been on Earth for 13,000 years.

Supporting ideas

This question requires recognizing what the passage indicates about a piece of information it offers. The passage states that *scientists generally agree* (line 5) that ALH84001 originated on Mars, which strongly suggests that there is not much dispute about it.

A While it is possible that McKay's team initially made the proposal, the passage does not say so.

B **Correct.** In stating that scientists generally agree ALH84001 originated on Mars, the passage indicates there is no real controversy on this matter.

C The skeptics mentioned in the passage are not described as calling into question that ALH84001 originated on Mars.

D The passage does not tie the existence of PAHs in ALH84001 to questions about its Martian origins.

E The passage makes no connection between the time ALH84001 has been on the Earth and questions as to its Martian origins.

The correct answer is B.

41. The passage suggests that the fact that ALH84001 has been on Earth for 13,000 years has been used by some scientists to support which of the following claims about ALH84001?

(A) ALH84001 may not have originated on Mars.

(B) ALH84001 contains PAHs that are the result of nonbiological processes.

(C) ALH84001 may not have contained PAHs when it landed on Earth.

(D) The organic molecules found in ALH84001 are not PAHs.

(E) The organic molecules found in ALH84001 could not be the result of terrestrial contamination.

Supporting ideas

This question requires recognizing how a particular fact is used to support a particular point of view reported in the passage. In the second paragraph, the passage presents various skeptics' arguments about whether the PAHs in ALH84001 originated on Mars. In lines 15–19, the passage indicates that some scientists see the fact that ALH84001 has been on Earth for 13,000 years as raising the possibility that the PAHs in ALH84001 *resulted from terrestrial contamination* or in other words that it did not contain PAHs when it landed on Earth.

A The passage indicates only that most scientists believe that ALH84001 originated on Mars.

B Although the passage indicates that skeptics have pointed out that PAHs can be formed by nonbiological processes, their point is not related to the length of time ALH84001 has been on Earth.

C **Correct.** The passage indicates that some scientists believe that the PAHs in ALH84001 may have been transferred to it during its 13,000 years on Earth.

D The passage does not indicate that any scientists doubt the presence of PAHs in ALH84001.

E The passage indicates that the fact that ALH84001 has been on Earth for 13,000 years is used by some scientists to support the idea of terrestrial contamination.

The correct answer is C.

42. The passage suggests that if a meteorite contained PAHs that were the result of terrestrial contamination, then one would expect which of the following to be true?

(A) The meteorite would have been on Earth for more than 13,000 years.

(B) The meteorite would have originated from a source other than Mars.

(C) The PAHs contained in the meteorite would have originated from nonbiological processes.

(D) The meteorite would contain fewer PAHs than most other meteorites contain.

(E) The PAHs contained in the meteorite would be concentrated toward the meteorite's surface.

Application

Answering this question involves applying information contained in the passage to a situation that is not described in the passage. According to the passage, some scientists believe that because ALH84001 has been on Earth for as long as 13,000 years, any PAHs contained in it may have been transferred from the Earth, a process the passage describes as *terrestrial contamination* (line 19). The passage also indicates that if terrestrial contamination occurred with ALH84001, then, contrary to the findings of McKay's team that showed PAH concentrations increasing *as one looks deeper into ALH84001* (lines 21–22), the PAHs would be expected to be concentrated more toward the outer parts, or surface, of ALH84001.

A The passage indicates that scientists believe that 13,000 years is sufficient time for terrestrial contamination to happen.

B The passage does not suggest that the origin of a meteorite affects its ability to become contaminated with terrestrial PAHs.

C The passage does not indicate whether PAHs resulting from terrestrial contamination would be nonbiological or not.

D The passage does not mention that different meteorites may contain different amounts of PAHs.

E **Correct.** The passage suggests that if ALH84001 experienced terrestrial contamination, then the PAHs would be more concentrated toward the outer surface of the meteorite.

The correct answer is E.

43. Which of the following best describes the function of the last sentence of the first paragraph?

(A) It identifies a possible organic source for the PAHs found in ALH84001.

(B) It describes a feature of PAHs that is not shared by other types of organic molecules.

(C) It explains how a characteristic common to most meteorites originates.

(D) It suggests how the terrestrial contamination of ALH84001 might have taken place.

(E) It presents evidence that undermines the claim that life once existed on Mars.

Evaluation

This question requires understanding how a part of the passage functions within the passage as a whole. The first paragraph begins by establishing that McKay's team believes that the PAHs found in ALH84001 provide compelling evidence that life existed on Mars. To explain this, the passage indicates that PAHs are a type of organic molecules, which form the basis for life. Furthermore, to connect PAHs to possible life on Mars, the final sentence of the first paragraph indicates that one source of PAHs is the decay of dead microbes.

A **Correct.** Without evidence of an organic source for the PAHs in ALH84001, the team's argument would not make sense.

B The passage indicates that PAHs can be formed by the decay of organic material from microbes but does not imply that other organic molecules cannot be formed this way.

C The sentence referred to explains one possible origin of a molecule found in ALH84001 but does not imply that most meteorites contain that molecule.

D The sentence referred to does not involve the process of terrestrial contamination.

E The sentence referred to provides information necessary to the team's argument that life may have existed on Mars.

The correct answer is A.

44. The passage suggests that McKay's team would agree with which of the following regarding the PAHs produced by nonorganic processes?

(A) These PAHs are not likely to be found in any meteorite that has been on Earth for 13,000 years or more.

(B) These PAHs are not likely to be found in any meteorite that originated from Mars.

(C) These PAHs are not likely to be produced by star formation.

(D) These PAHs are likely to be found in combinations that distinguish them from the PAHs produced by organic processes.

(E) These PAHs are likely to be found in fewer meteorites than the PAHs produced by organic processes.

Inference

This question involves understanding a particular point of view presented in the passage. The passage indicates in lines 11–13 that the organic molecules found in ALH84001 are PAHs. In lines 23–27, skeptics of McKay's team's findings point out that processes unrelated to organic life, including star formation, can produce PAHs. In the final sentence of the passage, McKay's team notes that the type of PAHs found in ALH84001 are more similar to those produced by organic processes than to those produced by nonorganic processes.

A McKay's team does not tie the presence of nonorganic PAHs in meteorites to the length of time the meteorites have been on Earth.

B McKay's team does not deny the possibility that at least some of the PAHs found in Martian meteorites are nonorganic in origin.

C McKay's team does not deny that PAHs can be produced by the formation of stars.

D Correct. McKay's team notes in lines 29–34 that the PAH combinations produced by organic processes can be distinguished from those produced by nonorganic processes.

E McKay's team does not address the probability of nonorganic PAHs being found in meteorites.

The correct answer is D.

Questions 45–53 refer to the passage on page 36.

45. The author of the passage draws conclusions about the fur trade in North America from all of the following sources EXCEPT

(A) Cartier's accounts of trading with Native Americans

(B) a seventeenth-century account of European settlements

(C) a sixteenth-century account written by a sailing vessel captain

(D) archaeological observations of sixteenth-century Native American sites

(E) a sixteenth-century account of Native Americans in what is now New England

Supporting idea

This question asks about the sources mentioned by the author of the passage. Answering the question correctly requires determining which answer option is NOT referred to in the passage as a source of evidence regarding the North American fur trade.

A Correct. The passage mentions Cartier's voyage but does not refer to Cartier's accounts of his trading.

B In the first paragraph, Nicolas Denys's 1672 account of European settlements provides evidence of fur trading by sixteenth-century European fishing crews.

C In the second paragraph, a Portuguese captain's records provide evidence that the fur trade was going on for some time prior to his 1501 account.

D In the first paragraph, archaeologists' observations of sixteenth-century Native American sites provide evidence of fur trading at that time.

E In the second paragraph, a 1524 account provides evidence that Native Americans living in what is now New England had become selective about which European goods they would accept in trade for furs.

The correct answer is A.

46. The passage suggests that which of the following is partially responsible for the difficulty in establishing the precise date when the fur trade in North America began?

(A) A lack of written accounts before that of Nicolas Denys in 1672

(B) A lack of written documentation before 1501

(C) Ambiguities in the evidence from Native American sources

(D) Uncertainty about Native American trade networks

(E) Uncertainty about the origin of artifacts supposedly traded by European fishing crews for furs

Inference

The question asks about information implied by the passage. The first paragraph points out the difficulty of establishing exactly when the fur trade between Native Americans and Europeans began. The second paragraph explains that the first written record of the fur trade (at least the earliest known to scholars who study the history of the trade) dates to 1501, but that trading was already well established by that time. Thus, it can be inferred that lack of written records prior to 1501 contributes to the difficulty in establishing an exact date for the beginning of the fur trade.

A Two written records of the fur trade prior to the account by Nicolas Denys are mentioned in the passage. The passage does not suggest that a lack of written records from before 1672 is a source of the difficulty in establishing the date.

B Correct. The passage indicates that the fur trade was well established by the time of the documentation dating from 1501 but strongly suggests that there is no known earlier documentation regarding that trade, so a lack of records before that time contributes to the difficulty in establishing an exact date.

C The only Native American sources mentioned in the passage are archaeological sites, and there is no indication of ambiguities at those sites.

D Native American trade networks are not mentioned in the passage.

E The passage mentions that fishing crews exchanged parts of their ships for furs and does not suggest any uncertainty about the origin of those artifacts.

The correct answer is B.

47. Which of the following, if true, most strengthens the author's assertion in the first sentence of the second paragraph?

(A) When Europeans retraced Cartier's voyage in the first years of the seventeenth century, they frequently traded with Native Americans.

(B) Furs from beavers, which were plentiful in North America but nearly extinct in Europe, became extremely fashionable in Europe in the final decades of the sixteenth century.

(C) Firing arms were rarely found on sixteenth-century Native American sites or on European lists of trading goods since such arms required frequent maintenance and repair.

(D) Europeans and Native Americans had established trade protocols, such as body language assuring one another of their peaceful intentions, that antedate the earliest records of trade.

(E) During the first quarter of the sixteenth century, an Italian explorer recorded seeing many Native Americans with what appeared to be copper beads, though they may have been made of indigenous copper.

Evaluation

The question depends on evaluating an assertion made in the passage and determining which additional evidence would most strengthen it. The first sentence of the second paragraph claims that the fur trade was well established by the time Europeans sailing the Atlantic coast of America first documented it. The passage then indicates that the first written documentation of the trade dates to 1501. Thus, evidence showing that trade had been going on for some time before 1501 would strengthen (support) the assertion.

A This evidence shows trade occurring in the first years of the seventeenth century, not prior to the first records from 1501.

B This evidence shows trade occurring in the final decades of the sixteenth century, not prior to the first records from 1501.

C This evidence does not indicate that trade took place prior to the first records from 1501.

D **Correct.** Evidence that trade protocols had developed before the trade was first recorded (in 1501) would strengthen support for the assertion that trade was taking place prior to the earliest documentation.

E Because the copper beads may have been made by Native Americans rather than acquired through trade with other societies, this observation would not provide evidence that trade with Europeans took place prior to 1501.

The correct answer is D.

48. Which of the following best describes the primary function of lines 11–16?

(A) It offers a reconsideration of a claim made in the preceding sentence.

(B) It reveals how archaeologists arrived at an interpretation of the evidence mentioned in the preceding sentence.

(C) It shows how scholars misinterpreted the significance of certain evidence mentioned in the preceding sentence.

(D) It identifies one of the first significant accounts of seventeenth-century European settlements in North America.

(E) It explains why Denys's account of seventeenth-century European settlements is thought to be significant.

Evaluation

This question depends on understanding how the last sentence of the first paragraph functions in relation to the larger passage. The first paragraph explains that the earliest Europeans to trade with Native Americans were fishing crews near Newfoundland. The second-to-last sentence of the paragraph describes archaeological artifacts from Native American sites. The last sentence then explains that Nicolas Denys's 1672 account helped archaeologists realize that the artifacts were evidence of trade with fishing crews. Thus, the last sentence of the passage shows how archaeologists learned to interpret the evidence mentioned in the previous sentence.

A The only claim made in the previous sentence is that archaeologists found a particular type of evidence. The final sentence of the paragraph does not suggest that this claim should be reconsidered.

B **Correct.** After reading Denys's account, archaeologists were able to interpret the archaeological evidence mentioned in the previous sentence.

C The passage suggests that archaeologists correctly interpreted the evidence, not misinterpreted it.

D Denys's account is mentioned primarily to explain how archaeologists learned to interpret the archaeological evidence, not primarily to identify an important early account of settlements.

E The passage does not discuss why Denys's account is significant, only that archaeologists used it to help understand the evidence mentioned in the previous sentence.

The correct answer is B.

49. It can be inferred from the passage that the author would agree with which of the following statements about the fur trade between Native Americans and Europeans in the early modern era?

(A) This trade may have begun as early as the 1480s.

(B) This trade probably did not continue much beyond the 1530s.
(C) This trade was most likely at its peak in the mid-1520s.
(D) This trade probably did not begin prior to 1500.
(E) There is no written evidence of this trade prior to the seventeenth century

Inference

The question requires determining which statement can most reasonably be inferred from the information in the passage. The passage argues that it is difficult to determine when the fur trade between Native Americans and Europeans began, since the earliest people to participate in that trade apparently left no written records. The second paragraph notes that at the time of the earliest known record in 1501, trade was already *well underway*. In the final two sentences of the passage, the author mentions an event that occurred in 1534 and then says that by that time the trade may have been going on for *perhaps half a century*.

A **Correct.** The next-to-last sentence of the passage cites evidence of fur trade between Native Americans and Europeans in 1524. In the final sentence of the passage, the author mentions an event that happened a decade after that date—thus in 1534—and expresses the opinion that the trade started *perhaps half a century* (fifty years) before that later date. Fifty years before 1534 would be 1484. This implies that the author accepts that the trade may have begun by the 1480s.

B The passage gives no indication that the author believes trade ended shortly after the 1530s.

C The passage does not discuss when the fur trade was at its peak.

D To the contrary, the passage argues that trade began well before 1501.

E The passage mentions written evidence of the trade from 1501 and 1524.

The correct answer is A.

50. Which of the following can be inferred from the passage about the Native Americans mentioned in line 24?

(A) They had little use for decorative objects such as earrings.
(B) They became increasingly dependent on fishing between 1501 and 1524.
(C) By 1524, only certain groups of Europeans were willing to trade with them.
(D) The selectivity of their trading choices made it difficult for them to engage in widespread trade with Europeans.
(E) The selectivity of their trading choices indicates that they had been trading with Europeans for a significant period of time prior to 1524.

Inference

The question asks about information that can be inferred from the passage. The Native Americans mentioned in the 1524 chronicles accepted only certain kinds of European goods in trade. The passage indicates that these Native Americans *had become selective* about which goods they would accept, which implies that by 1524 they had been trading long enough to determine which European goods were most valuable to them.

A The passage does not imply that these Native Americans had no use for decorative objects, only that they did not desire to obtain such items through trade with Europeans.

B The passage does not suggest that the Native Americans' dependency on fishing changed over time.

C There is no indication that any groups of Europeans were unwilling to trade with these Native Americans.

D The passage notes that the Native Americans were selective in their trade choices but does not suggest that such selectivity made widespread trade difficult.

E **Correct.** The passage notes that by 1524, the Native Americans had become selective about which European goods they would accept, and the passage takes this to indicate that the trade with Europeans significantly predated 1524.

The correct answer is E.

51. The passage supports which of the following statements about sixteenth-century European fishing crews working the waters off Newfoundland?

(A) They wrote no accounts of their fishing voyages.
(B) They primarily sailed under the flag of Portugal.
(C) They exchanged ship parts with Native Americans for furs.
(D) They commonly traded jewelry with Native Americans for furs.
(E) They carried surplus metal implements to trade with Native Americans for furs.

Inference

The question asks which statement is supported by information provided in the passage. The first paragraph states that European fishing crews around Newfoundland were the first Europeans to trade goods for furs with Native Americans in the modern period. The last sentence of the paragraph states that archaeological evidence indicates the crews had dismantled their ships to trade ship parts for furs.

A The second sentence states that the crews left no written accounts of their trade with Native Americans, but it does not suggest that they left no written accounts of their voyages.

B The passage mentions one Portuguese vessel but does not suggest that the European crews who fished off Newfoundland were mostly on Portuguese vessels.

C **Correct.** The last sentence of the first paragraph supports the conclusion that the crews traded ship parts for furs.

D The passage mentions one instance of a Native American acquiring earrings from Europeans but does not suggest that trades for such goods were common.

E The passage indicates that fishing crews traded metal implements with Native Americans but does not suggest that they brought surplus implements for that purpose—and in fact mentions that sometimes traded metal articles had been parts of their own ships.

The correct answer is C.

52. Which of the following can be inferred from the passage about evidence pertaining to the fur trade between Native Americans and Europeans in the early modern era?

(A) A lack of written evidence has made it difficult to establish which Europeans first participated in this trade.
(B) In general, the physical evidence pertaining to this trade has been more useful than the written evidence has been.
(C) There is more written evidence pertaining to this trade from the early part of the sixteenth century than from later in that century.
(D) The earliest written evidence pertaining to this trade dates from a time when the trade was already well established.
(E) Some important pieces of evidence pertaining to this trade, such as Denys's 1672 account, were long overlooked by archaeologists.

Inference

This question asks about information that can be inferred from the passage. Any suggestion that Native Americans may have produced written evidence of the early-modern trade with Europeans is absent from the passage. The second paragraph states that by the time Europeans first documented the fur trade, it was already well underway. This statement, in the context of the passage, implies that the earliest written records of the trade date to a time after it was well established.

A The first paragraph indicates that the first Europeans to participate in the trade were quite certainly fishing crews near Newfoundland.

B The passage gives no indication that physical evidence of the trade has been more useful than written evidence.

C Although the passage does not cite written evidence from the late sixteenth century, the passage gives no reason to believe that less written evidence exists from that time.

D **Correct.** According to the passage, the fur trade was well underway when written evidence of the trade was first documented by Europeans. The passage contains no suggestion that there might have been earlier documentation of that trade by anybody other than Europeans.

E The passage does not imply that archaeologists overlooked evidence for long periods of time.

The correct answer is D.

53. The passage suggests which of the following about the sixteenth-century Native Americans who traded with Europeans on the coast of what is now called New England?

(A) By 1524 they had become accustomed to exchanging goods with Europeans.

(B) They were unfamiliar with metals before encountering Europeans.

(C) They had no practical uses for European goods other than metals and metal implements.

(D) By 1524 they had become disdainful of European traders because such traders had treated them unfairly in the past.

(E) By 1524 they demanded only the most prized European goods because they had come to realize how valuable furs were on European markets.

Inference

The question asks about what is implied in the passage. The Native Americans trading with Europeans on the coast of what is now called New England are discussed in the 1524 chronicles mentioned in the second paragraph. The passage indicates that these Native Americans *had become selective* about which European goods they would accept in trade, which suggests they had become accustomed to trading with Europeans.

A **Correct.** By the time the chronicle was written, the Native Americans were familiar enough with trade to be able to specify which European goods they would accept.

B Although the Native Americans chose to trade furs for European metal goods, the passage does not imply they were unfamiliar with any metals prior to encountering Europeans.

C The passage does not suggest why Native Americans preferred certain goods over others.

D The passage does not attribute disdain for European traders to Native Americans.

E There is no indication in the passage that Native Americans were aware of furs' value in European markets.

The correct answer is A.

Questions 54–57 refer to the passage on page 38.

54. The passage is primarily concerned with

(A) describing the development of the biological species concept

(B) responding to a critique of reproductive compatibility as a criterion for defining a species

(C) considering two different approaches to identifying biological species

(D) pointing out the advantage of one method of distinguishing related species

(E) identifying an obstacle to the classification of biological species

Main idea

This question depends on understanding the passage as a whole. The passage begins by explaining that identifying a species can be difficult, because there are different ways of defining the term. The biological species concept is one approach, but it has problems. Phenotype is another approach that can be used when the biological species concept proves difficult.

A The first paragraph defines the biological species concept and identifies some problems with its application, but it does not explain how that concept developed.

B The passage presents some critiques of reproductive compatibility as a way of identifying a biological species; it does not concern itself with responding to those critiques.

C **Correct.** The passage considers the biological species concept and the idea of phenotype as ways of identifying biological species.

D While the passage identifies two ways of distinguishing species and states that some investigators use one of those methods—the phenotype method—when the biological method is difficult to apply, the passage is not primarily concerned with pointing out that either one is better than the other.

E The passage does discuss certain obstacles to the classification of species. First, it points out that there is no single accepted definition of *distinct species*. Second, it points out obstacles related to one particular approach to the classification of species. However, the passage considers these obstacles in service of its primary concern, namely considering two different approaches to identifying biological species.

The correct answer is C.

55. The author of the passage mentions "groups that live in different places" (line 21) most probably in order to

(A) point out a theoretical inconsistency in the biological species concept

(B) offer evidence in support of the biological species concept

(C) identify an obstacle to the application of the biological species concept

(D) note an instance in which phenotype classification is customarily used

(E) describe an alternative to the biological species concept

Evaluation

The author's mention of *groups that live in different places* comes at the end of the first paragraph, in the context of discussing a third problem with the biological species concept: that investigators may not know whether animals in such groups are able to interbreed.

A The author does not address theoretical inconsistencies in the biological species concept.

B The author mentions groups that live in different places in order to address a problem with the biological species concept, not to support it.

C **Correct.** One obstacle to applying the biological species concept is that those attempting to distinguish among species may not be able to determine whether geographically separated groups of animals can interbreed.

D The passage does mention that some investigators use phenotype classification when the biological species concept is difficult to apply, but it does not mention specifically that a situation in which groups live in different places is an instance in which phenotype classification is customarily used.

E Animal groups that live in different places pose a problem for the application of the biological species concept, according to the author. The author does not mention these groups in order to describe an alternative to that concept.

The correct answer is C.

56. With which of the following statements regarding the classification of individual species would the author most likely agree?

(A) Phenotype comparison may help to classify species when application of the biological species concept proves inconclusive.

(B) Because no standard definition exists for what constitutes a species, the classification of animal populations is inevitably an arbitrary process.

(C) The criteria used by biologists to classify species have not been based on adequate research.

(D) The existence of hybrids in wild animal species is the chief factor casting doubt on the usefulness of research into reproductive compatibility as a way of classifying species.

(E) Phenotype overlap should be used as the basic criterion for standardizing species classification.

Inference

This question depends on understanding the general points the author makes with regard to classification of individual species. The author explains that there is no single definition of species and then describes the biological species concept, which depends on reproductive compatibility. This approach has several problems, however, and the author goes on to say that phenotype may be used when the biological species concept is difficult to apply.

A **Correct.** The author states at the beginning of the second paragraph that some investigators use phenotype when they find it difficult to apply the biological species concept, and the passage provides no reason to believe that the author would disagree with the idea that phenotype comparison can be helpful in these situations.

B The author would most likely not agree that classification of animal populations is arbitrary. Investigators use clearly defined approaches, such as the biological species concept and phenotype classification, to make such classifications. That there may be problems with an approach does not make it arbitrary.

C The author states that the biological species concept can be too restrictive, but there is no suggestion that the author finds this approach, or phenotype classification, to be inadequately researched.

D The author mentions hybridization first as a factor casting doubt on the usefulness of the biological species concept, but nothing in the passage suggests that the author thinks that it is more significant than the other reasons offered for finding the biological species concept too restrictive.

E Phenotype overlap does not receive the author's endorsement as the best, or most basic, way of classifying species; instead, the author states merely that some investigators rely on this approach when they cannot apply the biological species concept.

The correct answer is A.

57. Which of the following best describes the function of lines 10–13?

(A) It elaborates the definition of the biological species concept given in a previous sentence.

(B) It develops a point about the biological species concept made in the previous sentence.

(C) It states the author's central point about the biological species concept.

(D) It identifies a central assumption underlying the biological species concept.

(E) It demonstrates why the biological species concept is invalid.

Evaluation

The highlighted sentence discusses hybridization as a first factor complicating the applicability of the biological species concept. Thus its function is to help explain why, as the previous sentence states, that concept is too restrictive.

A The highlighted sentence brings up a problem with the biological species concept; it does not elaborate the definition of that concept.

B Correct. According to the sentence that precedes the highlighted sentence, the biological species concept can be too restrictive. The author offers three reasons to develop this point, and the first reason is given in the highlighted sentence.

C The highlighted sentence could be said to support the author's central point about the biological species concept—that it is one (flawed) way of determining whether a population is a species—but it does not state that central point.

D The highlighted sentence expresses a problem with the biological species concept, not a central assumption of it.

E The highlighted sentence serves to indicate a problem with the biological species concept, but it does not go so far as to demonstrate that it is invalid.

The correct answer is B.

Questions 58–63 refer to the passage on page 40.

58. The primary purpose of the passage is to

(A) enumerate reasons why both traditional scholarly methods and newer scholarly methods have limitations
(B) identify a shortcoming in a scholarly approach and describe an alternative approach
(C) provide empirical data to support a long-held scholarly assumption
(D) compare two scholarly publications on the basis of their authors' backgrounds
(E) attempt to provide a partial answer to a long-standing scholarly dilemma

Main idea

To find the primary purpose, look at what the author is doing in the entire passage. In the first paragraph, the author examines two approaches to political history, both of which suffer from the same flaw, the exclusion of women. In the second paragraph, the author reviews an alternative, more inclusive way to understand political history.

A The first paragraph identifies only one reason that the two approaches are flawed; an alternative approach is discussed in the second paragraph.
B Correct. The author points to the flaw in earlier approaches to history and shows an alternative way of thinking about political history.
C No data are offered to support an assumption.
D Only one historian is mentioned by name; her background is not mentioned.
E No long-standing dilemma is discussed.

The correct answer is B.

59. The passage suggests which of the following concerning the techniques used by the new political historians described in the first paragraph of the passage?

(A) They involved the extensive use of the biographies of political party leaders and political theoreticians.
(B) They were conceived by political historians who were reacting against the political climates of the 1960's and 1970's.
(C) They were of more use in analyzing the positions of United States political parties in the nineteenth century than in analyzing the positions of those in the twentieth century.
(D) They were of more use in analyzing the political behavior of nineteenth-century voters than in analyzing the political activities of those who could not vote during that period.
(E) They were devised as a means of tracing the influence of nineteenth-century political trends on twentieth-century political trends.

Inference

The question's use of the verb *suggests* is an indication that an inference must be made. Examine the first paragraph, where the *new school of political history* is discussed. These historians used techniques such as *quantitative analyses of election returns* that the author describes as *useless in analyzing the political activities of women, who were denied the vote until 1920* (lines 9–12). It can, however, be assumed that the same techniques did prove useful in understanding the *mass political behavior* of voters.

A The first sentence explains that these historians *sought to go beyond the traditional focus . . . on leaders and government institutions.*
B The passage does not indicate that the new historians were reacting against the political climate of their own time.
C The new historians examined the *political practices of ordinary citizens* (line 5), not the positions of political parties.

D **Correct.** Lines 7–12 explicitly state that the new historians' techniques were *useless* in analyzing the political activities of those not allowed to vote; the same lines imply that the techniques were useful in analyzing the political behavior of voters.

E No information in the passage supports this explanation.

The correct answer is D.

60. It can be inferred that the author of the passage quotes Baker directly in the second paragraph primarily in order to

(A) clarify a position before providing an alternative to that position
(B) differentiate between a novel definition and traditional definitions
(C) provide an example of a point agreed on by different generations of scholars
(D) provide an example of the prose style of an important historian
(E) amplify a definition given in the first paragraph

Logical structure

To analyze why the author uses a direct quotation, look at the logical structure of the passage in relation to the quotation. The historians discussed in the first paragraph define political activity as voting. Paula Baker, however, has a new definition of political activity, one that includes the activities of those who were not allowed to vote. It is reasonable to infer that the author quotes Baker to draw attention to this new definition, which provides an innovative, alternative way of thinking about political history.

A Paula Baker's is the alternative position offered; no alternative to hers is discussed.

B **Correct.** Baker is quoted to emphasize that her definition is new and that it differs significantly from the traditional definition used by other historians.

C The contrasting views expressed in the first and second paragraphs show that different generations of scholars have not agreed.

D The author does not comment on Baker's prose style.

E Baker's definition contrasts with, rather than amplifies, the one offered in the first paragraph.

The correct answer is B.

61. According to the passage, Paula Baker and the new political historians of the 1960's and 1970's shared which of the following?

(A) A commitment to interest group politics
(B) A disregard for political theory and ideology
(C) An interest in the ways in which nineteenth-century politics prefigured contemporary politics
(D) A reliance on such quantitative techniques as the analysis of election returns
(E) An emphasis on the political involvement of ordinary citizens

Supporting ideas

Since the question uses the phrase *according to the passage*, the answer is explicitly stated in the passage. Look for a point on which the new political historians and Baker agree. The first sentence of the passage says that these new historians were interested in the political activities of *ordinary citizens* (line 5). Paula Baker is similarly interested in the political activities of *ordinary citizens* (lines 15–16), especially of female citizens, who were not allowed to vote.

A No mention at all is made of interest group politics, neither in relation to Baker nor in relation to the new historians.

B The passage does not show that they disregarded political theory and ideology.

C The passage only discusses Baker's interest in the way women's political activities in the nineteenth century prefigured twentieth-century trends (lines 16–18).

D The passage explains that new historians relied on such techniques but that Baker did not.

E **Correct.** Both the new historians and Baker are said to have studied the political activities of *ordinary citizens.*

The correct answer is E.

62. Which of the following best describes the structure of the first paragraph of the passage?

(A) Two scholarly approaches are compared, and a shortcoming common to both is identified.

(B) Two rival schools of thought are contrasted, and a third is alluded to.

(C) An outmoded scholarly approach is described, and a corrective approach is called for.

(D) An argument is outlined, and counterarguments are mentioned.

(E) A historical era is described in terms of its political trends.

Logical structure

To answer this question, analyze the structure of the first paragraph. It compares *the old approach* of studying political history through emphasis on leaders and government institutions with *the new school of political history*, which turned instead to the political practices of ordinary citizens. Both approaches suffered from the same drawback: the failure to include women in their analyses.

A **Correct.** Two approaches to history are discussed, and a flaw shared by both, the exclusion of women, is identified.

B The first paragraph does not allude to a third school of thought.

C A corrective approach is not discussed in the first paragraph.

D The first paragraph does present an argument, but no counterarguments are made.

E The political trends of an historical era are not detailed in the first paragraph.

The correct answer is A.

63. The information in the passage suggests that a pre-1960's political historian would have been most likely to undertake which of the following studies?

(A) An analysis of voting trends among women voters of the 1920's

(B) A study of male voters' gradual ideological shift from party politics to issue oriented politics

(C) A biography of an influential nineteenth-century minister of foreign affairs

(D) An analysis of narratives written by previously unrecognized women activists

(E) A study of voting trends among naturalized immigrant laborers in a nineteenth-century logging camp

Inference

In using *suggests*, this question asks the reader to apply information stated in the passage to make an inference about the methods of historians before the 1960's. These methods are discussed in the first paragraph. Lines 3–4 say that the *traditional focus of political historians* (before the advent of the new school of historians in the 1960's and 1970's) was *on leaders and government institutions.* It is reasonable to infer that the pre-1960's historian was likely to focus on a leader or government institution.

A Traditional historians did not focus on ordinary citizens, but on their leaders.

B Baker is interested in this group shift, but traditional historians were not.

C **Correct.** Traditional historians emphasized the work of leaders and government institutions; a biography of a foreign affairs minister fits this focus perfectly.

D Such an analysis would be of interest to Baker but not to traditional historians focusing on leaders and government.

E The new historians would be interested in such a study, but not traditional historians, who did not look at the activities of ordinary citizens.

The correct answer is C.

Questions 64–68 refer to the passage on page 42.

64. The passage is primarily concerned with

(A) identifying historical circumstances that led Du Bois to alter his long-term goals
(B) defining “accommodationism” and showing how Du Bois used this strategy to achieve certain goals
(C) accounting for a particular position adopted by Du Bois during the First World War
(D) contesting the view that Du Bois was significantly influenced by either Washington or Trotter
(E) assessing the effectiveness of a strategy that Du Bois urged African Americans to adopt

Main idea

This question asks what the passage as a whole is attempting to do. The passage opens by indicating that many African Americans were surprised by a political position taken by Du Bois in 1918, which seemed more accommodationist than expected. The passage then goes on to demonstrate that Du Bois often *shifted positions* (line 9) and states that Du Bois's 1918 position was pragmatic in that it responded to real social pressure. The passage then indicates that Du Bois's accommodationist stance *did not last* (line 31), and that he returned to a more confrontationist stance upon learning of the treatment of African Americans in the military.

A The passage indicates that Du Bois did not change his long-term goals (lines 22–24).

B *Accomodationism* is not defined in the passage but is associated with certain actions (community improvement), ideologies (solidarity), and leaders (Washington); the passage does not indicate if Du Bois was successful in achieving the accommodationist goals of 1895 (lines 11–15).

C Correct. The passage explains why Du Bois took his accommodationist position and why he eventually rejected it.

D The passage offers no judgment as to how much Du Bois was influenced by Washington or Trotter.

E The passage does not indicate that there was widespread adoption of any of the strategies Du Bois recommended.

The correct answer is C.

65. The passage indicates which of the following about Du Bois's attitude toward Washington?

(A) It underwent a shift during the First World War as Du Bois became more sympathetic with Trotter's views.
(B) It underwent a shift in 1903 for reasons other than Du Bois's disagreement with Washington's accommodationist views.
(C) It underwent a shift as Du Bois made a long-term commitment to the strategy of accommodation.
(D) It remained consistently positive even though Du Bois disagreed with Washington's efforts to control the African American press.
(E) It was shaped primarily by Du Bois's appreciation of Washington's pragmatic approach to the advancement of the interests of African Americans.

Supporting ideas

Answering this question involves recognizing what the passage indicates about a particular point of view it describes. In line 15, the passage indicates that Du Bois praised Washington's ideas, but that in 1903 Du Bois aligned himself with *Washington's militant opponent* (lines 16–17), a shift the passage describes as being due less to *ideological reasons* (lines 17–21) than to political reasons.

A The passage indicates that the shift described occurred in 1903, not during the First World War.

B Correct. The passage indicates Du Bois's shift was not due to differences he had with Washington's ideas or views.

C The passage indicates that Du Bois's accommodationist stance *did not last* (lines 30–31) and therefore was not a long-term commitment.

D The passage indicates in lines 16–17 that Du Bois at one point aligned himself with Washington's militant opponent.

E The passage indicates that Du Bois eventually rejected the accommodationist views of Washington.

The correct answer is B.

66. The passage suggests which of the following about the contributions of African Americans to the United States war effort during the First World War?

(A) The contributions were made largely in response to Du Bois's 1918 editorial.

(B) The contributions had much the same effect as African Americans' contributions to previous wars.

(C) The contributions did not end discrimination against African Americans in the military.

(D) The contributions were made in protest against Trotter's confrontationist tactics.

(E) The contributions were made primarily by civil rights activists who returned to activism after the war.

Inference

This question requires making an inference from information given in the passage. The passage begins by indicating that Du Bois called on African Americans to suspend their fight for equality and to help with the war effort during the First World War. The final sentence of the passage, however, indicates that Du Bois learned that African Americans were experiencing *systematic discrimination* in the military during this time.

A The passage does not indicate how African Americans responded to Du Bois's editorial other than that many African Americans were surprised by it.

B The passage indicates that African Americans' participation in previous wars brought legal and political advances but that African Americans experienced discrimination in the First World War.

C **Correct.** The passage indicates that African Americans experienced systematic discrimination in the military during the First World War.

D The passage does not describe how African Americans responded to Trotter's tactics during the First World War.

E The passage does not indicate whether African Americans involved in the war effort were primarily civil rights activists.

The correct answer is C.

67. The author of the passage refers to Washington's call to African Americans in 1895 primarily in order to

(A) identify Du Bois's characteristic position on the continuum between accommodationism and confrontationism

(B) explain why Du Bois was sympathetic with Washington's views in 1895

(C) clarify how Trotter's views differed from those of Washington in 1895

(D) support an assertion about Du Bois's tendency to shift his political positions

(E) dismiss the claim that Du Bois's position in his 1918 editorial was consistent with his previous views

Evaluation

This question requires understanding how a part of the passage functions within the passage as a whole. The passage begins by indicating that many African Americans were surprised by Du Bois's views in his 1918 editorial. The passage then explains that Du Bois *often shifted positions along the continuum* (lines 9–10). To demonstrate this, the passage indicates that Du Bois praised Washington's 1895 speech directed to African Americans, but that by 1903, Du Bois had aligned himself with Washington's *militant opponent* (lines 16–17).

A The passage indicates that Du Bois *shifted positions* (line 9) along the accommodationist-confrontationist continuum.

B The passage does not indicate why Du Bois praised Washington's 1895 speech.

C The passage does not indicate what Trotter's views of Washington's 1895 speech were.

D **Correct.** The passage uses Du Bois's praise for Washington's 1895 speech and subsequent support of Trotter to illustrate Du Bois's tendency to shift positions.

E The passage does not include any claims that Du Bois's 1918 editorial was consistent with his previous views.

The correct answer is D.

68. According to the passage, which of the following is true of the strategy that Du Bois's 1918 editorial urged African Americans to adopt during the First World War?

(A) It was a strategy that Du Bois had consistently rejected in the past.

(B) It represented a compromise between Du Bois's own views and those of Trotter.

(C) It represented a significant redefinition of the long-term goals Du Bois held prior to the war.

(D) It was advocated by Du Bois in response to his recognition of the discrimination faced by African Americans during the war.

(E) It was advocated by Du Bois in part because of his historical knowledge of gains African Americans had made during past wars.

Supporting ideas

This question requires recognizing how a part of the passage functions within the passage as a whole. The passage begins by indicating that Du Bois's 1918 editorial called on African Americans to abandon political and social activism and help with the war effort in the First World War. In the second paragraph, the passage indicates that Du Bois's wartime position, expressed in his 1918 speech, was at least partly motivated by his belief that *African Americans' contributions to past war efforts had brought them some legal and political advances* (lines 28–30).

A The passage does not discuss whether Du Bois recommended this strategy prior to 1918.

B The passage does not indicate that Du Bois consciously compromised with Trotter's views.

C The passage indicates that his 1918 wartime views were *not a change in his long-term goals* (lines 22–23).

D The passage indicates that Du Bois's recognition of discrimination in the military caused him to reject his own 1918 wartime views.

E **Correct.** The passage indicates that Du Bois's 1918 views were influenced partly by a belief that past war efforts helped African Americans both legally and politically.

The correct answer is E.

Questions 69–74 refer to the passage on page 44.

69. The primary purpose of the passage is to

(A) contrast possible outcomes of a type of business investment

(B) suggest more careful evaluation of a type of business investment

(C) illustrate various ways in which a type of business investment could fail to enhance revenues

(D) trace the general problems of a company to a certain type of business investment

(E) criticize the way in which managers tend to analyze the costs and benefits of business investments

Main idea

Look at the passage as a whole to find the primary purpose. This passage uses an example, described in the second paragraph, to illustrate the principle of business practice explained in the first paragraph. The author begins by saying that efforts to improve service do not always result in a *competitive advantage* for a company. Thus, an investment in service must be carefully evaluated to determine if it will reduce costs or increase revenues (lines 4–8).

A Only one outcome, failure to gain a competitive advantage, is examined.

B **Correct.** Investments in service must be carefully evaluated for the returns they will bring.

C Only one way, an unnecessary investment in improved service, is discussed.

D The example of the bank is used only to illustrate a general business principle; the bank itself is not the focus of the passage.

E The passage criticizes the absence of such an analysis, not the way it is conducted.

The correct answer is B.

70. According to the passage, investments in service are comparable to investments in production and distribution in terms of the

(A) tangibility of the benefits that they tend to confer

(B) increased revenues that they ultimately produce

(C) basis on which they need to be weighed

(D) insufficient analysis that managers devote to them

(E) degree of competitive advantage that they are likely to provide

Supporting ideas

The phrase *according to the passage* indicates that the question covers material that is explicitly stated in the passage. The answer to this question demands a careful reading of the second sentence (lines 4–8). Investments in service are like investments in production and distribution because they *must be balanced against other types of investments on the basis of direct, tangible benefits*. Thus, these investments should be weighed on the same basis.

A The author is not equating the tangible benefits the different kinds of investments reap but rather the basis on which decisions to make investments are made.

B Revenues generated from investing in service are not said to be comparable to revenues generated from investing in production and distribution.

C **Correct.** An evaluation of whether or not to make these investments must be made on the same basis.

D How managers analyze investments in production and distribution is not discussed.

E The competitive advantage of superior service is acknowledged, but not the degree of it; it is not mentioned at all in the context of production and distribution.

The correct answer is C.

71. The passage suggests which of the following about service provided by the regional bank prior to its investment in enhancing that service?

(A) It enabled the bank to retain customers at an acceptable rate.

(B) It threatened to weaken the bank's competitive position with respect to other regional banks.

(C) It had already been improved after having caused damage to the bank's reputation in the past.

(D) It was slightly superior to that of the bank's regional competitors.

(E) It needed to be improved to attain parity with the service provided by competing banks.

Inference

Because the question uses the word *suggests*, finding the answer depends on making an inference about service at the bank. The paragraph that discusses the bank begins with the transitional expression, *this truth*, which refers to the previous sentence (lines 8–15). The *truth* is that investing in improved service is a waste *if a company is already effectively on a par with its competitors because it provides service that avoids a damaging reputation and keeps customers from leaving at an unacceptable rate.* Because of the way the author has linked this generalization to the description of the bank after investment, it is reasonable to infer that the hypothetical company's situation describes the bank prior to its investment in improved service.

A **Correct.** The bank's service would have been good enough to avoid a damaging reputation and to retain customers at an acceptable rate.

B The passage does not suggest that the bank's service was either poor or deficient to that of its competitors.

C The passage implies that the bank's service avoided *a damaging reputation*.

D The bank would have been *on a par with its competitors*, not superior to them.

E The bank would have been *on a par with its competitors*, not inferior to them.

The correct answer is A.

72. The passage suggests that bank managers failed to consider whether or not the service improvement mentioned in lines 18–20

(A) was too complicated to be easily described to prospective customers

(B) made a measurable change in the experiences of customers in the bank's offices

(C) could be sustained if the number of customers increased significantly

(D) was an innovation that competing banks could have imitated

(E) was adequate to bring the bank's general level of service to a level that was comparable with that of its competitors

Inference

The question's use of the word *suggests* means that the answer depends on making an inference. To answer this question, look at the entire second paragraph. Managers failed to think ahead. Would the service improvement attract new customers because other banks would find it difficult to copy? Or would the service improvement be easily imitated by competitors? The managers should have investigated this area before investing in improved service.

A The passage states the improvement *could easily be described to customers* (lines 28–29).

B No evidence in the passage shows that the managers failed to think about their customers' experience in the bank.

C The passage does not imply that managers failed to consider an increase in clients.

D **Correct.** The managers did not wonder if other banks would copy their service improvement.

E Lines 8–12 imply that the bank enjoyed a comparable level of service before investing in service improvement.

The correct answer is D.

73. The discussion of the regional bank in the second paragraph serves which of the following functions within the passage as a whole?

(A) It describes an exceptional case in which investment in service actually failed to produce a competitive advantage.

(B) It illustrates the pitfalls of choosing to invest in service at a time when investment is needed more urgently in another area.

(C) It demonstrates the kind of analysis that managers apply when they choose one kind of service investment over another.

(D) It supports the argument that investments in certain aspects of service are more advantageous than investments in other aspects of service.

(E) It provides an example of the point about investment in service made in the first paragraph.

Logical structure

This question requires thinking about what the second paragraph contributes to the whole passage. The first paragraph makes a generalization about investing in improvements in service; in certain conditions, such improvements do not result in the *competitive advantage* a company hopes for. The second paragraph offers the bank as an example of this generalization.

A The first sentence of the passage explains that improving service does not necessarily bring a *competitive advantage*, so the bank is not exceptional.

B The bank illustrates the pitfall of not evaluating a service improvement on the basis of tangible benefits; other areas of the bank are not mentioned.

C The passage does not discuss how managers analyze and choose different service investments.

D Investments in different aspects of service are not evaluated in the passage.

E Correct. The bank is an example of the position stated in the first paragraph that investing in improved service can be a waste if the investment is not evaluated carefully.

The correct answer is E.

74. The author uses the word "only" in line 27 most likely in order to

(A) highlight the oddity of the service improvement

(B) emphasize the relatively low value of the investment in service improvement

(C) distinguish the primary attribute of the service improvement from secondary attributes

(D) single out a certain merit of the service improvement from other merits

(E) point out the limited duration of the actual service improvement

Logical structure

The question asks you to consider the logic of the author's word choice. The previous two sentences discuss why the service improvement was a wasted investment. In contrast, the final sentence turns to the sole advantage of the service improvement, which is trivial by comparison. The author uses *only* to modify *merit* in order to emphasize the minimal nature of this advantage.

A The passage does not indicate that the service improvement is somehow strange or peculiar.

B Correct. *Only* emphasizes the low value attached to the single benefit.

C No attributes of the service improvement are mentioned.

D *Only* signifies that there was one sole merit of the service improvement.

E The duration of the benefit is not discussed in the passage.

The correct answer is B.

Questions 75–81 refer to the passage on page 46.

75. The primary purpose of the passage is to

(A) review research demonstrating the benefits of corporate mergers and acquisitions and examine some of the drawbacks that acquisition behavior entails

(B) contrast the effects of corporate mergers and acquisitions on acquiring firms and on firms that are acquired

(C) report findings that raise questions about a reason for corporate mergers and acquisitions and suggest possible alternative reasons

(D) explain changes in attitude on the part of acquiring firms toward corporate mergers and acquisitions

(E) account for a recent decline in the rate of corporate mergers and acquisitions

Main idea

This question requires understanding what the passage as a whole is trying to do. The passage begins by citing three studies that demonstrate that when firms acquire other firms, there is not necessarily a worthwhile economic gain. The passage then cites economic interests as the reason given by firms when they acquire other firms but calls into question the veracity of this reasoning. The passage then goes on to speculate as to why mergers and acquisitions occur.

A The research cited in the passage calls into question whether mergers and acquisitions are beneficial to firms.

B The passage is not concerned with comparing the relative effects of mergers and acquisitions on the acquired and acquiring firms.

C Correct. The passage surveys reports that question the reasons given by firms when they acquire other firms and suggests other reasons for these acquisitions.

D The passage does not indicate that there has been a change in the attitude of acquiring firms toward mergers and acquisitions.

E The passage does not indicate that there has been a decline in the rate of mergers and acquisitions.

The correct answer is C.

76. The findings cited in the passage suggest which of the following about the outcomes of corporate mergers and acquisitions with respect to acquiring firms?

(A) They include a decrease in value of many acquiring firms' stocks.

(B) They tend to be more beneficial for small firms than for large firms.

(C) They do not fulfill the professed goals of most acquiring firms.

(D) They tend to be beneficial to such firms in the long term even though apparently detrimental in the short term.

(E) They discourage many such firms from attempting to make subsequent bids and acquisitions.

Inference

Answering this question requires recognizing what is inferable from information given in the passage. The passage begins by citing three studies that show that mergers and acquisitions often harm the economic goals of acquiring firms. The passage also indicates that, nonetheless, acquiring firms *continue to assert that their objectives are economic ones* (lines 15–16), suggesting that the goals of these firms are not met by acquiring other firms.

A The passage suggests that the stock of acquiring firms *tends to increase in value* (lines 12–13), albeit less than the firm it acquires.

B The three studies cited in the passage do contrast the effects of corporate mergers on acquiring firms and on acquired firms, but the effects in question are significant only insofar as they contribute to the wider investigation into why mergers take place at all.

C **Correct.** The passage indicates that even while acquiring firms cite economic goals, the results of the studies indicate that these goals are not being met.

D The passage makes no comparison between the long-term and short-term gains of acquiring firms.

E The passage does not indicate that firms have been affected by the results of the studies cited.

The correct answer is C.

77. It can be inferred from the passage that the author would be most likely to agree with which of the following statements about corporate acquisitions?

(A) Their known benefits to national economies explain their appeal to individual firms during the 1970's and 1980's.

(B) Despite their adverse impact on some firms, they are the best way to channel resources from less to more productive sectors of a nation's economy.

(C) They are as likely to occur because of poor monitoring by boards of directors as to be caused by incentive compensation for managers.

(D) They will be less prevalent in the future, since their actual effects will gain wider recognition.

(E) Factors other than economic benefit to the acquiring firm help to explain the frequency with which they occur.

Inference

This question requires understanding what view the author has about a particular issue. The three studies cited by the passage all suggest that mergers and acquisitions do not necessarily bring economic benefit to the acquiring firms. The author concludes therefore that *factors having little to do with corporate economic interests explain acquisitions* (lines 23–24) and then goes on to speculate as to what the reasons may actually be.

A The passage indicates that while mergers and acquisitions may benefit the national economy, the appeal of mergers and acquisitions must be tied to companies' *private economic interests* (lines 19–22).

B The passage makes no judgment as to the best way for firms to help channel resources from less to more efficient economic sectors.

C The passage makes no comparison between the influence of poor monitoring by boards and that of executive incentives.

D The passage makes no prediction as to future trends in the market for mergers and acquisitions.

E Correct. The passage states that factors other than economic interests drive mergers and acquisitions.

The correct answer is E.

78. The author of the passage mentions the effect of acquisitions on national economies most probably in order to

(A) provide an explanation for the mergers and acquisitions of the 1970's and 1980's overlooked by the findings discussed in the passage

(B) suggest that national economic interests played an important role in the mergers and acquisitions of the 1970's and 1980's

(C) support a noneconomic explanation for the mergers and acquisitions of the 1970's and 1980's that was cited earlier in the passage

(D) cite and point out the inadequacy of one possible explanation for the prevalence of mergers and acquisitions during the 1970's and 1980's

(E) explain how modeling affected the decisions made by managers involved in mergers and acquisitions during the 1970's and 1980's

Evaluation

This question requires understanding why a piece of information is included in the passage. After the passage cites the results of the three studies on mergers and acquisitions, which call into question the economic benefits of acquisitions, it indicates that firms nonetheless claim that their objectives are economic. The passage then states that while acquisitions *may well have* a desirable effect on national economies (lines 17–19), the results of the studies suggest that factors other than economic interest must drive executives to arrange mergers and acquisitions.

A The passage does not mention national economies as part of an explanation for the occurrence of mergers and acquisitions.

B The passage suggests that the effect of acquisitions on national economies is not tied to any explanations for why acquisitions occur.

C The effect of acquisitions on national economies is not mentioned in the passage as an explanation for why acquisitions occur.

D Correct. The passage uses the mention of national economies as part of a larger point questioning the stated motivations behind firms' efforts to acquire other firms.

E In the passage, modeling is unrelated to the idea that acquisitions may have a desirable effect on national economies.

The correct answer is D.

79. According to the passage, during the 1970's and 1980's, bidding firms differed from the firms for which they bid in that bidding firms

(A) tended to be more profitable before a merger than after a merger

(B) were more often concerned about the impact of acquisitions on national economies

(C) were run by managers whose actions were modeled on those of other managers

(D) anticipated greater economic advantages from prospective mergers

(E) experienced less of an increase in stock value when a prospective merger was announced

Supporting ideas

This question requires recognizing information contained in the passage. In lines 10–14, the passage describes the findings of the third study of mergers and acquisitions in the 1970's and 1980's. This study found that, after the announcement of a possible merger, the stock value of an acquiring, or bidding, firm increases much less than the stock value of the firm for which it is in the process of bidding.

A The passage does not indicate whether the profitability of acquiring firms tended to be greater or less after a merger.

B The passage does not indicate that acquiring firms were concerned about the impact of their actions on national economies.

C The passage does not mention the actions of managers at firms that are being acquired.

D The passage does not discuss whether acquiring firms tended to expect greater overall economic gains than actually occurred.

E Correct. The passage indicates that the stock value of acquiring firms grew less than that of the firms they were attempting to acquire.

The correct answer is E.

80. According to the passage, which of the following was true of corporate acquisitions that occurred during the 1970's and 1980's?

(A) Few of the acquisitions that firms made were subsequently divested.

(B) Most such acquisitions produced only small increases in acquired firms' levels of profitability.

(C) Most such acquisitions were based on an overestimation of the value of target firms.

(D) The gains realized by most acquiring firms did not equal the amounts expended in acquiring target firms.

(E) About half of such acquisitions led to long-term increases in the value of acquiring firms' stocks.

Supporting ideas

This question requires recognizing information contained in the passage. The passage reports on three studies of mergers and acquisitions in the 1970's and 1980's. In lines 7–10, the passage indicates that the second study found that the postacquisition gains to most of the acquiring firms did not offset, or at least equal, the price paid to acquire the firms.

A The passage does not discuss post-acquisition divesting.

B The passage indicates that on average, the profitability of acquired firms fell after being acquired (lines 5–7).

C The passage does not indicate whether most acquiring firms overestimated the value of the firms they acquired.

D Correct. The passage states that for most acquiring firms the costs of buying the acquired firm were greater than the gains derived from acquiring it.

E The passage does not indicate what percentage of acquiring firms, if any, experienced long-term gains in their stock value.

The correct answer is D.

81. The author of the passage implies that which of the following is a possible partial explanation for acquisition behavior during the 1970's and 1980's?

(A) Managers wished to imitate other managers primarily because they saw how financially beneficial other firms' acquisitions were.

(B) Managers miscalculated the value of firms that were to be acquired.

(C) Lack of consensus within boards of directors resulted in their imposing conflicting goals on managers.

(D) Total compensation packages for managers increased during that period.

(E) The value of bidding firms' stock increased significantly when prospective mergers were announced.

Inference

This question requires recognizing what can be inferred from the information in the passage. After providing the results of the studies of mergers and acquisitions, the author concludes that even though acquiring firms state that their objectives are economic, factors having little to do with corporate economic interests explain acquisitions (lines 22–24). Among alternative explanations, the author points to managerial error in estimating the value of firms targeted for acquisition (lines 27–28) as possibly contributing to acquisition behavior in the 1970's and 1980's.

A While the passage indicates that managers may have modeled their behavior on other managers, it does not provide a reason for why this would be so.

B **Correct.** The author states that one explanation for acquisition behavior may be that managers erred when they estimated the value of firms being acquired.

C The author discusses a lack of monitoring by boards of directors but makes no mention of consensus within these boards.

D The author does not discuss compensation packages for managers.

E The passage does not state how significantly the value of the bidding firm's stock increased upon announcing a merger but only that it increased less in value than did the stock of the prospective firm being acquired.

The correct answer is B.

Questions 82–88 refer to the passage on page 48.

82. According to the passage, conventional spiral galaxies differ from low-surface-brightness galaxies in which of the following ways?

(A) They have fewer stars than do low-surface-brightness galaxies.

(B) They evolve more quickly than low-surface-brightness galaxies.

(C) They are more diffuse than low-surface-brightness galaxies.

(D) They contain less helium than do low-surface-brightness galaxies.

(E) They are larger than low-surface-brightness galaxies.

Supporting ideas

This question requires recognizing information that is provided in the passage. The first paragraph describes and compares two types of galaxies: conventional galaxies and dim, or low-surface-brightness, galaxies. It states that dim galaxies have the same approximate number of stars as a common type of conventional galaxy but tend to be larger and more diffuse because their mass is spread over wider areas (lines 4–10). The passage also indicates that dim galaxies take longer than conventional galaxies to convert their primordial gases into stars, meaning that dim galaxies evolve much more slowly than conventional galaxies (lines 10–14), which entails that conventional galaxies evolve more quickly than dim galaxies.

A The passage states that dim galaxies have approximately the same numbers of stars as a common type of conventional galaxy.

B **Correct.** The passage indicates that dim galaxies evolve much more slowly than conventional galaxies, which entails that conventional galaxies evolve more quickly.

C The passage states that dim galaxies are more spread out, and therefore more diffuse, than conventional galaxies.

D The passage does not mention the relative amounts of helium in the two types of galaxies under discussion.

E The passage states that dim galaxies tend to be much larger than conventional galaxies.

The correct answer is B.

83. It can be inferred from the passage that which of the following is an accurate physical description of typical low-surface-brightness galaxies?

(A) They are large spiral galaxies containing fewer stars than conventional galaxies.

(B) They are compact but very dim spiral galaxies.

(C) They are diffuse spiral galaxies that occupy a large volume of space.

(D) They are small, young spiral galaxies that contain a high proportion of primordial gas.

(E) They are large, dense spirals with low luminosity.

Inference

This question requires drawing an inference from information given in the passage. The first paragraph compares dim galaxies and conventional galaxies. Dim galaxies are described as having the same general shape (lines 4–5) as a common type of conventional galaxy, the spiral galaxy, suggesting that dim galaxies are, themselves, spiral shaped. The passage also indicates that, although both types of galaxies tend to have approximately the same number of stars, dim galaxies tend to be much larger and spread out over larger areas of space (lines 4–10) than conventional galaxies.

A The passage states that the two types of galaxies have approximately the same number of stars.

B The passage indicates that dim galaxies are relatively large and spread out.

C **Correct.** The passage indicates that dim galaxies have the same general shape as spiral galaxies and that their mass is spread out over large areas of space.

D The passage indicates that dim galaxies are relatively large and spread out.

E The passage states that dim galaxies have few stars per unit of volume, suggesting that they are not dense but diffuse.

The correct answer is C.

84. It can be inferred from the passage that the "long-standing puzzle" refers to which of the following?

(A) The difference between the rate at which conventional galaxies evolve and the rate at which low-surface-brightness galaxies evolve

(B) The discrepancy between estimates of total baryonic mass derived from measuring helium and estimates based on measuring galactic luminosity

(C) The inconsistency between the observed amount of helium in the universe and the number of stars in typical low-surface-brightness galaxies

(D) Uncertainties regarding what proportion of baryonic mass is contained in intergalactic space and what proportion in conventional galaxies

(E) Difficulties involved in detecting very distant galaxies and in investigating their luminosity

Inference

This question requires drawing an inference from information given in the passage. The second paragraph describes *the long-standing puzzle of the missing baryonic mass in the universe*. The passage states that baryons are the source of galactic luminosity, and so scientists can estimate the amount of baryonic mass in the universe by measuring the luminosity of galaxies (lines 17–21). The puzzle is that spectroscopic measures of helium in the universe suggest that the baryonic mass in the universe is much higher than measures of luminosity would indicate (21–25).

A The differences between the rates of evolution of the two types of galaxies is not treated as being controversial in the passage.

B **Correct.** The passage indicates that measurements using spectroscopy and measurements using luminosity result in puzzling differences in estimates of the universe's baryonic mass.

C The passage does not suggest how helium might relate to the numbers of stars in dim galaxies.

D The passage indicates that astronomers have speculated that the missing baryonic mass might be discovered in intergalactic space or hard-to-detect galaxies but does not suggest that these speculations are constituents of the long-standing puzzle.

E The passage does not mention how the distance to galaxies affects scientists' ability to detect these galaxies.

The correct answer is B.

85. The author implies that low-surface-brightness galaxies could constitute an answer to the puzzle discussed in the second paragraph primarily because

(A) they contain baryonic mass that was not taken into account by researchers using galactic luminosity to estimate the number of baryons in the universe

(B) they, like conventional galaxies that contain many baryons, have evolved from massive, primordial gas clouds

(C) they may contain relatively more helium, and hence more baryons, than do galaxies whose helium content has been studied using spectroscopy

(D) they have recently been discovered to contain more baryonic mass than scientists had thought when low-surface-brightness galaxies were first observed

(E) they contain stars that are significantly more luminous than would have been predicted on the basis of initial studies of luminosity in low-surface-brightness galaxies

Inference

This question requires drawing an inference from information given in the passage. The puzzle is that estimates of the baryonic mass of the universe based on luminosity are lower than those based on spectroscopy (lines 21–25). The passage states that astronomers did not notice dim galaxies until recently (lines 2–3) and that these galaxies may help account for the missing baryonic mass in the universe (lines 15–17). The passage also suggests that astronomers measure the luminosity of specific galaxies (lines 19–21). Thus it can be inferred that, prior to their being noticed by astronomers, the luminosity of these dim galaxies was not measured, and their baryonic mass was not taken into account in the estimates of luminosity that led to the long-standing puzzle.

A **Correct.** The passage states that the missing baryonic mass in the universe may be discovered in the dim galaxies that have only recently been noticed by astronomers.

B The passage does not suggest that dim and conventional galaxies both originating from primordial gas clouds help solve the long-standing puzzle of the missing baryonic mass in the universe.

C The passage does not suggest that dim galaxies might contain more helium than do conventional galaxies or that measures of baryonic mass using spectroscopy do not take some dim galaxies into account.

D The passage does not suggest that dim galaxies contain more baryonic mass than scientists originally believed upon discovering these galaxies.

E The passage suggests that scientists measured the luminosity of galaxies, not of individual stars.

The correct answer is A.

86. The author mentions the fact that baryons are the source of stars' luminosity primarily in order to explain

(A) how astronomers determine that some galaxies contain fewer stars per unit volume than do others

(B) how astronomers are able to calculate the total luminosity of a galaxy

(C) why astronomers can use galactic luminosity to estimate baryonic mass

(D) why astronomers' estimates of baryonic mass based on galactic luminosity are more reliable than those based on spectroscopic studies of helium

(E) how astronomers know bright galaxies contain more baryons than do dim galaxies

Evaluation

This question requires understanding how one aspect of the passage relates to the reasoning in a larger portion of the passage. The second paragraph explains that scientists have been puzzled over missing baryonic mass in the universe as measured by luminosity (lines 21–25). Given that baryons are the source of luminosity in the galaxy (lines 17–19), astronomers can estimate the baryonic mass of a galaxy by measuring its luminosity.

A The passage discussion of baryons does not address the number of stars in individual galaxies.

B The passage discusses how the luminosity of galaxies can be used to estimate baryonic mass but does not address how total luminosity is measured.

C **Correct.** The passage indicates that because baryons are the source of galactic luminosity, measuring luminosity can be used to estimate baryonic mass of galaxies.

D The passage suggests that estimates based on luminosity may have been less accurate, not more accurate, than those based on spectroscopy.

E The passage does not indicate that bright galaxies contain more baryons than do dim galaxies.

The correct answer is C.

87. The author of the passage would be most likely to disagree with which of the following statements?

(A) Low-surface-brightness galaxies are more difficult to detect than are conventional galaxies.
(B) Low-surface-brightness galaxies are often spiral in shape.
(C) Astronomers have advanced plausible ideas about where missing baryonic mass might be found.
(D) Astronomers have devised a useful way of estimating the total baryonic mass in the universe.
(E) Astronomers have discovered a substantial amount of baryonic mass in intergalactic space.

Inference

This question involves identifying which answer option potentially conflicts with the information the author has provided in the passage. The second paragraph indicates that astronomers' estimates of the baryonic mass of the universe is lower when measured using luminosity than it is when measured using spectroscopy (lines 21–25). The final sentence states that astronomers have speculated that the missing baryonic mass might be discovered in intergalactic space or in hard-to-detect galaxies (lines 25–29). Although the passage does indicate that the discovery of dim, low-surface-brightness galaxies might help account for the missing baryonic mass (lines 15–17), the passage provides no support for the possibility that baryonic mass has been discovered in intergalactic space.

A The passage indicates that low-surface-brightness galaxies went unnoticed until recently, unlike conventional galaxies.

B The passage indicates that low-surface-brightness galaxies have the same general shape as spiral galaxies.

C The passage describes two possible explanations astronomers have given for the missing baryonic mass, one of which was made more plausible by the discovery of low-surface-brightness galaxies.

D The passage indicates that astronomers have used spectroscopy to estimate baryonic mass and gives no reason to suspect that this method is not useful.

E **Correct.** The passage does not indicate that astronomers have found any baryonic mass in intergalactic space.

The correct answer is E.

88. The primary purpose of the passage is to

(A) describe a phenomenon and consider its scientific significance
(B) contrast two phenomena and discuss a puzzling difference between them
(C) identify a newly discovered phenomenon and explain its origins
(D) compare two classes of objects and discuss the physical properties of each
(E) discuss a discovery and point out its inconsistency with existing theory

Main idea

This question requires understanding, in broad terms, the purpose of the passage as a whole. The first paragraph describes a phenomenon: the discovery of dim galaxies and some of their general attributes. The second paragraph describes how this discovery may help astronomers to solve a long-standing puzzle about the baryonic mass of the universe.

A **Correct.** The passage describes the phenomenon of dim galaxies and describes their significance in solving the long-standing puzzle of the missing baryonic mass in the universe.

B Although the passage discusses the puzzling difference between the two estimates of baryonic mass, this option does not account for the broader topic of dim galaxies.

C While the passage identifies the newly discovered phenomenon of dim galaxies, it does not offer a significant explanation for these galaxies' origins.

D Although the passage compares dim and conventional galaxies in the first paragraph, this option does not account for the important detail that dim galaxies may help solve a long-standing puzzle.

E The discovery of dim galaxies discussed in the passage is not said to be inconsistent with any existing scientific theory.

The correct answer is A.

Questions 89–91 refer to the passage on page 50.

89. The "apparent contradiction" mentioned in line 29 refers to the discrepancy between the

(A) legal status of Mexican women in territorial California and their status in the United States

(B) unflattering depiction of Mexicans in novels and the actual public sentiment about the Mexican-American War

(C) existence of many marriages between Californianas and non-Hispanic merchants and the strictures against them expressed in novels

(D) literary depiction of elite Californianas and the literary depiction of other Mexican individuals

(E) novelistic portrayals of elite Californianas' privileged lives and the actual circumstances of those lives

Supporting idea

The *apparent contradiction* in line 29 refers to the difference, noted in the previous sentence, between favorable literary portrayals of elite Californianas—that is, Mexican women of the California territory—on the one hand and novels' generally unflattering depictions of Mexicans on the other.

A The passage discusses the difference between the legal rights of Mexican women in the California territory and those of non-Hispanic women. The legal rights of Mexican women outside territorial California are not mentioned.

B The passage suggests that there is no contradiction between unflattering depictions of Mexicans in novels and public sentiment about the Mexican-American War: such depictions of Mexicans served to stir up sentiment in support of the war.

C According to the passage, novels expressed no strictures against marriages between Californianas and non-Hispanic merchants. Instead, the novels portrayed such marriages favorably.

D **Correct.** Non-Hispanic novelists glorified elite Californianas based on the importance of forging economic alliances with them, whereas novelists depicted other Mexicans in unflattering terms.

E The passage indicates that elite Californianas' lives were in fact privileged, at least in comparison to those of non-Hispanic women. It does not suggest that there was any contradiction between elite Californianas' lives and how those lives were portrayed in novels.

The correct answer is D.

90. Which of the following could best serve as an example of the kind of fictional plot discussed by Antonia Castañeda?

(A) A land speculator of English ancestry weds the daughter of a Mexican vineyard owner after the speculator has migrated to California to seek his fortune.

(B) A Californian woman of Hispanic ancestry finds that her agricultural livelihood is threatened when her husband is forced to seek work in a textile mill.

(C) A Mexican rancher who loses his land as a result of the Mexican-American War migrates to the northern United States and marries an immigrant schoolteacher.

(D) A wealthy Californiana whose father has bequeathed her all his property contends with avaricious relatives for her inheritance.

(E) A poor married couple emigrate from French Canada and gradually become wealthy as merchants in territorial California.

Application

According to the passage, Castañeda focuses on a particular plot in which an elite Californiana is pursued by a non-Hispanic merchant or trader for the purpose of gaining economic advantage.

A **Correct.** The story of a non-Hispanic land speculator wedding a Californiana who is likely, based on the inheritance rights granted her by the Hispanic law in territorial California, to inherit her father's vineyard would precisely fit the plot that Castañeda discusses.

B This description fails to identify the ethnicity of the Californiana's husband and the reason he married her, so there is no way to determine whether the story would fit Castañeda's plot.

C Castañeda's plot involves a non-Hispanic male protagonist, so a Mexican rancher could not play the main male role in such a story.

D The presence of a wealthy Californiana who inherits property might make this story seem to be an example of the fictional plot that Castañeda discusses, but there is no mention of a non-Hispanic merchant or trader who seeks her hand in marriage.

E Simply taking place in territorial California would not make a story an appropriate example of the plot discussed by Castañeda.

The correct answer is A.

91. Which of the following, if true, would provide the most support for Castañeda's explanation of the "stereotypical plot" mentioned in the lines 18–19?

(A) Non-Hispanic traders found business more profitable in California while it was a territory than when it became a state.

(B) Very few marriages between Hispanic women and non-Hispanic men in nineteenth-century territorial California have actually been documented.

(C) Records from the nineteenth century indicate that some large and valuable properties were owned by elite Californianas in their own right.

(D) Unmarried non-Hispanic women in the nineteenth-century United States were sometimes able to control property in their own right.

(E) Most of the property in nineteenth-century territorial California was controlled by Hispanic men.

Evaluation

Castañeda explains the *stereotypical plot* of a non-Hispanic merchant seeking to marry an elite Californiana based on economics: these women had property and inheritance rights equal to men. Novelists based their plots on the women's *real-life* economic power, which resulted in men's wishing to build economic alliances with them. Supporting this explanation requires supporting these economic ideas in some way.

A The profitability of non-Hispanic traders' business is not an issue in Castañeda's explanation; thus the change described has no significant relevance to that explanation.

B The lack of the type of documentation described, rather than providing support for Castañeda's explanation, signifies a deficit in documentary support for that explanation.

C **Correct.** If elite Californianas did in fact own valuable properties, Castañeda's economic explanation gains force. The women did have the real economic significance upon which Castañeda suggests the novelists drew.

D If it were true that some non-Hispanic women controlled property in this way, Castañeda's explanation of Californianas' uniqueness would be somewhat undermined.

E If most of the property in nineteenth-century territorial California was controlled by Hispanic men, that suggests that Californianas were less likely to possess the kind of economic power described in Castañeda's argument.

The correct answer is C.

Questions 92–94 refer to the passage on page 52.

92. The passage suggests that, in the early 1990s, Michaels would have been most likely to agree with which of the following statements about the disparity mentioned in the lines 3–4?

(A) This disparity is relatively less extreme in the Northern Hemisphere because of sulfate cooling.

(B) This disparity is only a short-term phenomenon brought about by sulfate cooling.

(C) This disparity is most significant in those parts of the world dominated by oceans.

(D) The extent of this disparity is being masked by the temporary effect of sulfate cooling.

(E) The disparity confirms that current models of global warming are correct.

Inference

The disparity highlighted in this question is between global warming models and actual climate data—that is, that the models predicted warming that has not occurred. In the early 1990s, according to the passage, Michaels tried to explain this disparity by saying that industrial sulfate emissions had a cooling effect that slowed global warming briefly.

A The passage does not indicate that Michaels came to distinguish between the Northern and Southern Hemispheres until he began to doubt his early 1990s explanation for the mentioned disparity.

B Correct. Michaels claimed in the early 1990s that the disparity was temporary, and that it occurred due to the cooling effect of sulfate emissions.

C Santer's contention, not Michaels's, is based on the effect of oceans on global warming.

D In the early 1990s, Michaels used the idea of sulfate cooling to explain the observed disparity, not to suggest that the disparity itself was larger than observed.

E In seeking to explain the disparity, Michaels seems to have assumed, in the early 1990s at least, that the models of global warming were correct. But he did not take the disparity as evidence of their correctness.

The correct answer is B.

93. According to the passage, Santer asserts which of the following about global warming?

(A) It will become a more serious problem in the Southern Hemisphere than in the Northern Hemisphere in spite of the cooling influence of oceans in the south.

(B) It is unlikely to be a serious problem in the future because of the pervasive effect of sulfate cooling.

(C) It will proceed at the same general rate in the Northern and Southern Hemispheres once the temporary influence of sulfate cooling comes to an end.

(D) Until the late 1980s, it was moderated in the Northern Hemisphere by the effect of sulfate cooling.

(E) Largely because of the cooling influence of oceans, it has had no discernible impact on the Southern Hemisphere.

Supporting idea

The second paragraph of the passage discusses Santer's take on global warming. He is concerned with the effect of oceans and of sulfate cooling on this process, and he argues that the rate of warming in the Southern and Northern Hemispheres has been differently affected by each of these. In general, oceans slow warming in the south, while sulfate cooling temporarily slowed warming in the north until the late 1980s.

A According to the passage, Santer has argued that since 1987 the Northern Hemisphere has warmed more significantly than the Southern Hemisphere.

B Santer maintains that sulfate cooling complicates our attempts to understand global warming. He notes, however, that sulfate cooling peaked in the Northern Hemisphere in the mid-1900s, and that that hemisphere's warming has increased considerably. So sulfate cooling's effect is not pervasive and has not mitigated the medium- and long-term problem of global warming.

C Santer argues that, in the absence of sulfate cooling, global warming would occur more slowly in the Southern Hemisphere due to the greater ocean coverage there.

D **Correct.** Santer says that sulfate cooling slowed warming in the Northern Hemisphere, but that in 1987, the influence of sulfate cooling was no longer significant.

E Santer maintains that global warming happens more slowly in the Southern Hemisphere due to the greater ocean coverage there, not that it has no discernible impact there.

The correct answer is D.

94. The passage suggests that Santer and Michaels would be most likely to DISAGREE over which of the following issues?

(A) Whether climatological data invalidates global warming models
(B) Whether warming in the Northern Hemisphere has intensified since 1987
(C) Whether disparities between global warming models and climatological data can be detected
(D) Whether landmasses warm more rapidly than oceans
(E) Whether oceans have a significant effect on global climate patterns

Inference

According to the end of the first paragraph, Michaels began to doubt that sulfate cooling had an effect on global warming, and, further, based on the fact that he could not find an answer for why climatological data did not line up with global warming models, he questioned the accuracy of those models. The second paragraph explains that Santer, in contrast, offered a more nuanced explanation for the effect of sulfate cooling, and that based on this explanation, he disputed the claim that climatological data were inconsistent with the models' predictions.

A **Correct.** Based on the passage, Santer and Michaels would clearly disagree about whether climatological data invalidate global warming models: Michaels came to question the models on the basis of those data, while Santer found the model predictions were in fact ultimately consistent with the observed data.

B Both Santer and Michaels accept the idea that warming in the north has accelerated since 1987.

C Santer and Michaels both offered reasons for why the seeming disparity between models and data occurred—thus they agreed that such disparities were in fact detected.

D According to the second paragraph, Santer holds that landmasses warm more rapidly than oceans. But the passage offers no indication that Michaels disagrees with this.

E Santer's argument is based in large part on the effect of oceans on global climate patterns, but nothing in the passage's discussion of Michaels's work indicates that Michaels would disagree that oceans have such an effect.

The correct answer is A.

Questions 95–101 refer to the passage on page 54.

95. According to the passage, Walker and Szalay disagree on which of the following points?

(A) The structure and composition of australopithecine teeth
(B) The kinds of conclusions that can be drawn from the micro-wear patterns on australopithecine teeth
(C) The idea that fruit was a part of the australopithecine diet
(D) The extent to which seed cracking and bone crunching produce similar micro-wear patterns on teeth
(E) The function of the heavy enamel on australopithecine teeth

Supporting idea

This question refers to the first paragraph, which states that Walker does not agree with Szalay's idea that *the heavy enamel of australopithecine teeth is an adaptation to bone crunching*.

A According to the passage, Walker and Szalay disagree about the function of heavy enamel on the teeth, not the structure and composition of the teeth.

B The passage does not indicate that Szalay has anything to say about the micro-wear patterns on the teeth.

C Walker does, according to the passage, believe that australopithecines ate fruit, but it gives no evidence about whether Szalay believes that they ate at least some fruit.

D According to the passage, Walker believes that seed cracking and bone crunching produce distinctive micro-wear patterns on teeth, but he does not necessarily believe that they are similar. The passage does not indicate Szalay's position on the difference between micro-wear patterns.

E **Correct.** The function of the heavy enamel on the teeth is the only idea about which the passage clearly indicates that Walker and Szalay disagree.

The correct answer is E.

96. The passage suggests that Walker's research indicated which of the following about australopithecine teeth?

(A) They had micro-wear characteristics indicating that fruit constituted only a small part of their diet.

(B) They lacked micro-wear characteristics associated with seed eating and bone crunching.

(C) They had micro-wear characteristics that differed in certain ways from the micro-wear patterns of chimpanzees and orangutans.

(D) They had micro-wear characteristics suggesting that the diet of australopithecines varied from one region to another.

(E) They lacked the micro-wear characteristics distinctive of modern frugivores.

Inference

According to the passage, Walker's research focuses on micro-wear patterns on the teeth of australopithecines. He draws several conclusions on the basis of these patterns: first, that australopithecines did not eat hard seeds; next, that they did not crunch bones; and finally, that they ate fruit.

A The passage indicates that Walker's observation of micro-wear patterns led him to conclude that australopithecines ate mostly fruit, not that *fruit constituted only a small part of their diet.*

B **Correct.** The first paragraph explains that Walker concluded from micro-wear patterns that australopithecines did not eat hard seeds and did not crunch bones; thus, his research must have indicated that they lacked micro-wear characteristics associated with such activities.

C According to the passage, the opposite is true: based on the observation that their micro-wear patterns were indistinguishable from those of chimpanzees and orangutans, Walker concluded that australopithecines ate fruit.

D The second paragraph of the passage complicates Walker's view by suggesting that australopithecines' diet might have varied from one region to another, but the passage says nothing about Walker's research from which to infer that it indicated such variation.

E Chimpanzees and orangutans are assumed to be frugivores, according to the passage, and Walker's research indicated that australopithecine teeth had micro-wear characteristics identical to theirs.

The correct answer is B.

97. The passage suggests that which of the following would be true of studies of tooth micro-wear patterns conducted on modern baboons?

(A) They would inaccurately suggest that some baboons eat more soft-bodied than hard-bodied insects.

(B) They would suggest that insects constitute the largest part of some baboons' diets.

(C) They would reveal that there are no significant differences in tooth micro-wear patterns among baboon populations.

(D) They would inadequately reflect the extent to which some baboons consume certain types of insects.

(E) They would indicate that baboons in certain regions eat only soft-bodied insects, whereas baboons in other regions eat hard-bodied insects.

Inference

The second paragraph states that modern baboons eat *only soft-bodied insects* and so would not exhibit tooth abrasion to indicate that they were insectivores. Thus, it would be difficult to determine exactly which soft-bodied insects they ate.

A The passage states that baboons eat only soft-bodied insects—so it is in fact accurate to suggest that all baboons eat more soft-bodied than hard-bodied insects.

B The passage says that baboons eat only soft-bodied insects. It also suggests that soft-bodied insects do not leave significant enough abrasions on baboons' teeth to provide evidence of this aspect of their diet. Therefore, the tooth-wear patterns would give little or no information regarding what proportion of the baboons' overall diet consists of insects.

C The passage does not provide grounds for inferring anything about the differences, or lack thereof, among baboon populations in terms of tooth micro-wear patterns.

D Correct. Because soft-bodied insects cause little tooth abrasion, micro-wear patterns would most likely not reflect the extent to which baboons consume soft-bodied insects.

E The passage states that baboons eat *only soft-bodied insects.* Nothing in the passage suggests that baboons in certain regions eat hard-bodied insects.

The correct answer is D.

98. The passage suggests which of the following about the micro-wear patterns found on the teeth of omnivorous primates?

(A) The patterns provide information about what kinds of foods are not eaten by the particular species of primate, but not about the foods actually eaten.

(B) The patterns of various primate species living in the same environment resemble one another.

(C) The patterns may not provide information about the extent to which a particular species' diet includes seeds.

(D) The patterns provide more information about these primates' diet than do the tooth micro-wear patterns of primates who are frugivores.

(E) The patterns may differ among groups within a species depending on the environment within which a particular group lives.

Inference

This question focuses mainly on the end of the second paragraph, which states that *the diets of current omnivorous primates vary considerably depending on the environments* in which they live. It goes on to conclude that australopithecines, if they were omnivores, would similarly consume varied diets, depending on environment, and exhibit varied tooth micro-wear patterns as well. Thus, it is reasonable to conclude that any omnivorous primates living in different environments and consuming different diets would exhibit varied micro-wear patterns.

A The passage indicates that the absence of certain types of micro-wear patterns can provide evidence about what foods a species does not eat. It also says that among omnivorous primates, one might expect to find considerable population variation in their tooth micro-wear patterns. Wherever micro-wear patterns are present, they provide evidence about what kinds of foods are eaten.

B The passage suggests that various primate species living in the same environment might consume a variety of different diets, so there is no reason to conclude that their micro-wear patterns would resemble one another.

C The passage indicates that seed-eating produces distinctive micro-wear patterns, so the patterns, or lack thereof, on the teeth of any species would most likely provide information about the extent to which the species' diet includes seeds.

D The end of the first paragraph suggests that frugivores' micro-wear patterns are distinctive; the passage provides no reason to believe that omnivores' diets provide more information.

E **Correct.** According to the passage, omnivorous primates of a particular species may consume different diets depending on where they live. Thus, their micro-wear patterns may differ on this basis.

The correct answer is E.

99. It can be inferred from the passage that if studies of tooth micro-wear patterns were conducted on modern baboons, which of the following would most likely be true of the results obtained?

    (A) There would be enough abrasion to allow a determination of whether baboons are frugivorous or insectivorous.

    (B) The results would suggest that insects constitute the largest part of the baboons' diet.

    (C) The results would reveal that there are no significant differences in tooth micro-wear patterns from one regional baboon population to another.

    (D) The results would provide an accurate indication of the absence of some kinds of insects from the baboons' diet.

    (E) The results would be unlikely to provide any indication of what inferences about the australopithecine diet can or cannot be drawn from micro-wear studies.

Inference

The second paragraph states that modern baboons eat soft-bodied insects but not hard-bodied ones—and it is hard-bodied insects, the passage suggests, that would cause particular micro-wear patterns on teeth. So the patterns on modern baboons' teeth most likely do not exhibit the patterns indicating hard-bodied insect consumption.

A The passage states that baboons' consumption of soft-bodied insects would not show up in the patterns on their teeth—so the abrasion would most likely not provide enough information for a determination of whether baboons are frugivorous or insectivorous.

B Since soft-bodied insects do not abrade the teeth significantly, it would be difficult to determine, based on micro-wear patterns, the part such insects play in the baboons' diet. Furthermore, the passage does not suggest that micro-wear patterns can indicate the quantity of food an animal might have eaten.

C There could be differences in tooth micro-wear patterns from one regional baboon population to another if they consumed anything in addition to soft-bodied insects.

D **Correct.** Studying tooth micro-wear patterns on baboons' teeth would most likely show that their teeth do not exhibit patterns typical of creatures that consume hard-bodied insects.

E The passage suggests that based on results from micro-wear patterns on modern baboons' teeth, one cannot infer from micro-wear studies whether australopithecines ate soft-bodied insects.

The correct answer is D.

100. It can be inferred from the passage that Walker's conclusion about the australopithecine diet would be called into question under which of the following circumstances?

    (A) The tooth enamel of australopithecines is found to be much heavier than that of modern frugivorous primates.

    (B) The micro-wear patterns of australopithecine teeth from regions other than east Africa are analyzed.

    (C) Orangutans are found to have a much broader diet than is currently recognized.

    (D) The environment of east Africa at the time australopithecines lived there is found to have been far more varied than is currently thought.

    (E) The area in which the australopithecine specimens were found is discovered to have been very rich in soft-bodied insects during the period when australopithecines lived there.

Inference

The passage explains that Walker bases his conclusion about the frugivorous nature of the australopithecine diet on the fact that the micro-wear patterns on australopithecine teeth are indistinguishable from those of chimpanzees and orangutans, both of which are presumed to have frugivorous diets.

A The passage indicates that Walker took into account the fact that australopithecines had relatively heavy tooth enamel and that he rejected the view that this heaviness was evidence against the hypothesis that they were frugivorous. For all we can tell from the information in the passage, the australopithecines' tooth enamel was already known to be much heavier than that of modern frugivorous primates.

B It could be the case that analyzing the micro-wear patterns of australopithecine teeth from other regions would yield the same data as those from east Africa.

C **Correct.** According to the passage, Walker bases the conclusion that australopithecines were frugivorous on the similarity between their micro-wear patterns and those of modern chimpanzees and orangutans. If orangutans were found to have a diet that included a greater range of non-fruit foods than is currently recognized, then the correspondence between their micro-wear patterns and australopithecines' micro-wear patterns would be consistent with the hypothesis that australopithecines' diet was broader as well.

D Even if the environment of east Africa were more varied, that would not mean the australopithecines necessarily ate a more varied diet. Many species that live in very varied environments specialize narrowly on particular foods in those environments.

E Just because many soft-bodied insects might have been available to australopithecines does not mean that australopithecines ate them.

The correct answer is C.

101. The author of the passage mentions the diets of baboons and other living primates most likely in order to

(A) provide evidence that refutes Walker's conclusions about the foods making up the diets of australopithecines

(B) suggest that studies of tooth micro-wear patterns are primarily useful for determining the diets of living primates

(C) suggest that australopithecines were probably omnivores rather than frugivores

(D) illustrate some of the limitations of using tooth micro-wear patterns to draw definitive conclusions about a group's diet

(E) suggest that tooth micro-wear patterns are caused by persistent, as opposed to occasional, consumption of particular foods

Evaluation

The passage discusses the diets of baboons and other living primates mainly in the second paragraph, which is concerned with explaining the limited utility of micro-wear studies.

A The author raises some doubts about Walker's conclusions but does not go as far as to try to refute them outright. The author argues only that, as the final sentence of the passage states, they may need to be expanded.

B The author discusses the diets of baboons and other living primates in relation to micro-wear research on extinct primates. Nothing in the discussion suggests that micro-wear studies would be more useful for determining the diets of living primates than for providing evidence regarding the diets of earlier primates or of other types of animals. Furthermore, the mention of baboon diets suggests that micro-wear studies may not be very useful for determining the diets of some living primates.

C The author leaves open the question of whether australopithecines were omnivores or frugivores. The passage suggests that some australopithecines might have been omnivores, if australopithecines' diets varied according to the environments they inhabited. Walker's conclusion regarding east African australopithecines' being frugivores might still hold, however.

D **Correct.** The author refers to baboons' diets and those of current omnivorous primates in order to suggest that there might be limitations to Walker's use of tooth micro-wear patterns to determine australopithecines' diet.

E The passage does not make a distinction between persistent and occasional consumption of particular foods.

The correct answer is D.

Questions 102–105 refer to the passage on page 57.

102. The primary purpose of the passage is to

(A) present recently discovered evidence that supports a conventional interpretation of a historical period

(B) describe how reinterpretations of available evidence have reinvigorated a once-discredited scholarly position

(C) explain why some historians have tended to emphasize change rather than continuity in discussing a particular period

(D) explore how changes in a particular occupation serve to counter the prevailing view of a historical period

(E) examine a particular area of historical research in order to exemplify a general scholarly trend

Main idea

This question asks about the passage's main purpose. The first paragraph initially describes a way in which historiography is changing: the idea of a consistent, monolithic decline in women's status is being complicated by *recent research*. The rest of the passage uses the example of Pinchbeck's interpretation of women's work in English cheesemaking to show the limits of earlier ideas about women's status: Pinchbeck's work illustrates the idea of consistent decline, but recent scholarship has called that work into question.

A The first paragraph suggests that Pinchbeck's work represents the conventional position that women's status declined consistently with the advent of capitalism; according to the passage, recent evidence undermines, rather than supports, that position.

B According to the passage, reinterpretations of evidence have inspired new interpretations; they have not reinvigorated a discredited position.

C The passage is concerned with noting both change and continuity, as stated in the first sentence.

D In the passage, continuity, not change, in a particular occupation—English farmhouse cheesemaking—helps to counter the prevailing view.

E **Correct.** The passage's main purpose is to examine women's work in English farmhouse cheesemaking so as to illustrate a trend in historiography of women's status under capitalism and industrialization.

The correct answer is E.

103. Regarding English local markets and fairs, which of the following can be inferred from the passage?

(A) Both before and after the agricultural revolution, the sellers of agricultural products at these venues were men.

(B) Knowing who the active sellers were at these venues may not give a reliable indication of who controlled the revenue from the sales.

(C) There were no parallel institutions at which American cheese makers could sell their own products.

(D) Prior to the agricultural revolution, the sellers of agricultural products at these venues were generally the producers themselves.

(E) Prior to the agricultural revolution, women sold not only cheese but also products of arable agriculture at these venues.

Inference

The passage discusses English local markets and fairs in the first and second paragraphs: the first paragraph states that before the agricultural revolution, women had sold cheese in such venues but that after that, factors, who were men, sold the cheese. The second paragraph argues that even though English women in precapitalist, preindustrial times may have at one point sold cheese at fairs, evidence indicates that in at least one case, a man appropriated most of the money his wife made from her sales.

A The first paragraph states that prior to the agricultural revolution, women sold cheese at local markets and fairs.

B Correct. As the second paragraph indicates, women may have sold the cheese, but there is evidence to suggest that they did not necessarily control the revenue from its sale.

C The passage does not provide evidence regarding any institutions at which American cheese makers sold their products.

D While the passage indicates that the producers of English farmhouse cheese may have been the ones who sold that cheese at local markets and fairs, there is no evidence to suggest that this was necessarily the case for other agricultural products.

E The passage provides no information regarding whether women sold products of arable agriculture in any venue.

The correct answer is B.

104. The passage describes the work of Pinchbeck primarily in order to

(A) demonstrate that some of the conclusions reached by recent historians were anticipated in earlier scholarship

(B) provide an instance of the viewpoint that, according to the passage's author, is being superseded

(C) illustrate the ways in which recent historians have built on the work of their predecessors

(D) provide a point of reference for subsequent scholarship on women's work during the agricultural revolution

(E) show the effect that the specialization introduced in the agricultural and industrial revolutions had on women's work

Evaluation

This question focuses on the function of Pinchbeck's work in the passage. Pinchbeck's study of women's work in cheese production is, according to the passage, an illustration of the view that women's status declined consistently with the advent of industrialization. That view, the author claims, is being challenged by current historiography.

A The passage indicates that the conclusions of Pinchbeck, who represents earlier scholarship, did not anticipate recent work, but rather that recent work argues against those conclusions.

B Correct. Pinchbeck's work illustrates earlier trends in historiography, trends that the author suggests are now giving way to newer ideas.

C The passage does not focus on any ways in which recent historians have built on Pinchbeck's work; instead, it discusses how they have argued against its conclusions.

D Pinchbeck's work provides a point of reference only insofar as subsequent scholarship is arguing against it.

E Pinchbeck makes the argument that specialization caused women's status to decline, but the passage is concerned with undermining this argument.

The correct answer is B.

105. It can be inferred from the passage that women did work in

(A) American cheesemaking at some point prior to industrialization

(B) arable agriculture in northern England both before and after the agricultural revolution

(C) arable agriculture in southeast England after the agricultural revolution, in those locales in which cultural values supported their participation

(D) the sale of cheese at local markets in England even after the agricultural revolution

(E) some areas of American cheese dairying after industrialization

Inference

This question focuses mainly on the final paragraph of the passage, in which women's continued work in English cheese dairying is contrasted with what the passage calls their *disappearance from arable agriculture in southeast England and from American cheese dairying*, presumably during the period of industrialization. The correct answer will be a conclusion that can be drawn from this information.

A **Correct.** That women "disappeared" from American cheese dairying during industrialization provides grounds for inferring that they did such dairying work at some point prior to industrialization.

B The passage says that women disappeared from arable agriculture in southeast England, but it gives no information about their participation in arable agriculture in northern England.

C The passage makes a blanket statement about women's *disappearance from arable agriculture in southeast England*, so there is no reason to infer that any locales supported women's participation in agriculture.

D The first paragraph states that factors, who were men, sold cheese after the agricultural revolution.

E The final paragraph explicitly states that women disappeared from American cheese dairying; thus, there is no basis for inferring that women worked in any areas of that field after industrialization.

The correct answer is A.

4.0 Critical Reasoning

4.0 Critical Reasoning

Critical reasoning questions appear in the Verbal section of the GMAT® exam. The Verbal section uses multiple-choice questions to measure your ability to read and comprehend written material, to reason and to evaluate arguments, and to correct written material to conform to standard written English. Because the Verbal section includes content from a variety of topics, you may be generally familiar with some of the material; however, neither the passages nor the questions assume knowledge of the topics discussed. Critical reasoning questions are intermingled with reading comprehension and sentence correction questions throughout the Verbal section of the test.

You will have 75 minutes to complete the Verbal section, or about 1¾ minutes to answer each question. Although critical reasoning questions are based on written passages, these passages are shorter than reading comprehension passages. They tend to be less than 100 words in length and generally are followed by one or two questions. For these questions, you will see a split computer screen. The written passage will remain visible at the top of the screen. In turn, each associated question will appear below the relevant passage.

Critical reasoning questions are designed to test the reasoning skills involved in (1) making arguments, (2) evaluating arguments, and (3) formulating or evaluating a plan of action. The materials on which questions are based are drawn from a variety of sources. The GMAT exam does not expect any familiarity with the subject matter of those materials.

In these questions, you are to analyze the situation on which each question is based, and then select the answer choice that most appropriately answers the question. Begin by reading the passages carefully, then reading the five answer choices. If the correct answer is not immediately obvious to you, see whether you can eliminate some of the wrong answers. Reading the passage a second time may be helpful in illuminating subtleties that were not immediately evident.

Answering critical reasoning questions requires no specialized knowledge of any particular field; you don't have to have knowledge of the terminology and conventions of formal logic. The sample critical reasoning questions in this chapter illustrate the variety of topics the test may cover, the kinds of questions it may ask, and the level of analysis it requires.

The following pages describe what critical reasoning questions are designed to measure and present the directions that will precede questions of this type. Sample questions and explanations of the correct answers follow.

4.1 What Is Measured

Critical reasoning questions are designed to provide one measure of your ability to reason effectively in the following areas:

- **Argument construction**
  Questions in this category may ask you to recognize such things as the basic structure of an argument, properly drawn conclusions, underlying assumptions, well-supported explanatory hypotheses, and parallels between structurally similar arguments.
- **Argument evaluation**
  These questions may ask you to analyze a given argument and to recognize such things as factors that would strengthen or weaken the given argument; reasoning errors committed in making that argument; and aspects of the method by which the argument proceeds.
- **Formulating and evaluating a plan of action**
  This type of question may ask you to recognize such things as the relative appropriateness, effectiveness, or efficiency of different plans of action, factors that would strengthen or weaken the prospects of success of a proposed plan of action, and assumptions underlying a proposed plan of action.

4.2 Test-Taking Strategies

1. **Read very carefully the set of statements on which a question is based.**
   Pay close attention to

   - what is put forward as factual information
   - what is not said but necessarily follows from what is said
   - what is claimed to follow from facts that have been put forward
   - how well substantiated are any claims that a particular conclusion follows from the facts that have been put forward

   In reading the arguments, it is important to pay attention to the logical reasoning used; the actual truth of statements portrayed as fact is not important.

2. **Identify the conclusion.**
   The conclusion does not necessarily come at the end of the text; it may come somewhere in the middle or even at the beginning. Be alert to clues in the text that an argument follows logically from another statement or statements in the text.

3. **Determine exactly what each question asks.**
   You might find it helpful to read the question first, before reading the material on which it is based; don't assume that you know what you will be asked about an argument. An argument may have obvious flaws, and one question may ask you to detect them. Other questions may direct you to select the one answer choice that does NOT describe a flaw in the argument.

4. **Read all the answer choices carefully.**
   Do not assume that a given answer is the best without first reading all the choices.

4.3 The Directions

These are the directions you will see for critical reasoning questions when you take the GMAT exam. If you read them carefully and understand them clearly before going to sit for the test, you will not need to spend too much time reviewing them when you are at the test center and the test is under way.

For these questions, select the best of the answer choices given.

4.4 Sample Questions

Each of the critical reasoning questions is based on a short argument, a set of statements, or a plan of action. For each question, select the best answer of the choices given.

106. PhishCo runs a number of farms in the arid province of Nufa, depending largely on irrigation. Now, as part of a plan to efficiently increase the farms' total production, it plans to drill down to an aquifer containing warm, slightly salty water that will be used to raise fish in ponds. The water from the ponds will later be used to supplement piped-in irrigation water for PhishCo's vegetable fields, and the ponds and accompanying vegetation should help reduce the heat in the area of the farms.

Which of the following would, if true, most strongly suggest that the plan, if implemented, would increase the overall efficiency of PhishCo's farms?

(A) Most of the vegetation to be placed around the ponds is native to Nufa.

(B) Fish raised on PhishCo's farms are likely to be saleable in the nearest urban areas.

(C) Organic waste from fish in the pond water will help to fertilize fields where it is used for irrigation.

(D) The government of Nufa will help to arrange loan financing to partially cover the costs of drilling.

(E) Ponds will be located on low-lying land now partially occupied by grain crops.

107. The sustained massive use of pesticides in farming has two effects that are especially pernicious. First, it often kills off the pests' natural enemies in the area. Second, it often unintentionally gives rise to insecticide-resistant pests, since those insects that survive a particular insecticide will be the ones most resistant to it, and they are the ones left to breed.

From the passage above, it can be properly inferred that the effectiveness of the sustained massive use of pesticides can be extended by doing which of the following, assuming that each is a realistic possibility?

(A) Using only chemically stable insecticides

(B) Periodically switching the type of insecticide used

(C) Gradually increasing the quantities of pesticides used

(D) Leaving a few fields fallow every year

(E) Breeding higher-yielding varieties of crop plants

108. Which of the following, if true, most logically completes the argument below?

Manufacturers are now required to make all cigarette lighters child-resistant by equipping them with safety levers. But this change is unlikely to result in a significant reduction in the number of fires caused by children playing with lighters, because children given the opportunity can figure out how to work the safety levers and _______.

(A) the addition of the safety levers has made lighters more expensive than they were before the requirement was instituted

(B) adults are more likely to leave child-resistant lighters than non-child-resistant lighters in places that are accessible to children

(C) many of the fires started by young children are quickly detected and extinguished by their parents

(D) unlike child-resistant lighters, lighters that are not child-resistant can be operated by children as young as two years old

(E) approximately 5,000 fires per year have been attributed to children playing with lighters before the safety levers were required

109. Which of the following most logically completes the passage?

A business analysis of the Appenian railroad system divided its long-distance passenger routes into two categories: rural routes and interurban routes. The analysis found that, unlike the interurban routes, few rural routes carried a high enough passenger volume to be profitable. Closing unprofitable rural routes, however, will not necessarily enhance the profitability of the whole system, since _______.

(A) a large part of the passenger volume on interurban routes is accounted for by passengers who begin or end their journeys on rural routes

(B) within the last two decades several of the least used rural routes have been closed and their passenger services have been replaced by buses

(C) the rural routes were all originally constructed at least one hundred years ago, whereas some of the interurban routes were constructed recently for new high-speed express trains

(D) not all of Appenia's large cities are equally well served by interurban railroad services

(E) the greatest passenger volume, relative to the routes' capacity, is not on either category of long-distance routes but is on suburban commuter routes

110. Although Ackerburg's subway system is currently operating at a deficit, the transit authority will lower subway fares next year. The authority projects that the lower fares will result in a ten percent increase in the number of subway riders. Since the additional income from the larger ridership will more than offset the decrease due to lower fares, the transit authority actually expects the fare reduction to reduce or eliminate the subway system's operating deficit for next year.

Which of the following, if true, provides the most support for the transit authority's expectation of reducing the subway system's operating deficit?

(A) Throughout the years that the subway system has operated, fares have never before been reduced.

(B) The planned fare reduction will not apply to students, who can already ride the subway for a reduced fare.

(C) Next year, the transit authority will have to undertake several large-scale track maintenance projects.

(D) The subway system can accommodate a ten percent increase in ridership without increasing the number of trains it runs each day.

(E) The current subway fares in Ackerburg are higher than subway fares in other cities in the region.

111. Patrick usually provides child care for six children. Parents leave their children at Patrick's house in the morning and pick them up after work. At the end of each workweek, the parents pay Patrick at an hourly rate for the child care provided that week. The weekly income Patrick receives is usually adequate but not always uniform, particularly in the winter, when children are likely to get sick and be unpredictably absent.

Which of the following plans, if put into effect, has the best prospect of making Patrick's weekly income both uniform and adequate?

(A) Pool resources with a neighbor who provides child care under similar arrangements, so that the two of them cooperate in caring for twice as many children as Patrick currently does.

(B) Replace payment by actual hours of child care provided with a fixed weekly fee based upon the number of hours of child care that Patrick would typically be expected to provide.

(C) Hire a full-time helper and invest in facilities for providing child care to sick children.

(D) Increase the hourly rate to a level that would provide adequate income even in a week when half of the children Patrick usually cares for are absent.

(E) Increase the number of hours made available for child care each day, so that parents can leave their children in Patrick's care for a longer period each day at the current hourly rate.

112. Editorial: Consumers in North America think that by drinking frozen concentrated orange juice, they are saving energy, because it takes fewer truckloads to transport it than it takes to transport an equivalent amount of not-from-concentrate juice. But they are mistaken, for the amount of energy required to concentrate the juice is far greater than the energy difference in the juices' transport.

Which of the following, if true, would provide the greatest additional support for the editorial's conclusion?

(A) Freezer trucks use substantially more energy per mile driven than do any other types of trucks.

(B) Frozen juice can be stored for several years, while not-from-concentrate juice lasts a much shorter time.

(C) Oranges grown in Brazil make up an increasing percentage of the fruit used in not-from-concentrate juice production.

(D) A serving of not-from-concentrate juice takes up to six times more space than a serving of frozen concentrated juice.

(E) Though frozen concentrated juice must be kept at a lower temperature, not-from-concentrate juice is far more sensitive to small temperature fluctuations.

113. A computer equipped with signature-recognition software, which restricts access to a computer to those people whose signatures are on file, identifies a person's signature by analyzing not only the form of the signature but also such characteristics as pen pressure and signing speed. Even the most adept forgers cannot duplicate all of the characteristics the program analyzes.

Which of the following can be logically concluded from the passage above?

(A) The time it takes to record and analyze a signature makes the software impractical for everyday use.

(B) Computers equipped with the software will soon be installed in most banks.

(C) Nobody can gain access to a computer equipped with the software solely by virtue of skill at forging signatures.

(D) Signature-recognition software has taken many years to develop and perfect.

(E) In many cases even authorized users are denied legitimate access to computers equipped with the software.

114. The rate at which a road wears depends on various factors, including climate, amount of traffic, and the size and weight of the vehicles using it. The only land transportation to Rittland's seaport is via a divided highway, one side carrying traffic to the seaport and one carrying traffic away from it. The side leading to the seaport has worn faster, even though each side has carried virtually the same amount of traffic, consisting mainly of large trucks.

Which of the following, if true, most helps to explain the difference in the rate of wear?

(A) The volume of traffic to and from Rittland's seaport has increased beyond the intended capacity of the highway that serves it.

(B) Wear on the highway that serves Rittland's seaport is considerably greater during the cold winter months.

(C) Wear on the side of the highway that leads to Rittland's seaport has encouraged people to take buses to the seaport rather than driving there in their own automobiles.

(D) A greater tonnage of goods is exported from Rittland's seaport than is imported through it.

(E) All of Rittland's automobiles are imported by ship.

115. In parts of South America, vitamin-A deficiency is a serious health problem, especially among children. In one region, agriculturists are attempting to improve nutrition by encouraging farmers to plant a new variety of sweet potato called SPK004 that is rich in beta-carotene, which the body converts into vitamin A. The plan has good chances of success, since sweet potato is a staple of the region's diet and agriculture, and the varieties currently grown contain little beta-carotene.

Which of the following, if true, most strongly supports the prediction that the plan will succeed?

(A) The growing conditions required by the varieties of sweet potato currently cultivated in the region are conditions in which SPK004 can flourish.

(B) The flesh of SPK004 differs from that of the currently cultivated sweet potatoes in color and texture, so traditional foods would look somewhat different when prepared from SPK004.

(C) There are no other varieties of sweet potato that are significantly richer in beta-carotene than SPK004 is.

(D) The varieties of sweet potato currently cultivated in the region contain some important nutrients that are lacking in SPK004.

(E) There are other vegetables currently grown in the region that contain more beta-carotene than the currently cultivated varieties of sweet potato do.

116. Which of the following most logically completes the argument?

The last members of a now-extinct species of a European wild deer called the giant deer lived in Ireland about 16,000 years ago. Prehistoric cave paintings in France depict this animal as having a large hump on its back. Fossils of this animal, however, do not show any hump. Nevertheless, there is no reason to conclude that the cave paintings are therefore inaccurate in this regard, since _________.

(A) some prehistoric cave paintings in France also depict other animals as having a hump

(B) fossils of the giant deer are much more common in Ireland than in France

(C) animal humps are composed of fatty tissue, which does not fossilize

(D) the cave paintings of the giant deer were painted well before 16,000 years ago

(E) only one currently existing species of deer has any anatomical feature that even remotely resembles a hump

117. High levels of fertilizer and pesticides, needed when farmers try to produce high yields of the same crop year after year, pollute water supplies. Experts therefore urge farmers to diversify their crops and to rotate their plantings yearly.

To receive governmental price-support benefits for a crop, farmers must have produced that same crop for the past several years.

The statements above, if true, best support which of the following conclusions?

(A) The rules for governmental support of farm prices work against efforts to reduce water pollution.
(B) The only solution to the problem of water pollution from fertilizers and pesticides is to take farmland out of production.
(C) Farmers can continue to make a profit by rotating diverse crops, thus reducing costs for chemicals, but not by planting the same crop each year.
(D) New farming techniques will be developed to make it possible for farmers to reduce the application of fertilizers and pesticides.
(E) Governmental price supports for farm products are set at levels that are not high enough to allow farmers to get out of debt.

118. Ten years ago the number of taxpayers in Greenspace County was slightly greater than the number of registered voters. The number of taxpayers has doubled over the last ten years, while the number of registered voters has increased, but at a lower rate than has the number of taxpayers.

Which of the following must be true in Greenspace County if the statements above are true?

(A) The number of taxpayers is now smaller than the number of registered voters.
(B) Everyone who is a registered voter is also a taxpayer.
(C) The proportion of registered voters to taxpayers has increased over the last ten years.
(D) The proportion of registered voters to taxpayers has decreased over the last ten years.
(E) The proportion of registered voters to taxpayers has remained unchanged over the last ten years.

119. The interview is an essential part of a successful hiring program because, with it, job applicants who have personalities that are unsuited to the requirements of the job will be eliminated from consideration.

The argument above logically depends on which of the following assumptions?

(A) A hiring program will be successful if it includes interviews.
(B) The interview is a more important part of a successful hiring program than is the development of a job description.
(C) Interviewers can accurately identify applicants whose personalities are unsuited to the requirements of the job.
(D) The only purpose of an interview is to evaluate whether job applicants' personalities are suited to the requirements of the job.
(E) The fit of job applicants' personalities to the requirements of the job was once the most important factor in making hiring decisions.

120. Many leadership theories have provided evidence that leaders affect group success rather than the success of particular individuals. So it is irrelevant to analyze the effects of supervisor traits on the attitudes of individuals whom they supervise. Instead, assessment of leadership effectiveness should occur only at the group level.

Which of the following would it be most useful to establish in order to evaluate the argument?

(A) Whether supervisors' documentation of individual supervisees' attitudes toward them is usually accurate
(B) Whether it is possible to assess individual supervisees' attitudes toward their supervisors without thereby changing those attitudes
(C) Whether any of the leadership theories in question hold that leaders should assess other leaders' attitudes
(D) Whether some types of groups do not need supervision in order to be successful in their endeavors
(E) Whether individuals' attitudes toward supervisors affect group success

121. A major health insurance company in Lagolia pays for special procedures prescribed by physicians only if the procedure is first approved as "medically necessary" by a company-appointed review panel. The rule is intended to save the company the money it might otherwise spend on medically unnecessary procedures. The company has recently announced that in order to reduce its costs, it will abandon this rule.

Which of the following, if true, provides the strongest justification for the company's decision?

(A) Patients often register dissatisfaction with physicians who prescribe nothing for their ailments.

(B) Physicians often prescribe special procedures that are helpful but not altogether necessary for the health of the patient.

(C) The review process is expensive and practically always results in approval of the prescribed procedure.

(D) The company's review process does not interfere with the prerogative of physicians, in cases where more than one effective procedure is available, to select the one they personally prefer.

(E) The number of members of the company-appointed review panel who review a given procedure depends on the cost of the procedure.

122. To evaluate a plan to save money on office-space expenditures by having its employees work at home, XYZ Company asked volunteers from its staff to try the arrangement for six months. During this period, the productivity of these employees was as high as or higher than before.

Which of the following, if true, would argue most strongly against deciding, on the basis of the trial results, to implement the company's plan?

(A) The employees who agreed to participate in the test of the plan were among the company's most self-motivated and independent workers.

(B) The savings that would accrue from reduced office-space expenditures alone would be sufficient to justify the arrangement for the company, apart from any productivity increases.

(C) Other companies that have achieved successful results from work-at-home plans have workforces that are substantially larger than that of XYZ.

(D) The volunteers who worked at home were able to communicate with other employees as necessary for performing the work.

(E) Minor changes in the way office work is organized at XYZ would yield increases in employee productivity similar to those achieved in the trial.

123. Consumer health advocate: Your candy company adds caffeine to your chocolate candy bars so that each one delivers a specified amount of caffeine. Since caffeine is highly addictive, this indicates that you intend to keep your customers addicted.

Candy manufacturer: Our manufacturing process results in there being less caffeine in each chocolate candy bar than in the unprocessed cacao beans from which the chocolate is made.

The candy manufacturer's response is flawed as a refutation of the consumer health advocate's argument because it

(A) fails to address the issue of whether the level of caffeine in the candy bars sold by the manufacturer is enough to keep people addicted
(B) assumes without warrant that all unprocessed cacao beans contain a uniform amount of caffeine
(C) does not specify exactly how caffeine is lost in the manufacturing process
(D) treats the consumer health advocate's argument as though it were about each candy bar rather than about the manufacturer's candy in general
(E) merely contradicts the consumer health advocate's conclusion without giving any reason to believe that the advocate's reasoning is unsound

124. Nutritionists are advising people to eat more fish, since the omega-3 fatty acids in fish help combat many diseases. If everyone took this advice, however, there would not be enough fish in oceans, rivers, and lakes to supply the demand; the oceans are already being overfished. The obvious method to ease the pressure on wild fish populations is for people to increase their consumption of farmed fish.

Which of the following, if true, raises the most serious doubt concerning the prospects for success of the solution proposed above?

(A) Aquaculture, or fish farming, raises more fish in a given volume of water than are generally present in the wild.
(B) Some fish farming, particularly of shrimp and other shellfish, takes place in enclosures in the ocean.
(C) There are large expanses of ocean waters that do not contain enough nutrients to support substantial fish populations.
(D) The feed for farmed ocean fish is largely made from small wild-caught fish, including the young of many popular food species.
(E) Some of the species that are now farmed extensively were not commonly eaten when they were only available in the wild.

125. Crops can be traded on the futures market before they are harvested. If a poor corn harvest is predicted, prices of corn futures rise; if a bountiful corn harvest is predicted, prices of corn futures fall. This morning meteorologists are predicting much-needed rain for the corn-growing region starting tomorrow. Therefore, since adequate moisture is essential for the current crop's survival, prices of corn futures will fall sharply today.

Which of the following, if true, most weakens the argument above?

(A) Corn that does not receive adequate moisture during its critical pollination stage will not produce a bountiful harvest.

(B) Futures prices for corn have been fluctuating more dramatically this season than last season.

(C) The rain that meteorologists predicted for tomorrow is expected to extend well beyond the corn-growing region.

(D) Agriculture experts announced today that a disease that has devastated some of the corn crop will spread widely before the end of the growing season.

(E) Most people who trade in corn futures rarely take physical possession of the corn they trade.

126. Large national budget deficits do not cause large trade deficits. If they did, countries with the largest budget deficits would also have the largest trade deficits. In fact, when deficit figures are adjusted so that different countries are reliably comparable to each other, there is no such correlation.

If the statements above are all true, which of the following can properly be inferred on the basis of them?

(A) Countries with large national budget deficits tend to restrict foreign trade.

(B) Reliable comparisons of the deficit figures of one country with those of another are impossible.

(C) Reducing a country's national budget deficit will not necessarily result in a lowering of any trade deficit that country may have.

(D) When countries are ordered from largest to smallest in terms of population, the smallest countries generally have the smallest budget and trade deficits.

(E) Countries with the largest trade deficits never have similarly large national budget deficits.

127. Which of the following best completes the passage below?

The more worried investors are about losing their money, the more they will demand a high potential return on their investment; great risks must be offset by the chance of great rewards. This principle is the fundamental one in determining interest rates, and it is illustrated by the fact that

(A) successful investors are distinguished by an ability to make very risky investments without worrying about their money

(B) lenders receive higher interest rates on unsecured loans than on loans backed by collateral

(C) in times of high inflation, the interest paid to depositors by banks can actually be below the rate of inflation

(D) at any one time, a commercial bank will have a single rate of interest that it will expect all of its individual borrowers to pay

(E) the potential return on investment in a new company is typically lower than the potential return on investment in a well-established company

128. It is often said that high rates of inflation tend to diminish people's incentive to save and invest. This view must be incorrect, however, because people generally saved and invested more of their income in the 1970's when inflation rates were high than they did in the 1980's when inflation rates were low.

Of the following, the best criticism of the argument above is that it overlooks the possibility that

(A) all people do not respond in the same way to a given economic stimulus

(B) certain factors operating in the 1980's but not in the 1970's diminished people's incentive to save and invest

(C) the population was larger in the 1980's than it was in the 1970's

(D) the proponents of the view cited would stand to gain if inflation rates become lower

(E) a factor that affects people's savings behavior in a certain way could affect people's investment behavior quite differently

129. Which of the following most logically completes the argument below?

Within the earth's core, which is iron, pressure increases with depth. Because the temperature at which iron melts increases with pressure, the inner core is solid and the outer core is molten. Physicists can determine the melting temperature of iron at any given pressure and the pressure for any given depth in the earth. Therefore, the actual temperature at the boundary of the earth's outer and inner cores—the melting temperature of iron there—can be determined, since __________.

(A) the depth beneath the earth's surface of the boundary between the outer and inner cores is known
(B) some of the heat from the earth's core flows to the surface of the earth
(C) pressures within the earth's outer core are much greater than pressures above the outer core
(D) nowhere in the earth's core can the temperature be measured directly
(E) the temperatures within the earth's inner core are higher than in the outer core

130. Which of the following most logically completes the reasoning?

Either food scarcity or excessive hunting can threaten a population of animals. If the group faces food scarcity, individuals in the group will reach reproductive maturity later than otherwise. If the group faces excessive hunting, individuals that reach reproductive maturity earlier will come to predominate. Therefore, it should be possible to determine whether prehistoric mastodons became extinct because of food scarcity or human hunting, since there are fossilized mastodon remains from both before and after mastodon populations declined, and __________.

(A) there are more fossilized mastodon remains from the period before mastodon populations began to decline than from after that period
(B) the average age at which mastodons from a given period reached reproductive maturity can be established from their fossilized remains
(C) it can be accurately estimated from fossilized remains when mastodons became extinct
(D) it is not known when humans first began hunting mastodons
(E) climate changes may have gradually reduced the food available to mastodons

131. Unlike the wholesale price of raw wool, the wholesale price of raw cotton has fallen considerably in the last year. Thus, although the retail price of cotton clothing at retail clothing stores has not yet fallen, it will inevitably fall.

Which of the following, if true, most seriously weakens the argument above?

(A) The cost of processing raw cotton for cloth has increased during the last year.
(B) The wholesale price of raw wool is typically higher than that of the same volume of raw cotton.
(C) The operating costs of the average retail clothing store have remained constant during the last year.
(D) Changes in retail prices always lag behind changes in wholesale prices.
(E) The cost of harvesting raw cotton has increased in the last year.

132. Many office buildings designed to prevent outside air from entering have been shown to have elevated levels of various toxic substances circulating through the air inside, a phenomenon known as sick building syndrome. Yet the air in other office buildings does not have elevated levels of these substances, even though those buildings are the same age as the "sick" buildings and have similar designs and ventilation systems.

Which of the following, if true, most helps to explain why not all office buildings designed to prevent outside air from entering have air that contains elevated levels of toxic substances?

(A) Certain adhesives and drying agents used in particular types of furniture, carpets, and paint contribute the bulk of the toxic substances that circulate in the air of office buildings.

(B) Most office buildings with sick building syndrome were built between 1950 and 1990.

(C) Among buildings designed to prevent outside air from entering, houses are no less likely than office buildings to have air that contains elevated levels of toxic substances.

(D) The toxic substances that are found in the air of "sick" office buildings are substances that are found in at least small quantities in nearly every building.

(E) Office buildings with windows that can readily be opened are unlikely to suffer from sick building syndrome.

133. Newsletter: **A condominium generally offers more value for its cost than an individual house because of economies of scale.** The homeowners in a condominium association can collectively buy products and services that they could not afford on their own. And since a professional management company handles maintenance of common areas, **condominium owners spend less time and money on maintenance than individual homeowners do.**

The two portions in boldface play which of the following roles in the newsletter's argument?

(A) The first is the argument's main conclusion; the second is another conclusion supporting the first.

(B) The first is a premise, for which no evidence is provided; the second is the argument's only conclusion.

(C) The first is a conclusion supporting the second; the second is the argument's main conclusion.

(D) The first is the argument's only conclusion; the second is a premise, for which no evidence is provided.

(E) Both are premises, for which no evidence is provided, and both support the argument's only conclusion.

134. Which of the following most logically completes the argument?

When officials in Tannersburg released their plan to widen the city's main roads, environmentalists protested that widened roads would attract more traffic and lead to increased air pollution. In response, city officials pointed out that today's pollution-control devices are at their most effective in vehicles traveling at higher speeds and that widening roads would increase the average speed of traffic. However, this effect can hardly be expected to offset the effect pointed out by environmentalists, since _________.

(A) increases in traffic volume generally produce decreases in the average speed of traffic unless roads are widened

(B) several of the roads that are slated for widening will have to be closed temporarily while construction is underway

(C) most of the air pollution generated by urban traffic comes from vehicles that do not have functioning pollution-control devices

(D) the newly widened roads will not have increased traffic volume if the roads that must be used to reach them are inadequate

(E) a vehicle traveling on a route that goes through Tannersburg will spend less time on Tannersburg's roads once the roads are widened

135. Premature babies who receive regular massages are more active than premature babies who do not. Even when all the babies drink the same amount of milk, the massaged babies gain more weight than do the unmassaged babies. This is puzzling because a more active person generally requires a greater food intake to maintain or gain weight.

Which of the following, if true, best reconciles the apparent discrepancy described above?

(A) Increased activity leads to increased levels of hunger, especially when food intake is not also increased.

(B) Massage increases premature babies' curiosity about their environment, and curiosity leads to increased activity.

(C) Increased activity causes the intestines of premature babies to mature more quickly, enabling the babies to digest and absorb more of the nutrients in the milk they drink.

(D) Massage does not increase the growth rate of babies over one year old, if the babies had not been previously massaged.

(E) Premature babies require a daily intake of nutrients that is significantly higher than that required by babies who were not born prematurely.

136. An eyeglass manufacturer tried to boost sales for the summer quarter by offering its distributors a special discount if their orders for that quarter exceeded those for last year's summer quarter by at least 20 percent. Many distributors qualified for this discount. Even with much merchandise discounted, sales increased enough to produce a healthy gain in net profits. The manufacturer plans to repeat this success by offering the same sort of discount for the fall quarter.

Which of the following, if true, most clearly points to a flaw in the manufacturer's plan to repeat the successful performance of the summer quarter?

(A) In general, a distributor's orders for the summer quarter are no higher than those for the spring quarter.

(B) Along with offering special discounts to qualifying distributors, the manufacturer increased newspaper and radio advertising in those distributors' sales areas.

(C) The distributors most likely to qualify for the manufacturer's special discount are those whose orders were unusually low a year earlier.

(D) The distributors who qualified for the manufacturer's special discount were free to decide how much of that discount to pass on to their own customers.

(E) The distributors' ordering more goods in the summer quarter left them overstocked for the fall quarter.

137. Which of the following, if true, most logically completes the argument?

Some dairy farmers in the province of Takandia want to give their cows a synthetic hormone that increases milk production. Many Takandians, however, do not want to buy milk from cows given the synthetic hormone. For this reason Takandia's legislature is considering a measure requiring milk from cows given the hormone to be labeled as such. Even if the measure is defeated, dairy farmers who use the hormone will probably lose customers, since __________.

(A) it has not been proven that any trace of the synthetic hormone exists in the milk of cows given the hormone

(B) some farmers in Takandia who plan to use the synthetic hormone will probably not do so if the measure were passed

(C) milk from cows that have not been given the synthetic hormone can be labeled as such without any legislative action

(D) the legislature's consideration of the bill has been widely publicized

(E) milk that comes from cows given the synthetic hormone looks and tastes the same as milk from cows that have not received the hormone

138. Budget constraints have made police officials consider reassigning a considerable number of officers from traffic enforcement to work on higher-priority, serious crimes. Reducing traffic enforcement for this reason would be counterproductive, however, in light of the tendency of criminals to use cars when engaged in the commission of serious crimes. An officer stopping a car for a traffic violation can make a search that turns up evidence of serious crime.

Which of the following, if true, most strengthens the argument given?

(A) An officer who stops a car containing evidence of the commission of a serious crime risks a violent confrontation, even if the vehicle was stopped only for a traffic violation.

(B) When the public becomes aware that traffic enforcement has lessened, it typically becomes lax in obeying traffic rules.

(C) Those willing to break the law to commit serious crimes are often in committing such crimes unwilling to observe what they regard as the lesser constraints of traffic law.

(D) The offenders committing serious crimes who would be caught because of traffic violations are not the same group of individuals as those who would be caught if the arresting officers were reassigned from traffic enforcement.

(E) The great majority of persons who are stopped by officers for traffic violations are not guilty of any serious crimes.

139. Conventional wisdom suggests vaccinating elderly people first in flu season, because they are at greatest risk of dying if they contract the virus. This year's flu virus poses particular risk to elderly people and almost none at all to younger people, particularly children. Nevertheless, health professionals are recommending vaccinating children first against the virus rather than elderly people.

Which of the following, if true, provides the strongest reason for the health professionals' recommendation?

(A) Children are vulnerable to dangerous infections when their immune systems are severely weakened by other diseases.

(B) Children are particularly unconcerned with hygiene and therefore are the group most responsible for spreading the flu virus to others.

(C) The vaccinations received last year will confer no immunity to this year's flu virus.

(D) Children who catch one strain of the flu virus and then recover are likely to develop immunity to at least some strains with which they have not yet come in contact.

(E) Children are no more likely than adults to have immunity to a particular flu virus if they have never lived through a previous epidemic of the same virus.

140. Pro-Tect Insurance Company has recently been paying out more on car-theft claims than it expected. Cars with special antitheft devices or alarm systems are much less likely to be stolen than are other cars. Consequently Pro-Tect, as part of an effort to reduce its annual payouts, will offer a discount to holders of car-theft policies if their cars have antitheft devices or alarm systems.

Which of the following, if true, provides the strongest indication that the plan is likely to achieve its goal?

(A) The decrease in the risk of car theft conferred by having a car alarm is greatest when only a few cars have such alarms.

(B) The number of policyholders who have filed a claim in the past year is higher for Pro-Tect than for other insurance companies.

(C) In one or two years, the discount that Pro-Tect is offering will amount to more than the cost of buying certain highly effective antitheft devices.

(D) Currently, Pro-Tect cannot legally raise the premiums it charges for a given amount of insurance against car theft.

(E) The amount Pro-Tect has been paying out on car-theft claims has been greater for some models of car than for others.

141. While the total enrollment of public elementary and secondary schools in Sondland is one percent higher this academic year than last academic year, the number of teachers there increased by three percent. Thus, the Sondland Education Commission's prediction of a teacher shortage as early as next academic year is unfounded.

Which of the following, if true, most seriously weakens the claim that the prediction of a teacher shortage as early as next academic year is unfounded?

(A) Funding for public elementary schools in Sondland is expected to increase over the next ten years.

(B) Average salaries for Sondland's teachers increased at the rate of inflation from last academic year to this academic year.

(C) A new law has mandated that there be ten percent more teachers per pupil in Sondland's public schools next academic year than there were this academic year.

(D) In the past, increases in enrollments in public elementary and secondary schools in Sondland have generally been smaller than increases in the number of teachers.

(E) Because of reductions in funding, the number of students enrolling in teacher-training programs in Sondland is expected to decline beginning in the next academic year.

142. Art restorers who have been studying the factors that cause Renaissance oil paintings to deteriorate physically when subject to climatic changes have found that the oil paint used in these paintings actually adjusts to these changes well. The restorers therefore hypothesize that it is a layer of material called gesso, which is under the paint, that causes the deterioration.

Which of the following, if true, most strongly supports the restorers' hypothesis?

(A) Renaissance oil paintings with a thin layer of gesso are less likely to show deterioration in response to climatic changes than those with a thicker layer.

(B) Renaissance oil paintings are often painted on wooden panels, which swell when humidity increases and contract when it declines.

(C) Oil paint expands and contracts readily in response to changes in temperature, but it absorbs little water and so is little affected by changes in humidity.

(D) An especially hard and nonabsorbent type of gesso was the raw material for moldings on the frames of Renaissance oil paintings.

(E) Gesso layers applied by Renaissance painters typically consisted of a coarse base layer onto which several increasingly fine-grained layers were applied.

143. Automobile Dealer's Advertisement: The Highway Traffic Safety Institute reports that the PZ 1000 has the fewest injuries per accident of any car in its class. This shows that the PZ 1000 is one of the safest cars available today.

Which of the following, if true, most seriously weakens the argument in the advertisement?

(A) The Highway Traffic Safety Institute report listed many cars in other classes that had more injuries per accident than did the PZ 1000.

(B) In recent years many more PZ 1000s have been sold than have any other kind of car in its class.

(C) Cars in the class to which the PZ 1000 belongs are more likely to be involved in accidents than are other types of cars.

(D) The difference between the number of injuries per accident for the PZ 1000 and that for other cars in its class is quite pronounced.

(E) The Highway Traffic Safety Institute issues reports only once a year.

144. Archaeologists working in the Andes Mountains recently excavated a buried 4,000-year-old temple containing structures that align with a stone carving on a distant hill to indicate the direction of the rising sun at the summer solstice. Alignments in the temple were also found to point toward the position, at the summer solstice, of a constellation known in Andean culture as the Fox. Since the local mythology represents the fox as teaching people how to cultivate and irrigate plants, the ancient Andeans may have built the temple as a religious representation of the fox.

Which of the following is an assumption on which the argument is based?

(A) The constellation known as the Fox has the same position at the summer solstice as it did 4,000 years ago.

(B) In the region around the temple, the summer solstice marks the time for planting.

(C) The temple was protected from looters by dirt and debris built up over thousands of years.

(D) Other structural alignments at the temple point to further constellations with agricultural significance.

(E) The site containing the temple was occupied for a significant amount of time before abandonment.

145. Which of the following most logically completes the passage?

It is generally believed that people receiving frequent medical checkups are likely to need hospitalization less frequently than they would otherwise; after all, many things can be done following a checkup to prevent problems that, if ignored, might become acute and then require hospitalization. But for people with chronic illnesses, frequent medical checkups are likely to lead to more frequent hospitalization since _________.

(A) the recommended treatments for complications of many chronic illnesses involve hospitalization even if those complications are detected while barely noticeable

(B) medical checkups sometimes do not reveal early symptoms of those chronic illnesses that are best treated in a hospital

(C) the average length of a hospital stay is the same for those who receive frequent checkups as for those who do not

(D) people with chronic illnesses generally receive medical checkups more frequently than people who are not chronically ill

(E) the average length of a hospital stay for people with a chronic illness tends to increase as the illness progresses

146. Meat from chickens contaminated with salmonella bacteria can cause serious food poisoning. Capsaicin, the chemical that gives chili peppers their hot flavor, has antibacterial properties. Chickens do not have taste receptors for capsaicin and will readily eat feed laced with capsaicin. When chickens were fed such feed and then exposed to salmonella bacteria, relatively few of them became contaminated with salmonella.

In deciding whether the feed would be useful in raising salmonella-free chicken for retail sale, it would be most helpful to determine which of the following?

(A) Whether feeding capsaicin to chickens affects the taste of their meat

(B) Whether eating capsaicin reduces the risk of salmonella poisoning for humans

(C) Whether chicken is more prone to salmonella contamination than other kinds of meat

(D) Whether appropriate cooking of chicken contaminated with salmonella can always prevent food poisoning

(E) Whether capsaicin can be obtained only from chili peppers

147. Laws requiring the use of headlights during daylight hours can prevent automobile collisions. However, since daylight visibility is worse in countries farther from the equator, any such laws would obviously be more effective in preventing collisions in those countries. In fact, the only countries that actually have such laws are farther from the equator than is the continental United States.

Which of the following conclusions could be most properly drawn from the information given above?

(A) Drivers in the continental United States who used their headlights during the day would be just as likely to become involved in a collision as would drivers who did not use their headlights.

(B) In many countries that are farther from the equator than is the continental United States, poor daylight visibility is the single most important factor in automobile collisions.

(C) The proportion of automobile collisions that occur in the daytime is greater in the continental United States than in the countries that have daytime headlight laws.

(D) Fewer automobile collisions probably occur each year in countries that have daytime headlight laws than occur within the continental United States.

(E) Daytime headlight laws would probably do less to prevent automobile collisions in the continental United States than they do in the countries that have the laws.

148. Which of the following most logically completes the argument below?

When mercury-vapor streetlights are used in areas inhabited by insect-eating bats, the bats feed almost exclusively around the lights, because the lights attract flying insects. In Greenville, the mercury-vapor streetlights are about to be replaced with energy-saving sodium streetlights, which do not attract insects. This change is likely to result in a drop in the population of insect-eating bats in Greenville, since __________.

(A) the bats do not begin to hunt until after sundown

(B) the bats are unlikely to feed on insects that do not fly

(C) the highway department will be able to replace mercury-vapor streetlights with sodium streetlights within a relatively short time and without disrupting the continuity of lighting at the locations of the streetlights

(D) in the absence of local concentrations of the flying insects on which bats feed, the bats expend much more energy on hunting for food, requiring much larger quantities of insects to sustain each bat

(E) bats use echolocation to catch insects and therefore gain no advantage from the fact that insects flying in the vicinity of streetlights are visible at night

149. Rats injected with morphine exhibit decreased activity of the immune system, the bodily system that fights off infections. These same rats exhibited heightened blood levels of corticosteroids, chemicals secreted by the adrenal glands. Since corticosteroids can interfere with immune-system activity, scientists hypothesized that the way morphine reduces immune responses in rats is by stimulating the adrenal glands to secrete additional corticosteroids into the bloodstream.

Which of the following experiments would yield the most useful results for evaluating the scientists' hypothesis?

(A) Injecting morphine into rats that already have heightened blood levels of corticosteroids and then observing their new blood levels of corticosteroids
(B) Testing the level of immune-system activity of rats, removing their adrenal glands, and then testing the rats' immune-system activity levels again
(C) Injecting rats with corticosteroids and then observing how many of the rats contracted infections
(D) Removing the adrenal glands of rats, injecting the rats with morphine, and then testing the level of the rats' immune-system responses
(E) Injecting rats with a drug that stimulates immune-system activity and then observing the level of corticosteroids in their bloodstreams

150. Curator: If our museum lends *Venus* to the Hart Institute for their show this spring, they will lend us their Rembrandt etchings for our print exhibition next fall. Having those etchings will increase attendance to the exhibition and hence increase revenue from our general admission fee.

Museum Administrator: But *Venus* is our biggest attraction. Moreover the Hart's show will run for twice as long as our exhibition. So on balance the number of patrons may decrease.

The point of the administrator's response to the curator is to question

(A) whether getting the Rembrandt etchings from the Hart Institute is likely to increase attendance at the print exhibition
(B) whether the Hart Institute's Rembrandt etchings will be appreciated by those patrons of the curator's museum for whom the museum's biggest attraction is *Venus*
(C) whether the number of patrons attracted by the Hart Institute's Rembrandt etchings will be larger than the number of patrons who do not come in the spring because *Venus* is on loan
(D) whether, if *Venus* is lent, the museum's revenue from general admission fees during the print exhibition will exceed its revenue from general admission fees during the Hart Institute's exhibition
(E) whether the Hart Institute or the curator's museum will have the greater financial gain from the proposed exchange of artworks

151. Which of the following most logically completes the passage?

Leaf beetles damage willow trees by stripping away their leaves, but a combination of parasites and predators generally keeps populations of these beetles in check. Researchers have found that severe air pollution results in reduced predator populations. The parasites, by contrast, are not adversely affected by pollution; nevertheless, the researchers' discovery probably does explain why leaf beetles cause particularly severe damage to willows in areas with severe air pollution, since __________.

(A) neither the predators nor the parasites of leaf beetles themselves attack willow trees

(B) the parasites that attack leaf beetles actually tend to be more prevalent in areas with severe air pollution than they are elsewhere

(C) the damage caused by leaf beetles is usually not enough to kill a willow tree outright

(D) where air pollution is not especially severe, predators have much more impact on leaf-beetle populations than parasites do

(E) willows often grow in areas where air pollution is especially severe

152. Which of the following best completes the passage below?

At a recent conference on environmental threats to the North Sea, most participating countries favored uniform controls on the quality of effluents, whether or not specific environmental damage could be attributed to a particular source of effluent. What must, of course, be shown, in order to avoid excessively restrictive controls, is that __________.

(A) any uniform controls that are adopted are likely to be implemented without delay

(B) any substance to be made subject to controls can actually cause environmental damage

(C) the countries favoring uniform controls are those generating the largest quantities of effluents

(D) all of any given pollutant that is to be controlled actually reaches the North Sea at present

(E) environmental damage already inflicted on the North Sea is reversible

153. On May first, in order to reduce the number of overdue books, a children's library instituted a policy of forgiving fines and giving bookmarks to children returning all of their overdue books. On July first there were twice as many overdue books as there had been on May first, although a record number of books had been returned during the interim.

Which of the following, if true, most helps to explain the apparent inconsistency in the results of the library's policy?

(A) The librarians did not keep accurate records of how many children took advantage of the grace period, and some of the children returning overdue books did not return all of their overdue books.

(B) Although the grace period enticed some children to return all of their overdue books, it did not convince all of the children with overdue books to return all of their books.

(C) The bookmarks became popular among the children, so in order to collect the bookmarks, many children borrowed many more books than they usually did and kept them past their due date.

(D) The children were allowed to borrow a maximum of five books for a two-week period, and hence each child could keep a maximum of fifteen books beyond their due date within a two-month period.

(E) Although the library forgave overdue fines during the grace period, the amount previously charged the children was minimal; hence, the forgiveness of the fines did not provide enough incentive for them to return their overdue books.

154. A certain species of desert lizard digs tunnels in which to lay its eggs. The eggs must incubate inside the tunnel for several weeks before hatching, and they fail to hatch if they are disturbed at any time during this incubation period. Yet these lizards guard their tunnels for only a few days after laying their eggs.

Which of the following, if true, most helps explain why there is no need for lizards to guard their tunnels for more than a few days?

(A) The eggs are at risk of being disturbed only during the brief egg-laying season when many lizards are digging in a relatively small area.

(B) The length of the incubation period varies somewhat from one tunnel to another.

(C) Each female lizard lays from 15 to 20 eggs, only about 10 of which hatch even if the eggs are not disturbed at any time during the incubation period.

(D) The temperature and humidity within the tunnels will not be suitable for the incubating eggs unless the tunnels are plugged with sand immediately after the eggs are laid.

(E) The only way to disturb the eggs of this lizard species is by opening up one of the tunnels in which they are laid.

155. Often patients with ankle fractures that are stable, and thus do not require surgery, are given follow-up x-rays because their orthopedists are concerned about possibly having misjudged the stability of the fracture. When a number of follow-up x-rays were reviewed, however, all the fractures that had initially been judged stable were found to have healed correctly. Therefore, it is a waste of money to order follow-up x-rays of ankle fractures initially judged stable.

Which of the following, if true, most strengthens the argument?

(A) Doctors who are general practitioners rather than orthopedists are less likely than orthopedists to judge the stability of an ankle fracture correctly.

(B) Many ankle injuries for which an initial x-ray is ordered are revealed by the x-ray not to involve any fracture of the ankle.

(C) X-rays of patients of many different orthopedists working in several hospitals were reviewed.

(D) The healing of ankle fractures that have been surgically repaired is always checked by means of a follow-up x-ray.

(E) Orthopedists routinely order follow-up x-rays for fractures of bones other than ankle bones.

156. In setting environmental standards for industry and others to meet, it is inadvisable to require the best results that state-of-the-art technology can achieve. Current technology is able to detect and eliminate even extremely minute amounts of contaminants, but at a cost that is exorbitant relative to the improvement achieved. So it would be reasonable instead to set standards by taking into account all of the current and future risks involved.

The argument given concerning the reasonable way to set standards presupposes that

(A) industry currently meets the standards that have been set by environmental authorities

(B) there are effective ways to take into account all of the relevant risks posed by allowing different levels of contaminants

(C) the only contaminants worth measuring are generated by industry

(D) it is not costly to prevent large amounts of contaminants from entering the environment

(E) minute amounts of some contaminants can be poisonous

157. Most scholars agree that King Alfred (A.D. 849–899) personally translated a number of Latin texts into Old English. One historian contends that Alfred also personally penned his own law code, arguing that the numerous differences between the language of the law code and Alfred's translations of Latin texts are outweighed by the even more numerous similarities. Linguistic similarities, however, are what one expects in texts from the same language, the same time, and the same region. Apart from Alfred's surviving translations and law code, there are only two other extant works from the same dialect and milieu, so it is risky to assume here that linguistic similarities point to common authorship.

The passage above proceeds by

(A) providing examples that underscore another argument's conclusion

(B) questioning the plausibility of an assumption on which another argument depends

(C) showing that a principle if generally applied would have anomalous consequences

(D) showing that the premises of another argument are mutually inconsistent

(E) using argument by analogy to undermine a principle implicit in another argument

158. A company plans to develop a prototype weeding machine that uses cutting blades with optical sensors and microprocessors that distinguish weeds from crop plants by differences in shade of color. The inventor of the machine claims that it will reduce labor costs by virtually eliminating the need for manual weeding.

Which of the following is a consideration in favor of the company's implementing its plan to develop the prototype?

(A) There is a considerable degree of variation in shade of color between weeds of different species.

(B) The shade of color of some plants tends to change appreciably over the course of their growing season.

(C) When crops are weeded manually, overall size and leaf shape are taken into account in distinguishing crop plants from weeds.

(D) Selection and genetic manipulation allow plants of virtually any species to be economically bred to have a distinctive shade of color without altering their other characteristics.

(E) Farm laborers who are responsible for the manual weeding of crops carry out other agricultural duties at times in the growing season when extensive weeding is not necessary.

159. A certain mayor has proposed a fee of five dollars per day on private vehicles entering the city, claiming that the fee will alleviate the city's traffic congestion. The mayor reasons that, since the fee will exceed the cost of round-trip bus fare from many nearby points, many people will switch from using their cars to using the bus.

Which of the following statements, if true, provides the best evidence that the mayor's reasoning is flawed?

(A) Projected increases in the price of gasoline will increase the cost of taking a private vehicle into the city.

(B) The cost of parking fees already makes it considerably more expensive for most people to take a private vehicle into the city than to take a bus.

(C) Most of the people currently riding the bus do not own private vehicles.

(D) Many commuters opposing the mayor's plan have indicated that they would rather endure traffic congestion than pay a five-dollar-per-day fee.

(E) During the average workday, private vehicles owned and operated by people living within the city account for 20 percent of the city's traffic congestion.

160. Aroca City currently funds its public schools through taxes on property. **In place of this system, the city plans to introduce a sales tax of 3 percent on all retail sales in the city.** Critics protest that 3 percent of current retail sales falls short of the amount raised for schools by property taxes. The critics are correct on this point. **Nevertheless, implementing the plan will probably not reduce the money going to Aroca's schools.** Several large retailers have selected Aroca City as the site for huge new stores, and these are certain to draw large numbers of shoppers from neighboring municipalities, where sales are taxed at rates of 6 percent and more. In consequence, retail sales in Aroca City are bound to increase substantially.

In the argument given, the two portions in **boldface** play which of the following roles?

(A) The first presents a plan that the argument concludes is unlikely to achieve its goal; the second expresses that conclusion.

(B) The first presents a plan that the argument concludes is unlikely to achieve its goal; the second presents evidence in support of that conclusion.

(C) The first presents a plan that the argument contends is the best available; the second is a conclusion drawn by the argument to justify that contention.

(D) The first presents a plan one of whose consequences is at issue in the argument; the second is the argument's conclusion about that consequence.

(E) The first presents a plan that the argument seeks to defend against a certain criticism; the second is that criticism.

161. Which of the following most logically completes the argument?

A photograph of the night sky was taken with the camera shutter open for an extended period. The normal motion of stars across the sky caused the images of the stars in the photograph to appear as streaks. However, one bright spot was not streaked. Even if the spot were caused, as astronomers believe, by a celestial object, that object could still have been moving across the sky during the time the shutter was open, since __________.

(A) the spot was not the brightest object in the photograph

(B) the photograph contains many streaks that astronomers can identify as caused by noncelestial objects

(C) stars in the night sky do not appear to shift position relative to each other

(D) the spot could have been caused by an object that emitted a flash that lasted for only a fraction of the time that the camera shutter was open

(E) if the camera shutter had not been open for an extended period, it would have recorded substantially fewer celestial objects

162. Economist: Paying extra for fair-trade coffee—coffee labeled with the Fairtrade logo—is intended to help poor farmers, because they receive a higher price for the fair-trade coffee they grow. But this practice may hurt more farmers in developing nations than it helps. By raising average prices for coffee, it encourages more coffee to be produced than consumers want to buy. This lowers prices for non-fair-trade coffee and thus lowers profits for non-fair-trade coffee farmers.

To evaluate the strength of the economist's argument, it would be most helpful to know which of the following?

(A) Whether there is a way of alleviating the impact of the increased average prices for coffee on non-fair-trade coffee farmers' profits

(B) What proportion of coffee farmers in developing nations produce fair-trade coffee

(C) Whether many coffee farmers in developing nations also derive income from other kinds of farming

(D) Whether consumers should pay extra for fair-trade coffee if doing so lowers profits for non-fair-trade coffee farmers

(E) How fair-trade coffee farmers in developing nations could be helped without lowering profits for non-fair-trade coffee farmers

163. Tanco, a leather manufacturer, uses large quantities of common salt to preserve animal hides. New environmental regulations have significantly increased the cost of disposing of salt water that results from this use, and, in consequence, Tanco is considering a plan to use potassium chloride in place of common salt. Research has shown that Tanco could reprocess the by-product of potassium chloride use to yield a crop fertilizer, leaving a relatively small volume of waste for disposal.

In determining the impact on company profits of using potassium chloride in place of common salt, it would be important for Tanco to research all of the following EXCEPT:

(A) What difference, if any, is there between the cost of the common salt needed to preserve a given quantity of animal hides and the cost of the potassium chloride needed to preserve the same quantity of hides?

(B) To what extent is the equipment involved in preserving animal hides using common salt suitable for preserving animal hides using potassium chloride?

(C) What environmental regulations, if any, constrain the disposal of the waste generated in reprocessing the by-product of potassium chloride?

(D) How closely does leather that results when common salt is used to preserve hides resemble that which results when potassium chloride is used?

(E) Are the chemical properties that make potassium chloride an effective means for preserving animal hides the same as those that make common salt an effective means for doing so?

164. Colorless diamonds can command high prices as gemstones. A type of less valuable diamonds can be treated to remove all color. Only sophisticated tests can distinguish such treated diamonds from naturally colorless ones. However, only 2 percent of diamonds mined are of the colored type that can be successfully treated, and many of those are of insufficient quality to make the treatment worthwhile. Surely, therefore, the vast majority of colorless diamonds sold by jewelers are naturally colorless.

A serious flaw in the reasoning of the argument is that

(A) comparisons between the price diamonds command as gemstones and their value for other uses are omitted

(B) information about the rarity of treated diamonds is not combined with information about the rarity of naturally colorless, gemstone diamonds

(C) the possibility that colored diamonds might be used as gemstones, even without having been treated, is ignored

(D) the currently available method for making colorless diamonds from colored ones is treated as though it were the only possible method for doing so

(E) the difficulty that a customer of a jeweler would have in distinguishing a naturally colorless diamond from a treated one is not taken into account

165. The Sumpton town council recently voted to pay a prominent artist to create an abstract sculpture for the town square. Critics of this decision protested that town residents tend to dislike most abstract art, and any art in the town square should reflect their tastes. But a town council spokesperson dismissed this criticism, pointing out that other public abstract sculptures that the same sculptor has installed in other cities have been extremely popular with those cities' local residents.

The statements above most strongly suggest that the main point of disagreement between the critics and the spokesperson is whether

(A) it would have been reasonable to consult town residents on the decision
(B) most Sumpton residents will find the new sculpture to their taste
(C) abstract sculptures by the same sculptor have truly been popular in other cities
(D) a more traditional sculpture in the town square would be popular among local residents
(E) public art that the residents of Sumpton would find desirable would probably be found desirable by the residents of other cities

166. Jay: Of course there are many good reasons to support the expansion of preventive medical care, but arguments claiming that it will lead to greater societal economic gains are misguided. Some of the greatest societal expenses arise from frequent urgent-care needs for people who have attained a long life due to preventive care.

Sunil: Your argument fails because you neglect economic gains outside the health care system: society suffers an economic loss when any of its productive members suffer preventable illnesses.

Sunil's response to Jay makes which of the following assumptions?

(A) Those who receive preventive care are not more likely to need urgent care than are those who do not receive preventive care.
(B) Jay intends the phrase "economic gains" to refer only to gains accruing to institutions within the health care system.
(C) Productive members of society are more likely than others to suffer preventable illnesses.
(D) The economic contributions of those who receive preventive medical care may outweigh the economic losses caused by preventive care.
(E) Jay is incorrect in stating that patients who receive preventive medical care are long-lived.

167. Boreal owls range over a much larger area than do other owls of similar size. The reason for this behavior is probably that the small mammals on which owls feed are especially scarce in the forests where boreal owls live, and the relative scarcity of prey requires the owls to range more extensively to find sufficient food.

Which of the following, if true, most helps to confirm the explanation above?

(A) Some boreal owls range over an area eight times larger than the area over which any other owl of similar size ranges.
(B) Boreal owls range over larger areas in regions where food of the sort eaten by small mammals is sparse than they do in regions where such food is abundant.
(C) After their young hatch, boreal owls must hunt more often than before in order to feed both themselves and their newly hatched young.
(D) Sometimes individual boreal owls hunt near a single location for many weeks at a time and do not range farther than a few hundred yards.
(E) The boreal owl requires less food, relative to its weight, than is required by members of other owl species.

168. Microbiologist: A lethal strain of salmonella recently showed up in a European country, causing an outbreak of illness that killed two people and infected twenty-seven others. Investigators blame the severity of the outbreak on the overuse of antibiotics, since the salmonella bacteria tested were shown to be drug-resistant. But this is unlikely because patients in the country where the outbreak occurred cannot obtain antibiotics to treat illness without a prescription, and the country's doctors prescribe antibiotics less readily than do doctors in any other European country.

Which of the following, if true, would most weaken the microbiologist's reasoning?

(A) Physicians in the country where the outbreak occurred have become hesitant to prescribe antibiotics since they are frequently in short supply.
(B) People in the country where the outbreak occurred often consume foods produced from animals that eat antibiotics-laden livestock feed.
(C) Use of antibiotics in two countries that neighbor the country where the outbreak occurred has risen over the past decade.
(D) Drug-resistant strains of salmonella have not been found in countries in which antibiotics are not generally available.
(E) Salmonella has been shown to spread easily along the distribution chains of certain vegetables, such as raw tomatoes.

169. Historian: Newton developed mathematical concepts and techniques that are fundamental to modern calculus. Leibniz developed closely analogous concepts and techniques. It has traditionally been thought that these discoveries were independent. Researchers have, however, recently discovered notes of Leibniz's that discuss one of Newton's books on mathematics. Several scholars have argued that since **the book includes a presentation of Newton's calculus concepts and techniques,** and since the notes were written before Leibniz's own development of calculus concepts and techniques, it is virtually certain **that the traditional view is false.** A more cautious conclusion than this is called for, however. Leibniz's notes are limited to early sections of Newton's book, sections that precede the ones in which Newton's calculus concepts and techniques are presented.

In the historian's reasoning, the two portions in **boldface** play which of the following roles?

(A) The first is a claim that the historian rejects; the second is a position that that claim has been used to support.
(B) The first is evidence that has been used to support a conclusion about which the historian expresses reservations; the second is that conclusion.
(C) The first provides evidence in support of a position that the historian defends; the second is that position.
(D) The first and the second each provide evidence in support of a position that the historian defends.
(E) The first has been used in support of a position that the historian rejects; the second is a conclusion that the historian draws from that position.

170. For over two centuries, no one had been able to make Damascus blades—blades with a distinctive serpentine surface pattern—but a contemporary sword maker may just have rediscovered how. Using iron with trace impurities that precisely matched those present in the iron used in historic Damascus blades, this contemporary sword maker seems to have finally hit on an intricate process by which he can produce a blade indistinguishable from a true Damascus blade.

Which of the following, if true, provides the strongest support for the hypothesis that trace impurities in the iron are essential for the production of Damascus blades?

(A) There are surface features of every Damascus blade—including the blades produced by the contemporary sword maker—that are unique to that blade.
(B) The iron with which the contemporary sword maker made Damascus blades came from a source of iron that was unknown two centuries ago.
(C) Almost all the tools used by the contemporary sword maker were updated versions of tools that were used by sword makers over two centuries ago.
(D) Production of Damascus blades by sword makers of the past ceased abruptly after those sword makers' original source of iron became exhausted.
(E) Although Damascus blades were renowned for maintaining a sharp edge, the blade made by the contemporary sword maker suggests that they may have maintained their edge less well than blades made using what is now the standard process for making blades.

171. Images from ground-based telescopes are invariably distorted by the Earth's atmosphere. Orbiting space telescopes, however, operating above Earth's atmosphere, should provide superbly detailed images. Therefore, ground-based telescopes will soon become obsolete for advanced astronomical research purposes.

Which of the following statements, if true, would cast the most doubt on the conclusion drawn above?

(A) An orbiting space telescope due to be launched this year is far behind schedule and over budget, whereas the largest ground-based telescope was both within budget and on schedule.

(B) Ground-based telescopes located on mountain summits are not subject to the kinds of atmospheric distortion which, at low altitudes, make stars appear to twinkle.

(C) By careful choice of observatory location, it is possible for large-aperture telescopes to avoid most of the kind of wind turbulence that can distort image quality.

(D) When large-aperture telescopes are located at high altitudes near the equator, they permit the best Earth-based observations of the center of the Milky Way Galaxy, a prime target of astronomical research.

(E) Detailed spectral analyses, upon which astronomers rely for determining the chemical composition and evolutionary history of stars, require telescopes with more light-gathering capacity than space telescopes can provide.

172. Generally scientists enter their field with the goal of doing important new research and accept as their colleagues those with similar motivation. Therefore, when any scientist wins renown as an expounder of science to general audiences, most other scientists conclude that this popularizer should no longer be regarded as a true colleague.

The explanation offered above for the low esteem in which scientific popularizers are held by research scientists assumes that

(A) serious scientific research is not a solitary activity, but relies on active cooperation among a group of colleagues

(B) research scientists tend not to regard as colleagues those scientists whose renown they envy

(C) a scientist can become a famous popularizer without having completed any important research

(D) research scientists believe that those who are well known as popularizers of science are not motivated to do important new research

(E) no important new research can be accessible to or accurately assessed by those who are not themselves scientists

173. Urban planner: When a city loses population due to migration, property taxes in that city tend to rise. This is because there are then fewer residents paying to maintain an infrastructure that was designed to support more people. Rising property taxes, in turn, drive more residents away, compounding the problem. Since the city of Stonebridge is starting to lose population, the city government should therefore refrain from raising property taxes.

Which of the following, if true, would most weaken the urban planner's argument?

(A) If Stonebridge does not raise taxes on its residents to maintain its infrastructure, the city will become much less attractive to live in as that infrastructure decays.

(B) Stonebridge at present benefits from grants provided by the national government to help maintain certain parts of its infrastructure.

(C) If there is a small increase in property taxes in Stonebridge and a slightly larger proportion of total revenue than at present is allocated to infrastructure maintenance, the funding will be adequate for that purpose.

(D) Demographers project that the population of a region that includes Stonebridge will start to increase substantially within the next several years.

(E) The property taxes in Stonebridge are significantly lower than those in many larger cities.

174. Which of the following most logically completes the argument?

Utrania was formerly a major petroleum exporter, but in recent decades economic stagnation and restrictive regulations inhibited investment in new oil fields. In consequence, Utranian oil exports dropped steadily as old fields became depleted. Utrania's currently improving economic situation, together with less-restrictive regulations, will undoubtedly result in the rapid development of new fields. However, it would be premature to conclude that the rapid development of new fields will result in higher oil exports, because __________.

(A) the price of oil is expected to remain relatively stable over the next several years

(B) the improvement in the economic situation in Utrania is expected to result in a dramatic increase in the proportion of Utranians who own automobiles

(C) most of the investment in new oil fields in Utrania is expected to come from foreign sources

(D) new technology is available to recover oil from old oil fields formerly regarded as depleted

(E) many of the new oil fields in Utrania are likely to be as productive as those that were developed during the period when Utrania was a major oil exporter

175. The use of growth-promoting antibiotics in hog farming can weaken their effectiveness in treating humans because such use can spread resistance to those antibiotics among microorganisms. But now the Smee Company, one of the largest pork marketers, may stop buying pork raised on feed containing these antibiotics. Smee has 60 percent of the pork market, and farmers who sell to Smee would certainly stop using antibiotics in order to avoid jeopardizing their sales. So if Smee makes this change, it will probably significantly slow the decline in antibiotics' effectiveness for humans.

Which of the following, if true, would most strengthen the argument above?

(A) Other major pork marketers will probably stop buying pork raised on feed containing growth-promoting antibiotics if Smee no longer buys such pork.
(B) The decline in hog growth due to discontinuation of antibiotics can be offset by improved hygiene.
(C) Authorities are promoting the use of antibiotics to which microorganisms have not yet developed resistance.
(D) A phaseout of use of antibiotics for hogs in one country reduced usage by over 50 percent over five years.
(E) If Smee stops buying pork raised with antibiotics, the firm's costs will probably increase.

176. In an experiment, volunteers walked individually through a dark, abandoned theater. Half of the volunteers had been told that the theater was haunted and the other half that it was under renovation. The first half reported significantly more unusual experiences than the second did. The researchers concluded that reports of encounters with ghosts and other supernatural entities generally result from prior expectations of such experiences.

Which of the following, if true, would most seriously weaken the researchers' reasoning?

(A) None of the volunteers in the second half believed that the unusual experiences they reported were supernatural.
(B) All of the volunteers in the first half believed that the researchers' statement that the theater was haunted was a lie.
(C) Before being told about the theater, the volunteers within each group varied considerably in their prior beliefs about supernatural experiences.
(D) Each unusual experience reported by the volunteers had a cause that did not involve the supernatural.
(E) The researchers did not believe that the theater was haunted.

177. In order to reduce dependence on imported oil, the government of Jalica has imposed minimum fuel-efficiency requirements on all new cars, beginning this year. The more fuel-efficient a car, the less pollution it produces per mile driven. As Jalicans replace their old cars with cars that meet the new requirements, annual pollution from car traffic is likely to decrease in Jalica.

Which of the following, if true, most seriously weakens the argument?

(A) In Jalica, domestically produced oil is more expensive than imported oil.
(B) The Jalican government did not intend the new fuel-efficiency requirement to be a pollution-reduction measure.
(C) Some pollution-control devices mandated in Jalica make cars less fuel-efficient than they would be without those devices.
(D) The new regulation requires no change in the chemical formulation of fuel for cars in Jalica.
(E) Jalicans who get cars that are more fuel-efficient tend to do more driving than before.

178. Plantings of cotton bioengineered to produce its own insecticide against bollworms, a major cause of crop failure, sustained little bollworm damage until this year. This year the plantings are being seriously damaged by bollworms. Bollworms, however, are not necessarily developing resistance to the cotton's insecticide. Bollworms breed on corn, and last year more corn than usual was planted throughout cotton-growing regions. So it is likely that the cotton is simply being overwhelmed by corn-bred bollworms.

In evaluating the argument, which of the following would it be most useful to establish?

(A) Whether corn could be bioengineered to produce the insecticide

(B) Whether plantings of cotton that does not produce the insecticide are suffering unusually extensive damage from bollworms this year

(C) Whether other crops that have been bioengineered to produce their own insecticide successfully resist the pests against which the insecticide was to protect them

(D) Whether plantings of bioengineered cotton are frequently damaged by insect pests other than bollworms

(E) Whether there are insecticides that can be used against bollworms that have developed resistance to the insecticide produced by the bioengineered cotton

179. Typically during thunderstorms most lightning strikes carry a negative electric charge; only a few carry a positive charge. Thunderstorms with unusually high proportions of positive-charge strikes tend to occur in smoky areas near forest fires. The fact that smoke carries positively charged smoke particles into the air above a fire suggests the hypothesis that the extra positive strikes occur because of the presence of such particles in the storm clouds.

Which of the following, if discovered to be true, most seriously undermines the hypothesis?

(A) Other kinds of rare lightning also occur with unusually high frequency in the vicinity of forest fires.

(B) The positive-charge strikes that occur near forest fires tend to be no more powerful than positive strikes normally are.

(C) A positive-charge strike is as likely to start a forest fire as a negative-charge strike is.

(D) Thunderstorms that occur in drifting clouds of smoke have extra positive-charge strikes weeks after the charge of the smoke particles has dissipated.

(E) The total number of lightning strikes during a thunderstorm is usually within the normal range in the vicinity of a forest fire.

180. Many gardeners believe that the variety of clematis vine that is most popular among gardeners in North America is *jackmanii*. This belief is apparently correct since, of the one million clematis plants sold per year by the largest clematis nursery in North America, ten percent are *jackmanii*.

Which of the following is an assumption on which the argument depends?

(A) The nursery sells more than ten different varieties of clematis.

(B) The largest clematis nursery in North America sells nothing but clematis plants.

(C) Some of the *jackmanii* sold by the nursery are sold to gardeners outside North America.

(D) Most North American gardeners grow clematis in their gardens.

(E) For all nurseries in North America that specialize in clematis, at least ten percent of the clematis plants they sell are *jackmanii*.

181. Since 1990 the percentage of bacterial sinus infections in Aqadestan that are resistant to the antibiotic perxicillin has increased substantially. Bacteria can quickly develop resistance to an antibiotic when it is prescribed indiscriminately or when patients fail to take it as prescribed. Since perxicillin has not been indiscriminately prescribed, health officials hypothesize that the increase in perxicillin-resistant sinus infections is largely due to patients' failure to take this medication as prescribed.

Which of the following, if true of Aqadestan, provides most support for the health officials' hypothesis?

(A) Resistance to several other commonly prescribed antibiotics has not increased since 1990 in Aqadestan.

(B) A large number of Aqadestanis never seek medical help when they have a sinus infection.

(C) When it first became available, perxicillin was much more effective in treating bacterial sinus infections than any other antibiotic used for such infections at the time.

(D) Many patients who take perxicillin experience severe side effects within the first few days of their prescribed regimen.

(E) Aqadestani health clinics provide antibiotics to their patients at cost.

182. Psychologist: In a study, researchers gave 100 volunteers a psychological questionnaire designed to measure their self-esteem. The researchers then asked each volunteer to rate the strength of his or her own social skills. The volunteers with the highest levels of self-esteem consistently rated themselves as having much better social skills than did the volunteers with moderate levels. This suggests that attaining an exceptionally high level of self-esteem greatly improves one's social skills.

The psychologist's argument is most vulnerable to criticism on which of the following grounds?

(A) It fails to adequately address the possibility that many of the volunteers may not have understood what the psychological questionnaire was designed to measure.

(B) It takes for granted that the volunteers with the highest levels of self-esteem had better social skills than did the other volunteers, even before the former volunteers had attained their high levels of self-esteem.

(C) It overlooks the possibility that people with very high levels of self-esteem may tend to have a less accurate perception of the strength of their own social skills than do people with moderate levels of self-esteem.

(D) It relies on evidence from a group of volunteers that is too small to provide any support for any inferences regarding people in general.

(E) It overlooks the possibility that factors other than level of self-esteem may be of much greater importance in determining the strength of one's social skills.

183. A product that represents a clear technological advance over competing products can generally command a high price. Because **technological advances tend to be quickly surpassed** and companies want to make large profits while they still can, **many companies charge the maximum possible price for such a product**. But large profits on the new product will give competitors a strong incentive to quickly match the new product's capabilities. Consequently, the strategy to maximize overall profit from a new product is to charge less than the greatest possible price.

In the argument above, the two portions in **boldface** play which of the following roles?

(A) The first is a consideration raised to argue that a certain strategy is counterproductive; the second presents that strategy.

(B) The first is a consideration raised to support the strategy that the argument recommends; the second presents that strategy.

(C) The first is a consideration raised to help explain the popularity of a certain strategy; the second presents that strategy.

(D) The first is an assumption, rejected by the argument, that has been used to justify a course of action; the second presents that course of action.

(E) The first is a consideration that has been used to justify adopting a certain strategy; the second presents the intended outcome of that strategy.

184. Gortland has long been narrowly self-sufficient in both grain and meat. However, as per capita income in Gortland has risen toward the world average, per capita consumption of meat has also risen toward the world average, and it takes several pounds of grain to produce one pound of meat. Therefore, since per capita income continues to rise, whereas domestic grain production will not increase, Gortland will soon have to import either grain or meat or both.

Which of the following is an assumption on which the argument depends?

(A) The total acreage devoted to grain production in Gortland will not decrease substantially.

(B) The population of Gortland has remained relatively constant during the country's years of growing prosperity.

(C) The per capita consumption of meat in Gortland is roughly the same across all income levels.

(D) In Gortland, neither meat nor grain is subject to government price controls.

(E) People in Gortland who increase their consumption of meat will not radically decrease their consumption of grain.

185. Political Advertisement:

Mayor Delmont's critics complain about the jobs that were lost in the city under Delmont's leadership. Yet the fact is that not only were more jobs created than were eliminated, but each year since Delmont took office the average pay for the new jobs created has been higher than that year's average pay for jobs citywide. So it stands to reason that throughout Delmont's tenure the average paycheck in this city has been getting steadily bigger.

Which of the following, if true, most seriously weakens the argument in the advertisement?

(A) The unemployment rate in the city is higher today than it was when Mayor Delmont took office.

(B) The average pay for jobs in the city was at a ten-year low when Mayor Delmont took office.

(C) Each year during Mayor Delmont's tenure, the average pay for jobs that were eliminated has been higher than the average pay for jobs citywide.

(D) Most of the jobs eliminated during Mayor Delmont's tenure were in declining industries.

(E) The average pay for jobs in the city is currently lower than it is for jobs in the suburbs surrounding the city.

186. To prevent a newly built dam on the Chiff River from blocking the route of fish migrating to breeding grounds upstream, the dam includes a fish pass, a mechanism designed to allow fish through the dam. Before the construction of the dam and fish pass, several thousand fish a day swam upriver during spawning season. But in the first season after the project's completion, only 300 per day made the journey. Clearly, the fish pass is defective.

Which of the following, if true, most seriously weakens the argument?

(A) Fish that have migrated to the upstream breeding grounds do not return down the Chiff River again.

(B) On other rivers in the region, the construction of dams with fish passes has led to only small decreases in the number of fish migrating upstream.

(C) The construction of the dam stirred up potentially toxic river sediments that were carried downstream.

(D) Populations of migratory fish in the Chiff River have been declining slightly over the last 20 years.

(E) During spawning season, the dam releases sufficient water for migratory fish below the dam to swim upstream.

187. Music critic: Fewer and fewer musicians are studying classical music, decreasing the likelihood that those with real aptitude for such music will be performing it. Audiences who hear these performances will not appreciate classical music's greatness and will thus decamp to other genres. So to maintain classical music's current meager popularity, we must encourage more young musicians to enter the field.

Which of the following, if true, most weakens the music critic's reasoning?

(A) Musicians who choose to study classical music do so because they believe they have an aptitude for the music.

(B) Classical music's current meager popularity is attributable to the profusion of other genres of music available to listeners.

(C) Most people who appreciate classical music come to do so through old recordings rather than live performances.

(D) It is possible to enjoy the music in a particular genre even when it is performed by musicians who are not ideally suited for that genre.

(E) The continued popularity of a given genre of music depends in part on the audiences being able to understand why that genre attained its original popularity.

188. Commemorative plaques cast from brass are a characteristic art form of the Benin culture of West Africa. Some scholars, noting that the oldest surviving plaques date to the 1400s, hypothesize that brass-casting techniques were introduced by the Portuguese, who came to Benin in 1485 A.D. But Portuguese records of that expedition mention cast-brass jewelry sent to Benin's king from neighboring Ife. So it is unlikely that Benin's knowledge of brass casting derived from the Portuguese.

Which of the following, if true, most strengthens the argument?

(A) The Portuguese records do not indicate whether their expedition of 1485 included metalworkers.

(B) The Portuguese had no contact with Ife until the 1500s.

(C) In the 1400s the Portuguese did not use cast brass for commemorative plaques.

(D) As early as 1500 A.D., Benin artists were making brass plaques incorporating depictions of Europeans.

(E) Copper, which is required for making brass, can be found throughout Benin territory.

4.5 Answer Key

106. C
107. B
108. B
109. A
110. D
111. B
112. A
113. C
114. D
115. A
116. C
117. A
118. D
119. C
120. E
121. C
122. A
123. A
124. D
125. D
126. C
127. B
128. B
129. A
130. B
131. A
132. A
133. A
134. C
135. C
136. E
137. C
138. C
139. B
140. C
141. C
142. A
143. C
144. A
145. A
146. A
147. E
148. D
149. D
150. C
151. D
152. B
153. C
154. A
155. C
156. B
157. B
158. D
159. B
160. D
161. D
162. B
163. E
164. B
165. B
166. D
167. B
168. B
169. B
170. D
171. E
172. D
173. A
174. B
175. A
176. B
177. E
178. B
179. D
180. A
181. D
182. C
183. C
184. E
185. C
186. C
187. C
188. B

4.6 Answer Explanations

The following discussion is intended to familiarize you with the most efficient and effective approaches to critical reasoning questions. The particular questions in this chapter are generally representative of the kinds of critical reasoning questions you will encounter on the GMAT. Remember that it is the problem solving strategy that is important, not the specific details of a particular question.

106. PhishCo runs a number of farms in the arid province of Nufa, depending largely on irrigation. Now, as part of a plan to efficiently increase the farms' total production, it plans to drill down to an aquifer containing warm, slightly salty water that will be used to raise fish in ponds. The water from the ponds will later be used to supplement piped-in irrigation water for PhishCo's vegetable fields, and the ponds and accompanying vegetation should help reduce the heat in the area of the farms.

Which of the following would, if true, most strongly suggest that the plan, if implemented, would increase the overall efficiency of PhishCo's farms?

(A) Most of the vegetation to be placed around the ponds is native to Nufa.

(B) Fish raised on PhishCo's farms are likely to be saleable in the nearest urban areas.

(C) Organic waste from fish in the pond water will help to fertilize fields where it is used for irrigation.

(D) The government of Nufa will help to arrange loan financing to partially cover the costs of drilling.

(E) Ponds will be located on low-lying land now partially occupied by grain crops.

Evaluation of a Plan

Situation A company plans to increase the total efficiency of its farms in an arid region by drilling down to an aquifer whose water will be used to raise fish in ponds and to help irrigate the farms' vegetable fields. The ponds and accompanying vegetation should help reduce the heat around the farms.

Reasoning *What would make it most likely that implementing the plan would increase the farms' overall efficiency?* The farms will become more efficient if the plan significantly increases their production for little or no added cost.

A Vegetation native to an arid region may be no more likely to thrive around ponds than non-native vegetation would be, and in any case would not clearly increase the farms' total crop production or efficiency.

B This makes it slightly more likely that the plan would increase the farms' profitability, not their efficiency or productivity.

C **Correct.** Fertilizing the fields with the waste while irrigating the crops might significantly improve crop production. But it would cost little or nothing extra, since the waste would already be in the irrigation water. Thus, this feature of the plan would likely enhance the farms' efficiency by increasing their productivity for no significant extra cost.

D This government assistance might slightly reduce the work the company has to do to procure a loan. But probably it would neither increase the farms' production nor reduce the overall expense of implementing the plan (including the expense incurred by the government).

E If anything, this suggests that the plan might reduce the farms' efficiency by eliminating productive crop land.

The correct answer is C.

107. The sustained massive use of pesticides in farming has two effects that are especially pernicious. First, it often kills off the pests' natural enemies in the area. Second, it often unintentionally gives rise to insecticide-resistant pests, since those insects that survive a particular insecticide will be the ones most resistant to it, and they are the ones left to breed.

From the passage above, it can be properly inferred that the effectiveness of the sustained massive use of pesticides can be extended by doing which of the following, assuming that each is a realistic possibility?

(A) Using only chemically stable insecticides
(B) Periodically switching the type of insecticide used
(C) Gradually increasing the quantities of pesticides used
(D) Leaving a few fields fallow every year
(E) Breeding higher-yielding varieties of crop plants

Evaluation of a Plan

Situation Continued high-level pesticide use often kills off the targeted pests' natural enemies. In addition, the pests that survive the application of the pesticide may become resistant to it, and these pesticide-resistant pests will continue breeding.

Reasoning *What can be done to prolong the effectiveness of pesticide use?* It can be inferred that the ongoing use of a particular pesticide will not continue to be effective against the future generations of pests with an inherent resistance to that pesticide. What would be effective against these future generations? If farmers periodically change the particular pesticide they use, then pests resistant to one kind of pesticide might be killed by another. This would continue, with pests being killed off in cycles as the pesticides are changed. It is also possible that this rotation might allow some of the pests' natural enemies to survive, at least until the next cycle.

A Not enough information about chemically stable insecticides is given to make a sound inference.

B Correct. This statement properly identifies an action that could extend the effectiveness of pesticide use.

C Gradually increasing the amount of the pesticides being used will not help the situation since the pests are already resistant to it.

D Continued use of pesticides is assumed as part of the argument. Since pesticides would be unnecessary for fallow fields, this suggestion is irrelevant.

E Breeding higher-yielding varieties of crops does nothing to extend the effectiveness of the use of pesticides.

The correct answer is B.

108. Which of the following, if true, most logically completes the argument below?

Manufacturers are now required to make all cigarette lighters child-resistant by equipping them with safety levers. But this change is unlikely to result in a significant reduction in the number of fires caused by children playing with lighters, because children given the opportunity can figure out how to work the safety levers and _______.

(A) the addition of the safety levers has made lighters more expensive than they were before the requirement was instituted

(B) adults are more likely to leave child-resistant lighters than non-child-resistant lighters in places that are accessible to children

(C) many of the fires started by young children are quickly detected and extinguished by their parents

(D) unlike child-resistant lighters, lighters that are not child-resistant can be operated by children as young as two years old

(E) approximately 5,000 fires per year have been attributed to children playing with lighters before the safety levers were required.

Argument Construction

Situation Manufacturers must equip all cigarette lighters with child-resistant safety levers, but children can figure out how to circumvent the safety levers and thereby often start fires.

Reasoning *What point would most logically complete the argument?* What would make it likely that the number of fires caused by children playing with lighters would remain the same? In order for children to start fires using lighters equipped with safety levers, they must be given the opportunity to figure out how the safety levers work and then to use them. They must, that is, have access to the lighters.

A If safety-lever-equipped lighters are more expensive than lighters that are not so equipped, fewer lighters might be sold. This would most likely afford children less access to lighters, thus giving them less opportunity to start fires with them.

B **Correct.** This statement properly identifies a point that logically completes the argument: it explains why children are likely to have access to lighters equipped with safety levers.

C The speed with which fires are extinguished does not have any bearing on the number of fires that are started.

D This provides a reason to believe that the number of fires started by children will most likely decrease, rather than stay the same: fewer children will be able to operate the lighters, and thus fewer fires are likely to be started.

E This information about how many fires were started by children before safety levers were required does not have any bearing on the question of how many fires are likely to be started by children now that the safety levers are required.

The correct answer is B.

109. Which of the following most logically completes the passage?

A business analysis of the Appenian railroad system divided its long-distance passenger routes into two categories: rural routes and interurban routes. The analysis found that, unlike the interurban routes, few rural routes carried a high enough passenger volume to be profitable. Closing unprofitable rural routes, however, will not necessarily enhance the profitability of the whole system, since _______.

(A) a large part of the passenger volume on interurban routes is accounted for by passengers who begin or end their journeys on rural routes

(B) within the last two decades several of the least used rural routes have been closed and their passenger services have been replaced by buses

(C) the rural routes were all originally constructed at least one hundred years ago, whereas some of the interurban routes were constructed recently for new high-speed express trains

(D) not all of Appenia's large cities are equally well served by interurban railroad services

(E) the greatest passenger volume, relative to the routes' capacity, is not on either category of long-distance routes but is on suburban commuter routes

Argument Construction

Situation In the Appenian railroad system, interurban routes generally carry enough passengers to be profitable, but few rural routes do.

Reasoning *What would suggest that closing unprofitable rural routes would not enhance the railroad system's profitability?* Any evidence that closing the unprofitable rural routes would indirectly reduce the profitability of other components of the railroad system would support the conclusion that closing those rural routes will not enhance the system's profitability. Thus, a statement providing such evidence would logically complete the passage.

A **Correct.** This suggests that closing the rural routes could discourage many passengers from traveling on the profitable interurban routes as well, thus reducing the profitability of the railroad system as a whole.

B Even if some of the least used rural routes have already been closed, it remains true that most of the remaining rural routes are too little used to be profitable.

C Closing very old routes would be at least as likely to enhance the railroad system's profitability as closing newer routes would be.

D Even if there is better railroad service to some large cities than others, closing unprofitable rural routes could still enhance the system's profitability.

E Even if suburban routes are the most heavily used and profitable, closing underused, unprofitable rural routes could still enhance the system's profitability.

The correct answer is A.

110. Although Ackerburg's subway system is currently operating at a deficit, the transit authority will lower subway fares next year. The authority projects that the lower fares will result in a ten percent increase in the number of subway riders. Since the additional income from the larger ridership will more than offset the decrease due to lower fares, the transit authority actually expects the fare reduction to reduce or eliminate the subway system's operating deficit for next year.

Which of the following, if true, provides the most support for the transit authority's expectation of reducing the subway system's operating deficit?

(A) Throughout the years that the subway system has operated, fares have never before been reduced.

(B) The planned fare reduction will not apply to students, who can already ride the subway for a reduced fare.

(C) Next year, the transit authority will have to undertake several large-scale track maintenance projects.

(D) The subway system can accommodate a ten percent increase in ridership without increasing the number of trains it runs each day.

(E) The current subway fares in Ackerburg are higher than subway fares in other cities in the region.

Argument Evaluation

Situation Ackerburg's transit authority plans to lower subway fares, projecting that this will increase ridership by 10 percent and thereby reduce or eliminate the subway system's operating deficit.

Reasoning *What evidence would support the expectation that lowering subway fares will reduce the operating deficit?* The passage says the additional income from the projected increase in ridership will more than offset the decrease due to the lowered fares. The claim that lowering fares will reduce the operating deficit could be supported either by additional evidence that lowering the fares will increase ridership at least as much as projected or by evidence that the plan will not increase overall operating expenses.

A The fact that fares have never been reduced provides no evidence about what would happen if they were reduced.

B This suggests that the planned fare reduction would not affect revenue from student riders, but it does not suggest how it would affect revenue from all other riders.

C These maintenance projects will probably increase the operating deficit, making it less likely that the fare reduction will reduce or eliminate that deficit.

D **Correct.** This indicates that the plan will not involve extra operating expenses for running trains and thus increases the likelihood that the plan will reduce the operating deficit.

E Ackerburg may differ from other cities in the region in ways that make the higher fares optimal for Ackerburg's subway system.

The correct answer is D.

111. Patrick usually provides child care for six children. Parents leave their children at Patrick's house in the morning and pick them up after work. At the end of each workweek, the parents pay Patrick at an hourly rate for the child care provided that week. The weekly income Patrick receives is usually adequate but not always uniform, particularly in the winter, when children are likely to get sick and be unpredictably absent.

Which of the following plans, if put into effect, has the best prospect of making Patrick's weekly income both uniform and adequate?

(A) Pool resources with a neighbor who provides child care under similar arrangements, so that the two of them cooperate in caring for twice as many children as Patrick currently does.

(B) Replace payment by actual hours of child care provided with a fixed weekly fee based upon the number of hours of child care that Patrick would typically be expected to provide.

(C) Hire a full-time helper and invest in facilities for providing child care to sick children.

(D) Increase the hourly rate to a level that would provide adequate income even in a week when half of the children Patrick usually cares for are absent.

(E) Increase the number of hours made available for child care each day, so that parents can leave their children in Patrick's care for a longer period each day at the current hourly rate.

Evaluation of a Plan

Situation At the end of the workweek, Patrick is paid a certain amount for each hour of child care he has provided. Patrick usually receives adequate weekly income under this arrangement, but in the winter Patrick's income fluctuates, because children are unpredictably absent due to illness.

Reasoning *Which plan would be most likely to meet the two goals of uniform weekly income and adequate weekly income?* Patrick must find a way to ensure that his weekly income is both adequate—that is, not reduced significantly from current levels—and uniform—that is, not subject to seasonal or other fluctuations. A successful plan would thus most likely be one that does not increase Patrick's costs. Further, the plan need not increase Patrick's weekly income; it must merely ensure that that income is more reliable. It should therefore also provide some way to mitigate the unexpected loss of income from children's absences.

A This plan might raise Patrick's income slightly, because he and the neighbor might pay out less in costs if they pool their resources. But this plan would have no effect on the problem that unpredictable absences pose for Patrick's weekly income.

B **Correct.** This statement properly identifies a plan that would most likely keep Patrick's income adequate (he would probably receive approximately the same amount of money per child as he does now) and uniform (he would receive the money regardless of whether a child was present or absent).

C While this plan might somewhat mitigate the unpredictability in Patrick's income that results from sick children's absences—because parents would be less likely to keep sick children at home—it would increase Patrick's costs. Paying a helper and investing in different facilities would reduce Patrick's income and might thus result in that income being inadequate.

D Under this plan, if we assume that parents did not balk at the increase in Patrick's hourly rate and find alternative child care, Patrick's income would most likely be adequate. But this plan would not help make Patrick's weekly income uniform. His income would continue to fluctuate when children are absent. Remember, there are two goals with regard to Patrick's income: adequacy and uniformity.

E This plan might increase Patrick's income, in that he might be paid for more hours of child care each week. The goals here, however, are to make Patrick's weekly income both adequate and uniform, and this plan does not address the issue of uniformity.

The correct answer is B.

112. Editorial: Consumers in North America think that by drinking frozen concentrated orange juice, they are saving energy, because it takes fewer truckloads to transport it than it takes to transport an equivalent amount of not-from-concentrate juice. But they are mistaken, for the amount of energy required to concentrate the juice is far greater than the energy difference in the juices' transport.

Which of the following, if true, would provide the greatest additional support for the editorial's conclusion?

(A) Freezer trucks use substantially more energy per mile driven than do any other types of trucks.

(B) Frozen juice can be stored for several years, while not-from-concentrate juice lasts a much shorter time.

(C) Oranges grown in Brazil make up an increasing percentage of the fruit used in not-from-concentrate juice production.

(D) A serving of not-from-concentrate juice takes up to six times more space than a serving of frozen concentrated juice.

(E) Though frozen concentrated juice must be kept at a lower temperature, not-from-concentrate juice is far more sensitive to small temperature fluctuations.

Argument Evaluation

Situation North American consumers think that drinking frozen concentrated orange juice saves energy because the concentrated juice can be transported in fewer truckloads than an equivalent amount of not-from-concentrate juice. But more energy is required to concentrate the juice than is saved by this reduction in the number of truckloads used for transportation.

Reasoning *What additional evidence would most help to support the conclusion that drinking frozen concentrated orange juice rather than not-from-concentrate juice does not save energy?* Factors other than the concentration process and the number of truckloads used for transportation may also affect the amounts of energy used to provide the two types of juice. Evidence of any such factor that increases the amount of energy needed to provide frozen concentrated juice more than it increases the amount needed to provide the same amount of not-from-concentrate juice would help to support the editorial's conclusion.

A **Correct.** This suggests that it takes much more energy per truckload to transport frozen concentrated juice than to transport not-from-concentrate juice, which is not frozen.

B If anything, this suggests that a higher proportion of not-from-concentrate juice goes bad and is discarded rather than being drunk. This waste would increase the amount of energy used to provide each glass of not-from-concentrate juice that is drunk.

C Since Brazil is far from North America, this suggests that the average amount of energy used to transport each serving of not-from-concentrate juice may be increasing.

D Since both types of juice must be kept cold until ready to drink, this suggests that a much larger amount of space must be refrigerated to provide each serving of not-from-concentrate juice. That may mean that more energy needs to be used to keep each serving of not-from-concentrate juice cold.

E It may take extra energy to keep the temperature of not-from-concentrate juice more constant. If it does, that would increase the amount of energy used to provide each serving of not-from-concentrate juice.

The correct answer is A.

113. A computer equipped with signature-recognition software, which restricts access to a computer to those people whose signatures are on file, identifies a person's signature by analyzing not only the form of the signature but also such characteristics as pen pressure and signing speed. Even the most adept forgers cannot duplicate all of the characteristics the program analyzes.

Which of the following can be logically concluded from the passage above?

(A) The time it takes to record and analyze a signature makes the software impractical for everyday use.

(B) Computers equipped with the software will soon be installed in most banks.

(C) Nobody can gain access to a computer equipped with the software solely by virtue of skill at forging signatures.

(D) Signature-recognition software has taken many years to develop and perfect.

(E) In many cases even authorized users are denied legitimate access to computers equipped with the software.

Argument Construction

Situation Forgers cannot duplicate all the characteristics that signature-recognition software analyzes, including the form of a signature, pen pressure, and signing speed. Computers equipped with this software restrict access to those whose signatures are on file.

Reasoning *What conclusion can be reached about computers equipped with this software?* The passage states that the software detects more characteristics in a signature than the most accomplished forger can possibly reproduce. Thus, skill at forging signatures is not enough to allow someone to gain access to a computer equipped with the software.

A No information about the speed of the analysis is given, so no such conclusion can be drawn.

B Although the software would likely be of benefit to banks, we cannot conclude that it will be installed in most banks because the passage doesn't rule out, e.g., that the software may be too costly or that there may be proprietary constraints.

C **Correct.** This statement properly identifies a conclusion that can be drawn from the passage.

D Although it seems reasonable to think that the software took a long time to develop, nothing in the passage justifies the claim that it took years.

E Nothing in the passage rules out the possibility that the software functions so well that authorized users will never be denied legitimate access to computers equipped with the software.

The correct answer is C.

114. The rate at which a road wears depends on various factors, including climate, amount of traffic, and the size and weight of the vehicles using it. The only land transportation to Rittland's seaport is via a divided highway, one side carrying traffic to the seaport and one carrying traffic away from it. The side leading to the seaport has worn faster, even though each side has carried virtually the same amount of traffic, consisting mainly of large trucks.

Which of the following, if true, most helps to explain the difference in the rate of wear?

(A) The volume of traffic to and from Rittland's seaport has increased beyond the intended capacity of the highway that serves it.

(B) Wear on the highway that serves Rittland's seaport is considerably greater during the cold winter months.

(C) Wear on the side of the highway that leads to Rittland's seaport has encouraged people to take buses to the seaport rather than driving there in their own automobiles.

(D) A greater tonnage of goods is exported from Rittland's seaport than is imported through it.

(E) All of Rittland's automobiles are imported by ship.

Argument Construction

Situation The side of a divided highway leading to a seaport has worn faster than the side leading away from the seaport. Both sides carry roughly the same amount of traffic, mainly consisting of large trucks.

Reasoning *What could explain why the side of the highway leading to the seaport has worn faster than the other side?* We are told that climate, amount of traffic, and the size and weight of vehicles on a road affect how quickly the road wears. We are also told that the amounts of traffic on the two sides of the highway are almost identical. Probably the climate on the two sides is also almost identical. Thus, the most likely explanation for the different rates of wear is that the size or weight of the vehicles driving on the two sides differs significantly. So any factor that would make the vehicles' size or weight greater on the side leading to the seaport than on the other side could help explain the difference in wearing.

A The increased traffic volume affects both sides of the highway, so it does not help explain why one side is wearing faster than the other.

B The winter weather affects both sides of the highway, so it does not help explain why one side is wearing faster than the other.

C The buses may contribute to wear on the side of the highway leading to the seaport, but not necessarily more than the car traffic they are replacing would (though the increased use of buses instead of cars may decrease the amount of traffic, buses would be heavier than cars and thus may result in an equal or greater amount of wear). Furthermore, the buses have to come back on the other side, probably carrying the returning travelers who have not left their cars at the airport.

D **Correct.** This suggests that the many trucks visiting the seaport tend to be more heavily laden with goods when traveling on the side of the highway leading to the seaport than when returning on the other side. The resulting difference in the trucks' weight when traveling on the two sides could explain the different rates of wear.

E These automobiles would be transported along the side of the highway leading from the seaport, but not along the side leading to it. This would likely create a pattern of wear opposite to the one observed.

The correct answer is D.

115. In parts of South America, vitamin-A deficiency is a serious health problem, especially among children. In one region, agriculturists are attempting to improve nutrition by encouraging farmers to plant a new variety of sweet potato called SPK004 that is rich in beta-carotene, which the body converts into vitamin A. The plan has good chances of success, since sweet potato is a staple of the region's diet and agriculture, and the varieties currently grown contain little beta-carotene.

Which of the following, if true, most strongly supports the prediction that the plan will succeed?

(A) The growing conditions required by the varieties of sweet potato currently cultivated in the region are conditions in which SPK004 can flourish.

(B) The flesh of SPK004 differs from that of the currently cultivated sweet potatoes in color and texture, so traditional foods would look somewhat different when prepared from SPK004.

(C) There are no other varieties of sweet potato that are significantly richer in beta-carotene than SPK004 is.

(D) The varieties of sweet potato currently cultivated in the region contain some important nutrients that are lacking in SPK004.

(E) There are other vegetables currently grown in the region that contain more beta-carotene than the currently cultivated varieties of sweet potato do.

Evaluation of a Plan

Situation Agriculturists believe that if farmers in a particular South American region plant a new beta-carotene-rich variety of sweet potato, SPK004, the vitamin-A deficiency suffered in that region can be alleviated. Even though sweet potatoes are a staple of the region and the body can convert a sweet potato's beta-carotene into vitamin A, the varieties currently grown there contain little beta-carotene.

Reasoning *What would most support the success of the plan to improve nutrition by encouraging farmers to plant SPK004?* What, that is, would make farmers respond positively to encouragement to plant SPK004? Farmers in the region would probably be inclined to substitute SPK004 for the varieties of sweet potato they currently grow if they could be assured that SPK004 would grow as well as those other varieties do. This would in turn most likely lead to SPK004 being substituted for current varieties of sweet potato in staple dishes, and thus to an improvement in nutrition in the region.

A **Correct.** This statement properly identifies a factor that would support a prediction of the plan's success.

B If dishes made with SPK004 look different than traditional sweet potato dishes in the region do, people might be less likely to eat those dishes; in such a situation, the plan's success would be less likely, rather than more likely.

C It is SPK004's beta-carotene content relative to the beta-carotene content of the sweet potatoes currently grown in the region that is relevant here, so it does not matter if there are other varieties of sweet potato that are richer in beta-carotene than SPK004 is.

D This suggests that switching from currently grown sweet potatoes to SPK004 could negatively affect nutrition in the region; this undermines, rather than supports, the prediction that the plan to improve nutrition will succeed.

E These other vegetables, despite their beta-carotene content being higher than that of the currently cultivated varieties of sweet potato, are clearly not sufficient to prevent a vitamin-A deficiency in the region. This information does nothing to support the prediction that encouraging farmers to plant SPK004 will help to meet those beta-carotene needs.

The correct answer is A.

116. Which of the following most logically completes the argument?

The last members of a now-extinct species of a European wild deer called the giant deer lived in Ireland about 16,000 years ago. Prehistoric cave paintings in France depict this animal as having a large hump on its back. Fossils of this animal, however, do not show any hump. Nevertheless, there is no reason to conclude that the cave paintings are therefore inaccurate in this regard, since __________.

(A) some prehistoric cave paintings in France also depict other animals as having a hump
(B) fossils of the giant deer are much more common in Ireland than in France
(C) animal humps are composed of fatty tissue, which does not fossilize
(D) the cave paintings of the giant deer were painted well before 16,000 years ago
(E) only one currently existing species of deer has any anatomical feature that even remotely resembles a hump

Argument Construction

Situation — Representations found in prehistoric cave paintings in France of the now-extinct giant deer species—the last members of which lived in Ireland about 16,000 years ago—depict the deer as having a hump on its back. Fossils of the deer, however, do not feature a hump.

Reasoning — *What point would most logically complete the argument? That is, what would show that the cave paintings are not inaccurate even though fossils of the giant deer show no hump?* How could it be the case that the paintings show a hump while the fossils do not? One way in which this could be so is if the humps are not part of the fossils—that is, if there is some reason why a hump would not be preserved with the rest of an animal's remains.

A We do not know whether these other cave paintings accurately depict the animals as having humps, so this provides no reason to think that the depictions of giant deer are accurate.

B Where giant deer fossils are found has no bearing on whether cave paintings of giant deer that show a hump on the animal's back are inaccurate. It could be that this suggests that the painters responsible for the representations would not be very familiar with the species; if this were so, it would give some reason to conclude that the representations *were* inaccurate.

C **Correct.** This statement properly identifies a point that logically completes the argument. A hump would not be found as part of a giant deer's fossilized remains if the humps were fatty tissue that would not be fossilized.

D That the cave paintings were painted well before 16,000 years ago shows that they were executed before the giant deer became extinct, but this does not help to explain the discrepancy between the paintings' depiction of a hump on the deer's back and the fossil record's lack of such a hump. It could be that even though the cave painters coexisted with the giant deer, they were not sufficiently familiar with them to depict them accurately.

E That currently existing species of deer lack humps, or even that one species does have a feature resembling a hump, has little bearing on whether cave paintings in France accurately depict the giant deer as having a hump.

The correct answer is C.

117. High levels of fertilizer and pesticides, needed when farmers try to produce high yields of the same crop year after year, pollute water supplies. Experts therefore urge farmers to diversify their crops and to rotate their plantings yearly.

To receive governmental price-support benefits for a crop, farmers must have produced that same crop for the past several years.

The statements above, if true, best support which of the following conclusions?

(A) The rules for governmental support of farm prices work against efforts to reduce water pollution.

(B) The only solution to the problem of water pollution from fertilizers and pesticides is to take farmland out of production.

(C) Farmers can continue to make a profit by rotating diverse crops, thus reducing costs for chemicals, but not by planting the same crop each year.

(D) New farming techniques will be developed to make it possible for farmers to reduce the application of fertilizers and pesticides.

(E) Governmental price supports for farm products are set at levels that are not high enough to allow farmers to get out of debt.

Argument Construction

Situation Farmers are urged to rotate crops annually because the chemicals they must use when continuing to produce the same crops pollute water supplies. On the other hand, farmers may receive federal price-support benefits only if they have been producing the same crop for the past several years.

Reasoning *What conclusion can be drawn from this information?* Farmers wish to receive the price-support benefits offered by the government, so they grow the same crop for several years. In order to continue getting good yields, they use the high levels of chemicals necessary when the same crop is grown from year to year. The result is water pollution. The government's rules for price-support benefits work against the efforts to reduce water pollution.

A **Correct.** This statement properly identifies the conclusion supported by the evidence.

B The experts cited in the passage believe that the rotation of crops is the solution, not the removal of farmland from production.

C The conclusion that farmers cannot make a profit by producing the same crop year after year is not justified by the information given in the premises. The information given suggests that this conclusion would actually be false, since these farmers would benefit by price-support measures for such a crop.

D No information in the passage supports a conclusion about farming techniques other than crop diversification and rotation, which are clearly existing farming techniques and not new or yet to be developed.

E This conclusion is unwarranted because there is no information in the two statements about the levels of the price supports and of the farmers' debts.

The correct answer is A.

118. Ten years ago the number of taxpayers in Greenspace County was slightly greater than the number of registered voters. The number of taxpayers has doubled over the last ten years, while the number of registered voters has increased, but at a lower rate than has the number of taxpayers.

Which of the following must be true in Greenspace County if the statements above are true?

(A) The number of taxpayers is now smaller than the number of registered voters.

(B) Everyone who is a registered voter is also a taxpayer.

(C) The proportion of registered voters to taxpayers has increased over the last ten years.

(D) The proportion of registered voters to taxpayers has decreased over the last ten years.

(E) The proportion of registered voters to taxpayers has remained unchanged over the last ten years.

Argument Evaluation

Situation Ten years ago a county had slightly more taxpayers than registered voters. Since then the number of taxpayers has doubled, while the number of registered voters has increased less.

Reasoning *What can be deduced from the information about the changing numbers of taxpayers and registered voters?* There were already slightly more taxpayers than registered voters ten years ago, but since then the number of taxpayers has increased more than proportionately to the number of registered voters. It follows that there must still be more taxpayers than registered voters, that the absolute number of taxpayers must have increased more than the absolute number of registered voters has, and that the ratio of taxpayers to registered voters must have increased.

A Since there were already more taxpayers than registered voters ten years ago, and since the number of taxpayers has increased more than the number of registered voters, there must still be more taxpayers than registered voters.

B Although there are more taxpayers than registered voters overall, there could still be many individual registered voters who are not taxpayers.

C Since the number of taxpayers has doubled while the number of registered voters has less than doubled, the proportion of registered voters to taxpayers must have decreased, not increased as this option claims.

D **Correct.** Since the number of taxpayers has doubled while the number of registered voters has less than doubled, the proportion of registered voters to taxpayers must have decreased.

E Since the number of taxpayers has doubled while the number of registered voters has less than doubled, the proportion of registered voters to taxpayers must have decreased, not remained unchanged.

The correct answer is D.

119. The interview is an essential part of a successful hiring program because, with it, job applicants who have personalities that are unsuited to the requirements of the job will be eliminated from consideration.

The argument above logically depends on which of the following assumptions?

(A) A hiring program will be successful if it includes interviews.

(B) The interview is a more important part of a successful hiring program than is the development of a job description.

(C) Interviewers can accurately identify applicants whose personalities are unsuited to the requirements of the job.

(D) The only purpose of an interview is to evaluate whether job applicants' personalities are suited to the requirements of the job.

(E) The fit of job applicants' personalities to the requirements of the job was once the most important factor in making hiring decisions.

Argument Construction

Situation The interview is a necessary part of hiring because candidates with unsuitable personalities are eliminated from consideration.

Reasoning *What is being assumed in this argument?* The argument puts forth one reason that the interview is important: it eliminates candidates with unsuitable personalities. This presupposes that interviewers can, with a fair degree of accuracy, rule out those candidates whose personalities do not fit the needs of the job.

A The argument does not go so far as to say that interviews guarantee a successful hiring program.

B The argument does not prioritize the parts of a hiring program.

C **Correct.** This statement properly identifies the assumption underlying the argument.

D The argument gives one reason that the interview is important, but it does not say it is the *only* reason.

E This concerns past practices in hiring, and is irrelevant to the argument.

The correct answer is C.

120. Many leadership theories have provided evidence that leaders affect group success rather than the success of particular individuals. So it is irrelevant to analyze the effects of supervisor traits on the attitudes of individuals whom they supervise. Instead, assessment of leadership effectiveness should occur only at the group level.

Which of the following would it be most useful to establish in order to evaluate the argument?

(A) Whether supervisors' documentation of individual supervisees' attitudes toward them is usually accurate

(B) Whether it is possible to assess individual supervisees' attitudes toward their supervisors without thereby changing those attitudes

(C) Whether any of the leadership theories in question hold that leaders should assess other leaders' attitudes

(D) Whether some types of groups do not need supervision in order to be successful in their endeavors

(E) Whether individuals' attitudes toward supervisors affect group success

Argument Evaluation

Situation Many leadership theories have provided evidence that leaders affect the success of groups but not of individuals.

Reasoning *What would be most helpful to know in order to evaluate how well the stated fact supports the conclusion that leadership effectiveness should be assessed only at the group level without considering supervisors' influence on the attitudes of the individuals they supervise?* Even if leaders do not affect the success of the individuals they lead, they might still affect those individuals' attitudes. And those attitudes in turn might affect group success. If so, the argument would be weak. So any evidence about the existence or strength of these possible effects in the relationship between supervisors and their supervisees would be helpful in evaluating the argument.

A How accurately supervisors document their supervisees' attitudes is not clearly relevant to how much the supervisors affect those attitudes, nor to how much the attitudes affect group success.

B Even if assessing supervisees' attitudes would in itself change those attitudes, the person doing the assessment might be able to predict this change and take it into account. Thus, considering individual supervisees' attitudes might still be worthwhile.

C The argument is not about interactions among leaders, but rather about interactions between supervisors and supervisees.

D The argument is not about groups without supervisors, or whether certain groups might be effective without a supervisor, but rather about how to assess the effectiveness of supervisors in groups that do have them.

E **Correct.** As explained above, if individual supervisees' attitudes affect group success, the argument would be weak. And probably individual supervisees' attitudes toward their supervisors are influenced by those supervisors. So knowing whether individual attitudes toward supervisors affect group success would be helpful in evaluating the argument

The correct answer is E.

121. A major health insurance company in Lagolia pays for special procedures prescribed by physicians only if the procedure is first approved as "medically necessary" by a company-appointed review panel. The rule is intended to save the company the money it might otherwise spend on medically unnecessary procedures. The company has recently announced that in order to reduce its costs, it will abandon this rule.

Which of the following, if true, provides the strongest justification for the company's decision?

(A) Patients often register dissatisfaction with physicians who prescribe nothing for their ailments.

(B) Physicians often prescribe special procedures that are helpful but not altogether necessary for the health of the patient.

(C) The review process is expensive and practically always results in approval of the prescribed procedure.

(D) The company's review process does not interfere with the prerogative of physicians, in cases where more than one effective procedure is available, to select the one they personally prefer.

(E) The number of members of the company-appointed review panel who review a given procedure depends on the cost of the procedure.

Evaluation of a Plan

Situation In order to cut costs, a major health insurance company is abandoning a rule stating that it will pay for special procedures only if the procedure is approved as medically necessary by a review panel.

Reasoning *What piece of information would most help to justify the company's decision?* For the company to save money, it would need to be in some way cutting its costs by abandoning the rule. Under what circumstances might the rule cost, rather than save, the company money? The panel itself might be expensive to convene, for example. Further, the cost savings achieved by the panel might be minimal if the panel did not deny significant numbers of procedures.

A This suggests that patients might be pressuring their physicians to prescribe certain unnecessary procedures for their ailments, which in turn suggests that the panel is reviewing these procedures and denying them. But if so, then the panel is probably saving the insurance company money, so abandoning the panel's review would not reduce the company's costs.

B This suggests that certain procedures that are being prescribed by physicians are not medically necessary, which in turn suggests that the panel reviewing these procedures may be denying them. If this is the case, then the panel is probably saving the insurance company a significant amount of money, so abandoning the panel's review may well increase rather than decrease the company's costs.

C **Correct.** This statement properly identifies information that would help to justify the company's decision.

D Even if the panel does not interfere with physicians' choices when more than one medically effective procedure is available, the panel may still be denying pay for many procedures that are not medically necessary. In such cases the panel may be saving the insurance company money, and abandoning the review process would not reduce the company's costs.

E This suggests that the more expensive the procedure under review, the more expensive the panel itself is. Even so, if the panel denies payment for very expensive procedures, it may nonetheless save the company significantly more than the company has to pay to convene the panel, so abandoning the review process would not reduce the company's costs.

The correct answer is C.

122. To evaluate a plan to save money on office-space expenditures by having its employees work at home, XYZ Company asked volunteers from its staff to try the arrangement for six months. During this period, the productivity of these employees was as high as or higher than before.

Which of the following, if true, would argue most strongly against deciding, on the basis of the trial results, to implement the company's plan?

(A) The employees who agreed to participate in the test of the plan were among the company's most self-motivated and independent workers.

(B) The savings that would accrue from reduced office-space expenditures alone would be sufficient to justify the arrangement for the company, apart from any productivity increases.

(C) Other companies that have achieved successful results from work-at-home plans have workforces that are substantially larger than that of XYZ.

(D) The volunteers who worked at home were able to communicate with other employees as necessary for performing the work.

(E) Minor changes in the way office work is organized at XYZ would yield increases in employee productivity similar to those achieved in the trial.

Evaluation of a Plan

Situation To save money on office space expenditures, a company considers having employees work at home. A six-month trial with employees who have volunteered to test the plan shows their productivity to be as high as or higher than before.

Reasoning *Why would the trial results NOT provide a good reason to implement the plan?* Generalizing from a small sample to the group depends on having a sample that is representative. In this case, the employees who participated in the trial are not representative of all employees. The employees who volunteered for the trial may be the type of employees who would be most likely to work successfully at home. It would not be wise to base a generalization about all employees on this sample.

A **Correct.** This statement properly identifies a flaw in the trial that is the basis for the plan.

B This statement supports the implementation of the plan. Moreover, it is not based on the trial results, so it does not answer the question.

C The passage gives no information about how company size might affect the implementation of the plan or the reliability of the trial results.

D If anything, this would tend to support the plan.

E The goal of the plan is to save money on office space, not to increase productivity, so an alternative plan to increase productivity is irrelevant.

The correct answer is A.

123. Consumer health advocate: Your candy company adds caffeine to your chocolate candy bars so that each one delivers a specified amount of caffeine. Since caffeine is highly addictive, this indicates that you intend to keep your customers addicted.

Candy manufacturer: Our manufacturing process results in there being less caffeine in each chocolate candy bar than in the unprocessed cacao beans from which the chocolate is made.

The candy manufacturer's response is flawed as a refutation of the consumer health advocate's argument because it

(A) fails to address the issue of whether the level of caffeine in the candy bars sold by the manufacturer is enough to keep people addicted

(B) assumes without warrant that all unprocessed cacao beans contain a uniform amount of caffeine

(C) does not specify exactly how caffeine is lost in the manufacturing process

(D) treats the consumer health advocate's argument as though it were about each candy bar rather than about the manufacturer's candy in general

(E) merely contradicts the consumer health advocate's conclusion without giving any reason to believe that the advocate's reasoning is unsound

Argument Evaluation

Situation A candy manufacturer is accused of adding caffeine, an addictive substance, to its chocolate candy bars with the intent of keeping its customers addicted. The candy manufacturer responds to this accusation by saying that there is less caffeine in each chocolate candy bar than in the unprocessed cacao beans from which the chocolate is made.

Reasoning *What is the flaw in the candy manufacturer's response?* First consider whether the response indeed refutes the advocate's charge. In actuality, instead of focusing on the details of the accusation—adding caffeine to its chocolate bars to keep customers addicted—the manufacturer substitutes an entirely different subject, the amount of caffeine in cacao beans. The manufacturer's response is a diversion, not an answer.

A **Correct.** This statement properly identifies the flaw in the response. The candy manufacturer does not answer the question whether adding caffeine to candy bars is designed to make them addictive.

B Even if the manufacturer did make this assumption, the information is not relevant to the accusation, which is not concerned with naturally occurring caffeine in cacao beans.

C The precise amount of caffeine lost in the manufacturing process is not at issue.

D The manufacturer does not treat the health advocate's argument this way.

E The manufacturer does not contradict the accusation, but rather avoids it.

The correct answer is A.

124. Nutritionists are advising people to eat more fish, since the omega-3 fatty acids in fish help combat many diseases. If everyone took this advice, however, there would not be enough fish in oceans, rivers, and lakes to supply the demand; the oceans are already being overfished. The obvious method to ease the pressure on wild fish populations is for people to increase their consumption of farmed fish.

Which of the following, if true, raises the most serious doubt concerning the prospects for success of the solution proposed above?

(A) Aquaculture, or fish farming, raises more fish in a given volume of water than are generally present in the wild.
(B) Some fish farming, particularly of shrimp and other shellfish, takes place in enclosures in the ocean.
(C) There are large expanses of ocean waters that do not contain enough nutrients to support substantial fish populations.
(D) The feed for farmed ocean fish is largely made from small wild-caught fish, including the young of many popular food species.
(E) Some of the species that are now farmed extensively were not commonly eaten when they were only available in the wild.

Argument Evaluation

Situation Nutritionists advise people to eat fish for the omega-3 fatty acids, but there would not be enough fish to meet the demand if everyone followed this advice. Therefore, people should increase their consumption of farmed fish to ease pressure of wild fish populations.

Reasoning *What evidence would suggest that increasing consumption of farmed fish would not ease pressure on wild fish populations?* Any evidence suggesting that significantly increasing consumption of farmed fish would diminish the habitat or food available for wild fish would also suggest that increasing consumption of farmed fish would not ease pressure on wild fish populations.

A Probably the less space fish farming requires, the less pressure it creates on wild fish habitats and populations, other things being equal.

B Whether any fish farming takes place in enclosures in the ocean is not clearly relevant to whether it eases pressure on wild fish populations.

C Substantial fish populations may thrive in other large expanses of ocean water that contain more nutrients, and in rivers and lakes.

D **Correct.** This suggests that increasing consumption of farmed fish would require increased use of wild fish as feed for farmed fish and therefore would not ease pressure on wild fish populations.

E Even if some farmed fish are different species from the wild fish that are commonly eaten, increased consumption of the farmed fish could reduce demand for the wild fish and thereby ease pressure on wild fish populations.

The correct answer is D.

125. Crops can be traded on the futures market before they are harvested. If a poor corn harvest is predicted, prices of corn futures rise; if a bountiful corn harvest is predicted, prices of corn futures fall. This morning meteorologists are predicting much-needed rain for the corn-growing region starting tomorrow. Therefore, since adequate moisture is essential for the current crop's survival, prices of corn futures will fall sharply today.

Which of the following, if true, most weakens the argument above?

(A) Corn that does not receive adequate moisture during its critical pollination stage will not produce a bountiful harvest.

(B) Futures prices for corn have been fluctuating more dramatically this season than last season.

(C) The rain that meteorologists predicted for tomorrow is expected to extend well beyond the corn-growing region.

(D) Agriculture experts announced today that a disease that has devastated some of the corn crop will spread widely before the end of the growing season.

(E) Most people who trade in corn futures rarely take physical possession of the corn they trade.

Argument Evaluation

Situation Crop futures rise when a harvest is expected to be small and drop when a harvest is expected to be large. Today's weather forecast for the corn-growing area predicts much-needed rain, so corn futures will fall today.

Reasoning *What information weakens the argument that corn futures will fall?* The prediction that corn futures will drop sharply today is made solely on the basis of the forecast of rain, which would lead futures buyers to expect an abundant crop. However, if it becomes known that some harmful circumstance such as a devastating disease will severely affect the corn crop before the end of the growing season, this knowledge may lead buyers of futures to expect a smaller harvest, causing prices of futures to rise rather than fall.

A This statement tells at what exact point in the growing cycle rain is critical to a good harvest, but it gives no information about this year's harvest.

B This comparison of past price fluctuations does not affect what will happen to today's corn futures on account of the predicted rain. The argument is not weakened.

C The only rain that matters is the rain that affects the corn-growing region, not areas beyond it; this statement is irrelevant to the prediction.

D **Correct.** This statement properly identifies information that weakens the argument.

E Physical possession of the corn is irrelevant to the price of corn futures.

The correct answer is D.

126. Large national budget deficits do not cause large trade deficits. If they did, countries with the largest budget deficits would also have the largest trade deficits. In fact, when deficit figures are adjusted so that different countries are reliably comparable to each other, there is no such correlation.

If the statements above are all true, which of the following can properly be inferred on the basis of them?

(A) Countries with large national budget deficits tend to restrict foreign trade.
(B) Reliable comparisons of the deficit figures of one country with those of another are impossible.
(C) Reducing a country's national budget deficit will not necessarily result in a lowering of any trade deficit that country may have.
(D) When countries are ordered from largest to smallest in terms of population, the smallest countries generally have the smallest budget and trade deficits.
(E) Countries with the largest trade deficits never have similarly large national budget deficits.

Argument Construction

Situation No correlation is found between large national budget deficits and large trade deficits.

Reasoning *What inference can be drawn from this information?* Since the passage states that national budget deficits do not correlate with trade deficits, it is logical to anticipate an inference about the independent nature of the relationship between the two kinds of deficits. One possible inference is that reducing one deficit need not result in a reduction of the other.

A This would receive some support if there were information indicating that there was a correlation between large budget deficits and small trade deficits, but no such information is given.

B The passage states that reliable comparisons have been developed.

C **Correct.** This statement properly identifies an inference that can be drawn from the given information.

D The passage gives no indication as to whether either type of deficit correlates in any way with the population size of a country.

E Though there is no general correlation between the two kinds of deficits, it cannot be inferred that there are no countries in which both kinds of deficits are large.

The correct answer is C.

127. Which of the following best completes the passage below?

The more worried investors are about losing their money, the more they will demand a high potential return on their investment; great risks must be offset by the chance of great rewards. This principle is the fundamental one in determining interest rates, and it is illustrated by the fact that

(A) successful investors are distinguished by an ability to make very risky investments without worrying about their money

(B) lenders receive higher interest rates on unsecured loans than on loans backed by collateral

(C) in times of high inflation, the interest paid to depositors by banks can actually be below the rate of inflation

(D) at any one time, a commercial bank will have a single rate of interest that it will expect all of its individual borrowers to pay

(E) the potential return on investment in a new company is typically lower than the potential return on investment in a well-established company

Argument Construction

Situation The principle of determining interest rates is related to the risk involved in making the investment of a loan. Potentially greater rewards will lead lenders (investors) to accept greater risks.

Reasoning *Which example illustrates the principle that greater risks should produce greater rewards?* The example must be about the relationship of risk to benefit. Lenders take a greater risk when loans are unsecured (not backed by collateral) because there is a chance they could lose their money entirely. The principle indicates that the lenders—who by definition are investors—would demand the reward of higher interest rates.

A The freedom from anxiety enjoyed by some investors is not relevant. While risky investments are mentioned, this statement does not mention their return.

B **Correct.** This statement properly identifies an example that shows that riskier loans—those not backed by collateral—receive the benefit of higher interest rates.

C This discussion of interest rates in times of inflation does not mention potential risk or potential benefit.

D A single rate of interest for all investments, no matter the level of risk, contradicts the principle and so cannot possibly be an example of it.

E New companies are generally riskier than established ones. A lower rate of return for such riskier new companies contradicts the principle.

The correct answer is B.

128. It is often said that high rates of inflation tend to diminish people's incentive to save and invest. This view must be incorrect, however, because people generally saved and invested more of their income in the 1970's when inflation rates were high than they did in the 1980's when inflation rates were low.

Of the following, the best criticism of the argument above is that it overlooks the possibility that

(A) all people do not respond in the same way to a given economic stimulus
(B) certain factors operating in the 1980's but not in the 1970's diminished people's incentive to save and invest
(C) the population was larger in the 1980's than it was in the 1970's
(D) the proponents of the view cited would stand to gain if inflation rates become lower
(E) a factor that affects people's savings behavior in a certain way could affect people's investment behavior quite differently

Argument Evaluation

Situation People generally saved and invested more in the 1970's when inflation was high than in the 1980s when inflation was low, despite the fact that it is commonly believed that high inflation discourages savings and investment.

Reasoning *Why does the observation about savings, investment, and inflation rates in the 1970's and 1980's not justify the conclusion that high inflation does not generally diminish people's incentive to save and invest?* The argument observes that over the course of two decades there was a positive rather than a negative correlation between inflation on the one hand and savings and investment on the other. It infers from this that high rates of inflation do not tend to diminish people's incentive to save and invest. Is this inference justified? Note that the claim that this argument is trying to discredit is not that high rates of inflation always diminished people's incentive to save and invest. Rather, the claim is merely that high rates of inflation tend to do this. The argument overlooks the possibility that during the two decades in question other factors may have caused a positive correlation to briefly appear even if in general the correlation is negative.

A The argument is compatible with the hypothesis that some people respond to inflation by saving and investing more, while others do not.

B Correct. If these other factors, unrelated to the inflation rate, that operated in the 1980's but not the 1970's, created an even greater disincentive to savings and investment than high inflation rates provide, then those trends do not provide evidence about the general relationship among savings, investment, and inflation.

C The argument appears to concern savings and investment per capita, so total population size should be irrelevant. But increasing population would not explain declining total amounts of savings and investment, either.

D If anything, the possibility that the proponents' ulterior motives distorted their reasoning would help to support the argument's conclusion that the proponents' view is incorrect.

E The argument addresses this possibility by presenting evidence that inflation was positively correlated with both savings and investment during the 1970's and 1980's.

The correct answer is B.

129. Which of the following most logically completes the argument below?

Within the earth's core, which is iron, pressure increases with depth. Because the temperature at which iron melts increases with pressure, the inner core is solid and the outer core is molten. Physicists can determine the melting temperature of iron at any given pressure and the pressure for any given depth in the earth. Therefore, the actual temperature at the boundary of the earth's outer and inner cores—the melting temperature of iron there—can be determined, since ________.

(A) the depth beneath the earth's surface of the boundary between the outer and inner cores is known

(B) some of the heat from the earth's core flows to the surface of the earth

(C) pressures within the earth's outer core are much greater than pressures above the outer core

(D) nowhere in the earth's core can the temperature be measured directly

(E) the temperatures within the earth's inner core are higher than in the outer core

Argument Construction

Situation Pressure within the earth's iron core increases with depth. Because the melting temperature of iron increases with pressure, the inner core is solid and the outer core molten. Physicists can determine iron's melting temperature at any pressure and the pressure it is under at any depth.

Reasoning *What further premise, combined with the information provided, would support the conclusion that physicists can determine the temperature at the boundary between the outer and inner cores?* Since physicists can determine iron's melting temperature at any pressure and the pressure it is under at any depth, they must be able to determine its melting temperature at any depth. The temperature at the boundary between the inner and outer cores must exactly equal the melting temperature there, since that is the boundary between the molten and solid parts of the core. To determine the temperature at the boundary, therefore, it would suffice to know the depth of the boundary.

A **Correct.** If physicists know the depth of the boundary between the inner and outer cores, they can determine the temperature at the boundary.

B The fact that *some heat* flows from the core to the surface is too vague to help in determining exact temperatures anywhere.

C The difference in pressures between the outer core and the region above it is only vaguely described here and is not clearly relevant to the temperature at the boundary between the outer core and the inner core below it.

D An absence of information would not be helpful in determining the temperature at the boundary between the outer and inner cores.

E This information is not sufficiently specific to show that the temperature at the boundary between the outer and inner cores can be determined.

The correct answer is A.

130. Which of the following most logically completes the reasoning?

Either food scarcity or excessive hunting can threaten a population of animals. If the group faces food scarcity, individuals in the group will reach reproductive maturity later than otherwise. If the group faces excessive hunting, individuals that reach reproductive maturity earlier will come to predominate. Therefore, it should be possible to determine whether prehistoric mastodons became extinct because of food scarcity or human hunting, since there are fossilized mastodon remains from both before and after mastodon populations declined, and ________.

(A) there are more fossilized mastodon remains from the period before mastodon populations began to decline than from after that period
(B) the average age at which mastodons from a given period reached reproductive maturity can be established from their fossilized remains
(C) it can be accurately estimated from fossilized remains when mastodons became extinct
(D) it is not known when humans first began hunting mastodons
(E) climate changes may have gradually reduced the food available to mastodons

Argument Construction

Situation In a population of animals, food scarcity causes later reproductive maturity; if that population is hunted excessively, earlier-maturing animals will be more numerous in the population.

Reasoning *What point would most logically complete the argument?* For the information given to be of use in determining what caused mastodons' extinction, mastodon fossils would need to indicate the age at which mastodons reached reproductive maturity, since that is what the argument suggests can indicate cause of extinction. If fossilized remains exist from before and after mastodon populations began to decline, and if the age at which those fossilized mastodons reached reproductive maturity can be determined, then we will have a good idea of what caused their extinction: if they reached reproductive maturity late, it was probably food scarcity, but if they matured earlier, it was most likely hunting.

A This fact only helps indicate that there was a decline; it tells us nothing about what caused the decline.

B Correct. This statement properly identifies a point that logically completes the argument: it explains how the fossilized mastodon remains could be used to help determine what caused mastodons' extinction.

C The point at which mastodons became extinct is not part of this argument, which is concerned with the cause of their extinction. The only way in which this could be relevant to the issue at hand is if mastodons became extinct before humans took up hunting mastodons—but the argument includes no information on whether this was so.

D Not knowing when humans began hunting mastodons would have no effect on the argument, which is concerned with how mastodon fossils, combined with knowledge about how food scarcity and hunting affect mastodon reproductive maturity, can help determine how mastodons became extinct.

E This fact only shows that food scarcity *may* have led to mastodon's decline. It tells us nothing about whether fossilized remains can help determine whether it was food scarcity or human hunting that actually led to the decline.

The correct answer is B.

131. Unlike the wholesale price of raw wool, the wholesale price of raw cotton has fallen considerably in the last year. Thus, although the retail price of cotton clothing at retail clothing stores has not yet fallen, it will inevitably fall.

Which of the following, if true, most seriously weakens the argument above?

(A) The cost of processing raw cotton for cloth has increased during the last year.

(B) The wholesale price of raw wool is typically higher than that of the same volume of raw cotton.

(C) The operating costs of the average retail clothing store have remained constant during the last year.

(D) Changes in retail prices always lag behind changes in wholesale prices.

(E) The cost of harvesting raw cotton has increased in the last year.

Argument Evaluation

Situation Since the wholesale price of raw cotton has fallen significantly, the retail price of cotton clothing in stores will inevitably fall.

Reasoning *What point weakens this argument?* Consider carefully the difference between the two products for which costs are being compared: cotton and cloth. This argument assumes that lower wholesale prices for a raw product must necessarily result in lower retail prices for a processed product. What other factors could have an impact on the final retail prices of cotton clothing? If any of the costs of transforming the raw product into a processed product increase, then the retail prices of cotton clothing will not necessarily fall.

A **Correct.** This statement properly identifies a weakness in the argument.

B The relative prices of raw wool and raw cotton are irrelevant to price changes in raw cotton and processed cotton.

C One step between wholesale and retail prices is the operating cost of the retail store. If that operating cost has been constant rather than rising, it is possible that the retail prices could follow the lower wholesale prices. Thus the argument is not weakened.

D The argument notes that the wholesale price has fallen *in the last year* and that though the retail price *has not yet fallen, it will inevitably fall.* The argument has already taken the lag into account and is not weakened by this statement.

E Harvesting costs are part of the assumed increased price of raw cotton and do not affect current retail prices.

The correct answer is A.

132. Many office buildings designed to prevent outside air from entering have been shown to have elevated levels of various toxic substances circulating through the air inside, a phenomenon known as sick building syndrome. Yet the air in other office buildings does not have elevated levels of these substances, even though those buildings are the same age as the "sick" buildings and have similar designs and ventilation systems.

Which of the following, if true, most helps to explain why not all office buildings designed to prevent outside air from entering have air that contains elevated levels of toxic substances?

(A) Certain adhesives and drying agents used in particular types of furniture, carpets, and paint contribute the bulk of the toxic substances that circulate in the air of office buildings.

(B) Most office buildings with sick building syndrome were built between 1950 and 1990.

(C) Among buildings designed to prevent outside air from entering, houses are no less likely than office buildings to have air that contains elevated levels of toxic substances.

(D) The toxic substances that are found in the air of "sick" office buildings are substances that are found in at least small quantities in nearly every building.

(E) Office buildings with windows that can readily be opened are unlikely to suffer from sick building syndrome.

Argument Evaluation

Situation Many office buildings designed to prevent outside air from entering have elevated levels of toxic substances in their interior air, but other such buildings similar in age, design, and ventilation do not.

Reasoning *What would help to explain the difference in air quality among buildings similar in age, design, and ventilation?* If office buildings are designed to prevent outside air from entering, toxic substances emitted into the interior air might not be ventilated out quickly, and thus might become more concentrated inside the building. But if such toxic substances are not emitted into a building's interior air in the first place, they will not become concentrated there, even if the building is poorly ventilated. So any factor that suggests why toxic substances are emitted into the interior air of some buildings but not others of similar age and design would help to explain the difference in the buildings' air quality.

A **Correct.** Some buildings may have these types of furniture, carpets, and paint, while other buildings similar in age, design, and ventilation do not.

B Since all these buildings were built during the same period, this does not help to explain the difference in air quality among buildings similar in age.

C The passage concerns air quality in office buildings only, not in houses.

D This does not help to explain why these toxic substances are more concentrated in some office buildings than in others.

E The passage concerns the differences in air quality only among office buildings that were designed to prevent outside air from entering.

The correct answer is A.

133. Newsletter: **A condominium generally offers more value for its cost than an individual house because of economies of scale.** The homeowners in a condominium association can collectively buy products and services that they could not afford on their own. And since a professional management company handles maintenance of common areas, **condominium owners spend less time and money on maintenance than individual homeowners do.**

The two portions in boldface play which of the following roles in the newsletter's argument?

(A) The first is the argument's main conclusion; the second is another conclusion supporting the first.

(B) The first is a premise, for which no evidence is provided; the second is the argument's only conclusion.

(C) The first is a conclusion supporting the second; the second is the argument's main conclusion.

(D) The first is the argument's only conclusion; the second is a premise, for which no evidence is provided.

(E) Both are premises, for which no evidence is provided, and both support the argument's only conclusion.

Argument Construction

Situation Homeowners in a condominium association can buy products and services collectively. A management company handles maintenance of condominium common areas.

Reasoning *What roles are played in the argument by the statement that a condominium generally offers more value for its cost than a house because of economies of scale and by the statement that condominium owners spend less time and money on maintenance than owners of individual homes do?* In the passage, the first sentence (the first boldface statement) is a generalization. The second sentence provides an example of the economies of scale mentioned in the first sentence, so it helps support the first sentence as a conclusion. In the third sentence, the word *since* indicates that the first clause is a premise supporting the second clause (the second boldface statement) as a conclusion. That conclusion itself provides another example of the economies of scale mentioned in the first sentence, so it also helps support that first sentence as a conclusion.

A **Correct.** As explained above, the first boldface statement is supported by the rest of the statements in the argument, so it is the main conclusion. The second boldface statement supports the first, but is itself a conclusion supported by the *since* clause preceding it.

B The second and third sentences in the argument provide examples of economies of scale. These examples are evidence supporting the first boldface statement as a conclusion.

C Since the second boldface statement provides evidence of the economies of scale described by the first, it supports the first as a conclusion.

D The *since* clause immediately preceding the second boldface statement provides evidence that supports it, so the second boldface statement is a conclusion.

E Both the second and the third sentences of the argument support the first boldface statement as a conclusion. And the *since* clause immediately preceding the second boldface statement supports it as a conclusion.

The correct answer is A.

134. Which of the following most logically completes the argument?

When officials in Tannersburg released their plan to widen the city's main roads, environmentalists protested that widened roads would attract more traffic and lead to increased air pollution. In response, city officials pointed out that today's pollution-control devices are at their most effective in vehicles traveling at higher speeds and that widening roads would increase the average speed of traffic. However, this effect can hardly be expected to offset the effect pointed out by environmentalists, since __________.

(A) increases in traffic volume generally produce decreases in the average speed of traffic unless roads are widened

(B) several of the roads that are slated for widening will have to be closed temporarily while construction is underway

(C) most of the air pollution generated by urban traffic comes from vehicles that do not have functioning pollution-control devices

(D) the newly widened roads will not have increased traffic volume if the roads that must be used to reach them are inadequate

(E) a vehicle traveling on a route that goes through Tannersburg will spend less time on Tannersburg's roads once the roads are widened

Argument Evaluation

Situation Environmentalists protested a plan to widen a city's main roads on the grounds that it would increase traffic and air pollution. City officials replied that widening the roads would increase average traffic speeds, which would improve the effectiveness of vehicles' pollution-control devices.

Reasoning *What would most support the conclusion that the improved effectiveness of the pollution-control devices would be insufficient to prevent the increased traffic from increasing air pollution?* The word *since* preceding the blank space at the end of the argument indicates that the space should be filled with a premise supporting the conclusion stated immediately before the *since*. To support this conclusion, we would need evidence that widening the roads and increasing traffic speeds would not improve the pollution-control devices' effectiveness enough to compensate for the amount of added air pollution generated by the additional traffic on the widened roads.

A It is unclear whether traffic volume would increase if the roads were not widened. But if it did, this would cast doubt on the conclusion by suggesting that a combination of higher traffic volume and lower speeds could make air pollution worse if the roads were not widened than if they were widened.

B The argument is about the long-term effects of widening the roads, not about the temporary effects of closing them during construction.

C **Correct.** If most vehicles in the area lack air-pollution devices altogether or have ones that do not work, then it is highly questionable whether the greater efficiency of the few functioning devices would be sufficient to compensate for the increase in air pollution that would result from increased traffic.

D If anything, this casts doubt on the conclusion by suggesting that widening the roads may not increase traffic volume or air pollution at all.

E If anything, this casts doubt on the conclusion by suggesting that widening the roads will decrease the amount of time each vehicle spends generating air pollution on those roads.

The correct answer is C.

135. Premature babies who receive regular massages are more active than premature babies who do not. Even when all the babies drink the same amount of milk, the massaged babies gain more weight than do the unmassaged babies. This is puzzling because a more active person generally requires a greater food intake to maintain or gain weight.

Which of the following, if true, best reconciles the apparent discrepancy described above?

(A) Increased activity leads to increased levels of hunger, especially when food intake is not also increased.

(B) Massage increases premature babies' curiosity about their environment, and curiosity leads to increased activity.

(C) Increased activity causes the intestines of premature babies to mature more quickly, enabling the babies to digest and absorb more of the nutrients in the milk they drink.

(D) Massage does not increase the growth rate of babies over one year old, if the babies had not been previously massaged.

(E) Premature babies require a daily intake of nutrients that is significantly higher than that required by babies who were not born prematurely.

Argument Construction

Situation Premature babies who receive regular massages are more active and gain more weight than unmassaged premature babies do, even when they drink the same amount of milk.

Reasoning *What would help to explain how the massaged babies could be more active than the unmassaged babies and yet still gain more weight without consuming more milk?* If the massaged babies are burning more calories than unmassaged babies through their extra activity, but are not consuming more calories in the form of milk, then how are they gaining more weight than the unmassaged babies? Possible explanations could cite factors suggesting how the massaged babies might not actually burn more calories despite their greater activity; how they might consume or absorb more calories even without consuming more milk; or how they might gain more weight without extra calorie intake.

A Increased hunger without increased food intake would not help to explain why the massaged babies are gaining more weight.

B This only helps to explain why the massaged babies are more active, not why they are gaining more weight without consuming more milk.

C **Correct.** This suggests that the increased activity of the massaged babies could increase their calorie and nutrient intake from a given amount of milk, thereby explaining how they could gain extra weight without drinking more milk.

D This suggests that the apparent discrepancy is only present in premature babies under one year old, but it does not explain why that discrepancy exists.

E The passage does not compare premature babies to babies that were not born prematurely, but rather only compares premature babies that are massaged to premature babies that are not massaged.

The correct answer is C.

136. An eyeglass manufacturer tried to boost sales for the summer quarter by offering its distributors a special discount if their orders for that quarter exceeded those for last year's summer quarter by at least 20 percent. Many distributors qualified for this discount. Even with much merchandise discounted, sales increased enough to produce a healthy gain in net profits. The manufacturer plans to repeat this success by offering the same sort of discount for the fall quarter.

Which of the following, if true, most clearly points to a flaw in the manufacturer's plan to repeat the successful performance of the summer quarter?

(A) In general, a distributor's orders for the summer quarter are no higher than those for the spring quarter.

(B) Along with offering special discounts to qualifying distributors, the manufacturer increased newspaper and radio advertising in those distributors' sales areas.

(C) The distributors most likely to qualify for the manufacturer's special discount are those whose orders were unusually low a year earlier.

(D) The distributors who qualified for the manufacturer's special discount were free to decide how much of that discount to pass on to their own customers.

(E) The distributors' ordering more goods in the summer quarter left them overstocked for the fall quarter.

Evaluation of a Plan

Situation A manufacturer successfully boosted sales and gained net profits for the summer quarter by giving distributors a discount if their orders exceeded the previous summer's orders by 20 percent. The manufacturer plans to repeat the success by offering the discount again in the fall quarter.

Reasoning *What is the flaw in the manufacturer's plan?* The plan assumes that an action that succeeded once will work a second time. Why might the plan not work this time? If the distributors increased their orders during the summer simply because they were eager to take advantage of the discount, the result may be that they are now overstocked for the fall quarter. If so, they will not need to place orders for more goods, and the plan of continuing the discount will have less chance of success now.

A This is irrelevant to the plan since relevant quarters—fall and summer—are not being compared.

B Increased advertising should continue to contribute to the plan's success.

C Even if the qualifying distributors reached only normal levels of sales, there may be other distributors who will qualify in the fall because they had low sales one year earlier.

D The distributors' freedom to decide how much of the discount to pass on to customers is equally true in both summer and fall quarters and should not affect the success of the plan.

E **Correct.** This statement properly identifies a flaw in the plan.

The correct answer is E.

137. Which of the following, if true, most logically completes the argument?

Some dairy farmers in the province of Takandia want to give their cows a synthetic hormone that increases milk production. Many Takandians, however, do not want to buy milk from cows given the synthetic hormone. For this reason Takandia's legislature is considering a measure requiring milk from cows given the hormone to be labeled as such. Even if the measure is defeated, dairy farmers who use the hormone will probably lose customers, since __________.

(A) it has not been proven that any trace of the synthetic hormone exists in the milk of cows given the hormone

(B) some farmers in Takandia who plan to use the synthetic hormone will probably not do so if the measure were passed

(C) milk from cows that have not been given the synthetic hormone can be labeled as such without any legislative action

(D) the legislature's consideration of the bill has been widely publicized

(E) milk that comes from cows given the synthetic hormone looks and tastes the same as milk from cows that have not received the hormone

Argument Construction

Situation Some dairy farmers in a province want to give their dairy cows a synthetic hormone, but many people in the province do not want to buy milk that is from cows given the hormone. The provincial legislature is considering a measure requiring milk from cows given the hormone to be labeled as such.

Reasoning *What would be a reason to believe that dairy farmers who use the hormone will lose customers even if the measure is defeated?* If the measure passes, the dairy farmers who give cows the hormone may lose the many customers who do not want to buy such milk. If the measure is defeated, then milk produced with the hormone will not have to be labeled—so what would lead one to believe that hormone-using farmers would nevertheless lose customers? A statement that provides an answer to this question would logically complete the argument.

A At best, this lack of proof might mitigate hormone-using farmers' loss of customers, whatever the outcome of the legislature's consideration of the measure.

B The argument's conclusion is mainly about what will happen if the measure is defeated, not what will happen if it passes.

C **Correct.** If the measure is defeated, the milk produced by farmers who avoid using the hormone would likely gain a market advantage if the milk was labeled as produced without use of the hormone. As a result, dairy farmers who use the hormone would probably lose customers.

D Publicity could affect consumers' attitudes about hormone-produced milk, but if the measure is defeated and labeling practices do not change, customers would have no way of knowing which milk was produced by use of the hormone.

E This suggests that, in the absence of labeling, consumers would be unable to decide which milk was produced by use of the hormone, so dairy farmers who used the hormone would be unlikely to lose customers if the labeling measure is defeated.

The correct answer is C.

138. Budget constraints have made police officials consider reassigning a considerable number of officers from traffic enforcement to work on higher-priority, serious crimes. Reducing traffic enforcement for this reason would be counterproductive, however, in light of the tendency of criminals to use cars when engaged in the commission of serious crimes. An officer stopping a car for a traffic violation can make a search that turns up evidence of serious crime.

Which of the following, if true, most strengthens the argument given?

(A) An officer who stops a car containing evidence of the commission of a serious crime risks a violent confrontation, even if the vehicle was stopped only for a traffic violation.

(B) When the public becomes aware that traffic enforcement has lessened, it typically becomes lax in obeying traffic rules.

(C) Those willing to break the law to commit serious crimes are often in committing such crimes unwilling to observe what they regard as the lesser constraints of traffic law.

(D) The offenders committing serious crimes who would be caught because of traffic violations are not the same group of individuals as those who would be caught if the arresting officers were reassigned from traffic enforcement.

(E) The great majority of persons who are stopped by officers for traffic violations are not guilty of any serious crimes.

Argument Construction

Situation Budget constraints have made police officials consider reassigning many officers from traffic enforcement to work on serious crimes. But criminals often drive when committing serious crimes, and police who stop cars for traffic violations can find evidence of those crimes.

Reasoning *What additional information, when combined with the argument provided, would suggest that it would be counterproductive to reassign officers from traffic enforcement to work on serious crimes?* The argument implicitly reasons that because officers working on traffic enforcement can turn up evidence of serious crimes by searching cars that commit traffic violations, reassigning those officers would hinder police efforts to prevent serious crime, even if the officers were reassigned to work directly on serious crime. The argument could be strengthened by information suggesting that traffic enforcement may increase the probability that evidence relating to serious crimes will be discovered.

A If anything, this risk of violence might discourage traffic enforcement officers from stopping and searching as many cars, thus reducing their effectiveness at preventing serious crimes.

B This suggests that reassigning officers from traffic enforcement to work on serious crimes would increase the number of unpunished minor traffic violations, not the number of unpunished serious crimes.

C **Correct.** This suggests that people committing serious crimes often commit traffic violations as well, increasing the likelihood that traffic enforcement officers will stop and search their cars and find evidence of those crimes.

D The question at issue is not whether the same offenders would be caught if the officers were reassigned, but rather whether more or fewer offenders would be caught.

E This weakens the argument by suggesting that most work by traffic enforcement officers is unrelated to preventing serious crimes.

The correct answer is C.

139. Conventional wisdom suggests vaccinating elderly people first in flu season, because they are at greatest risk of dying if they contract the virus. This year's flu virus poses particular risk to elderly people and almost none at all to younger people, particularly children. Nevertheless, health professionals are recommending vaccinating children first against the virus rather than elderly people.

Which of the following, if true, provides the strongest reason for the health professionals' recommendation?

(A) Children are vulnerable to dangerous infections when their immune systems are severely weakened by other diseases.

(B) Children are particularly unconcerned with hygiene and therefore are the group most responsible for spreading the flu virus to others.

(C) The vaccinations received last year will confer no immunity to this year's flu virus.

(D) Children who catch one strain of the flu virus and then recover are likely to develop immunity to at least some strains with which they have not yet come in contact.

(E) Children are no more likely than adults to have immunity to a particular flu virus if they have never lived through a previous epidemic of the same virus.

Argument Construction

Situation Although this year's flu virus poses particular risk to elderly people and almost no risk to children, health professionals are recommending vaccinating children before elderly people, contrary to what conventional wisdom recommends.

Reasoning *What would help justify the health professionals' recommendation?* Since children will experience almost no risk from the virus, vaccinating them first for their own sake appears unnecessary. However, individuals at no personal risk from a virus can still transmit it to more-vulnerable individuals. If children are especially likely to transmit the virus, it could be reasonable to vaccinate them first in order to protect others, including elderly people, by preventing the virus from spreading.

A This might be a reason to vaccinate certain children with severely weakened immune systems, if their weak immune systems would even respond effectively to the vaccine. However, it is not clearly a reason to vaccinate the vast majority of children.

B **Correct.** This suggests that children are especially likely to transmit the virus even if it does not endanger them. So as explained above, it provides a good reason for the health professionals' recommendation.

C This might be a good reason to vaccinate everyone, but it is not clearly a reason to vaccinate children before vaccinating elderly people.

D If anything, this would suggest that there might be a reason not to vaccinate children against this year's strain at all: unvaccinated children who catch this year's strain, which the argument claims is relatively harmless to children, may develop immunity to more dangerous strains that might arise in the future.

E The argument claims that this year's virus poses almost no risk to children. So even if they are not technically immune to it, it does not affect them significantly enough to justify vaccinating them before vaccinating elderly people.

The correct answer is B.

140. Pro-Tect Insurance Company has recently been paying out more on car-theft claims than it expected. Cars with special antitheft devices or alarm systems are much less likely to be stolen than are other cars. Consequently Pro-Tect, as part of an effort to reduce its annual payouts, will offer a discount to holders of car-theft policies if their cars have antitheft devices or alarm systems.

Which of the following, if true, provides the strongest indication that the plan is likely to achieve its goal?

(A) The decrease in the risk of car theft conferred by having a car alarm is greatest when only a few cars have such alarms.

(B) The number of policyholders who have filed a claim in the past year is higher for Pro-Tect than for other insurance companies.

(C) In one or two years, the discount that Pro-Tect is offering will amount to more than the cost of buying certain highly effective antitheft devices.

(D) Currently, Pro-Tect cannot legally raise the premiums it charges for a given amount of insurance against car theft.

(E) The amount Pro-Tect has been paying out on car-theft claims has been greater for some models of car than for others.

Evaluation of a Plan

Situation An insurance company is paying more money on car-theft claims than anticipated. To reduce these payments, the company is planning to offer discounts to customers whose cars have antitheft devices or alarm systems, because such cars are less likely to be stolen.

Reasoning *What piece of information would indicate that the plan is likely to succeed?* Pro-Tect wishes to reduce its annual payouts, and one way for that to happen is for fewer cars insured by Pro-Tect to be stolen. To help accomplish this, Pro-Tect is offering discounts to policyholders whose cars are so equipped, because cars equipped with antitheft devices or alarm systems are less likely to be stolen than are cars without such devices. What would interfere with the success of Pro-Tect's plan? Car owners would probably resist investing in antitheft devices or alarm systems if the cost of such systems is higher than the discount they will receive. So if Pro-Tect sets the discount at a level that makes installing antitheft devices seem like a bargain to car owners, the plan will most likely succeed.

A Pro-Tect's plan is designed to increase the number of cars equipped with car alarms. If having more cars equipped with car alarms reduces those alarms' effectivity in preventing thefts, then Pro-Tect's plan is unlikely to achieve its goal.

B Pro-Tect's claims in relation to those of other insurance companies are not relevant to whether Pro-Tect's plan to reduce its own car-theft claims will achieve its goal.

C **Correct.** This statement suggests that Pro-Tect's plan will provide an effective incentive for car owners to install antitheft devices; this statement therefore properly identifies information that indicates the plan is likely to achieve its goal.

D Because Pro-Tect's plan does not involve raising the premiums it charges, restrictions on its ability to do so are irrelevant to whether that plan will achieve its goal.

E Pro-Tect's plan does not distinguish among different models of car, so this statement indicates nothing about whether the proposed plan will succeed.

The correct answer is C.

141. While the total enrollment of public elementary and secondary schools in Sondland is one percent higher this academic year than last academic year, the number of teachers there increased by three percent. Thus, the Sondland Education Commission's prediction of a teacher shortage as early as next academic year is unfounded.

Which of the following, if true, most seriously weakens the claim that the prediction of a teacher shortage as early as next academic year is unfounded?

(A) Funding for public elementary schools in Sondland is expected to increase over the next ten years.

(B) Average salaries for Sondland's teachers increased at the rate of inflation from last academic year to this academic year.

(C) A new law has mandated that there be 10 percent more teachers per pupil in Sondland's public schools next academic year than there were this academic year.

(D) In the past, increases in enrollments in public elementary and secondary schools in Sondland have generally been smaller than increases in the number of teachers.

(E) Because of reductions in funding, the number of students enrolling in teacher-training programs in Sondland is expected to decline beginning in the next academic year.

Argument Evaluation

Situation In Sondland's public schools this academic year, the number of students is one percent higher and the number of teachers three percent higher than they were last academic year. For this reason, the Sondland Education Commission's prediction of a teacher shortage as early as next academic year is questionable.

Reasoning *What evidence would most weaken support for the claim that there will be no teacher shortage next academic year?* A teacher shortage will arise next academic year if the number of teachers needed will exceed the number of teachers employed. This will happen if the number of teachers needed increases without a sufficient increase in the number employed, or if the number employed decreases without a sufficient decrease in the number needed. Evidence that either or both of these changes will occur next academic year is evidence that the predicted shortage will occur, so any such evidence will weaken support for the claim that the prediction is unfounded.

A Increased funding will likely allow more teachers to be hired but will not necessarily increase the need for teachers, so it does not support the prediction of a teacher shortage (and indeed it very slightly undermines the prediction). Also, the funding is expected to increase over ten years, not necessarily next year. Furthermore, we are not told who expects this increase or why. Their expectation may be unjustifiable.

B A salary increase at the rate of inflation is equivalent to no change in the salary's actual value. The absence of a change in real salary in the past academic year does not by itself support any prediction of a change in the number of teachers needed or employed next academic year.

C **Correct.** The schools will need a lot more teachers next academic year to satisfy this mandate. It may be difficult for the schools to hire enough teachers in time. This provides at least some reason to predict that a teacher shortage will result.

D This means the number of students per teacher has been generally declining. It does not suggest that next academic year the number of teachers needed will increase, nor that the number employed will decrease.

E This does support the prediction that a shortage of trained teachers will arise eventually. But the declining number of students in teacher-training programs next academic year probably will not reduce the number of teachers available to teach during that same year.

The correct answer is C.

142. Art restorers who have been studying the factors that cause Renaissance oil paintings to deteriorate physically when subject to climatic changes have found that the oil paint used in these paintings actually adjusts to these changes well. The restorers therefore hypothesize that it is a layer of material called gesso, which is under the paint, that causes the deterioration.

Which of the following, if true, most strongly supports the restorers' hypothesis?

(A) Renaissance oil paintings with a thin layer of gesso are less likely to show deterioration in response to climatic changes than those with a thicker layer.

(B) Renaissance oil paintings are often painted on wooden panels, which swell when humidity increases and contract when it declines.

(C) Oil paint expands and contracts readily in response to changes in temperature, but it absorbs little water and so is little affected by changes in humidity.

(D) An especially hard and nonabsorbent type of gesso was the raw material for moldings on the frames of Renaissance oil paintings.

(E) Gesso layers applied by Renaissance painters typically consisted of a coarse base layer onto which several increasingly fine-grained layers were applied.

Argument Evaluation

Situation Renaissance paintings are subject to deterioration due to changes in climate, but their actual paint is not a factor in this deterioration. Instead, restorers hypothesize, it is gesso, the material under the paint, that causes problems for the paintings.

Reasoning *What would most strongly support the hypothesis that gesso is causing the deterioration?* An indication that gesso is affected by climatic changes would be most helpful in supporting the hypothesis. What could show that gesso is affected in this way? If the extent of a painting's deterioration is directly related to the amount of gesso used under that painting, then the gesso clearly plays some part in that deterioration.

A **Correct.** This statement properly identifies a point supporting the hypothesis.

B This suggests that another factor—the wood of the panels—has a role in the paintings' deterioration. Thus it weakens the hypothesis that gesso causes the deterioration.

C This merely reinforces given information, that the paint itself is not responsible for the paintings' deterioration.

D Because this gives no information about any connection between this especially hard and nonabsorbent type of gesso and the type of gesso used under the paint in Renaissance paintings, the properties and usage of the former type of gesso are irrelevant to the question of whether gesso is responsible for the paintings' deterioration.

E Because we are told nothing about whether this technique of gesso application increases or decreases the likelihood that gesso will be affected by climatic change, it does not support the restorers' hypothesis.

The correct answer is A.

143. Automobile Dealer's Advertisement:

The Highway Traffic Safety Institute reports that the PZ 1000 has the fewest injuries per accident of any car in its class. This shows that the PZ 1000 is one of the safest cars available today.

Which of the following, if true, most seriously weakens the argument in the advertisement?

(A) The Highway Traffic Safety Institute report listed many cars in other classes that had more injuries per accident than did the PZ 1000.

(B) In recent years many more PZ 1000s have been sold than have any other kind of car in its class.

(C) Cars in the class to which the PZ 1000 belongs are more likely to be involved in accidents than are other types of cars.

(D) The difference between the number of injuries per accident for the PZ 1000 and that for other cars in its class is quite pronounced.

(E) The Highway Traffic Safety Institute issues reports only once a year.

Argument Evaluation

Situation An advertisement claims that the PZ 1000 is one of the safest cars available; it bases this claim on the Highway Traffic Safety Institute's report that this model had the fewest injuries per accident of any car in its class.

Reasoning *What point weakens the advertisement's claim?* Examine closely the difference between the report and the conclusion the advertisement draws from it. While the Highway Traffic Safety Institute compares the PZ 1000 to other cars *in its class,* the advertisement compares the PZ 1000 to *all cars available today.* What if the class of cars to which the PZ 1000 belongs is a more dangerous class of cars? In that case, while the PZ 1000 may the safest car of a dangerous class, it cannot be said to be one of the safest cars available.

A The higher incidence of injuries per accident in other classes of cars supports rather than weakens the advertisement's argument.

B The fact that the PZ 1000 is the best selling car in its class might be explained by the fact that it is the safest car in its class, but if this has any effect on the argument at all, it would be to strengthen rather than weaken it.

C **Correct.** This statement properly identifies a weakness in the advertisement's argument.

D This slightly strengthens, rather than weakens, the argument.

E The frequency of the reports is irrelevant to the advertisement's claim.

The correct answer is C.

144. Archaeologists working in the Andes Mountains recently excavated a buried 4,000-year-old temple containing structures that align with a stone carving on a distant hill to indicate the direction of the rising sun at the summer solstice. Alignments in the temple were also found to point toward the position, at the summer solstice, of a constellation known in Andean culture as the Fox. Since the local mythology represents the fox as teaching people how to cultivate and irrigate plants, the ancient Andeans may have built the temple as a religious representation of the fox.

Which of the following is an assumption on which the argument is based?

(A) The constellation known as the Fox has the same position at the summer solstice as it did 4,000 years ago.
(B) In the region around the temple, the summer solstice marks the time for planting.
(C) The temple was protected from looters by dirt and debris built up over thousands of years.
(D) Other structural alignments at the temple point to further constellations with agricultural significance.
(E) The site containing the temple was occupied for a significant amount of time before abandonment.

Argument Construction

Situation A recently excavated 4,000-year-old temple contains structures that point toward the positions at the summer solstice of both the rising sun and a constellation known in local culture as the Fox. Local mythology represents the fox as teaching people how to cultivate and irrigate plants.

Reasoning *What must be true in order for the argument's premises to suggest that the temple was built to religiously represent the fox?* The argument's premises are all observations about current conditions: the current alignment at the summer solstice of the temple relative to the sunrise and to the constellation known as the Fox, the current local name for a constellation, and current local mythology. To support the conclusion about the temple's original purpose, the argument has to assume that all these conditions may still be essentially the same as they were 4,000 years ago when the temple was built.

A **Correct.** If the constellation's position at the summer solstice relative to the temple is different from what it was 4,000 years ago, the temple must not have been aligned to point toward it when it was built. In that case, the argument's justification for associating the temple with that constellation and with the fox is undermined.

B This does not have to be assumed for the argument to succeed, though if true, it might strengthen the argument by providing additional evidence associating the temple with the mythological fox as a teacher of agriculture. But the argument could be just as strong if the solstice were instead associated with agricultural activities other than planting.

C Even if the temple was not protected from looters, the conditions described in the argument's premises may still be the same as they were 4,000 years ago.

D This is not assumed. Additional structural alignments pointing to different constellations associated with mythological beings other than the fox might weaken or even undermine the argument's justification for associating the temple with the fox specifically.

E The argument makes no assumption regarding how long the temple was occupied, or even regarding whether the temple was ever occupied.

The correct answer is A.

145. Which of the following most logically completes the passage?

It is generally believed that people receiving frequent medical checkups are likely to need hospitalization less frequently than they would otherwise; after all, many things can be done following a checkup to prevent problems that, if ignored, might become acute and then require hospitalization. But for people with chronic illnesses, frequent medical checkups are likely to lead to more frequent hospitalization since _________.

(A) the recommended treatments for complications of many chronic illnesses involve hospitalization even if those complications are detected while barely noticeable

(B) medical checkups sometimes do not reveal early symptoms of those chronic illnesses that are best treated in a hospital

(C) the average length of a hospital stay is the same for those who receive frequent checkups as for those who do not

(D) people with chronic illnesses generally receive medical checkups more frequently than people who are not chronically ill

(E) the average length of a hospital stay for people with a chronic illness tends to increase as the illness progresses

Argument Construction

Situation Actions taken after medical checkups can prevent problems that might otherwise become acute and require hospitalization. But for people with chronic illnesses, frequent medical checkups tend to lead to more frequent hospitalizations.

Reasoning *What would help to explain why more frequent medical checkups tend to lead to more frequent hospitalizations for people with chronic illnesses?* The first sentence of the passage suggests that medical checkups should make hospitalization less frequent by catching medical problems before they become severe enough to require hospitalization. But if the medical problems that checkups typically catch in people with chronic illnesses already require hospitalization when they are caught, the checkups might result in such people being hospitalized more frequently rather than less frequently.

A **Correct.** This suggests that in people with chronic illnesses, checkups may more often result in treatments that require hospitalization than in treatments that could prevent hospitalization.

B The fact that occasionally a checkup fails to reveal early symptoms of a chronic illness best treated in a hospital does not indicate that frequent checkups of people with chronic illnesses would lead to more frequent hospitalization than less frequent checkups would.

C The question at issues concerns the frequency of hospitalization, not the average length of hospital stays.

D The question at issue is why people with chronic illnesses who have more frequent checkups tend to be hospitalized more frequently than other chronically ill people, not why they tend to be hospitalized more frequently than people who are not chronically ill.

E Again, the question at issue concerns the frequency of hospitalization, not the average length of hospital stays. In any case, we are not told whether people with chronic illnesses tend to have checkups more or less frequently as their illnesses progress.

The correct answer is A.

146. Meat from chickens contaminated with salmonella bacteria can cause serious food poisoning. Capsaicin, the chemical that gives chili peppers their hot flavor, has antibacterial properties. Chickens do not have taste receptors for capsaicin and will readily eat feed laced with capsaicin. When chickens were fed such feed and then exposed to salmonella bacteria, relatively few of them became contaminated with salmonella.

In deciding whether the feed would be useful in raising salmonella-free chicken for retail sale, it would be most helpful to determine which of the following?

(A) Whether feeding capsaicin to chickens affects the taste of their meat
(B) Whether eating capsaicin reduces the risk of salmonella poisoning for humans
(C) Whether chicken is more prone to salmonella contamination than other kinds of meat
(D) Whether appropriate cooking of chicken contaminated with salmonella can always prevent food poisoning
(E) Whether capsaicin can be obtained only from chili peppers

Argument Evaluation

Situation Chickens will readily eat feed laced with capsaicin, which appears to protect them from contamination with salmonella bacteria that can cause food poisoning.

Reasoning *What information would help determine whether using the feed would be an effective strategy for raising salmonella-free chicken for retail sale?* In order for the strategy to be effective, it must be economically feasible for farmers to raise chickens using the feed, and there must be enough consumer demand for chickens raised this way. So any information about factors likely to affect either the economic feasibility of raising the chickens or consumer demand for them could be helpful in determining how useful the feed would be.

A **Correct.** If chicken producers tried to market meat from capsaicin-fed chickens without knowing whether the taste is affected, they would risk alienating consumers. Of course, if they found that the taste is affected, they would then need to do further investigations to determine how consumers would likely respond to the difference. If consumers did not like the taste, this could negatively affect demand for the chickens. In that case, using the feed would not be an effective way to raise chickens for retail sale.

B There are two ways this might be considered relevant. First, it might be thought that because capsaicin reduces the risk of salmonella poisoning in humans, it will also do so in chickens; but we already have good evidence of that in the argument. Second, it might be thought that, if the capsaicin does not produce chickens that are totally salmonella free, then if any capsaicin remains in the chickens, it will help prevent any humans who consume the chicken from getting salmonella poisoning. But the relevant issue is whether the capsaicin will make the chickens salmonella free, not whether humans will be protected whether the chickens are salmonella free or not.

C The susceptibility of other types of meat to salmonella contamination would not affect the usefulness of the feed for preventing such contamination in chicken.

D Presumably many people do not cook contaminated chicken appropriately, so consumers could still benefit from salmonella-free chicken whether or not appropriate cooking methods could prevent food poisoning.

E Regardless of whether capsaicin can be obtained from other sources, chili peppers may be a perfectly viable source.

The correct answer is A.

147. Laws requiring the use of headlights during daylight hours can prevent automobile collisions. However, since daylight visibility is worse in countries farther from the equator, any such laws would obviously be more effective in preventing collisions in those countries. In fact, the only countries that actually have such laws are farther from the equator than is the continental United States.

Which of the following conclusions could be most properly drawn from the information given above?

(A) Drivers in the continental United States who used their headlights during the day would be just as likely to become involved in a collision as would drivers who did not use their headlights.

(B) In many countries that are farther from the equator than is the continental United States, poor daylight visibility is the single most important factor in automobile collisions.

(C) The proportion of automobile collisions that occur in the daytime is greater in the continental United States than in the countries that have daytime headlight laws.

(D) Fewer automobile collisions probably occur each year in countries that have daytime headlight laws than occur within the continental United States.

(E) Daytime headlight laws would probably do less to prevent automobile collisions in the continental United States than they do in the countries that have the laws.

Argument Construction

Situation Laws requiring the use of headlights during the daytime are more effective at preventing car collisions in countries with lower daylight visibility, that is, in countries at greater distances from the equator. The only countries having these laws are those located farther from the equator than is the continental United States.

Reasoning *What conclusion can be drawn from this information?* Countries with daytime headlight laws are all farther from the equator than is the continental United States. The location is significant because daytime visibility is worse in those countries than it is in the continental United States. How effective at preventing collisions would such laws be in the continental United States with its greater proximity to the equator? It is reasonable to conclude that such laws would be less effective at preventing collisions there than they are in the countries farther from the equator.

A Although daytime headlight use may be less effective in countries with more daylight, it cannot be concluded that U.S. drivers using daytime headlights would gain no benefit from them and would be just as likely to have collisions as those who do not use them.

B The passage offers no evidence for the conclusion that poor visibility is the *greatest* cause for collisions in these countries.

C Many factors besides use of headlights during daylight hours influence accident rates, and these factors may vary widely from one country to another. We are given no information about these other factors or about their relative impact in various countries.

D Without specific data, no conclusion can be drawn about the relative number of accidents that occur.

E **Correct.** This statement properly identifies a conclusion to be drawn from the given information.

The correct answer is E.

148. Which of the following most logically completes the argument below?

When mercury-vapor streetlights are used in areas inhabited by insect-eating bats, the bats feed almost exclusively around the lights, because the lights attract flying insects. In Greenville, the mercury-vapor streetlights are about to be replaced with energy-saving sodium streetlights, which do not attract insects. This change is likely to result in a drop in the population of insect-eating bats in Greenville, since __________.

(A) the bats do not begin to hunt until after sundown

(B) the bats are unlikely to feed on insects that do not fly

(C) the highway department will be able to replace mercury-vapor streetlights with sodium streetlights within a relatively short time and without disrupting the continuity of lighting at the locations of the streetlights

(D) in the absence of local concentrations of the flying insects on which bats feed, the bats expend much more energy on hunting for food, requiring much larger quantities of insects to sustain each bat

(E) bats use echolocation to catch insects and therefore gain no advantage from the fact that insects flying in the vicinity of streetlights are visible at night

Argument Construction

Situation In areas with mercury-vapor streetlights, any insect-eating bats feed almost exclusively around the lights, which attract flying insects. In Greenville, mercury-vapor streetlights will soon be replaced with sodium streetlights that do not attract insects.

Reasoning *What evidence would suggest that the change in streetlights will reduce Greenville's population of insect-eating bats?* Since the sodium streetlights will not attract flying insects, the bats will probably stop focusing their feeding around Greenville's streetlights after the lights are changed. A statement providing evidence that this will make it harder for the bats to get enough food to sustain themselves would support the conclusion that the change is likely to reduce Greenville's bat population and thus would logically complete the argument.

A Insect-eating bats existed long before streetlights did, so they can probably find insects away from streetlights even if they hunt only after sundown.

B Greenville will almost certainly still have flying insects for the bats to eat after the change, even if those insects no longer gather around the streetlights.

C If anything, such a smooth transition would be less likely to disturb the bats and therefore less likely to reduce their population.

D **Correct.** Since there will be no local concentrations of flying insects around Greenville streetlights after the change, the bats will most likely have more trouble getting enough to eat, and that their local population will therefore fall.

E The advantage that the bats gain from mercury-vapor streetlights comes from the high concentration of insects. The fact that the bats get no additional advantage from the insects' visibility tells us nothing about what affect the change to a different type of light might have.

The correct answer is D.

149. Rats injected with morphine exhibit decreased activity of the immune system, the bodily system that fights off infections. These same rats exhibited heightened blood levels of corticosteroids, chemicals secreted by the adrenal glands. Since corticosteroids can interfere with immune-system activity, scientists hypothesized that the way morphine reduces immune responses in rats is by stimulating the adrenal glands to secrete additional corticosteroids into the bloodstream.

Which of the following experiments would yield the most useful results for evaluating the scientists' hypothesis?

(A) Injecting morphine into rats that already have heightened blood levels of corticosteroids and then observing their new blood levels of corticosteroids

(B) Testing the level of immune-system activity of rats, removing their adrenal glands, and then testing the rats' immune-system activity levels again

(C) Injecting rats with corticosteroids and then observing how many of the rats contracted infections

(D) Removing the adrenal glands of rats, injecting the rats with morphine, and then testing the level of the rats' immune-system responses

(E) Injecting rats with a drug that stimulates immune-system activity and then observing the level of corticosteroids in their bloodstreams

Argument Evaluation

Situation Rats injected with morphine exhibit decreased immune-system activity and increased levels of corticosteroids, which are secreted by the adrenal glands and can interfere with immune-system activity.

Reasoning *What further experiment would help determine whether morphine reduces immune responses in rats by stimulating the adrenal glands to release more corticosteroids?* Contrary to the scientists' hypothesis, the experimental results might have occurred because the morphine injections directly reduced immune-system activity. Or the injections might have blocked some mechanism that reduces corticosteroid levels in the blood, even if the morphine did not stimulate the adrenal glands to produce more corticosteroids. To evaluate whether the scientists' hypothesis is more plausible than these rival hypotheses, it would be helpful to know whether similar experimental results would occur after morphine injections even if adrenal gland activity did not change.

A Morphine could stimulate the adrenal glands of rats with normal corticosteroid levels to produce more corticosteroids, whether or not it does so in rats whose corticosteroid levels are already heightened.

B Such an experiment would not involve morphine and thus would not help to determine how morphine affects immune-system activity in rats.

C Whether or not rats contract infections may not reliably indicate their levels of immune-system activity.

D **Correct.** If the immune system responses decreased after the morphine injections in this experiment, the hypothesis that it was by stimulation of the adrenal glands that morphine reduced immune-system activity would be undermined. But if no decrease in immune-system responses occurred, the hypothesis would be confirmed.

E Even if the mechanism by which a drug other than morphine increases immune-system activity were discovered, this discovery would not necessarily reveal the mechanism by which morphine reduces immune-system activity.

The correct answer is D.

150. Curator: If our museum lends *Venus* to the Hart Institute for their show this spring, they will lend us their Rembrandt etchings for our print exhibition next fall. Having those etchings will increase attendance to the exhibition and hence increase revenue from our general admission fee.

Museum Administrator: But *Venus* is our biggest attraction. Moreover the Hart's show will run for twice as long as our exhibition. So on balance the number of patrons may decrease.

The point of the administrator's response to the curator is to question

(A) whether getting the Rembrandt etchings from the Hart Institute is likely to increase attendance at the print exhibition

(B) whether the Hart Institute's Rembrandt etchings will be appreciated by those patrons of the curator's museum for whom the museum's biggest attraction is *Venus*

(C) whether the number of patrons attracted by the Hart Institute's Rembrandt etchings will be larger than the number of patrons who do not come in the spring because *Venus* is on loan

(D) whether, if *Venus* is lent, the museum's revenue from general admission fees during the print exhibition will exceed its revenue from general admission fees during the Hart Institute's exhibition

(E) whether the Hart Institute or the curator's museum will have the greater financial gain from the proposed exchange of artworks

Argument Construction

Situation A curator and a museum administrator debate whether lending a particular artwork to the Hart Institute in exchange for a loan of some of the Hart Institute's artworks would increase or decrease attendance and revenue at the museum.

Reasoning *Which of the curator's explicit or implicit claims is the museum administrator questioning?* The administrator's statements that *Venus* is the museum's biggest attraction and that the Hart Institute's show will run twice as long as the museum's exhibition do not directly conflict with any statement or assumption made by the curator. However, the administrator's conclusion is that on balance the number of patrons at the museum may decrease if the curator's proposal is followed. This conclusion calls into question the curator's claim that the proposal will increase revenue from the general admission fee, since that claim presupposes that on balance the proposal will increase the number of visitors to the museum. (The context suggests that the administrator is using the term *patrons* to mean visitors rather than donors.)

A The administrator does not dispute that the Rembrandt etchings would probably increase attendance at the print exhibition but rather suggests that this increase would be exceeded by the loss of visitors to the museum while the Hart Institute borrows *Venus*.

B Neither the curator nor the administrator comments on whether the patrons attracted to the Rembrandt etchings would be the same people attracted to *Venus*.

C **Correct.** The curator implicitly infers that the former number will be larger than the latter, whereas the administrator questions this by asserting that the latter number may be larger than the former.

D The administrator does not question whether the revenue during the print exhibition will exceed the revenue during the Hart Institute's exhibition, but rather whether it will exceed the loss of revenue during the Hart Institute's exhibition.

E Neither the curator nor the administrator comments on whether the museum would gain more or less from the exchange than the Hart Institute would.

The correct answer is C.

151. Which of the following most logically completes the passage?

Leaf beetles damage willow trees by stripping away their leaves, but a combination of parasites and predators generally keeps populations of these beetles in check. Researchers have found that severe air pollution results in reduced predator populations. The parasites, by contrast, are not adversely affected by pollution; nevertheless, the researchers' discovery probably does explain why leaf beetles cause particularly severe damage to willows in areas with severe air pollution, since __________.

(A) neither the predators nor the parasites of leaf beetles themselves attack willow trees

(B) the parasites that attack leaf beetles actually tend to be more prevalent in areas with severe air pollution than they are elsewhere

(C) the damage caused by leaf beetles is usually not enough to kill a willow tree outright

(D) where air pollution is not especially severe, predators have much more impact on leaf-beetle populations than parasites do

(E) willows often grow in areas where air pollution is especially severe

Argument Construction

Situation Leaf beetles damage willow trees, but predators and parasites keep leaf beetle populations in check. Air pollution reduces populations of predators but not of parasites. Leaf beetles damage willows especially severely in areas with severe air pollution.

Reasoning *What would support the conclusion that air pollution's effects on the predator populations (but not on the parasite populations) explains why leaf beetles damage willows the most in areas with severe air pollution?* The word *since* preceding the blank space at the end of the passage indicates that the space should be filled with a premise supporting the conclusion stated immediately before the *since*. To support this conclusion, it would help to have evidence that predators play a predominant role in keeping leaf beetle populations in check, and thus that the reduction of predator populations by air pollution could be sufficient to enable leaf beetle populations to grow and cause especially severe damage.

A The fact that neither the predators nor the parasites directly contribute to harming the trees offers no reason to conclude that a difference in how they are affected by pollution would contribute to the harm that the beetles cause to the trees.

B If the parasites are more prevalent in areas with severe air pollution, then they are more likely to keep leaf beetle populations in check in those areas, despite the reduced predator populations. Thus, the decline in predator populations would more likely be insufficient to explain why the leaf beetles cause more damage in those areas.

C This observation is irrelevant to whether the decline in predator populations explains why leaf beetles damage willow trees more severely in areas with severe air pollution.

D **Correct.** This indicates that predators play a predominant role in keeping leaf beetle populations in check, so, as explained above, it supports the argument's conclusion.

E This is not clearly relevant to whether the decline in predator populations explains why leaf beetles damage willow trees more severely in areas with severe air pollution. The argument's conclusion could just as easily be true regardless of whether willows grow in such polluted areas frequently or infrequently.

The correct answer is D.

152. Which of the following best completes the passage below?

At a recent conference on environmental threats to the North Sea, most participating countries favored uniform controls on the quality of effluents, whether or not specific environmental damage could be attributed to a particular source of effluent. What must, of course, be shown, in order to avoid excessively restrictive controls, is that __________.

(A) any uniform controls that are adopted are likely to be implemented without delay
(B) any substance to be made subject to controls can actually cause environmental damage
(C) the countries favoring uniform controls are those generating the largest quantities of effluents
(D) all of any given pollutant that is to be controlled actually reaches the North Sea at present
(E) environmental damage already inflicted on the North Sea is reversible

Argument Construction

Situation In the face of environmental threats to the North Sea, restrictions on effluents are considered.

Reasoning *How can excessively restrictive controls be avoided?* To prevent pollutants from entering the North Sea, countries decide to control the quality of effluents. They need to control only those effluents that cause environmental damage. There is no need to restrict harmless effluents.

A The immediacy of adopting controls does not prevent the controls from being overly restrictive.

B **Correct.** This statement properly identifies the fact that controls on harmless effluents would be excessively restrictive and so should be avoided.

C Avoiding unnecessary restrictions involves analyzing the quality of the effluents, not the composition of the countries favoring the restrictions.

D It is not necessary to prove that all of a pollutant reaches the North Sea. It is necessary to prove only that some of it does.

E The environmental damage that has already been caused is outside the scope of the restrictions. Finding that the damage is reversible will do nothing to prevent unnecessary restrictions.

The correct answer is B.

153. On May first, in order to reduce the number of overdue books, a children's library instituted a policy of forgiving fines and giving bookmarks to children returning all of their overdue books. On July first there were twice as many overdue books as there had been on May first, although a record number of books had been returned during the interim.

Which of the following, if true, most helps to explain the apparent inconsistency in the results of the library's policy?

(A) The librarians did not keep accurate records of how many children took advantage of the grace period, and some of the children returning overdue books did not return all of their overdue books.

(B) Although the grace period enticed some children to return all of their overdue books, it did not convince all of the children with overdue books to return all of their books.

(C) The bookmarks became popular among the children, so in order to collect the bookmarks, many children borrowed many more books than they usually did and kept them past their due date.

(D) The children were allowed to borrow a maximum of five books for a two-week period, and hence each child could keep a maximum of fifteen books beyond their due date within a two-month period.

(E) Although the library forgave overdue fines during the grace period, the amount previously charged the children was minimal; hence, the forgiveness of the fines did not provide enough incentive for them to return their overdue books.

Argument Construction

Situation After a library started forgiving fines and giving bookmarks to children who returned all their overdue books, the number of books returned greatly increased, but so did the number of overdue books.

Reasoning *Why might the policy have simultaneously increased the number of overdue books and the number of books being returned?* In order to increase both these numbers, the policy must have resulted in more books being checked out, kept past their due dates, and then returned. But why would the policy have promoted that behavior? One possibility is that it rewarded the behavior. The policy involved giving children bookmarks as rewards for returning overdue books, while removing the fines that penalized the children for doing so. If the children liked the bookmarks, they might have tried to get more of them by deliberately checking books out in order to keep them past their due dates before returning them to get the bookmarks.

A Failing to keep accurate records of the number of children would not clearly increase the number of books being returned. And the policy change did not apply to children who returned only some of their overdue books.

B This suggests that the policy had limited effects, but does not help to explain why it had apparently inconsistent effects.

C **Correct.** This explains how the policy gave the children a motive to check out and return more books while also allowing them to keep more of the books past the due dates.

D This restriction would have limited the number of overdue books and thus would not help to explain why that number increased.

E This suggests that the policy had little effect but does not help to explain why it had apparently inconsistent effects.

The correct answer is C.

154. A certain species of desert lizard digs tunnels in which to lay its eggs. The eggs must incubate inside the tunnel for several weeks before hatching, and they fail to hatch if they are disturbed at any time during this incubation period. Yet these lizards guard their tunnels for only a few days after laying their eggs.

Which of the following, if true, most helps explain why there is no need for lizards to guard their tunnels for more than a few days?

(A) The eggs are at risk of being disturbed only during the brief egg-laying season when many lizards are digging in a relatively small area.

(B) The length of the incubation period varies somewhat from one tunnel to another.

(C) Each female lizard lays from 15 to 20 eggs, only about 10 of which hatch even if the eggs are not disturbed at any time during the incubation period.

(D) The temperature and humidity within the tunnels will not be suitable for the incubating eggs unless the tunnels are plugged with sand immediately after the eggs are laid.

(E) The only way to disturb the eggs of this lizard species is by opening up one of the tunnels in which they are laid.

Argument Construction

Situation Lizards of a certain species dig tunnels in which they lay their eggs. Although the eggs fail to hatch if disturbed during their several weeks of incubation, the lizards guard the tunnels for only a few days after laying the eggs.

Reasoning *What would help to explain why the lizards have to guard their tunnels for only a few days?* For the lizards to survive as a species, their behaviors must ensure that enough of their eggs hatch. Thus, they must successfully prevent enough of their eggs from being disturbed in the tunnels throughout the several weeks of incubation. If guarding the tunnels for only a few days accomplishes this, then some other factor must prevent the eggs from being disturbed during the remaining weeks. Evidence of any such factor would help to explain why the lizards do not have to guard the tunnels longer. For example, to protect the eggs without guarding them, the lizards might conceal the tunnel entrances after the first few days. Or animals likely to disturb the eggs might only be present for those first days, in which case there would be nothing for the lizards to guard against thereafter.

A **Correct.** This suggests that the only creatures likely to disturb the eggs are other lizards of the same species digging tunnels to lay their own eggs at around the same time. If so, each lizard can safely leave its eggs unguarded after a few days because all the other lizards will have finished digging.

B Even if the incubation period varies somewhat, the passage says it always lasts several weeks. So this does not explain why the lizards have to guard the tunnels for only a few days.

C If many eggs fail to hatch even when undisturbed, that is all the more reason for the lizards to protect the remaining eggs from disturbance throughout the incubation period so that at least some will hatch. So it does not explain why the lizards guard their tunnels only for a few days.

D Whether or not immediately plugging the tunnels with sand is enough to protect the eggs, this behavior does not explain why the lizards subsequently guard the tunnels for a few days and then leave for the rest of the incubation period.

E Even if it is impossible to disturb the eggs without opening the tunnels, that does not explain why the lizards guard the tunnels for a few days and then leave for the rest of the incubation period.

The correct answer is A.

155. Often patients with ankle fractures that are stable, and thus do not require surgery, are given follow-up x-rays because their orthopedists are concerned about possibly having misjudged the stability of the fracture. When a number of follow-up x-rays were reviewed, however, all the fractures that had initially been judged stable were found to have healed correctly. Therefore, it is a waste of money to order follow-up x-rays of ankle fractures initially judged stable.

Which of the following, if true, most strengthens the argument?

(A) Doctors who are general practitioners rather than orthopedists are less likely than orthopedists to judge the stability of an ankle fracture correctly.

(B) Many ankle injuries for which an initial x-ray is ordered are revealed by the x-ray not to involve any fracture of the ankle.

(C) X-rays of patients of many different orthopedists working in several hospitals were reviewed.

(D) The healing of ankle fractures that have been surgically repaired is always checked by means of a follow-up x-ray.

(E) Orthopedists routinely order follow-up x-rays for fractures of bones other than ankle bones.

Argument Evaluation

Situation Often patients with ankle fractures that their orthopedists have judged not to require surgery are given follow-up x-rays to check whether the fracture healed correctly. An examination of a sample of those x-rays found that the ankle had, in each case, healed properly.

Reasoning *The question is which of the options, if true, would most strengthen the argument.* The argument is based on data concerning follow-up x-rays, each of which revealed no problem with the orthopedist's initial judgment that the ankle fracture was stable (and would heal without surgery). This invites the question whether the follow-up x-rays are really needed. The argument concludes that they are a waste of money. But was the x-ray data truly representative of orthopedists generally? After all, some orthopedists—perhaps more experienced, better-trained, or employed at a facility with better staff or facilities—may be much better than others at judging ankle fractures. If we add the information that the data for the conclusion comes from many orthopedists working at many different hospitals, we have greater assurance that the x-ray data is representative, and the argument will be made much stronger.

A Neither the study nor the conclusion that is drawn from it concerns general practitioners, so this point is irrelevant.

B Naturally many ankle injuries do not involve fractures—x-rays may sometimes be used to determine this—but the argument concerns only cases where there have been ankle fractures.

C **Correct.** This shows that the sample of x-ray data examined was probably sufficiently representative of cases of ankle fracture judged to be stable by orthopedists.

D The argument does not concern cases of ankle fracture that have been surgically repaired.

E The argument concerns only x-rays of ankles. From the information given here, we cannot infer that orthopedists are generally wasteful in routinely ordering follow-up x-rays.

The correct answer is C.

156. In setting environmental standards for industry and others to meet, it is inadvisable to require the best results that state-of-the-art technology can achieve. Current technology is able to detect and eliminate even extremely minute amounts of contaminants, but at a cost that is exorbitant relative to the improvement achieved. So it would be reasonable instead to set standards by taking into account all of the current and future risks involved.

The argument given concerning the reasonable way to set standards presupposes that

(A) industry currently meets the standards that have been set by environmental authorities
(B) there are effective ways to take into account all of the relevant risks posed by allowing different levels of contaminants
(C) the only contaminants worth measuring are generated by industry
(D) it is not costly to prevent large amounts of contaminants from entering the environment
(E) minute amounts of some contaminants can be poisonous

Argument Construction

Situation State-of-the-art technology can detect and eliminate even tiny amounts of environmental contaminants, but at a cost that is exorbitant relative to its benefits.

Reasoning *What must be true in order for the argument's premises to support its conclusion?* The argument is that environmental standards requiring the best results that state-of-the-art technology can provide are unreasonably expensive relative to their benefits, so it would be reasonable instead to set environmental standards that take into account all present and future risks from contaminants. In order for the premise to support the conclusion, the environmental standards based on present and future risks would have to be less expensive relative to their benefits than the *best results* environmental standards are. Furthermore, setting the *current and future risks* environmental standards cannot be reasonable unless it is feasible to assess present and future risks as those standards require.

A The argument does not say which standards, if any, environmental authorities have set. In any case, such standards could be reasonable or unreasonable regardless of whether industry currently meets them.

B **Correct.** If taking future risks into account were infeasible, then applying the *current and future risks* standards would also be infeasible. And setting those standards would be unreasonable if they could not feasibly be applied.

C According to the stimulus, the proposed *current and future risks* standards would apply to industry *and others*. So those standards could be reasonable even if the unspecified *others* also generated contaminants worth measuring, and even if the standards required measuring those contaminants.

D Even if it were costly to prevent large amounts of contaminants from entering the environment, the benefits of doing so to prevent present and future risks might outweigh the costs.

E The *current and future risks* standards could take into account any poisoning risks posed by minute amounts of contaminants.

The correct answer is B.

157. Most scholars agree that King Alfred (A.D. 849–899) personally translated a number of Latin texts into Old English. One historian contends that Alfred also personally penned his own law code, arguing that the numerous differences between the language of the law code and Alfred's translations of Latin texts are outweighed by the even more numerous similarities. Linguistic similarities, however, are what one expects in texts from the same language, the same time, and the same region. Apart from Alfred's surviving translations and law code, there are only two other extant works from the same dialect and milieu, so it is risky to assume here that linguistic similarities point to common authorship.

The passage above proceeds by

(A) providing examples that underscore another argument's conclusion
(B) questioning the plausibility of an assumption on which another argument depends
(C) showing that a principle if generally applied would have anomalous consequences
(D) showing that the premises of another argument are mutually inconsistent
(E) using argument by analogy to undermine a principle implicit in another argument

Argument Evaluation

Situation A historian argues that King Alfred must have written his own law code, since there are more similarities than differences between the language in the law code and that in Alfred's translations of Latin texts. Apart from Alfred's translations and law code, there are only two other extant works in the same dialect and from the same milieu.

Reasoning *How does the reasoning in the passage proceed?* The first sentence presents a claim that is not disputed in the passage. The second sentence presents a historian's argument. Implicitly citing the undisputed claim in the passage's first sentence as evidence, the historian proposes an analogy between the law code and Alfred's translations, arguing on the basis of this analogy that Alfred wrote the law code. The third sentence of the passage casts doubt on this analogy, pointing out that it could plausibly apply to texts that Alfred did not write. The fourth sentence suggests that too few extant texts are available as evidence to rule out the possibility raised in the third sentence. Thus, the third and fourth sentences are intended to undermine the historian's argument.

A As explained above, the passage is intended to undermine the conclusion of the historian's argument, not to *underscore* (emphasize) it.

B **Correct.** The passage's third and fourth sentences question the plausibility of the historian's assumption that no one but Alfred would have been likely to write a text whose language has more similarities to than differences from the language in Alfred's translations.

C Although there might well be anomalous consequences from generalizing the assumption on which the historian's argument relies, the passage does not mention or allude to any such consequences.

D The passage does not mention, or suggest the existence of, any inconsistencies among the premises of the historian's argument.

E Although the historian argues by analogy, the passage does not itself argue by analogy; it does not suggest any specific counteranalogy to undermine the historian's argument.

The correct answer is B.

158. A company plans to develop a prototype weeding machine that uses cutting blades with optical sensors and microprocessors that distinguish weeds from crop plants by differences in shade of color. The inventor of the machine claims that it will reduce labor costs by virtually eliminating the need for manual weeding.

Which of the following is a consideration in favor of the company's implementing its plan to develop the prototype?

(A) There is a considerable degree of variation in shade of color between weeds of different species.

(B) The shade of color of some plants tends to change appreciably over the course of their growing season.

(C) When crops are weeded manually, overall size and leaf shape are taken into account in distinguishing crop plants from weeds.

(D) Selection and genetic manipulation allow plants of virtually any species to be economically bred to have a distinctive shade of color without altering their other characteristics.

(E) Farm laborers who are responsible for the manual weeding of crops carry out other agricultural duties at times in the growing season when extensive weeding is not necessary.

Evaluation of a Plan

Situation A company plans to develop an automated weeding machine that would distinguish weeds from crop plants by differences in shade of color. It is supposed to reduce labor costs by eliminating the need for manual weeding.

Reasoning *Which option describes a consideration that would favor the company's plan?* The passage supports the plan by claiming that the machine would reduce labor costs by virtually eliminating weeding by hand. The correct option will be one that adds to this support. Labor costs will be reduced only if the machine works well. The machine relies on shade of color to distinguish between weeds and crop plants. If crop plants can be bred to have distinctive color without sacrificing other qualities, it would be more likely that the machine could be used effectively.

A Greater variation among weed plants would make it more difficult for the machine to distinguish between weeds and crop plants, and this would make it less likely that the machine would be effective.

B This option tends to disfavor the effectiveness of the machine. The more changeable the colors of the plants to be distinguished, the more complex the task of distinguishing between weeds and crop plants based on their color.

C This option tends to disfavor the likely benefits of the machine because it indicates that manual weeding distinguishes weeds from crop plants by using criteria that the machine does not take into account. If the machine does not distinguish weeds from crop plants as accurately and reliably as manual weeding does, then the machine is less apt to make manual weeding unnecessary.

D **Correct.** Making crop plants easily distinguishable from weeds would facilitate the effective use of the weeding machine.

E This does not favor the company's implementing the plan to develop the machine. There would still be tasks other than weeding that would require hiring staff. Thus there would still be labor costs even if the need for manual weeding were eliminated.

The correct answer is D.

159. A certain mayor has proposed a fee of five dollars per day on private vehicles entering the city, claiming that the fee will alleviate the city's traffic congestion. The mayor reasons that, since the fee will exceed the cost of round-trip bus fare from many nearby points, many people will switch from using their cars to using the bus.

Which of the following statements, if true, provides the best evidence that the mayor's reasoning is flawed?

(A) Projected increases in the price of gasoline will increase the cost of taking a private vehicle into the city.

(B) The cost of parking fees already makes it considerably more expensive for most people to take a private vehicle into the city than to take a bus.

(C) Most of the people currently riding the bus do not own private vehicles.

(D) Many commuters opposing the mayor's plan have indicated that they would rather endure traffic congestion than pay a five-dollar-per-day fee.

(E) During the average workday, private vehicles owned and operated by people living within the city account for 20 percent of the city's traffic congestion.

Evaluation of a Plan

Situation In order to alleviate traffic congestion, the mayor proposes a five-dollar daily fee on private vehicles entering the city. Since the fee is more than the round-trip bus fare, the mayor believes many drivers will switch to buses.

Reasoning *What flaw exists in the mayor's reasoning?* The mayor apparently believes that saving money is the decisive issue for drivers. If, however, drivers are already paying considerably more in parking fees than they would in fares as bus commuters, then saving money is not the primary reason they are choosing to drive their cars rather than take the bus. This suggests that drivers may not change their behavior simply to save money.

A This statement does not indicate whether the increased cost will dissuade people from taking private vehicles into the city, and therefore does not indicate whether the mayor's reasoning is flawed.

B **Correct.** This statement properly identifies a flaw in the mayor's reasoning.

C Current bus riders are not relevant to the mayor's plan, which anticipates only that people currently driving private vehicles into the city will become bus riders.

D Many drivers may continue to commute in their private vehicles, but others might switch to buses. The mayor's plan does not anticipate a switch by all drivers.

E The 20 percent figure shows that most congestion is caused by vehicles entering from outside the city; this does not point out a weakness in the mayor's plan.

The correct answer is B.

160. Aroca City currently funds its public schools through taxes on property. **In place of this system, the city plans to introduce a sales tax of 3 percent on all retail sales in the city.** Critics protest that 3 percent of current retail sales falls short of the amount raised for schools by property taxes. The critics are correct on this point. **Nevertheless, implementing the plan will probably not reduce the money going to Aroca's schools.** Several large retailers have selected Aroca City as the site for huge new stores, and these are certain to draw large numbers of shoppers from neighboring municipalities, where sales are taxed at rates of 6 percent and more. In consequence, retail sales in Aroca City are bound to increase substantially.

In the argument given, the two portions in **boldface** play which of the following roles?

(A) The first presents a plan that the argument concludes is unlikely to achieve its goal; the second expresses that conclusion.

(B) The first presents a plan that the argument concludes is unlikely to achieve its goal; the second presents evidence in support of that conclusion.

(C) The first presents a plan that the argument contends is the best available; the second is a conclusion drawn by the argument to justify that contention.

(D) The first presents a plan one of whose consequences is at issue in the argument; the second is the argument's conclusion about that consequence.

(E) The first presents a plan that the argument seeks to defend against a certain criticism; the second is that criticism.

Argument Evaluation

Situation Aroca City plans to switch the source of its public school funding from property taxes to a new local sales tax.

Reasoning *What argumentative roles do the two portions in boldface play in the passage?* The first boldface portion simply describes the city's plan. The next two sentences in the passage describe an observation some critics have made in objecting to the plan and say that the observation is correct. But then the second boldface portion rejects the critics' implicit conclusion that the plan will reduce school funding. The final two sentences in the passage present reasons to accept the statement in the second boldface portion, so they are premises supporting it as a conclusion.

A The argument concludes that the plan is unlikely to reduce funding for the schools. The passage does not mention the plan's goal, but presumably that goal is not to reduce school funding.

B The second boldface portion presents the argument's conclusion, not evidence to support the conclusion. The passage does not mention the plan's goal, but presumably that goal is not to reduce school funding.

C The passage does not say whether the plan is better than any other possible school funding plans.

D **Correct.** The plan's likely effect on the amount of school funding is at issue in the argument, whose conclusion is that the plan probably will not reduce that funding.

E The second boldface portion does not criticize the plan, but rather rejects a criticism of the plan by stating that the plan will probably not reduce school funding.

The correct answer is D.

161. Which of the following most logically completes the argument?

A photograph of the night sky was taken with the camera shutter open for an extended period. The normal motion of stars across the sky caused the images of the stars in the photograph to appear as streaks. However, one bright spot was not streaked. Even if the spot were caused, as astronomers believe, by a celestial object, that object could still have been moving across the sky during the time the shutter was open, since _________.

(A) the spot was not the brightest object in the photograph

(B) the photograph contains many streaks that astronomers can identify as caused by noncelestial objects

(C) stars in the night sky do not appear to shift position relative to each other

(D) the spot could have been caused by an object that emitted a flash that lasted for only a fraction of the time that the camera shutter was open

(E) if the camera shutter had not been open for an extended period, it would have recorded substantially fewer celestial objects

Argument Construction

Situation In a photograph of the night sky taken with the camera shutter open for an extended period, the images of stars appeared as streaks because of the stars' normal motion across the sky, but one bright spot was not streaked.

Reasoning *What would most strongly suggest that a celestial object moving across the sky could have caused the spot?* An object moving across the sky that was bright throughout the time the camera shutter was open should have appeared as a streak in the photograph, just as the stars did. But if the moving object was bright for only a very brief moment, and thus not for an extended time while the camera shutter was open, the object's movement may not have been captured in the photograph, and thus would appear in the photograph as an unstreaked bright spot.

A The argument is not about how bright the spot was compared to other objects in the photograph.

B Streaks caused by noncelestial objects such as satellites or airplanes do not explain how only one of many celestial objects moving across the sky could have produced the unstreaked spot.

C The passage indicates that the stars were shifting position relative to the camera, not relative to one another. In any case, this observation does not help to explain how a celestial object that may not have been a star but that was moving across the sky could have produced the unstreaked spot in the photograph.

D **Correct.** As explained above, a moving celestial object that only produced a momentary flash of light would produce an unstreaked bright spot in the photograph.

E This may be true, given that fewer celestial objects might have moved into the camera's range of view if the camera shutter had not been open as long. But it does not provide any evidence that a moving celestial object could have produced the unstreaked spot.

The correct answer is D.

162. Economist: Paying extra for fair-trade coffee—coffee labeled with the Fairtrade logo—is intended to help poor farmers, because they receive a higher price for the fair-trade coffee they grow. But this practice may hurt more farmers in developing nations than it helps. By raising average prices for coffee, it encourages more coffee to be produced than consumers want to buy. This lowers prices for non-fair-trade coffee and thus lowers profits for non-fair-trade coffee farmers.

To evaluate the strength of the economist's argument, it would be most helpful to know which of the following?

(A) Whether there is a way of alleviating the impact of the increased average prices for coffee on non-fair-trade coffee farmers' profits
(B) What proportion of coffee farmers in developing nations produce fair-trade coffee
(C) Whether many coffee farmers in developing nations also derive income from other kinds of farming
(D) Whether consumers should pay extra for fair-trade coffee if doing so lowers profits for non-fair-trade coffee farmers
(E) How fair-trade coffee farmers in developing nations could be helped without lowering profits for non-fair-trade coffee farmers

Argument Evaluation

Situation Poor farmers receive higher prices for fair-trade coffee. But paying extra for fair-trade coffee lowers prices for non-fair-trade coffee and thus lowers profits for non-fair-trade coffee farmers.

Reasoning *What would be most helpful to know to evaluate how well the economist's observations support the conclusion that buying fair-trade coffee hurts more farmers in developing nations than it helps?* The economist suggests that buying fair-trade coffee benefits farmers who grow it because they receive higher prices, but that it hurts non-fair-trade coffee farmers by reducing their profits. So to know whether the practice hurts more farmers in developing nations than it helps, it would be helpful to know whether developing nations have more farmers who produce non-fair-trade coffee than produce fair-trade coffee.

A Even if there were some potential way of alleviating the negative impact from buying fair-trade coffee on non-fair-trade coffee farmers, it still could be that the practice hurts more developing-nation farmers than it helps. Alleviating the negative impact does not entail that there is no negative impact.

B **Correct.** If fewer than half of these farmers produce fair-trade coffee, then the economist's observations do suggest that buying fair-trade coffee hurts more coffee farmers in developing nations than it helps. But if more than half do, those observations suggest the contrary.

C Although knowing this could be helpful in determining how intensely many farmers are economically affected by people buying fair-trade coffee, it is not helpful in determining whether more farmers are hurt than are helped.

D The argument's conclusion is only about the economic impact of buying fair-trade coffee, not about how consumers should or should not respond to that impact.

E Knowing how the fair-trade coffee farmers could potentially be helped without hurting the other coffee farmers is irrelevant to assessing whether the practice of buying fair-trade coffee hurts more developing-nation farmers than it helps.

The correct answer is B.

163. Tanco, a leather manufacturer, uses large quantities of common salt to preserve animal hides. New environmental regulations have significantly increased the cost of disposing of salt water that results from this use, and, in consequence, Tanco is considering a plan to use potassium chloride in place of common salt. Research has shown that Tanco could reprocess the by-product of potassium chloride use to yield a crop fertilizer, leaving a relatively small volume of waste for disposal.

In determining the impact on company profits of using potassium chloride in place of common salt, it would be important for Tanco to research all of the following EXCEPT:

(A) What difference, if any, is there between the cost of the common salt needed to preserve a given quantity of animal hides and the cost of the potassium chloride needed to preserve the same quantity of hides?

(B) To what extent is the equipment involved in preserving animal hides using common salt suitable for preserving animal hides using potassium chloride?

(C) What environmental regulations, if any, constrain the disposal of the waste generated in reprocessing the by-product of potassium chloride?

(D) How closely does leather that results when common salt is used to preserve hides resemble that which results when potassium chloride is used?

(E) Are the chemical properties that make potassium chloride an effective means for preserving animal hides the same as those that make common salt an effective means for doing so?

Evaluation of a Plan

Situation New environmental regulations will increase the costs of disposing of the salt water that results from the use of large amounts of common salt in leather manufacturing. The manufacturer is considering switching from common salt to potassium chloride, because the by-product of the latter could be reprocessed to yield a crop fertilizer, with little waste left over to be disposed.

Reasoning *In order to determine whether it would be profitable to switch from using common salt to using potassium chloride, which of the five questions does the manufacturer NOT need to answer?* The chemical properties making potassium chloride an effective means of preserving animal hides might be quite different from those that make common salt effective, but there is no particular reason for thinking that this would impact the profitability of switching to potassium chloride. The relevant effects on the preserved hides might be the same even if the properties that brought about those effects were quite different. Thus, without more information than is provided in the passage, this question is irrelevant.

A The savings in waste disposal costs that would be gained by switching to potassium chloride could be cancelled out if the cost of potassium chloride needed far exceeded that for common salt.

B If switching to potassium chloride would force the manufacturer to replace the equipment it uses for preserving hides, then it might be less profitable to switch.

C Even though there is said to be relatively little waste associated with using potassium chloride in the process, if the costs of this disposal are very high due to environmental regulations, it might be less profitable to switch.

D If the leather that results from the use of potassium chloride looks substantially different from that which results when common salt has been used, then the leather might be less attractive to consumers, which would adversely affect the economics of switching to potassium chloride.

E **Correct.** Note that the question as stated here presupposes that potassium chloride and salt are both effective means for preserving animal hides—so it does not raise any issue as to whether potassium chloride is adequately effective or as effective as salt (clearly, an issue of effectiveness *would* be relevant to profitability).

The correct answer is E.

164. Colorless diamonds can command high prices as gemstones. A type of less valuable diamonds can be treated to remove all color. Only sophisticated tests can distinguish such treated diamonds from naturally colorless ones. However, only 2 percent of diamonds mined are of the colored type that can be successfully treated, and many of those are of insufficient quality to make the treatment worthwhile. Surely, therefore, the vast majority of colorless diamonds sold by jewelers are naturally colorless.

A serious flaw in the reasoning of the argument is that

(A) comparisons between the price diamonds command as gemstones and their value for other uses are omitted
(B) information about the rarity of treated diamonds is not combined with information about the rarity of naturally colorless, gemstone diamonds
(C) the possibility that colored diamonds might be used as gemstones, even without having been treated, is ignored
(D) the currently available method for making colorless diamonds from colored ones is treated as though it were the only possible method for doing so
(E) the difficulty that a customer of a jeweler would have in distinguishing a naturally colorless diamond from a treated one is not taken into account

Argument Evaluation

Situation Colored diamonds of a type that comprises 2 percent of all mined diamonds can be treated so that they are not easily distinguishable from more valuable, naturally colorless diamonds, but many are too low in quality for the treatment to be worthwhile.

Reasoning *Why do the argument's premises not justify the conclusion that the vast majority of colorless diamonds sold by jewelers are naturally colorless?* Since the type of colored diamonds that can be treated make up only 2 percent of all mined diamonds, and many diamonds of that type are too low in quality for treatment to be worthwhile, the vast majority of mined diamonds must not be treated to have their color removed. However, we are not told what proportion of all mined diamonds are naturally colorless. Naturally colorless diamonds may be far rarer even than the uncommon diamonds that have been treated to have their color removed. Thus, for all we can tell from the passage, it could well be that most colorless diamonds sold by jewelers have been treated to remove all color.

A Even if some types of diamonds command higher prices for uses other than as gemstones, the types discussed in the passage evidently command high enough prices as gemstones to be sold as such by jewelers.

B **Correct.** The argument does not work if naturally colorless diamonds are rarer than treated diamonds, as they may be for all we can tell from the information provided.

C The argument's conclusion is only that jewelers sell more naturally colorless diamonds than diamonds treated to be colorless. Whether jewelers sell any colored diamonds or other gemstones is irrelevant.

D The argument only concerns the types of colorless diamonds sold now, not the types that may be sold in the future if other treatment methods are discovered.

E The argument does suggest this difficulty but implies that even so there are too few treated diamonds available for jewelers to sell in place of naturally colorless ones.

The correct answer is B.

165. The Sumpton town council recently voted to pay a prominent artist to create an abstract sculpture for the town square. Critics of this decision protested that town residents tend to dislike most abstract art, and any art in the town square should reflect their tastes. But a town council spokesperson dismissed this criticism, pointing out that other public abstract sculptures that the same sculptor has installed in other cities have been extremely popular with those cities' local residents.

The statements above most strongly suggest that the main point of disagreement between the critics and the spokesperson is whether

(A) it would have been reasonable to consult town residents on the decision
(B) most Sumpton residents will find the new sculpture to their taste
(C) abstract sculptures by the same sculptor have truly been popular in other cities
(D) a more traditional sculpture in the town square would be popular among local residents
(E) public art that the residents of Sumpton would find desirable would probably be found desirable by the residents of other cities

Argument Construction

Situation After the Sumpton town council voted to pay a prominent sculptor to create an abstract sculpture for the town square, critics protested the decision. A town council spokesperson responded to the critics.

Reasoning *What do the critics and the spokesperson mainly disagree about?* The critics argue that Sumpton residents dislike most abstract art and that art in the town square should reflect their taste. Since the critics are protesting the town council's decision, they are clearly inferring from the residents' general attitude toward abstract art that the residents will dislike the specific sculpture the prominent sculptor will create. The spokesperson replies by arguing that in other cities, sculptures by the same sculptor have been very popular with local residents. The spokesperson implicitly infers from this that the sculpture the prominent sculptor will create for Sumpton will be popular with Sumpton residents—and therefore that the critics are mistaken.

A Neither the critics nor the spokesperson mentions consultation with the town residents on the decision.

B Correct. As explained above, the critics raise points implicitly suggesting that the residents will dislike the sculpture, whereas the spokesperson responds with a point implicitly supporting the opposite conclusion.

C The critics could concede that the sculptor's work has been popular in other cities, but nonetheless hold that Sumpton residents have different tastes from those of the other cities' residents.

D The spokesperson gives no indication regarding the attitudes of Sumpton residents regarding traditional sculpture.

E It may be that neither the critics nor the spokesperson holds this view. The spokesperson may hold that Sumpton residents are easier to please than residents of most other cities, whereas the critics may hold that Sumpton residents are far more traditional in their tastes than other cities' residents.

The correct answer is B.

166. Jay: Of course there are many good reasons to support the expansion of preventive medical care, but arguments claiming that it will lead to greater societal economic gains are misguided. Some of the greatest societal expenses arise from frequent urgent-care needs for people who have attained a long life due to preventive care.

Sunil: Your argument fails because you neglect economic gains outside the health care system: society suffers an economic loss when any of its productive members suffer preventable illnesses.

Sunil's response to Jay makes which of the following assumptions?

(A) Those who receive preventive care are not more likely to need urgent care than are those who do not receive preventive care.
(B) Jay intends the phrase "economic gains" to refer only to gains accruing to institutions within the health care system.
(C) Productive members of society are more likely than others to suffer preventable illnesses.
(D) The economic contributions of those who receive preventive medical care may outweigh the economic losses caused by preventive care.
(E) Jay is incorrect in stating that patients who receive preventive medical care are long-lived.

Argument Construction

Situation Some of the greatest societal expenses arise from frequent urgent-care needs for people who have reached old age thanks to preventive medical care. But society also suffers economic loss when any of its productive members suffer preventable illnesses.

Reasoning *What is Sunil assuming in his argument that Jay's argument fails?* Jay implies that by helping people live longer, expanding preventive medical care may actually increase the amount of urgent medical care people need over the course of their lives, and that societal expenses for this additional urgent care may equal or exceed any societal economic benefits from expanding preventive care. Sunil responds by implying that expanding preventive care would allow society to avoid economic losses from lost productivity caused by preventable illnesses. In order for Sunil's argument to establish that Jay's argument fails, the potential economic benefits that Sunil implies would arise from expanded preventive care must be greater than the economic losses from the increased need for urgent care that Jay points out.

A This is not an assumption that underpins Sunil's suggestion that the societal economic benefits from expanded preventive care may exceed any resulting economic losses from urgent care.

B If Jay intends the phrase "economic gains" to refer only to gains within the health care system, then Sunil's point about economic gains outside the health care system is not even relevant to Jay's argument about economic gains within it.

C Even if productive members of society are not more likely than others to suffer preventable illnesses, it still may be true, as Sunil suggests, that the economic benefits of preventing productive members of society from suffering those illnesses may outweigh the economic losses of doing so. In that case, Jay's argument could still fail in the way Sunil indicates.

D **Correct.** Sunil must assume this in order to rebut Jay's argument. As explained above, if the economic contributions of those receiving preventive care definitely do not outweigh the economic losses caused by preventive care, then Sunil's implicit point that expanding preventive care would help to prevent the loss of such contributions is insufficient to rebut Jay's argument.

E Whether Jay is correct or incorrect in this respect, Sunil may be correct that Jay's argument fails because Jay has neglected to consider how preventive care produces larger economic gains outside the health care system.

The correct answer is D.

167. Boreal owls range over a much larger area than do other owls of similar size. The reason for this behavior is probably that the small mammals on which owls feed are especially scarce in the forests where boreal owls live, and the relative scarcity of prey requires the owls to range more extensively to find sufficient food.

Which of the following, if true, most helps to confirm the explanation above?

(A) Some boreal owls range over an area eight times larger than the area over which any other owl of similar size ranges.

(B) Boreal owls range over larger areas in regions where food of the sort eaten by small mammals is sparse than they do in regions where such food is abundant.

(C) After their young hatch, boreal owls must hunt more often than before in order to feed both themselves and their newly hatched young.

(D) Sometimes individual boreal owls hunt near a single location for many weeks at a time and do not range farther than a few hundred yards.

(E) The boreal owl requires less food, relative to its weight, than is required by members of other owl species.

Argument Evaluation

Situation The small mammals on which owls prey are relatively scarce in the forests where boreal owls live. That is why boreal owls range more extensively than do other, similarly sized owls in search of food.

Reasoning *Which choice, if true, would most help confirm the proposed explanation?* One way to confirm an explanation is by finding further information that one would expect to be true *if* the explanation is valid. If the explanation in the passage is valid, then one would expect that variations in the population density of available small-animal prey for boreal owls would be accompanied by variations in the ranges of the boreal owls. Naturally the population density of available small-animal prey is likely to be affected by how plentiful food is for those small animals.

A The comparison between different groups of boreal owls is not relevant to the comparison between boreal owls and other owls.

B **Correct.** This indicates that abundance of food for the boreal owls' small-animal prey in an area (and therefore abundance of small animals in that area) correlates with a smaller range for the boreal owls there. This strengthens the proposed explanation.

C This option concerns a correlation between owls' need for food and the frequency with which owls hunt, whereas the phenomenon described in the passage and the proposed explanation have to do with the range over which owls hunt.

D If one were to assume that boreal owls never hunt near a single location for weeks, that would in no way undermine the proposed explanation.

E If anything, this option tends to undermine the proposed explanation, because it suggests the possibility that boreal owls need not make up for the relative scarcity of prey in their habitats by ranging over larger areas.

The correct answer is B.

168. Microbiologist: A lethal strain of salmonella recently showed up in a European country, causing an outbreak of illness that killed two people and infected twenty-seven others. Investigators blame the severity of the outbreak on the overuse of antibiotics, since the salmonella bacteria tested were shown to be drug-resistant. But this is unlikely because patients in the country where the outbreak occurred cannot obtain antibiotics to treat illness without a prescription, and the country's doctors prescribe antibiotics less readily than do doctors in any other European country.

Which of the following, if true, would most weaken the microbiologist's reasoning?

(A) Physicians in the country where the outbreak occurred have become hesitant to prescribe antibiotics since they are frequently in short supply.

(B) People in the country where the outbreak occurred often consume foods produced from animals that eat antibiotics-laden livestock feed.

(C) Use of antibiotics in two countries that neighbor the country where the outbreak occurred has risen over the past decade.

(D) Drug-resistant strains of salmonella have not been found in countries in which antibiotics are not generally available.

(E) Salmonella has been shown to spread easily along the distribution chains of certain vegetables, such as raw tomatoes.

Argument Evaluation

Situation Antibiotic-resistant salmonella caused an outbreak of illness in a European country where patients need prescriptions to obtain antibiotics and where doctors dispense such prescriptions less readily than in other European countries.

Reasoning *What evidence would most strongly suggest that overuse of antibiotics was likely responsible for the outbreak, despite the cited facts?* The microbiologist reasons that because patients need prescriptions to obtain antibiotics in the country where the outbreak occurred, and the country's doctors dispense such prescriptions less readily than doctors in other European countries do, antibiotics are probably not being overused in the country—so antibiotic overuse was probably not responsible for the outbreak. Implicit in the microbiologist's reasoning is the assumption that overuse of antibiotics, if it had occurred, could probably have resulted only from overprescribing of antibiotics by physicians to treat illness in people in the country in question. Any evidence casting doubt on this complex assumption would suggest a weakness in the microbiologist's reasoning.

A This strengthens the argument by providing additional evidence that antibiotics are not being overprescribed in the country.

B **Correct.** This weakens the microbiologist's argument by indicating that an assumption implicit in the argument may be false: the salmonella outbreak could easily by explained by overuse of antibiotics in livestock feed (perhaps imported from other countries).

C Even if antibiotic use has risen in the two neighboring countries, antibiotics still might be underused in both countries.

D This suggests that antibiotic-resistant salmonella arises only in countries where antibiotics are used; even if this were true it would be quite compatible with the microbiologist's argument and does not weaken that argument.

E This describes one mechanism by which salmonella can spread in a population; it says nothing about whether an outbreak of antibiotic-resistant strains of salmonella might have been caused by antibiotic overuse.

The correct answer is B.

169. Historian: Newton developed mathematical concepts and techniques that are fundamental to modern calculus. Leibniz developed closely analogous concepts and techniques. It has traditionally been thought that these discoveries were independent. Researchers have, however, recently discovered notes of Leibniz's that discuss one of Newton's books on mathematics. Several scholars have argued that since **the book includes a presentation of Newton's calculus concepts and techniques,** and since the notes were written before Leibniz's own development of calculus concepts and techniques, it is virtually certain **that the traditional view is false.** A more cautious conclusion than this is called for, however. Leibniz's notes are limited to early sections of Newton's book, sections that precede the ones in which Newton's calculus concepts and techniques are presented.

In the historian's reasoning, the two portions in **boldface** play which of the following roles?

(A) The first is a claim that the historian rejects; the second is a position that that claim has been used to support.

(B) The first is evidence that has been used to support a conclusion about which the historian expresses reservations; the second is that conclusion.

(C) The first provides evidence in support of a position that the historian defends; the second is that position.

(D) The first and the second each provide evidence in support of a position that the historian defends.

(E) The first has been used in support of a position that the historian rejects; the second is a conclusion that the historian draws from that position.

Argument Construction

Situation A historian discusses a controversy about whether or not Leibniz developed calculus concepts and techniques independently of Newton.

Reasoning *What argumentative roles do the two portions in boldface play in the passage?* The first four sentences of the passage simply provide background information. Both boldface sections are within the fifth sentence, which reports an argument by *several scholars*. The key word *since* indicates that the first boldface section is a premise in the scholars' argument. A second premise preceded by another *since* follows in the next clause. The final clause of the fifth sentence reveals that the second boldface section is the conclusion of the scholars' argument. In the sixth sentence, the historian expresses misgivings about the scholars' conclusion, for reasons presented in the seventh and final sentence.

A The historian does not reject the claim that Newton's book includes a presentation of Newton's calculus concepts and techniques. Instead, the historian merely points out that Leibniz's notes do not cover those sections of Newton's book.

B **Correct.** The first boldface section is one of two premises in the scholars' argument, and the second boldface section is that argument's conclusion. In the following sentence the historian expresses reservations about that conclusion.

C The historian does not defend the scholars' conclusion but rather expresses misgivings about it.

D The second boldface section is the scholars' conclusion and does not present any evidence. Nor does it support the historian's position that a more cautious conclusion is called for.

E The second boldface section presents not the historian's conclusion but rather the scholars' conclusion, about which the historian expresses misgivings.

The correct answer is B.

170. For over two centuries, no one had been able to make Damascus blades—blades with a distinctive serpentine surface pattern—but a contemporary sword maker may just have rediscovered how. Using iron with trace impurities that precisely matched those present in the iron used in historic Damascus blades, this contemporary sword maker seems to have finally hit on an intricate process by which he can produce a blade indistinguishable from a true Damascus blade.

Which of the following, if true, provides the strongest support for the hypothesis that trace impurities in the iron are essential for the production of Damascus blades?

(A) There are surface features of every Damascus blade—including the blades produced by the contemporary sword maker—that are unique to that blade.

(B) The iron with which the contemporary sword maker made Damascus blades came from a source of iron that was unknown two centuries ago.

(C) Almost all the tools used by the contemporary sword maker were updated versions of tools that were used by sword makers over two centuries ago.

(D) Production of Damascus blades by sword makers of the past ceased abruptly after those sword makers' original source of iron became exhausted.

(E) Although Damascus blades were renowned for maintaining a sharp edge, the blade made by the contemporary sword maker suggests that they may have maintained their edge less well than blades made using what is now the standard process for making blades.

Argument Evaluation

Situation A sword maker may have recently rediscovered how to make Damascus blades using iron with trace impurities matching those in the iron from which historic Damascus blades were wrought.

Reasoning *What evidence would suggest that the trace impurities are essential for producing Damascus blades?* The passage says the sword maker seems to have created blades indistinguishable from historic Damascus blades by using iron with the same trace impurities found in those blades. But that does not prove the trace impurities are essential to the process. Evidence suggesting that Damascus blades have never been made from iron without the trace impurities would support the hypothesis that the trace impurities are essential to their manufacture.

A Damascus blades could vary in their surface features whether or not trace impurities are essential for their manufacture.

B Whatever the source of the iron the contemporary sword maker used, it contains the same trace impurities as the iron historically used to make Damascus blades, which is what the hypothesis is about.

C If anything, this might cast doubt on the hypothesis by suggesting that the special tools rather than the trace impurities could account for the distinctive features of Damascus blades.

D **Correct.** This suggests that when the historic sword makers lost access to the special iron with its trace impurities, they could no longer make Damascus blades. Thus, it supports the hypothesis that the trace impurities are necessary for manufacturing Damascus blades.

E Even if Damascus blades maintained their edges less well than most contemporary blades do, the trace impurities may not have been essential for manufacturing them.

The correct answer is D.

171. Images from ground-based telescopes are invariably distorted by the Earth's atmosphere. Orbiting space telescopes, however, operating above Earth's atmosphere, should provide superbly detailed images. Therefore, ground-based telescopes will soon become obsolete for advanced astronomical research purposes.

Which of the following statements, if true, would cast the most doubt on the conclusion drawn above?

(A) An orbiting space telescope due to be launched this year is far behind schedule and over budget, whereas the largest ground-based telescope was both within budget and on schedule.

(B) Ground-based telescopes located on mountain summits are not subject to the kinds of atmospheric distortion which, at low altitudes, make stars appear to twinkle.

(C) By careful choice of observatory location, it is possible for large-aperture telescopes to avoid most of the kind of wind turbulence that can distort image quality.

(D) When large-aperture telescopes are located at high altitudes near the equator, they permit the best Earth-based observations of the center of the Milky Way Galaxy, a prime target of astronomical research.

(E) Detailed spectral analyses, upon which astronomers rely for determining the chemical composition and evolutionary history of stars, require telescopes with more light-gathering capacity than space telescopes can provide.

Argument Evaluation

Situation Earth's atmosphere distorts images from ground-based telescopes, whereas space telescopes orbiting above the atmosphere should provide superbly detailed images.

Reasoning *What evidence would undermine the claim that ground-based telescopes will soon become obsolete for advanced astronomical research?* The argument implicitly assumes that advanced astronomical research can be accomplished more effectively with the more detailed, less distorted images produced by space telescopes and that therefore almost all advanced astronomical research will soon be conducted with space telescopes. This reasoning would be undermined by evidence that ground-based telescopes have substantial advantages for advanced astronomical research despite their distorted images or by evidence that space telescopes will not soon become common or affordable enough to support most advanced astronomical research.

A Even if this is true, there may be several orbiting space telescopes that will be, or have been, launched on schedule and within budget, so this option does not cast doubt on the conclusion of the argument.

B Ground-based telescopes on mountain summits are still subject to more atmospheric distortion than are space telescopes orbiting above the atmosphere.

C Atmospheric distortion of telescopic images may result mainly from factors other than wind turbulence.

D Even the best Earth-based observations of the center of the Milky Way Galaxy may be vastly inferior to space-based observations.

E **Correct.** This indicates an inherent limitation of space-based telescopes: unlike Earth-based telescopes, they lack the light-gathering capacity that astronomers need to perform one of their primary tasks, i.e., detailed spectral analyses. So Earth-based telescopes are unlikely to soon become obsolete.

The correct answer is E.

172. Generally scientists enter their field with the goal of doing important new research and accept as their colleagues those with similar motivation. Therefore, when any scientist wins renown as an expounder of science to general audiences, most other scientists conclude that this popularizer should no longer be regarded as a true colleague.

The explanation offered above for the low esteem in which scientific popularizers are held by research scientists assumes that

(A) serious scientific research is not a solitary activity, but relies on active cooperation among a group of colleagues
(B) research scientists tend not to regard as colleagues those scientists whose renown they envy
(C) a scientist can become a famous popularizer without having completed any important research
(D) research scientists believe that those who are well known as popularizers of science are not motivated to do important new research
(E) no important new research can be accessible to or accurately assessed by those who are not themselves scientists

Argument Construction

Situation Research scientists desire to do important new research and treat as colleagues just those who have a similar desire. When a scientist becomes popular among a general audience for explaining principles of science, other scientists have less esteem for this popularizer, no longer regarding such a scientist as a serious colleague.

Reasoning *What assumption do research scientists make about scientists who become popularizers?* The community of scientists shares a common goal: to do important new research. What would cause this community to disapprove of a popularizer and to cease to regard the popularizer as a colleague? It must be because many scientists believe that becoming a popularizer is incompatible with desiring to do important new research.

A Many scientists make this assumption, of course—but it is not an assumption on which the explanation specifically depends. The explanation concerns the scientists' motivation, not their style of doing research.

B This statement gives another reason that scientists may reject a popularizer, but because it is not the reason implied in the passage, it is not assumed.

C Even if this is true, it does not address the core issue of the argument: what scientists believe about the *motivation* of popularizers.

D **Correct.** This statement properly identifies an assumption on which the explanation for scientists' rejection of popularizers depends.

E The passage is not concerned with whether nonscientists can understand new research, but rather with the beliefs and motivations of scientists who reject popularizers as colleagues.

The correct answer is D.

173. Urban planner: When a city loses population due to migration, property taxes in that city tend to rise. This is because there are then fewer residents paying to maintain an infrastructure that was designed to support more people. Rising property taxes, in turn, drive more residents away, compounding the problem. Since the city of Stonebridge is starting to lose population, the city government should therefore refrain from raising property taxes.

Which of the following, if true, would most weaken the urban planner's argument?

(A) If Stonebridge does not raise taxes on its residents to maintain its infrastructure, the city will become much less attractive to live in as that infrastructure decays.

(B) Stonebridge at present benefits from grants provided by the national government to help maintain certain parts of its infrastructure.

(C) If there is a small increase in property taxes in Stonebridge and a slightly larger proportion of total revenue than at present is allocated to infrastructure maintenance, the funding will be adequate for that purpose.

(D) Demographers project that the population of a region that includes Stonebridge will start to increase substantially within the next several years.

(E) The property taxes in Stonebridge are significantly lower than those in many larger cities.

Argument Evaluation

Situation When a city loses population due to migration, fewer residents remain to pay to maintain the city's infrastructure, so property taxes tend to rise. These rising property taxes then drive even more residents away. The city of Stonebridge is starting to lose population, so Stonebridge's government should not raise property taxes.

Reasoning *What would weaken the urban planner's justification for concluding that Stonebridge's government should refrain from raising property taxes?* The urban planner implicitly reasons that raising property taxes in Stonebridge in order to maintain the city's infrastructure would make the city lose even more residents, leaving even fewer paying to maintain the infrastructure, and that this would worsen the funding problem the tax increase would have been intended to solve. The urban planner's argument would be weakened by any evidence that raising property taxes in Stonebridge would not drive residents away or that refraining from raising property taxes would cause the same problems as raising them would cause, or worse.

A **Correct.** This suggests that refraining from raising property taxes could drive more residents out of Stonebridge than raising them would, and thus would not help the city avoid the problem the urban planner describes.

B This does slightly weaken the argument because the grants may still be provided to maintain certain parts of the infrastructure, even if increased property taxes drive more residents away. But losing more residents could still make it harder to raise enough funds to maintain the rest of the city's infrastructure, as the urban planner argues.

C Even if this approach would address the immediate maintenance funding problem, the small increase in property taxes could still drive more residents away, forcing additional future tax increases on those who remain, just as the urban planner suggests.

D This does slightly weaken the argument, but the residents who will move to the region might still avoid moving to Stonebridge if the property taxes there are too high, and those who live in Stonebridge might still move to other cities in the region.

E Residents fleeing Stonebridge because of high property taxes would likely avoid moving to the many larger cities with even higher property taxes, but they might be happy to move to many other places with low property taxes.

The correct answer is A.

174. Which of the following most logically completes the argument?

Utrania was formerly a major petroleum exporter, but in recent decades economic stagnation and restrictive regulations inhibited investment in new oil fields. In consequence, Utranian oil exports dropped steadily as old fields became depleted. Utrania's currently improving economic situation, together with less-restrictive regulations, will undoubtedly result in the rapid development of new fields. However, it would be premature to conclude that the rapid development of new fields will result in higher oil exports, because __________.

(A) the price of oil is expected to remain relatively stable over the next several years
(B) the improvement in the economic situation in Utrania is expected to result in a dramatic increase in the proportion of Utranians who own automobiles
(C) most of the investment in new oil fields in Utrania is expected to come from foreign sources
(D) new technology is available to recover oil from old oil fields formerly regarded as depleted
(E) many of the new oil fields in Utrania are likely to be as productive as those that were developed during the period when Utrania was a major oil exporter

Argument Construction

Situation A country that had been a major oil exporter has seen its exports decline in recent decades due to economic stagnation, a failure to invest in new fields, and the steady depletion of its old fields. But looser regulations and an improving economy will bring rapid development of new oil fields in the country.

Reasoning *Which of the options would most logically complete the argument?* The passage describes the conditions that led to Utrania's no longer being a major oil exporter: a lack of investment in new oil fields due to a stagnant economy and restrictive regulations. The passage then says that due to changed regulatory and economic conditions, there will now be rapid development of new oil fields. Nonetheless, this might not bring about an increase in Utrania's oil exports. To logically complete the argument, one must explain how oil exports might not increase even when the condition that led to decreased oil exports has been removed. Suppose there were an increase in domestic oil consumption. A dramatic increase in the rate of car ownership in Utrania could reasonably be expected to significantly increase domestic oil consumption, which could eat up the added oil production from the new fields.

A This choice is incorrect. There is no reason why stable oil prices should prevent Utrania's oil exports from increasing.

B Correct. An increase in car ownership would increase Utrania's oil consumption—and this supports the claim that oil exports might not increase.

C If anything, this suggests that oil exports should increase. So it would not be a good choice for completion of the argument.

D The advent of new technology allowing oil to be extracted from fields previously thought to be depleted would mean that there is even more reason to think that Utrania's oil exports will increase.

E This does not help to explain why exports would not increase. On the contrary, it suggests that the new fields will lead to increased exports.

The correct answer is B.

175. The use of growth-promoting antibiotics in hog farming can weaken their effectiveness in treating humans because such use can spread resistance to those antibiotics among microorganisms. But now the Smee Company, one of the largest pork marketers, may stop buying pork raised on feed containing these antibiotics. Smee has 60 percent of the pork market, and farmers who sell to Smee would certainly stop using antibiotics in order to avoid jeopardizing their sales. So if Smee makes this change, it will probably significantly slow the decline in antibiotics' effectiveness for humans.

Which of the following, if true, would most strengthen the argument above?

(A) Other major pork marketers will probably stop buying pork raised on feed containing growth-promoting antibiotics if Smee no longer buys such pork.

(B) The decline in hog growth due to discontinuation of antibiotics can be offset by improved hygiene.

(C) Authorities are promoting the use of antibiotics to which microorganisms have not yet developed resistance.

(D) A phaseout of use of antibiotics for hogs in one country reduced usage by over 50 percent over five years.

(E) If Smee stops buying pork raised with antibiotics, the firm's costs will probably increase.

Argument Evaluation

Situation Using growth-promoting antibiotics in hog farming can produce widespread resistance to antibiotics among microorganisms, thereby making the antibiotics less effective in treating humans. The Smee Company, a pork marketer with 60 percent of the pork market, may stop buying pork raised on feed containing these antibiotics.

Reasoning *What additional evidence would most help to support the conclusion that if Smee makes the change, it will significantly slow the decline in antibiotics' effectiveness for humans?* We are already informed that if Smee makes the change, it will eliminate the use of antibiotics in hog feed by farmers supplying at least 60 percent of the pork market. The argument would be strengthened by evidence that Smee's decision would indirectly cause use of the antibiotics to stop more broadly, for example in hog farms supplying significantly more than 60 percent of the total amount of pork marketed.

A **Correct.** This suggests that if Smee makes the change, hog farmers supplying other major pork marketers will also have to stop using antibiotics in hog feed, making the change more widespread and thus probably more effective.

B Even if the decline in hog growth from discontinuing the antibiotics cannot be offset, many hog farmers will still have to stop using the antibiotics as a result of Smee's decision. On the other hand, even if the decline can be offset with improved hygiene, that change might be too expensive or difficult to be worth its benefits for most hog farmers.

C Whatever new antibiotics authorities are promoting, microorganisms may soon develop resistance to them as well. Smee may or may not refuse to buy pork raised on feed containing these new antibiotics.

D This is evidence that Smee's decision may significantly reduce antibiotic use in hogs, but it provides no evidence of how this reduction may affect antibiotics' effectiveness for humans.

E If anything, this provides reason to suspect that Smee will not stick with the change for long after the costs increase, so it weakens rather than strengthens the argument that the change will significantly slow the decline in antibiotics' effectiveness.

The correct answer is A.

176. In an experiment, volunteers walked individually through a dark, abandoned theater. Half of the volunteers had been told that the theater was haunted and the other half that it was under renovation. The first half reported significantly more unusual experiences than the second did. The researchers concluded that reports of encounters with ghosts and other supernatural entities generally result from prior expectations of such experiences.

Which of the following, if true, would most seriously weaken the researchers' reasoning?

(A) None of the volunteers in the second half believed that the unusual experiences they reported were supernatural.

(B) All of the volunteers in the first half believed that the researchers' statement that the theater was haunted was a lie.

(C) Before being told about the theater, the volunteers within each group varied considerably in their prior beliefs about supernatural experiences.

(D) Each unusual experience reported by the volunteers had a cause that did not involve the supernatural.

(E) The researchers did not believe that the theater was haunted.

Argument Evaluation

Situation Volunteers in an experiment walked through a dark, abandoned theater. Those who had been told the theater was haunted reported more unusual experiences than those who had been told it was under renovation.

Reasoning *What evidence would most strongly suggest that the experimental results do not indicate that reports of supernatural encounters result from prior expectations of such experiences?* The researcher assumes that the half of the volunteers who had been told the theater was haunted were more inclined to expect supernatural experiences in the theater than were the other half of the volunteers. Based on this assumption and the greater incidence of reports of unusual experiences among the first half of the volunteers, the researcher concludes that prior expectation of supernatural experiences makes people more likely to report such experiences. The researchers' reasoning would be weakened by evidence that the volunteers did not actually have the expectations the researchers assumed them to have, or by evidence that any such expectations did not influence their reports.

A This strengthens the argument by indicating that the volunteers whom the researchers did not lead to expect supernatural experiences reported no such experiences.

B **Correct.** If none of the volunteers believed the researchers' claim that the theater was haunted, then the implicit assumption that several of those volunteers expected supernatural experiences in the theater is flawed, and so the inference that their prior expectations probably account for their reports of supernatural experiences is flawed.

C This is compatible with the researchers' inference and does not undermine it. Even if the volunteers' initial beliefs about supernatural experiences varied, the researchers' claims about the theater might have strongly influenced how many volunteers in each group expected to have such experiences in the theater specifically.

D The researchers argue that the volunteers' prior expectations account for all the reports of unusual experiences, and this is compatible with there being no genuine supernatural occurrences in the theater.

E Whatever the researchers personally believed about the theater, they might still have successfully influenced the volunteers' beliefs about it.

The correct answer is B.

177. In order to reduce dependence on imported oil, the government of Jalica has imposed minimum fuel-efficiency requirements on all new cars, beginning this year. The more fuel-efficient a car, the less pollution it produces per mile driven. As Jalicans replace their old cars with cars that meet the new requirements, annual pollution from car traffic is likely to decrease in Jalica.

Which of the following, if true, most seriously weakens the argument?

(A) In Jalica, domestically produced oil is more expensive than imported oil.

(B) The Jalican government did not intend the new fuel-efficiency requirement to be a pollution-reduction measure.

(C) Some pollution-control devices mandated in Jalica make cars less fuel-efficient than they would be without those devices.

(D) The new regulation requires no change in the chemical formulation of fuel for cars in Jalica.

(E) Jalicans who get cars that are more fuel-efficient tend to do more driving than before.

Argument Evaluation

Situation The Jalican government is requiring all new cars to meet minimum fuel-efficiency requirements starting this year. Cars that are more fuel efficient produce less pollution per mile driven.

Reasoning *What evidence would suggest that annual pollution from car traffic will not decrease in Jalica, despite the new policy?* Air pollution from car traffic is unlikely to decrease if the new standards will result in more cars on the road or more miles driven per car; or if air pollution from car traffic in Jalica is increasing because of unrelated factors such as growing numbers of Jalicans who can afford cars, construction of more roads, etc. Evidence that any of these factors is present would cast doubt on the argument's conclusion and thus weaken the argument.

A The question at issue is not whether the new policy will reduce dependence on imported oil as the government intends, but rather whether it will reduce air pollution from car traffic.

B A government policy may have consequences that the government did not intend it to have.

C Even if these pollution-control devices make cars less fuel efficient, the new fuel-efficiency standards may still improve cars' average fuel efficiency and thereby reduce air pollution.

D Even if the fuel is unchanged, the new fuel-efficiency standards may still result in cars using less fuel and may thereby reduce air pollution.

E **Correct.** If the new fuel-efficient cars are driven more miles per year than older cars are, they may produce as much or more pollution per year than older cars do even though they produce less pollution per mile driven.

The correct answer is E.

178. Plantings of cotton bioengineered to produce its own insecticide against bollworms, a major cause of crop failure, sustained little bollworm damage until this year. This year the plantings are being seriously damaged by bollworms. Bollworms, however, are not necessarily developing resistance to the cotton's insecticide. Bollworms breed on corn, and last year more corn than usual was planted throughout cotton-growing regions. So it is likely that the cotton is simply being overwhelmed by corn-bred bollworms.

In evaluating the argument, which of the following would it be most useful to establish?

(A) Whether corn could be bioengineered to produce the insecticide

(B) Whether plantings of cotton that does not produce the insecticide are suffering unusually extensive damage from bollworms this year

(C) Whether other crops that have been bioengineered to produce their own insecticide successfully resist the pests against which the insecticide was to protect them

(D) Whether plantings of bioengineered cotton are frequently damaged by insect pests other than bollworms

(E) Whether there are insecticides that can be used against bollworms that have developed resistance to the insecticide produced by the bioengineered cotton

Argument Evaluation

Situation Although plantings of cotton bioengineered to produce an insecticide to combat bollworms were little damaged by the pests in previous years, they are being severely damaged this year. Since the bollworms breed on corn, and there has been more corn planted this year in cotton-growing areas, the cotton is probably being overwhelmed by the corn-bred bollworms.

Reasoning *In evaluating the argument, which question would it be most useful to have answered?* The argument states that the bioengineered cotton crop failures this year (1) have likely been due to the increased corn plantings and (2) not due to the pests having developed a resistance to the insecticide. This also implies (3) that the failures are not due to some third factor.

It would be useful to know how the bioengineered cotton is faring in comparison to the rest of this year's cotton crop. If the bioengineered cotton is faring better against the bollworms, that fact would support the argument because it would suggest that the insecticide is still combating bollworms. If, on the other hand, the bioengineered cotton is being more severely ravaged by bollworms than is other cotton, that suggests that there is some third cause that is primarily at fault.

A This would probably be useful information to those trying to alleviate the bollworm problem in bioengineered cotton. But whether such corn could be developed has no bearing on what is causing the bioengineered cotton to be damaged by bollworms this year.

B **Correct.** If bollworm damage on non-bioengineered cotton is worse than usual this year, then bollworm infestation in general is simply worse than usual, so pesticide resistance does not need to be invoked to explain the bollworm attacks on the bioengineered cotton.

C Even if other crops that have been bioengineered to resist pests have not successfully resisted them, that fact would not mean that the same is true of this cotton. Furthermore, the facts already suggest that the bioengineered cotton has resisted bollworms.

D Whether other types of pests often damage bioengineered cotton has no bearing on why bollworms are damaging this type of cotton more this year than in the past.

E This, too, might be useful information to those trying to alleviate the bollworm problem in bioengineered cotton, but it is not particularly useful in evaluating the argument. Even if there are pesticides that could be used against bollworms that have developed resistance to the insecticide of the bioengineered cotton, that does not mean that such pesticides are being used this year.

The correct answer is B.

179. Typically during thunderstorms most lightning strikes carry a negative electric charge; only a few carry a positive charge. Thunderstorms with unusually high proportions of positive-charge strikes tend to occur in smoky areas near forest fires. The fact that smoke carries positively charged smoke particles into the air above a fire suggests the hypothesis that the extra positive strikes occur because of the presence of such particles in the storm clouds.

Which of the following, if discovered to be true, most seriously undermines the hypothesis?

(A) Other kinds of rare lightning also occur with unusually high frequency in the vicinity of forest fires.

(B) The positive-charge strikes that occur near forest fires tend to be no more powerful than positive strikes normally are.

(C) A positive-charge strike is as likely to start a forest fire as a negative-charge strike is.

(D) Thunderstorms that occur in drifting clouds of smoke have extra positive-charge strikes weeks after the charge of the smoke particles has dissipated.

(E) The total number of lightning strikes during a thunderstorm is usually within the normal range in the vicinity of a forest fire.

Argument Evaluation

Situation Thunderstorms with unusually high proportions of positive-charge lightning strikes tend to occur in smoky areas near forest fires. Smoke carries positively charged particles into the air above fires, suggesting that smoke particles in storm clouds are responsible for the higher proportion of positive strikes.

Reasoning *What would cast doubt on the hypothesis that the extra positive-charge lightning strikes in thunderstorms near forest fires result from positively charged smoke particles carried into the storm clouds?* The hypothesis would be weakened by evidence that the positively charged smoke particles do not enter the storm clouds in the first place, or that they do not retain their charge in the clouds long enough to produce an effect, or that their positive charge cannot affect the charges of the storm's lightning strikes in any case, or that some other factor tends to make the lightning strikes above these storms positively charged.

A It could be that positively charged smoke particles cause these other kinds of rare lightning, too, so this does not seriously undermine the hypothesis.

B The hypothesis is not about the power of the positive-charge lightning strikes, only about why a high proportion of them occur in thunderstorms near forest fires.

C The hypothesis is about why positive-charge strikes tend to occur in smoky areas near forest fires that have already started before the strikes occur. Furthermore, an equal likelihood of positive-charge and negative-charge strikes starting fires cannot explain a correlation between fires and positive-charge strikes specifically.

D **Correct.** This means that even when drifting clouds of smoke persist for weeks after a fire, when the charge of their particles has already dissipated, the smoke somehow still makes the strikes positively charged in any thunderstorms arising within it. If so, some factor other than positively charged smoke particles must affect the strikes' charge.

E This information does not undermine the hypothesis. The hypothesis does not concern the possibility that there might be more lightning strikes in the vicinity of forest fires; rather it concerns the proportion of all such lightning strikes that are positively charged.

The correct answer is D.

180. Many gardeners believe that the variety of clematis vine that is most popular among gardeners in North America is *jackmanii*. This belief is apparently correct since, of the one million clematis plants sold per year by the largest clematis nursery in North America, ten percent are *jackmanii*.

Which of the following is an assumption on which the argument depends?

(A) The nursery sells more than ten different varieties of clematis.

(B) The largest clematis nursery in North America sells nothing but clematis plants.

(C) Some of the *jackmanii* sold by the nursery are sold to gardeners outside North America.

(D) Most North American gardeners grow clematis in their gardens.

(E) For all nurseries in North America that specialize in clematis, at least ten percent of the clematis plants they sell are *jackmanii*.

Argument Construction

Situation Of the clematis plants sold by the largest clematis nursery in North America, 10 percent are *jackmanii*, which many gardeners believe to be the most popular variety of clematis in North America.

Reasoning *What must be true in order for the fact that 10 percent of the clematis sold at the nursery are* jackmanii *to provide evidence that jackmanii is the most popular variety of clematis in North America?* The argument assumes that sales of different varieties of clematis at the nursery reflect the relative levels of popularity of those varieties among North American gardeners. It also assumes that *jackmanii* is the best-selling clematis variety at the nursery, an assumption which requires that less than 10 percent of the nursery's clematis sales are of any one variety other than *jackmanii*.

A **Correct.** Suppose the nursery sold ten or fewer varieties of clematis. Then at least one variety other than *jackmanii* would have to account for at least 10 percent of the nursery's clematis sales, so *jackmanii* would not be the best-selling clematis variety at the nursery as the argument assumes.

B The argument only concerns how popular *jackmanii* is relative to other varieties of clematis, not relative to any plants other than clematis that the nursery may sell.

C If anything, this would weaken the argument by suggesting that the nursery's *jackmanii* sales might reflect *jackmanii*'s popularity outside North America more than its popularity within North America.

D This would indicate that clematis is a popular plant among North American gardeners, not that *jackmanii* is the most popular variety of clematis.

E Even if *jackmanii* accounts for less than 10 percent of clematis sales at a few individual nurseries, it may still account for 10 percent or more of North American clematis sales overall.

The correct answer is A.

181. Since 1990 the percentage of bacterial sinus infections in Aqadestan that are resistant to the antibiotic perxicillin has increased substantially. Bacteria can quickly develop resistance to an antibiotic when it is prescribed indiscriminately or when patients fail to take it as prescribed. Since perxicillin has not been indiscriminately prescribed, health officials hypothesize that the increase in perxicillin-resistant sinus infections is largely due to patients' failure to take this medication as prescribed.

Which of the following, if true of Aqadestan, provides most support for the health officials' hypothesis?

(A) Resistance to several other commonly prescribed antibiotics has not increased since 1990 in Aqadestan.

(B) A large number of Aqadestanis never seek medical help when they have a sinus infection.

(C) When it first became available, perxicillin was much more effective in treating bacterial sinus infections than any other antibiotic used for such infections at the time.

(D) Many patients who take perxicillin experience severe side effects within the first few days of their prescribed regimen.

(E) Aqadestani health clinics provide antibiotics to their patients at cost.

Argument Construction

Situation In Aqadestan the percentage of bacterial sinus infections resistant to the antibiotic perxicillin has been increasing even though perxicillin has not been indiscriminately prescribed.

Reasoning *What evidence most strongly suggests that the main reason perxicillin-resistant sinus infections are becoming more common is that patients are failing to take perxicillin as prescribed?* Any evidence suggesting that patients have in fact been failing to take perxicillin as prescribed would support the hypothesis, as would any evidence casting doubt on other possible explanations for the increasing proportion of perxicillin-resistant sinus infections.

A This suggests that some factor specific to perxicillin is increasing bacterial resistance to it, but that could be true whether or not the factor is patients' failure to take perxicillin as prescribed.

B If anything, this weakens the argument by suggesting that most people with sinus infections are never prescribed perxicillin, and that therefore relatively few people are getting prescriptions and then failing to follow them.

C The relative effectiveness of perxicillin when it first became available does not suggest that the reason it is now becoming less effective is that many patients are failing to take it as prescribed.

D **Correct.** These side effects would discourage patients from taking perxicillin as prescribed, so their existence provides evidence that many patients are not taking it as prescribed.

E If the clinics do not charge extra for perxicillin, that would make it more affordable and hence easier for many patients to take as prescribed.

The correct answer is D.

182. Psychologist: In a study, researchers gave 100 volunteers a psychological questionnaire designed to measure their self-esteem. The researchers then asked each volunteer to rate the strength of his or her own social skills. The volunteers with the highest levels of self-esteem consistently rated themselves as having much better social skills than did the volunteers with moderate levels. This suggests that attaining an exceptionally high level of self-esteem greatly improves one's social skills.

The psychologist's argument is most vulnerable to criticism on which of the following grounds?

(A) It fails to adequately address the possibility that many of the volunteers may not have understood what the psychological questionnaire was designed to measure.

(B) It takes for granted that the volunteers with the highest levels of self-esteem had better social skills than did the other volunteers, even before the former volunteers had attained their high levels of self-esteem.

(C) It overlooks the possibility that people with very high levels of self-esteem may tend to have a less accurate perception of the strength of their own social skills than do people with moderate levels of self-esteem.

(D) It relies on evidence from a group of volunteers that is too small to provide any support for any inferences regarding people in general.

(E) It overlooks the possibility that factors other than level of self-esteem may be of much greater importance in determining the strength of one's social skills.

Argument Evaluation

Situation In a psychological study of 100 volunteers, those found to have the highest self-esteem consistently rated themselves as having much better social skills than did those found to have moderate self-esteem.

Reasoning *What is wrong with the psychologist citing the study's results to justify the conclusion that exceptionally high self-esteem greatly improves social skills?* The psychologist reasons that the study shows a correlation between very high self-esteem and how highly one rates one's social skills, and that this correlation in turn suggests that very high self-esteem improves social skills. This argument is vulnerable to at least two criticisms: First, the argument assumes that the volunteers' ratings of their own social skills are generally accurate. But very high self-esteem might in many cases result from a tendency to overestimate oneself and one's skills, including one's social skills. Second, the argument fails to address the possibility that good social skills promote high self-esteem rather than vice versa, as well as the possibility that some third factor (such as a sunny disposition or fortunate circumstances) promotes both high self-esteem and good social skills.

A An experiment's subjects do not have to understand the experiment's design in order for the experimental results to be accurate.

B To the contrary, the argument concludes that the volunteers with the highest self-esteem attained their enhanced social skills as a result of attaining such high self-esteem.

C **Correct.** As explained above, very high self-esteem may often result from a tendency to overestimate oneself in general, and thus to overestimate one's social skills.

D A group of 100 volunteers is large enough for an experiment to provide at least a little support for at least some inferences regarding people in general.

E As explained above, the argument overlooks the possibility that some third factor may play a significant role in determining the strength of one's social skills. But even if some factor other than self-esteem is more important in determining the strength of social skills, that would still be compatible with very high self-esteem being of some importance in improving one's social skills.

The correct answer is C.

183. A product that represents a clear technological advance over competing products can generally command a high price. Because **technological advances tend to be quickly surpassed** and companies want to make large profits while they still can, **many companies charge the maximum possible price for such a product**. But large profits on the new product will give competitors a strong incentive to quickly match the new product's capabilities. Consequently, the strategy to maximize overall profit from a new product is to charge less than the greatest possible price.

In the argument above, the two portions in **boldface** play which of the following roles?

(A) The first is a consideration raised to argue that a certain strategy is counterproductive; the second presents that strategy.

(B) The first is a consideration raised to support the strategy that the argument recommends; the second presents that strategy.

(C) The first is a consideration raised to help explain the popularity of a certain strategy; the second presents that strategy.

(D) The first is an assumption, rejected by the argument, that has been used to justify a course of action; the second presents that course of action.

(E) The first is a consideration that has been used to justify adopting a certain strategy; the second presents the intended outcome of that strategy.

Argument Construction

Situation Often, when a company comes out with an innovative product, it will price the product as high as it can to maximize profits before the competitors quickly catch up. But this is not a good strategy because the very high price of the new product only encourages competitors to match the technological advance more quickly.

Reasoning *Which option best describes the roles that the boldface portions play in the argument?* This type of item concerns only the argument's structure—the way it is intended to work, not the quality of the argument or what might strengthen or weaken the argument. So even if a boldface portion could be used by the argument in a certain way, all that matters is its actual intended role. The fact that *technological advances tend to be quickly surpassed* serves to partly explain why *many companies charge the maximum possible price for such a product*. In other words, the first boldface portion helps explain the popularity of the strategy presented in the second boldface portion. The conclusion of the argument, however, is that the strategy exemplified in this latter boldface portion is unwise, so the argument as a whole opposes that strategy.

A Although the first boldface portion could be used as part of an argument that the strategy presented in the second boldface portion is counterproductive, that is not how it is used here. Rather, it immediately follows the word *because* and serves to explain the occurrence of what is described in the second boldface portion.

B This is clearly wrong because the second boldface portion presents the strategy that the argument opposes.

C **Correct.** It is the only choice that is consistent with the analysis of the reasoning presented above.

D The first boldface portion is not an assumption rejected by the argument; rather, it is affirmed in the argument.

E The argument does not expressly claim that the first boldface portion has been used to justify the strategy of setting the price as high as possible, although it implies that this is part of the justification that those adopting the strategy would give. More clearly, the second boldface portion does not describe the intended outcome of the strategy, but rather the means of bringing about that intended outcome (maximizing profits, by means of high prices).

The correct answer is C.

184. Gortland has long been narrowly self-sufficient in both grain and meat. However, as per capita income in Gortland has risen toward the world average, per capita consumption of meat has also risen toward the world average, and it takes several pounds of grain to produce one pound of meat. Therefore, since per capita income continues to rise, whereas domestic grain production will not increase, Gortland will soon have to import either grain or meat or both.

Which of the following is an assumption on which the argument depends?

(A) The total acreage devoted to grain production in Gortland will not decrease substantially.

(B) The population of Gortland has remained relatively constant during the country's years of growing prosperity.

(C) The per capita consumption of meat in Gortland is roughly the same across all income levels.

(D) In Gortland, neither meat nor grain is subject to government price controls.

(E) People in Gortland who increase their consumption of meat will not radically decrease their consumption of grain.

Argument Construction

Situation A country previously self-sufficient in grain and meat will soon have to import one or the other or both because its consumption of meat has risen as per capita income has risen. It takes several pounds of grain to produce one pound of meat.

Reasoning *What conditions must be true for the conclusion to be true?* Meat consumption is rising. What about grain consumption? A sharp reduction in the amount of grain directly consumed by meat eaters could compensate for increased meat consumption, making the conclusion false. If people did radically decrease their grain consumption, it might not be necessary to import grain or meat. Since the argument concludes that the imports are necessary, it assumes that direct consumption of grain by those who begin to eat meat will not plunge.

A The argument makes no assumptions about the acreage devoted to grain; it assumes only that the demand for grain will rise.

B The argument is based on rising per capita income, not population levels.

C The argument involves only meat consumption in general, not its distribution by income level.

D Since the argument does not refer to price controls, it cannot depend on an assumption about them.

E **Correct.** This statement properly identifies the assumption that those who begin to eat meat do not then greatly decrease their direct consumption of grains.

The correct answer is E.

185. Political Advertisement:

Mayor Delmont's critics complain about the jobs that were lost in the city under Delmont's leadership. Yet the fact is that not only were more jobs created than were eliminated, but each year since Delmont took office the average pay for the new jobs created has been higher than that year's average pay for jobs citywide. So it stands to reason that throughout Delmont's tenure the average paycheck in this city has been getting steadily bigger.

Which of the following, if true, most seriously weakens the argument in the advertisement?

(A) The unemployment rate in the city is higher today than it was when Mayor Delmont took office.

(B) The average pay for jobs in the city was at a ten-year low when Mayor Delmont took office.

(C) Each year during Mayor Delmont's tenure, the average pay for jobs that were eliminated has been higher than the average pay for jobs citywide.

(D) Most of the jobs eliminated during Mayor Delmont's tenure were in declining industries.

(E) The average pay for jobs in the city is currently lower than it is for jobs in the suburbs surrounding the city.

Argument Evaluation

Situation Every year since Mayor Delmont took office, average pay for new jobs has exceeded average pay for jobs citywide. So, the average paycheck in the city has been increasing since Delmont took office.

Reasoning *Which option, if true, would most seriously weaken the argument?* If average pay for new jobs continually exceeds that for jobs generally, new jobs pay better (on average) than old jobs that still exist. But suppose the following occurred. Every year all of the highest paying jobs are eliminated and replaced with somewhat lower-paying jobs that still pay more than the average job. The result would be that every year the average pay for a new job would be greater than that for existing jobs, but the average pay for all jobs would nonetheless decrease. Thus, if every year during the mayor's tenure the jobs that were eliminated paid better on average than jobs citywide, that would seriously weaken the argument: the conclusion could be false even if the information on which it is based is true.

A The percentage of people in the city who have a job has no direct bearing on whether the average pay for jobs citywide is increasing or decreasing.

B Whether the average pay was low when the mayor took office in comparison to the ten preceding years is immaterial to the comparison addressed in the argument's conclusion.

C Correct. This information weakens the argument because it opens up the possibility that the jobs eliminated had higher average pay than the jobs created during Mayor Delmont's tenure. This in turn would mean that the average pay was not increasing during Mayor Delmont's tenure.

D This, too, has no bearing on the argument, because we have no information about the average pay for jobs in those declining industries.

E This is also irrelevant. No comparison is made (or implied) in the argument between jobs in the city and jobs in the suburbs.

The correct answer is C.

186. To prevent a newly built dam on the Chiff River from blocking the route of fish migrating to breeding grounds upstream, the dam includes a fish pass, a mechanism designed to allow fish through the dam. Before the construction of the dam and fish pass, several thousand fish a day swam upriver during spawning season. But in the first season after the project's completion, only 300 per day made the journey. Clearly, the fish pass is defective.

Which of the following, if true, most seriously weakens the argument?

(A) Fish that have migrated to the upstream breeding grounds do not return down the Chiff River again.

(B) On other rivers in the region, the construction of dams with fish passes has led to only small decreases in the number of fish migrating upstream.

(C) The construction of the dam stirred up potentially toxic river sediments that were carried downstream.

(D) Populations of migratory fish in the Chiff River have been declining slightly over the last 20 years.

(E) During spawning season, the dam releases sufficient water for migratory fish below the dam to swim upstream.

Argument Evaluation

Situation A new dam includes a mechanism called a fish pass designed to allow fish to migrate upstream past the dam to their breeding grounds. The number of migrating fish fell from several thousand per day before the dam was built to three hundred per day in the first season after it was built, indicating—according to the argument—that the fish pass is defective.

Reasoning *What evidence would suggest that the fish pass is not defective?* The argument implicitly reasons that a defective fish pass would make it difficult for the fish to migrate, which would explain why the number of migrating fish fell when the dam was completed. Any evidence suggesting an alternative explanation for the reduced number of migrating fish, such as an environmental change that occurred when the dam was built, would cast doubt on the argument's reasoning.

A A defective fish pass could prevent most of the fish from migrating upstream regardless of whether those that succeed ever return downstream.

B This would suggest that dams with properly functioning fish passes do not greatly reduce the number of migrating fish, so it would provide further evidence that the fish pass in this particular dam is defective.

C **Correct.** This suggests that the toxic sediments may have poisoned the fish and reduced their population. A smaller fish population could be sufficient to explain the reduced number of fish migrating, which casts doubt on the argument's assumption that the explanation for their declining numbers involves the fish pass.

D A slight and gradual ongoing decline in migratory fish populations would not explain an abrupt and extreme decline right after the dam was built.

E This supports the argument's proposed explanation for the declining fish population by ruling out the alternative explanation that the dam does not release enough water for the fish to migrate.

The correct answer is C.

187. Music critic: Fewer and fewer musicians are studying classical music, decreasing the likelihood that those with real aptitude for such music will be performing it. Audiences who hear these performances will not appreciate classical music's greatness and will thus decamp to other genres. So to maintain classical music's current meager popularity, we must encourage more young musicians to enter the field.

Which of the following, if true, most weakens the music critic's reasoning?

(A) Musicians who choose to study classical music do so because they believe they have an aptitude for the music.

(B) Classical music's current meager popularity is attributable to the profusion of other genres of music available to listeners.

(C) Most people who appreciate classical music come to do so through old recordings rather than live performances.

(D) It is possible to enjoy the music in a particular genre even when it is performed by musicians who are not ideally suited for that genre.

(E) The continued popularity of a given genre of music depends in part on the audience's being able to understand why that genre attained its original popularity.

Argument Evaluation

Situation Fewer musicians are studying classical music. This reduces the likelihood that those performing the music will have real aptitude for it, which in turn reduces audience's appreciation of classical music performances.

Reasoning *What evidence would cast the most doubt on the support provided for the conclusion that encouraging more young musicians to study classical music is necessary in order to maintain the genre's meager popularity?* The music critic's argument is that because fewer talented classical musicians are performing, audiences hearing their performances will fail to appreciate the genre, and thus will abandon it. The critic reasons that to solve this problem, it will be necessary to encourage more young musicians to study classical music so that audiences will eventually be exposed to more talented classical performers and decide the genre is worthwhile after all. The argument would be weakened, for example, by evidence that hearing unremarkable live performances does not really drive many people away from classical music, or that the number of audience members hearing great performances does not depend much on the number of talented performers, or that encouraging young musicians to study classical music is either ineffective or not the only effective way to increase the number of talented classical performers.

A This does not weaken the critic's reasoning. However much confidence musicians studying classical music have in their own talent, a decline in the total number of classical musicians will probably result in a decline in the number of truly talented classical musicians, just as the critic assumes.

B The critic is only proposing a way to at least maintain classical music's current meager popularity, which might be accomplished even if the profusion of other genres prevents classical music's popularity from increasing.

C **Correct.** This suggests that classical music's meager popularity could at least be maintained by encouraging people to listen to great old recordings of classical music rather than by increasing the supply of great live performances.

D This does weaken the argument slightly. But even if a few audience members manage to enjoy mediocre classical music performances, they might still be more strongly drawn to other genres with more talented performers.

E Listeners exposed to more impressive live performances of classical music by talented performers would probably better understand why classical music was once popular than would listeners exposed only to mediocre classical performances.

The correct answer is C.

188. Commemorative plaques cast from brass are a characteristic art form of the Benin culture of West Africa. Some scholars, noting that the oldest surviving plaques date to the 1400s, hypothesize that brass-casting techniques were introduced by the Portuguese, who came to Benin in 1485 A.D. But Portuguese records of that expedition mention cast-brass jewelry sent to Benin's king from neighboring Ife. So it is unlikely that Benin's knowledge of brass casting derived from the Portuguese.

Which of the following, if true, most strengthens the argument?

(A) The Portuguese records do not indicate whether their expedition of 1485 included metalworkers.
(B) The Portuguese had no contact with Ife until the 1500s.
(C) In the 1400s the Portuguese did not use cast brass for commemorative plaques.
(D) As early as 1500 A.D., Benin artists were making brass plaques incorporating depictions of Europeans.
(E) Copper, which is required for making brass, can be found throughout Benin territory.

Argument Construction

Situation The oldest surviving cast-brass plaques from the Benin culture date to the 1400s. Records of a Portuguese expedition to Benin in 1485 mention cast-brass jewelry sent to Benin's king from neighboring Ife.

Reasoning *What additional evidence, when combined with the argument's premises, would most help support the conclusion that Benin's knowledge of brass casting did not derive from the Portuguese?* The argument is that since the expedition records indicate that cast-brass jewelry from Ife was already known in Benin when the Portuguese first came there, Benin's knowledge of brass casting probably did not derive from the Portuguese. This argument assumes that receiving the brass-cast jewelry from Ife could have transmitted knowledge of brass casting to Benin, and also that knowledge of brass casting in Ife did not itself derive from the Portuguese. Any evidence supporting either of these assumptions would strengthen the argument.

A This is compatible with a Portuguese origin for brass-casting in Benin. The expedition might well have included metalworkers even if the records do not mention whether it did. Furthermore, other Portuguese expeditions with metalworkers might have quickly followed the initial expedition.

B **Correct.** If the Portuguese had no contact with Ife before 1500, then Ife's earlier knowledge of brass casting did not derive directly from the Portuguese. This increases the likelihood that knowledge of brass-casting in Benin did not derive from the Portuguese, even if it derived from Ife.

C This is compatible with a Portuguese origin for brass-casting in Benin. Even if the Portuguese did not use cast brass for commemorative plaques, they could have used it for jewelry or other items they brought to Benin or manufactured there, and thus they could have transmitted the knowledge to the Benin culture.

D This leaves open the possibility that the Benin culture learned about brass casting from the Portuguese in 1485 and started using it to produce plaques of this type by 1500.

E Even if copper has always been common in the Benin territory, brass-casting techniques could have been introduced by the Portuguese.

The correct answer is B.

5.0 Sentence Correction

5.0 Sentence Correction

Sentence correction questions appear in the Verbal section of the GMAT® exam. The Verbal section uses multiple-choice questions to measure your ability to read and comprehend written material, to reason and evaluate arguments, and to correct written material to conform to standard written English. Because the Verbal section includes passages from several different content areas, you may be generally familiar with some of the material; however, neither the passages nor the questions assume detailed knowledge of the topics discussed. Sentence correction questions are intermingled with critical reasoning and reading comprehension questions throughout the Verbal section of the test. You will have 75 minutes to complete the Verbal section or about 1¾ minutes to answer each question.

Sentence correction questions present a statement in which words are underlined. The questions ask you to select the best expression of the idea or relationship described in the underlined section from the answer options. The first answer choice always repeats the original phrasing, whereas the other four provide alternatives. In some cases, the original phrasing is the best choice. In other cases, the underlined section has obvious or subtle errors that require correction. These questions require you to be familiar with the stylistic conventions and grammatical rules of standard written English and to demonstrate your ability to improve incorrect or ineffective expressions.

You should begin these questions by reading the sentence carefully. Note whether there are any obvious grammatical errors as you read the underlined section. Then read the five answer choices carefully. If there was a subtle error you did not recognize the first time you read the sentence, it may become apparent after you have read the answer choices. If the error is still unclear, see whether you can eliminate some of the answers as being incorrect. Remember that in some cases, the original selection may be the best answer.

5.1 Basic English Grammar Rules

Sentence correction questions ask you to recognize and potentially correct at least one of the following grammar rules. However, these rules are not exhaustive. If you are interested in learning more about English grammar as a way to prepare for the GMAT exam, there are several resources available on the Internet.

Agreement

Standard English requires elements within a sentence to be consistent. There are two types of agreement: noun-verb and pronoun.

Noun-verb agreement: Singular subjects take singular verbs, whereas plural subjects take plural verbs.
Examples:
Correct: "I walk to the store." Incorrect: "I walks to the store."
Correct: "We go to school." Incorrect: "We goes to school."
Correct: "The number of residents has grown." Incorrect: "The number of residents have grown."
Correct: "The masses have spoken." Incorrect: "The masses has spoken."

Pronoun agreement: A pronoun must agree with the noun or pronoun it refers to in person, number, and gender.
Examples:
Correct: "When you dream, you are usually asleep." Incorrect: "When one dreams, you are usually asleep."
Correct: "When the kids went to sleep, they slept like logs."
Incorrect: "When the kids went to sleep, he slept like a log."

Diction

Words should be chosen to reflect correctly and effectively the appropriate part of speech. There are several words that are commonly used incorrectly. When answering sentence correction questions, pay attention to the following conventions.

Among/between: Among is used to refer to relationships involving more than two objects. *Between* is used to refer to relationships involving only two objects.
Examples:
Correct: "We divided our winnings among the three of us." Incorrect: "We divided our winnings between the three of us."
Correct: "She and I divided the cake between us." Incorrect: "She and I divided the cake among us."

As/like: As can be a preposition meaning "in the capacity of," but more often is a conjunction of manner and is followed by a verb. *Like* is generally used as a preposition and therefore is followed by a noun, an object pronoun, or a verb ending in *ing.*
Examples:
Correct: "I work as a librarian." Incorrect: "I work like a librarian."
Correct: "Do as I say, not as I do." Incorrect: "Do like I say, not like I do."
Correct: "It felt like a dream." Incorrect: "It felt as a dream."
Correct: "People like you inspire me." Incorrect: "People as you inspire me."
Correct: "There's nothing like biking on a warm, autumn day." Incorrect: "There's nothing as biking on a warm autumn day."

Mass and count words: Mass words are nouns quantified by an amount rather than by a number. *Count* nouns can be quantified by a number.
Examples:
Correct: "We bought a loaf of bread." Incorrect: "We bought one bread."
Correct: "He wished me much happiness." Incorrect: "He wished me many happinesses."
Correct: "We passed many buildings." Incorrect: "We passed much buildings."

Pronouns: Myself should not be used as a substitute for *I* or *me.*
Examples:
Correct: "Mom and I had to go to the store." Incorrect: "Mom and myself had to go to the store."
Correct: "He gave the present to Dad and me." Incorrect: "He gave the present to Dad and myself."

Grammatical Construction

Good grammar requires complete sentences. Be on the lookout for improperly formed constructions.

Fragments: Parts of a sentence that are disconnected from the main clause are called fragments.
Example:
Correct: "We saw the doctor and his nurse at the party." Incorrect: "We saw the doctor at the party. And his nurse."

Run-on sentences: A run-on sentence is two or more independent clauses that run together without proper punctuation.
Examples:
Correct: "Jose Canseco is still a feared batter; most pitchers don't want to face him." Incorrect: "Jose Canseco is still a feared batter most pitchers don't want to face him."

Constructions: Avoid wordy, redundant constructions.
Example:
Correct: "We could not come to the meeting because of a conflict." Incorrect: "The reason we could not come to the meeting is because of a conflict."

Idiom

It is important to avoid nonstandard expressions, although English idioms sometimes do not follow conventional grammatical rules. Be careful to use the correct idiom when using the constructions and parts of speech.

Prepositions: Specific prepositions have specific purposes.
Examples:
Correct: "She likes to jog in the morning." Incorrect: "She likes to jog on the morning."
Correct: "They ranged in age from 10 to 15." Incorrect: "They ranged in age from 10 up to 15."

Correlatives: Word combinations such as "not only . . . but also" should be followed by an element of the same grammatical type.
Examples:
Correct: "I have called not only to thank her but also to tell her about the next meeting."
Incorrect: "I have called not only to thank her but also I told her about the next meeting."

Forms of comparison: Many forms follow precise constructions. *Fewer* refers to a specific number, whereas *less than* refers to a continuous quantity. *Between . . . and* is the correct form to designate a choice. *Farther* refers to distance, whereas *further* refers to degree.
Examples:
Correct: "There were fewer children in my class this year." Incorrect: "There were less children in my class this year."
Correct: "There was less devastation than I was told." Incorrect: "There was fewer devastation than I was told."
Correct: "We had to choose between chocolate and vanilla." Incorrect: "We had to choose between chocolate or vanilla." (It is also correct to say, "We had to choose chocolate or vanilla.")
Correct: "I ran farther than John, but he took his weight training further than I did." Incorrect: "I ran further than John, but he took his weight training farther than I did."

Logical Predication

Watch out for phrases that detract from the logical argument.

Modification problems: Modifiers should be positioned so it is clear what word or words they are meant to modify. If modifiers are not positioned clearly, they can cause illogical references or comparisons or distort the meaning of the statement.

Examples:
Correct: "I put the cake that I baked by the door." Incorrect: "I put the cake by the door that I baked."
Correct: "Reading my mind, she gave me the delicious cookie." Incorrect: "Reading my mind, the cookie she gave me was delicious."
Correct: "In the Middle Ages, the world was believed to be flat." Incorrect: "In the Middle Ages, the world was flat."

Parallelism

Constructing a sentence that is parallel in structure depends on making sure that the different elements in the sentence balance each other; this is a little bit like making sure that the two sides of a mathematical equation are balanced. To make sure that a sentence is grammatically correct, check to ensure that phrases, clauses, verbs, and other sentence elements parallel each other.

Examples:
Correct: "I took a bath, went to sleep, and woke up refreshed." Incorrect: "I took a bath, sleeping, and waking up refreshed."
Correct: "The only way to know is to take the plunge." Incorrect: "The only way to know is taking the plunge."

Rhetorical Construction

Good sentence structure avoids constructions that are awkward, wordy, redundant, imprecise, or unclear, even when they are free of grammatical errors.

Example:
Correct: "Before we left on vacation, we watered the plants, checked to see that the stove was off, and set the burglar alarm." Incorrect: "Before we left to go on our vacation, we watered, checked to be sure that the stove had been turned off, and set it."

Verb Form

In addition to watching for problems of agreement or parallelism, make sure that verbs are used in the correct tense. Be alert to whether a verb should reflect past, present, or future tense.

Example:
Correct: "I went to school yesterday." "I go to school every weekday." "I will go to school tomorrow."

Each tense also has a perfect form (used with the past participle—e.g., walked, ran), a progressive form (used with the present participle—e.g., walking, running), and a perfect progressive form (also used with the present participle—e.g., walking, running).

Present perfect: Used with *has* or *have,* the present perfect tense describes an action that occurred at an indefinite time in the past or that began in the past and continues into the present.
Examples:
Correct: "I have traveled all over the world." (at an indefinite time)
Correct: "He has gone to school since he was five years old." (continues into the present)

Past perfect: This verb form is used with *had* to show the order of two events that took place in the past.
Example:
Correct: "By the time I left for school, the cake had been baked."

Future perfect: Used with *will have,* this verb form describes an event in the future that will precede another event.
Example:
Correct: "By the end of the day, I will have studied for all my tests."

Present progressive: Used with *am, is,* or *are,* this verb form describes an ongoing action that is happening now.
Example:
Correct: "I am studying for exams." "The student is studying for exams." "We are studying for exams."

Past progressive: Used with *was* or *were,* this verb form describes something that was happening when another action occurred.
Example:
Correct: "The student was studying when the fire alarm rang." "They were studying when the fire broke out."

Future progressive: Used with *will be* or *shall be,* this verb tense describes an ongoing action that will continue into the future.
Example:
Correct: "The students will be studying for exams throughout the month of December."

Present perfect progressive: Used with *have been* or *has been*, this verb tense describes something that began in the past, continues into the present, and may continue into the future.
Example:
Correct: "The student has been studying hard in the hope of acing the test."

Past perfect progressive: Used with *had been,* this verb form describes an action of some duration that was completed before another past action occurred.
Example:
Correct: "Before the fire alarm rang, the student had been studying."

Future perfect progressive: Used with *will have been*, this verb form describes a future, ongoing action that will occur before a specified time.
Example:
Correct: "By the end of next year, the students will have been studying math for five years."

5.2 Study Suggestions

There are two basic ways you can study for sentence correction questions:

- **Read material that reflects standard usage.**
One way to gain familiarity with the basic conventions of standard written English is simply to read. Suitable material will usually be found in good magazines and nonfiction books, editorials in outstanding newspapers, and the collections of essays used by many college and university writing courses.

- **Review basic rules of grammar and practice with writing exercises.**
Begin by reviewing the grammar rules laid out in this chapter. Then, if you have school assignments (such as essays and research papers) that have been carefully evaluated for grammatical errors, it may be helpful to review the comments and corrections.

5.3 What Is Measured

Sentence correction questions test three broad aspects of language proficiency:

- **Correct expression**
A correct sentence is grammatically and structurally sound. It conforms to all the rules of standard written English, including noun-verb agreement, noun-pronoun agreement, pronoun consistency, pronoun case, and verb tense sequence. A correct sentence will not have dangling, misplaced, or improperly formed modifiers; unidiomatic or inconsistent expressions; or faults in parallel construction.

- **Effective expression**
An effective sentence expresses an idea or relationship clearly and concisely as well as grammatically. This does not mean that the choice with the fewest and simplest words is necessarily the best answer. It means that there are no superfluous words or needlessly complicated expressions in the best choice.

- **Proper diction**
An effective sentence also uses proper diction. (Diction refers to the standard dictionary meanings of words and the appropriateness of words in context.) In evaluating the diction of a sentence, you must be able to recognize whether the words are well chosen, accurate, and suitable for the context.

5.4 Test-Taking Strategies

1. **Read the entire sentence carefully.**
Try to understand the specific idea or relationship that the sentence should express.

2. **Evaluate the underlined passage for errors and possible corrections before reading the answer choices.**
This strategy will help you discriminate among the answer choices. Remember, in some cases the underlined passage is correct.

3. **Read each answer choice carefully**
   The first answer choice always repeats the underlined portion of the original sentence. Choose this answer if you think that the sentence is best as originally written, but do so only after examining all the other choices.

4. **Try to determine how to correct what you consider to be wrong with the original sentence.**
   Some of the answer choices may change things that are not wrong, whereas others may not change everything that is wrong.

5. **Make sure that you evaluate the sentence and the choices thoroughly.**
   Pay attention to general clarity, grammatical and idiomatic usage, economy and precision of language, and appropriateness of diction.

6. **Read the whole sentence, substituting the choice that you prefer for the underlined passage.**
   A choice may be wrong because it does not fit grammatically or structurally with the rest of the sentence. Remember that some sentences will require no correction. When the given sentence requires no correction, choose the first answer.

5.5 The Directions

These are the directions that you will see for sentence correction questions when you take the GMAT exam. If you read them carefully and understand them clearly before going to sit for the test, you will not need to spend too much time reviewing them once you are at the test center and the test is under way.

Sentence correction questions present a sentence, part or all of which is underlined. Beneath the sentence, you will find five ways of phrasing the underlined passage. The first answer choice repeats the original underlined passage; the other four are different. If you think the original phrasing is best, choose the first answer; otherwise, choose one of the others.

This type of question tests your ability to recognize the correctness and effectiveness of expression in standard written English. In choosing your answer, follow the requirements of standard written English; that is, pay attention to grammar, choice of words, and sentence construction. Choose the answer that produces the most effective sentence; this answer should be clear and exact, without awkwardness, ambiguity, redundancy, or grammatical error.

5.6 Sample Questions

Each of the sentence correction questions presents a sentence, part of or all of which is underlined. Beneath the sentence you will find five ways of phrasing the underlined part. The first of these repeats the original; the other four are different. Follow the requirements of standard written English to choose your answer, paying attention to grammar, word choice, and sentence construction. Select the answer that produces the most effective sentence; your answer should make the sentence clear, exact, and free of grammatical error. It should also minimize awkwardness, ambiguity, and redundancy.

189. Using digital enhancements of skull fragments from five prehistoric hominids dating to more than 350,000 years ago, anthropologists argue that these human ancestors probably had hearing similar to that of people today.

    (A) anthropologists argue that these human ancestors
    (B) anthropologists argue, so these human ancestors
    (C) anthropologists argue, these human ancestors
    (D) these human ancestors, anthropologists argue,
    (E) these human ancestors are argued by anthropologists to have

190. The interior minister explained that one of the village planning proposal's best characteristics was their not detracting from the project's overall benefit by being a burden on the development budget.

    (A) one of the village planning proposal's best characteristics was their not detracting
    (B) one of the village's planning proposal's best characteristics were its not taking
    (C) one of the best characteristics of the village's planning proposal was that it did not detract
    (D) a best characteristic of the village planning proposal was, it did not take
    (E) among the village planning proposal's best characteristics, one was, it did not detract

191. Like ants, termites have an elaborate social structure in which a few individuals reproduce and the rest are serving the colony by tending juveniles, gathering food, building the nest, or they battle intruders.

    (A) are serving the colony by tending juveniles, gathering food, building the nest, or they battle
    (B) are serving the colony in that they tend juveniles, gather food, build the nest, or battle
    (C) serve the colony, tending juveniles, gathering food, building the nest, or by battling
    (D) serve the colony by tending juveniles, gathering food, by building the nest, or by battling
    (E) serve the colony by tending juveniles, gathering food, building the nest, or battling

192. Global warming is said to be responsible for extreme weather changes, which, like the heavy rains that caused more than $2 billion in damages and led to flooding throughout the state of California, and the heat wave in the northeastern and midwestern United States, which was also the cause of a great amount of damage and destruction.

    (A) which, like the heavy rains that caused more than $2 billion in damages and led to flooding throughout the state of California,
    (B) which, like the heavy rains that throughout the state of California caused more than $2 billion in damages and led to flooding,
    (C) like the heavy flooding that, because of rains throughout the state of California, caused more than $2 billion in damages,
    (D) such as the heavy flooding that led to rains throughout the state of California causing more than $2 billion in damages,
    (E) such as the heavy rains that led to flooding throughout the state of California, causing more than $2 billion in damages,

193. The voluminous personal papers of Thomas Alva Edison reveal that his inventions typically sprang to life not in a flash of inspiration but evolved slowly from previous works.

(A) sprang to life not in a flash of inspiration but evolved slowly

(B) sprang to life not in a flash of inspiration but were slowly evolved

(C) did not spring to life in a flash of inspiration but evolved slowly

(D) did not spring to life in a flash of inspiration but had slowly evolved

(E) did not spring to life in a flash of inspiration but they were slowly evolved

194. Hundreds of species of fish generate and discharge electric currents, in bursts or as steady electric fields around their bodies, using their power either to find and attack prey, to defend themselves, or also for communicating and navigating.

(A) either to find and attack prey, to defend themselves, or also for communicating and navigating

(B) either for finding and attacking prey, defend themselves, or for communication and navigation

(C) to find and attack prey, for defense, or communication and navigation

(D) for finding and attacking prey, to defend themselves, or also for communication and navigation

(E) to find and attack prey, to defend themselves, or to communicate and navigate

195. Native to South America, when peanuts were introduced to Africa by Portuguese explorers early in the sixteenth century they were quickly adopted into Africa's agriculture, probably because of being so similar to the Bambarra groundnut, a popular indigenous plant.

(A) when peanuts were introduced to Africa by Portuguese explorers early in the sixteenth century they were quickly adopted into Africa's agriculture, probably because of being

(B) peanuts having been introduced to Africa by Portuguese explorers early in the sixteenth century and quickly adopted into Africa's agriculture, probably because of being

(C) peanuts were introduced to Africa by Portuguese explorers early in the sixteenth century and were quickly adopted into Africa's agriculture, probably because they were

(D) peanuts, introduced to Africa by Portuguese explorers early in the sixteenth century and quickly adopted into Africa's agriculture, probably because they were

(E) peanuts, introduced to Africa by Portuguese explorers early in the sixteenth century and having been quickly adopted into Africa's agriculture, probably because they were

196. It stood twelve feet tall, weighed nine thousand pounds, and wielded seven-inch claws, and *Megatherium americanum*, a giant ground sloth, may have been the largest hunting mammal ever to walk the Earth.

(A) It stood twelve feet tall, weighed nine thousand pounds, and wielded seven-inch claws, and *Megatherium americanum*, a giant ground sloth,

(B) It stood twelve feet tall, weighing nine thousand pounds, and wielding seven-inch claws, *Megatherium americanum* was a giant ground sloth and

(C) The giant ground sloth *Megatherium americanum*, having stood twelve feet tall, weighing nine thousand pounds, and wielding seven-inch claws, it

(D) Standing twelve feet tall, weighing nine thousand pounds, and wielding seven-inch claws, *Megatherium americanum*, a giant ground sloth,

(E) Standing twelve feet tall, weighing nine thousand pounds, it wielded seven-inch claws, and the giant ground sloth *Megatherium americanum*

197. Delighted by the reported earnings for the first quarter of the fiscal year, it was decided by the company manager to give her staff a raise.

(A) it was decided by the company manager to give her staff a raise
(B) the decision of the company manager was to give her staff a raise
(C) the company manager decided to give her staff a raise
(D) the staff was given a raise by the company manager
(E) a raise was given to the staff by the company manager

198. Studying skeletons unearthed near Rome, DNA evidence was recovered by scientists, who were able to deduce from this that an epidemic of malaria struck in the empire's waning days.

(A) Studying skeletons unearthed near Rome, DNA evidence was recovered by scientists, who were able to deduce from this
(B) In studying skeletons unearthed near Rome, DNA evidence was recovered by scientists, who were able to deduce from this
(C) Scientists recovered DNA evidence from studying skeletons unearthed near Rome, being able to deduce from this
(D) Skeletons unearthed near Rome allowed scientists to recover DNA evidence, and they were able to deduce from it
(E) Scientists studying skeletons unearthed near Rome recovered DNA evidence from which they were able to deduce

199. Coffee prices rose sharply Monday, posting their biggest one-day gain in almost three years, after a weekend cold snap in Brazil raised concern that there could be damage to the world's largest crop when at a time with supplies already tight.

(A) that there could be damage to the world's largest crop when at a time with supplies
(B) that the world's largest crop could be damaged at a time such as when supplies are
(C) that the world's largest crop could be damaged at a time when supplies are
(D) of the world's largest crop possibly being damaged at a time with supplies
(E) of possibly damaging the world's largest crop at a time that supplies were

200. Growing competitive pressures may be encouraging auditors to bend the rules in favor of clients; auditors may, for instance, allow a questionable loan to remain on the books in order to maintain a bank's profits on paper.

(A) clients; auditors may, for instance, allow
(B) clients, as an instance, to allow
(C) clients, like to allow
(D) clients, such as to be allowing
(E) clients; which might, as an instance, be the allowing of

201. A March 2000 Census Bureau survey showed that Mexico accounted for more than a quarter of all foreign-born residents of the United States, the largest share for any country to contribute since 1890, when about 30 percent of the country's foreign-born population was from Germany.

(A) the largest share for any country to contribute
(B) the largest share that any country has contributed
(C) which makes it the largest share for any country to contribute
(D) having the largest share to be contributed by any country
(E) having the largest share to have been contributed by any country

202. Recently declassified information from military satellites in orbit thousands of miles above the Earth show the planet continually bombarded by large meteoroids that explode with the power of atomic bomb blasts.

(A) show the planet continually bombarded by

(B) show continual bombarding of the planet by

(C) show a continual bombardment of the planet from

(D) shows continually that the planet is bombarded from

(E) shows that the planet is continually bombarded by

203. The themes that Rita Dove explores in her poetry is universal, encompassing much of the human condition while occasionally she deals with racial issues.

(A) is universal, encompassing much of the human condition while occasionally she deals

(B) is universal, encompassing much of the human condition, also occasionally it deals

(C) are universal, they encompass much of the human condition and occasionally deals

(D) are universal, encompassing much of the human condition while occasionally dealing

(E) are universal, they encompass much of the human condition, also occasionally are dealing

204. Child development specialists believe that, in confining babies much of the time to strollers, high chairs, playpens, and walkers, muscle development can be inhibited.

(A) that, in confining babies much of the time to strollers, high chairs, playpens, and walkers, muscle development can be inhibited

(B) that, in their confinement much of the time to strollers, high chairs, playpens, and walkers, muscle development can be inhibited in babies

(C) that confining babies much of the time to strollers, high chairs, playpens, and walkers can inhibit muscle development

(D) that babies, if confined much of the time to strollers, high chairs, playpens, and walkers can inhibit muscle development

(E) that strollers, high chairs, playpens, and walkers can, if babies are confined to them much of the time, result in muscle development being inhibited

205. Travelers to Mars would have to endure low levels of gravity for long periods of time, avoid large doses of radiation, contend with the chemically reactive Martian soil, and perhaps even having to ward off contamination by Martian life-forms.

(A) contend with the chemically reactive Martian soil, and perhaps even having to ward

(B) contend with the chemically reactive Martian soil, and perhaps even warding

(C) contend with the chemically reactive Martian soil, and perhaps even ward

(D) contending with the chemically reactive Martian soil, and perhaps even to ward

(E) contending with the chemically reactive Martian soil, and perhaps even warding

206. The personal income tax did not become permanent in the United States until the First World War; before that time the federal government was dependent on tariffs to be their main source of revenue.

(A) the federal government was dependent on tariffs to be their main source of revenue

(B) the federal government had depended on tariffs as its main source of revenue

(C) tariffs were what the federal government was dependent on to be its main source of revenue

(D) the main source of revenue for the federal government was dependent on tariffs

(E) for their main source of revenue, tariffs were depended on by the federal government

207. In 1776 Adam Smith wrote that it is young people who have "the contempt of risk and the presumptuous hope of success" needed to found new businesses.

(A) who have

(B) with

(C) having

(D) who are those with

(E) who are the ones to have

208. The gyrfalcon, an Arctic bird of prey, has survived a close brush with extinction; its numbers are now five times greater than when the use of DDT was sharply restricted in the early 1970's.

(A) extinction; its numbers are now five times greater than

(B) extinction; its numbers are now five times more than

(C) extinction, their numbers now fivefold what they were

(D) extinction, now with fivefold the numbers they had

(E) extinction, now with numbers five times greater than

209. In his *Uses of Enchantment* (1976), it was psychologist Bruno Bettelheim's assertion that the apparently cruel and arbitrary nature of many fairy tales actually are an instructive reflection of a child's natural and necessary "killing off" of successive phases in his or her own development.

(A) it was psychologist Bruno Bettelheim's assertion that the apparently cruel and arbitrary nature of many fairy tales actually are

(B) it was the assertion of psychologist Bruno Bettelheim that what is apparently the cruel and arbitrary nature of many fairy tales actually is

(C) psychologist Bruno Bettelheim's assertion that what is apparently the cruel and arbitrary nature of many fairy tales actually is

(D) psychologist Bruno Bettelheim asserted that the apparently cruel and arbitrary nature of many fairy tales actually are

(E) psychologist Bruno Bettelheim asserted that the apparently cruel and arbitrary nature of many fairy tales is actually

210. After weeks of uncertainty about the course the country would pursue to stabilize its troubled economy, officials reached a revised agreement with the International Monetary Fund, pledging the enforcement of substantially greater budget discipline as that which was originally promised and to keep inflation below ten percent.

(A) the enforcement of substantially greater budget discipline as that which was originally promised and to keep inflation below ten percent

(B) the enforcement of substantially greater budget discipline than originally promised and keeping inflation below the ten percent figure

(C) to enforce substantially greater budget discipline than originally promised and to keep inflation below ten percent

(D) to enforce substantially greater budget discipline than that which was originally promised and keeping inflation less than the ten percent figure

(E) to enforce substantially greater budget discipline as that which was originally promised and to keep inflation less than ten percent

211. A new satellite sweeping over the poles at altitudes of up to 32,000 miles is called POLAR, giving scientists their best look yet at the magnetosphere, the region of space under the invisible influence of Earth's magnetic field.

(A) A new satellite sweeping over the poles at altitudes of up to 32,000 miles is called POLAR, giving scientists their best look yet at the magnetosphere, the region of space under the invisible influence of Earth's magnetic field.

(B) A new satellite called POLAR that is giving scientists their best look yet at the magnetosphere, the region of space under the invisible influence of Earth's magnetic field, sweeping over the poles at altitudes of up to 32,000 miles.

(C) Scientists are getting their best look yet at the magnetosphere, the region of space under the invisible influence of Earth's magnetic field, from a new satellite sweeping over the poles at altitudes of up to 32,000 miles called POLAR.

(D) Sweeping over the poles at altitudes of up to 32,000 miles, a new satellite called POLAR is giving scientists their best look yet at the magnetosphere, the region of space under the invisible influence of Earth's magnetic field.

(E) Sweeping over the poles at altitudes of up to 32,000 miles, scientists' best look yet at the magnetosphere, the region of space under the invisible influence of Earth's magnetic field, is coming from a new satellite called POLAR.

212. The treasury market dropped in response to a decrease in the value of the dollar and to continued concern that the economy might be growing as fast as to accelerate inflation and drive interest rates higher.

(A) that the economy might be growing as fast as

(B) that the economy might be growing fast enough

(C) with the economy's possibly growing so fast as

(D) with the possibility of the economy growing fast enough so as

(E) with the possibility of the economy possibly growing fast enough

213. Like Rousseau, Tolstoi rebelled against the unnatural complexity of human relations in modern society.

(A) Like Rousseau, Tolstoi rebelled

(B) Like Rousseau, Tolstoi's rebellion was

(C) As Rousseau, Tolstoi rebelled

(D) As did Rousseau, Tolstoi's rebellion was

(E) Tolstoi's rebellion, as Rousseau's, was

214. Japanese researchers are producing a series of robots that can identify human facial expressions, to which they will then respond; their goal is primarily creating a robot that will empathize with us.

(A) expressions, to which they will then respond; their goal is primarily creating

(B) expressions, then responding to them; primarily to create

(C) expressions and then respond to them; the researchers' primary goal is to create

(D) expressions as well as giving a response to them; their primary goal is creation of

(E) expressions and responding to them; primarily, the researchers' goal is creating

215. Despite a growing population, in 1998 the United States used 38 billion fewer gallons of water a day when comparing it to the period of all-time highest consumption almost 20 years earlier.

(A) day when comparing it to the period of all-time highest consumption almost 20 years earlier

(B) day than it did during the period of all-time highest consumption almost 20 years earlier

(C) day than were used almost 20 years earlier, which had been the all-time high consumption

(D) day, compared to almost 20 years earlier, that having been the all-time high consumption

(E) day, which is in comparison to the period of all-time highest consumption almost 20 years earlier

216. Analysts believe that whereas bad decisions by elected leaders can certainly hurt the economy, no administration can really be said to control or manage all of the complex and interrelated forces that determine the nation's economic strength.

(A) no administration can really be said to control
(B) no administration can be said that it really controls
(C) that no administration can really be said to control
(D) that no administration can really be said that it controls
(E) that it cannot be said that any administration really controls

217. Except for a concert performance that the composer himself staged in 1911, Scott Joplin's ragtime opera *Treemonisha* was not produced until 1972, sixty-one years after its completion.

(A) Except for a concert performance that the composer himself staged
(B) Except for a concert performance with the composer himself staging it
(C) Besides a concert performance being staged by the composer himself
(D) Excepting a concert performance that the composer himself staged
(E) With the exception of a concert performance with the staging done by the composer himself

218. Nearly unrivaled in their biological diversity, coral reefs provide a host of benefits that includes the supply of protein for people, protecting shorelines, and they contain biochemical sources for new life-saving medicines.

(A) coral reefs provide a host of benefits that includes the supply of protein for people, protecting shorelines,
(B) coral reefs provide a host of benefits: they supply people with protein, they protect the shorelines,
(C) coral reefs provide a host of benefits that include supplying protein for people, as well as shoreline protection,
(D) a coral reef provides a host of benefits; they supply protein for people, the protecting of shorelines,
(E) a coral reef provides a host of benefits, including protein for people, protecting shorelines,

219. Literacy opened up entire realms of verifiable knowledge to ordinary men and women having been previously considered incapable of discerning truth for themselves.

(A) having been previously considered incapable of discerning truth for themselves
(B) who had previously been considered incapable of discerning truth for themselves
(C) previously considered incapable of discerning truth for himself or herself
(D) of whom it had previously been considered they were incapable of discerning truth for themselves
(E) who had previously been considered incapable of discerning truth for himself or herself

220. In early Mesopotamian civilization, castor oil served not only as a laxative, but also a skin-softening lotion and it was a construction lubricant for sliding giant stone blocks over wooden rollers.

(A) not only as a laxative, but also a skin-softening lotion and it was a construction
(B) as not only a laxative, but also a skin-softening lotion, and it was a construction
(C) not only as a laxative but also as a skin-softening lotion and as a construction
(D) as not only a laxative but as a skin-softening lotion and in construction, as a
(E) not only as a laxative, but a skin-softening lotion and in construction, a

221. An analysis of tree bark all over the globe shows that chemical insecticides have often spread thousands of miles from where they were originally used.

(A) that chemical insecticides have often spread thousands of miles from where they were originally used
(B) that chemical insecticides have spread, often thousands of miles from their original use
(C) chemical insecticides, having often spread thousands of miles from where they were used originally
(D) chemical insecticides, often spreading thousands of miles from where their original use
(E) chemical insecticides, often spreading thousands of miles from where they were originally used

222. Consumers may not think of household cleaning products to be hazardous substances, but many of them can be harmful to health, especially if they are used improperly.

(A) Consumers may not think of household cleaning products to be

(B) Consumers may not think of household cleaning products being

(C) A consumer may not think of their household cleaning products being

(D) A consumer may not think of household cleaning products as

(E) Household cleaning products may not be thought of, by consumers, as

223. According to the Economic Development Corporation of Los Angeles County, if one were to count the Los Angeles metropolitan area as a separate nation, it would have the world's eleventh largest gross national product, that is bigger than that of Australia, Mexico, or the Netherlands.

(A) if one were to count the Los Angeles metropolitan area as a separate nation, it would have the world's eleventh largest gross national product, that is

(B) if the Los Angeles metropolitan area is counted as a separate nation, it has the world's eleventh largest gross national product, that being

(C) if the Los Angeles metropolitan area were a separate nation, it would have the world's eleventh largest gross national product,

(D) were the Los Angeles metropolitan area a separate nation, it will have the world's eleventh largest gross national product, which is

(E) when the Los Angeles metropolitan area is counted as a separate nation, it has the world's eleventh largest gross national product, thus

224. Initiated five centuries after Europeans arrived in the New World on Columbus Day 1992, Project SETI pledged a $100 million investment in the search for extraterrestrial intelligence.

(A) Initiated five centuries after Europeans arrived in the New World on Columbus Day 1992, Project SETI pledged a $100 million investment in the search for extraterrestrial intelligence.

(B) Initiated on Columbus Day 1992, five centuries after Europeans arrived in the New World, a $100 million investment in the search for extraterrestrial intelligence was pledged by Project SETI.

(C) Initiated on Columbus Day 1992, five centuries after Europeans arrived in the New World, Project SETI pledged a $100 million investment in the search for extraterrestrial intelligence.

(D) Pledging a $100 million investment in the search for extraterrestrial intelligence, the initiation of Project SETI five centuries after Europeans arrived in the New World on Columbus Day 1992.

(E) Pledging a $100 million investment in the search for extraterrestrial intelligence five centuries after Europeans arrived in the New World, on Columbus Day 1992, the initiation of Project SETI took place.

225. According to some economists, the July decrease in unemployment so that it was the lowest in two years suggests that the gradual improvement in the job market is continuing.

(A) so that it was the lowest in two years

(B) so that it was the lowest two-year rate

(C) to what would be the lowest in two years

(D) to a two-year low level

(E) to the lowest level in two years

226. Developed by Pennsylvania's Palatine Germans about 1750, Conestoga wagons, with high wheels capable of crossing rutted roads, muddy flats, and the nonroads of the prairie and they had a floor curved upward on either end so as to prevent cargo from shifting on steep grades.

(A) wagons, with high wheels capable of crossing rutted roads, muddy flats, and the nonroads of the prairie and they had a floor curved upward on either end so as to prevent

(B) wagons, with high wheels capable of crossing rutted roads, muddy flats, and the nonroads of the prairie, and with a floor that was curved upward at both ends to prevent

(C) wagons, which had high wheels capable of crossing rutted roads, muddy flats, and the nonroads of the prairie, and floors curved upward on their ends so that they prevented

(D) wagons had high wheels capable of crossing rutted roads, muddy flats, and the nonroads of the prairie, and a floor that was curved upward at both ends to prevent

(E) wagons had high wheels capable of crossing rutted roads, muddy flats, and the nonroads of the prairie and floors curving upward at their ends so that it prevented

227. The Baldrick Manufacturing Company has for several years followed a policy aimed at decreasing operating costs and improving the efficiency of its distribution system.

(A) aimed at decreasing operating costs and improving

(B) aimed at the decreasing of operating costs and to improve

(C) aiming at the decreasing of operating costs and improving

(D) the aim of which is the decreasing of operating costs and improving

(E) with the aim to decrease operating costs and to improve

228. Some buildings that were destroyed and heavily damaged in the earthquake last year were constructed in violation of the city's building code.

(A) Some buildings that were destroyed and heavily damaged in the earthquake last year were

(B) Some buildings that were destroyed or heavily damaged in the earthquake last year had been

(C) Some buildings that the earthquake destroyed and heavily damaged last year have been

(D) Last year the earthquake destroyed or heavily damaged some buildings that have been

(E) Last year some of the buildings that were destroyed or heavily damaged in the earthquake had been

229. Because the collagen fibers in skin line up in the direction of tension, surgical cuts made along these so-called Langer's lines sever fewer fibers and is less likely to leave an unsightly scar.

(A) Because the collagen fibers in skin line up in the direction of tension, surgical cuts made along these so-called Langer's lines sever fewer

(B) Because the collagen fibers in skin line up in the direction of tension, a surgical cut having been made along these so-called Langer's lines severs less

(C) Because the collagen fibers in skin line up in the direction of tension, a surgical cut made along these so-called Langer's lines severs fewer

(D) With the collagen fibers in skin lining up in the direction of tension, surgical cuts made along these so-called Langer's lines sever less

(E) With the collagen fibers in skin lining up in the direction of tension, a surgical cut made along these so-called Langer's lines sever fewer

230. In A.D. 391, resulting from the destruction of the largest library of the ancient world at Alexandria, later generations lost all but the *Iliad* and *Odyssey* among Greek epics, most of the poetry of Pindar and Sappho, and dozens of plays by Aeschylus and Euripides.

(A) resulting from the destruction of the largest library of the ancient world at Alexandria,

(B) the destroying of the largest library of the ancient world at Alexandria resulted and

(C) because of the result of the destruction of the library at Alexandria, the largest of the ancient world,

(D) as a result of the destruction of the library at Alexandria, the largest of the ancient world,

(E) Alexandria's largest library of the ancient world was destroyed, and the result was

231. The nephew of Pliny the Elder wrote the only eyewitness account of the great eruption of Vesuvius in two letters to the historian Tacitus.

(A) The nephew of Pliny the Elder wrote the only eyewitness account of the great eruption of Vesuvius in two letters to the historian Tacitus.

(B) To the historian Tacitus, the nephew of Pliny the Elder wrote two letters, being the only eyewitness accounts of the great eruption of Vesuvius.

(C) The only eyewitness account is in two letters by the nephew of Pliny the Elder writing to the historian Tacitus an account of the great eruption of Vesuvius.

(D) Writing the only eyewitness account, Pliny the Elder's nephew accounted for the great eruption of Vesuvius in two letters to the historian Tacitus.

(E) In two letters to the historian Tacitus, the nephew of Pliny the Elder wrote the only eyewitness account of the great eruption of Vesuvius.

232. Nearly two tons of nuclear-reactor fuel have already been put into orbit around the Earth, and the chances of a collision involving such material increase greatly as the amount of both space debris and satellites continue to rise.

(A) as the amount of both space debris and satellites continue to rise

(B) as the rise continues in both the amount of satellites and space debris

(C) as the amount of space debris and the number of satellites continue to rise

(D) with the continually increasing amount of space debris and the number of satellites

(E) with the amount of space debris continuing to increase along with the number of satellites

233. Though being tiny, blind, and translucent, a recently discovered species of catfish lessens their vulnerability with thickened bones and armor plates on their sides.

(A) Though being tiny, blind, and translucent, a recently discovered species of catfish lessens their vulnerability with thickened bones and armor plates on their sides.

(B) Though tiny, blind, and translucent, a recently discovered species of catfish has thickened bones and armor plates on its sides that lessen its vulnerability.

(C) A recently discovered species of catfish has thickened bones and armor plates on its sides that lessen their vulnerability, though tiny, blind, and translucent.

(D) Thickened bones and armor plates on their sides lessen the vulnerability of a recently discovered species of catfish that is tiny, blind, and translucent.

(E) Tiny, blind, and translucent, thickened bones and armor plates on its sides lessen the vulnerability of a recently discovered species of catfish.

234. A recent court decision has qualified a 1998 ruling that workers cannot be laid off if they have been given reason to believe that their jobs will be safe, provided that their performance remains satisfactory.

(A) if they have been given reason to believe that their jobs will
(B) if they are given reason for believing that their jobs would still
(C) having been given reason for believing that their jobs would
(D) having been given reason to believe their jobs to
(E) given reason to believe that their jobs will still

235. Thomas Eakins' powerful style and his choices of subject—the advances in modern surgery, the discipline of sport, the strains of individuals in tension with society or even with themselves—was as disturbing to his own time as it is compelling for ours.

(A) was as disturbing to his own time as it is
(B) were as disturbing to his own time as they are
(C) has been as disturbing in his own time as they are
(D) had been as disturbing in his own time as it was
(E) have been as disturbing in his own time as

236. As well as heat and light, the sun is the source of a continuous stream of atomic particles known as the solar wind.

(A) As well as heat and light, the sun is the source of a continuous stream
(B) Besides heat and light, also the sun is the source of a continuous stream
(C) Besides heat and light, the sun is also the source of a continuous streaming
(D) The sun is the source not only of heat and light, but also of a continuous stream
(E) The sun is the source of not only heat and light but, as well, of a continuous streaming

237. The psychologist William James believed that facial expressions not only provide a visible sign of an emotion, actually contributing to the feeling itself.

(A) emotion, actually contributing to the feeling itself
(B) emotion but also actually contributing to the feeling itself
(C) emotion but also actually contribute to the feeling itself
(D) emotion; they also actually contribute to the feeling of it
(E) emotion; the feeling itself is also actually contributed to by them

238. Inspired by the Helsinki Accords and outraged by the harsh sentences meted out to a group of Czech rock musicians called the Plastic People of the Universe, Charter 77 was established by dissident writers, philosophers, and other professionals to be a human rights group.

(A) Charter 77 was established by dissident writers, philosophers, and other professionals to be
(B) Charter 77 had been established by dissident writers, philosophers, and other professionals as
(C) Charter 77, established by dissident writers, philosophers, and other professionals, was
(D) dissident writers, philosophers, and other professionals established Charter 77 as
(E) dissident writers, philosophers, and other professionals had established Charter 77 to be

239. According to research covering the last decade, the average number of rooms added by high-end hotel chains was lower than what the hotel industry average did for this period, but their occupancy and room rates grew faster than the average hotel.

(A) than what the hotel industry average did for this period, but their occupancy and room rates grew faster than
(B) than the hotel industry average for this period, but occupancy and room rates grew faster for these chains than for
(C) as compared to the hotel industry average for this period, but occupancy and room rates for them grew faster than with
(D) as compared to what the hotel industry average had been for this period, but occupancy and room rates for these chains grew faster than did
(E) as compared to the hotel industry average for this period, but their occupancy and room rates grew faster than they did for

240. Of all the record companies involved in early jazz, the three most prominent were Columbia, Victor, and OKeh.

(A) Of all the record companies involved in early jazz, the three most prominent were Columbia, Victor, and OKeh.
(B) Three most prominent record companies of all the ones that were involved in early jazz were Columbia, Victor, and OKeh.
(C) Columbia, Victor, and OKeh were, of all the record companies involved in early jazz, the three of them that were most prominent.
(D) Columbia, Victor, and OKeh were three most prominent of all the record companies involved in early jazz.
(E) Out of all the record companies that were involved in early jazz, three of them that were the most prominent were Columbia, Victor, and OKeh.

241. Analysts blamed May's sluggish retail sales on unexciting merchandise as well as the weather, colder and wetter than was usual in some regions, which slowed sales of barbecue grills and lawn furniture.

(A) colder and wetter than was usual in some regions, which slowed
(B) which was colder and wetter than usual in some regions, slowing
(C) since it was colder and wetter than usually in some regions, which slowed
(D) being colder and wetter than usually in some regions, slowing
(E) having been colder and wetter than was usual in some regions and slowed

242. Twenty-two feet long and 10 feet in diameter, the AM-1 is one of the many new satellites that is a part of 15 years effort of subjecting the interactions of Earth's atmosphere, oceans, and land surfaces to detailed scrutiny from space.

(A) satellites that is a part of 15 years effort of subjecting the interactions of Earth's atmosphere, oceans, and land surfaces
(B) satellites, which is a part of a 15-year effort to subject how Earth's atmosphere, oceans, and land surfaces interact
(C) satellites, part of 15 years effort of subjecting how Earth's atmosphere, oceans, and land surfaces are interacting
(D) satellites that are part of an effort for 15 years that has subjected the interactions of Earth's atmosphere, oceans, and land surfaces
(E) satellites that are part of a 15-year effort to subject the interactions of Earth's atmosphere, oceans, and land surfaces

243. On the tournament roster are listed several tennis students, most all of which play as good as their instructors.

(A) most all of which play as good
(B) most all of whom play as good
(C) almost all of which play as well
(D) almost all of whom play as good
(E) almost all of whom play as well

244. Recently discovered fossil remains strongly suggest that the Australian egg-laying mammals of today are a branch of the main stem of mammalian evolution rather than developing independently from a common ancestor of mammals more than 220 million years ago.

(A) rather than developing independently from
(B) rather than a type that developed independently from
(C) rather than a type whose development was independent of
(D) instead of developing independently from
(E) instead of a development that was independent of

245. In 1974 a large area of the surface of Mercury was photographed from varying distances, which revealed a degree of cratering similar to that of the Moon's.

(A) which revealed a degree of cratering similar to that of the Moon's
(B) to reveal a degree of cratering similar to the Moon
(C) revealing a degree of cratering similar to that of the Moon
(D) and revealed cratering similar in degree to the Moon
(E) that revealed cratering similar in degree to that of the Moon

246. The energy source on *Voyager 2* is not a nuclear reactor, in which atoms are actively broken apart; rather a kind of nuclear battery that uses natural radioactive decay to produce power.

(A) apart; rather
(B) apart, but rather
(C) apart, but rather that of
(D) apart, but that of
(E) apart; it is that of

247. Many kitchens today are equipped with high-speed electrical gadgets, such as blenders and food processors, which are able to inflict as serious injuries as those caused by an industrial wood-planing machine.

(A) which are able to inflict as serious injuries as those
(B) which can inflict serious injuries such as those
(C) inflicting injuries as serious as that having been
(D) capable to inflict injuries as serious as that
(E) capable of inflicting injuries as serious as those

248. Under high pressure and intense heat, graphite, the most stable form of pure carbon, changes into the substance commonly referred to as diamond and remaining this way whether or not the heat and pressure are removed.

(A) remaining this way whether or not
(B) remaining like that even as
(C) remaining as such whether or not
(D) remains in this way although
(E) remains thus even when

249. The computer company reported strong second-quarter earnings that surpassed Wall Street's estimates and announced the first in a series of price cuts intended to increase sales further.

(A) The computer company reported strong second-quarter earnings that surpassed Wall Street's estimates and announced the first in a series of price cuts intended to increase sales further.
(B) The report of the computer company showed strong second-quarter earnings, surpassing Wall Street's estimates, and they announced the first in a series of price cuts that they intend to increase sales further.
(C) Surpassing Wall Street's estimates, the report of the computer company showed strong second-quarter earnings, and, for the purpose of increasing sales further, they announced the first in a series of price cuts.
(D) The computer company reported strong second-quarter earnings, surpassing Wall Street's estimates, and announcing the first in a series of price cuts for the purpose of further increasing sales.
(E) The computer company, surpassing Wall Street's estimates, reported strong second-quarter earnings, while announcing that to increase sales further there would be the first in a series of price cuts.

250. Being a United States citizen since 1988 and born in Calcutta in 1940, author Bharati Mukherjee has lived in England and Canada, and first came to the United States in 1961 to study at the Iowa Writers' Workshop.

(A) Being a United States citizen since 1988 and born in Calcutta in 1940, author Bharati Mukherjee has
(B) Having been a United States citizen since 1988, she was born in Calcutta in 1940; author Bharati Mukherjee
(C) Born in Calcutta in 1940, author Bharati Mukherjee became a United States citizen in 1988; she has
(D) Being born in Calcutta in 1940 and having been a United States citizen since 1988, author Bharati Mukherjee
(E) Having been born in Calcutta in 1940 and being a United States citizen since 1988, author Bharati Mukherjee

251. As a result of record low temperatures, the water pipes on the third floor froze, which caused the heads of the sprinkler system to burst, which released torrents of water into offices on the second floor.

(A) which caused the heads of the sprinkler system to burst, which released torrents of water
(B) which caused the heads of the sprinkler system to burst and which released torrents of water
(C) which caused the heads of the sprinkler system to burst, torrents of water were then released
(D) causing the heads of the sprinkler system to burst, then releasing torrents of water
(E) causing the heads of the sprinkler system to burst and release torrents of water

252. Archaeologists in Ireland believe that a recently discovered chalice, which dates from the eighth century, was probably buried to keep from being stolen by invaders.

(A) to keep from
(B) to keep it from
(C) to avoid
(D) in order that it would avoid
(E) in order to keep from

253. The bank holds $3 billion in loans that are seriously delinquent or in such trouble that they do not expect payments when due.

(A) they do not expect payments when
(B) it does not expect payments when it is
(C) it does not expect payments to be made when they are
(D) payments are not to be expected to be paid when
(E) payments are not expected to be paid when they will be

254. Faced with an estimated $2 billion budget gap, the city's mayor proposed a nearly 17 percent reduction in the amount allocated the previous year to maintain the city's major cultural institutions and to subsidize hundreds of local arts groups.

(A) proposed a nearly 17 percent reduction in the amount allocated the previous year to maintain the city's major cultural institutions and to subsidize
(B) proposed a reduction from the previous year of nearly 17 percent in the amount it was allocating to maintain the city's major cultural institutions and for subsidizing
(C) proposed to reduce, by nearly 17 percent, the amount from the previous year that was allocated for the maintenance of the city's major cultural institutions and to subsidize
(D) has proposed a reduction from the previous year of nearly 17 percent of the amount it was allocating for maintaining the city's major cultural institutions, and to subsidize
(E) was proposing that the amount they were allocating be reduced by nearly 17 percent from the previous year for maintaining the city's major cultural institutions and for the subsidization

255. In the textbook publishing business, the second quarter is historically weak, because revenues are low and marketing expenses are high as companies prepare for the coming school year.

(A) low and marketing expenses are high as companies prepare
(B) low and their marketing expenses are high as they prepare
(C) low with higher marketing expenses in preparation
(D) low, while marketing expenses are higher to prepare
(E) low, while their marketing expenses are higher in preparation

256. Ms. Chambers is among the forecasters who predict that the rate of addition to arable lands will drop while those of loss rise.

(A) those of loss rise
(B) it rises for loss
(C) those of losses rise
(D) the rate of loss rises
(E) there are rises for the rate of loss

257. Less than 400 Sumatran rhinos survive on the Malay peninsula and on the islands of Sumatra and Borneo, and they occupy a small fraction of the species' former range.

(A) Less than 400 Sumatran rhinos survive on the Malay peninsula and on the islands of Sumatra and Borneo, and they occupy a small fraction of the species' former range.
(B) Less than 400 Sumatran rhinos, surviving on the Malay peninsula and on the islands of Sumatra and Borneo, occupy a small fraction of the species' former range.
(C) Occupying a small fraction of the species' former range, the Malay peninsula and the islands of Sumatra and Borneo are where fewer than 400 Sumatran rhinos survive.
(D) Occupying a small fraction of the species' former range, fewer than 400 Sumatran rhinos survive on the Malay peninsula and on the islands of Sumatra and Borneo.
(E) Surviving on the Malay peninsula and on the islands of Sumatra and Borneo, less than 400 Sumatran rhinos occupy a small fraction of the species' former range.

258. Certain pesticides can become ineffective if used repeatedly in the same place; one reason is suggested by the finding that there are much larger populations of pesticide-degrading microbes in soils with a relatively long history of pesticide use than in soils that are free of such chemicals.

(A) Certain pesticides can become ineffective if used repeatedly in the same place; one reason is suggested by the finding that there are much larger populations of pesticide-degrading microbes in soils with a relatively long history of pesticide use than in soils that are free of such chemicals.
(B) If used repeatedly in the same place, one reason that certain pesticides can become ineffective is suggested by the finding that there are much larger populations of pesticide-degrading microbes in soils with a relatively long history of pesticide use than in soils that are free of such chemicals.
(C) If used repeatedly in the same place, one reason certain pesticides can become ineffective is suggested by the finding that much larger populations of pesticide-degrading microbes are found in soils with a relatively long history of pesticide use than those that are free of such chemicals.
(D) The finding that there are much larger populations of pesticide-degrading microbes in soils with a relatively long history of pesticide use than in soils that are free of such chemicals is suggestive of one reason, if used repeatedly in the same place, certain pesticides can become ineffective.
(E) The finding of much larger populations of pesticide-degrading microbes in soils with a relatively long history of pesticide use than in those that are free of such chemicals suggests one reason certain pesticides can become ineffective if used repeatedly in the same place.

259. While some academicians believe that business ethics should be integrated into every business course, others say that students will take ethics seriously only if it would be taught as a separately required course.

(A) only if it would be taught as a separately required course
(B) only if it is taught as a separate, required course
(C) if it is taught only as a course required separately
(D) if it was taught only as a separate and required course
(E) if it would only be taught as a required course, separately

260. Whether they will scale back their orders to pre-2003 levels or stop doing business with us altogether depends on whether the changes that their management has proposed will be fully implemented.

(A) Whether they will scale back their orders to pre-2003 levels or stop doing business with us altogether depends on whether the changes that their management has proposed will be fully implemented.
(B) Whether they scale back their orders to pre-2003 levels or whether they discontinue their business with us altogether depends on the changes their management has proposed, if fully implemented or not.
(C) Their either scaling back their orders in the future to pre-2003 levels, or their outright termination of business with us, depends on their management's proposed changes being fully implemented or not.
(D) Whether they will scale back their orders to pre-2003 levels or stop doing business with us altogether depends if the changes that their management has proposed become fully implemented.
(E) They will either scale back their orders to pre-2003 levels, or they will stop doing business with us altogether dependent on whether the changes their management has proposed will be fully implemented, or not.

261. Until 1868 and Disraeli, Great Britain had no prime ministers not coming from a landed family.

(A) Until 1868 and Disraeli, Great Britain had no prime ministers not coming
(B) Until 1868 and Disraeli, Great Britain had had no prime ministers who have not come
(C) Until Disraeli in 1868, there were no prime ministers in Great Britain who have not come
(D) It was not until 1868 that Great Britain had a prime minister—Disraeli—who did not come
(E) It was only in 1868 and Disraeli that Great Britain had one of its prime ministers not coming

262. Around 1900, fishermen in the Chesapeake Bay area landed more than seventeen million pounds of shad in a single year, but by 1920, overfishing and the proliferation of milldams and culverts that have blocked shad migrations up their spawning streams had reduced landings to less than four million pounds.

(A) that have blocked shad migrations up their spawning streams had reduced landings to less
(B) that blocked shad from migrating up their spawning streams had reduced landings to less
(C) that blocked shad from migrating up their spawning streams reduced landings to a lower amount
(D) having blocked shad from migrating up their spawning streams reduced landings to less
(E) having blocked shad migrations up their spawning streams had reduced landings to an amount lower

263. By offering lower prices and a menu of personal communications options, such as caller identification and voice mail, the new telecommunications company has not only captured customers from other phone companies but also forced them to offer competitive prices.

(A) has not only captured customers from other phone companies but also forced them
(B) has not only captured customers from other phone companies, but it also forced them
(C) has not only captured customers from other phone companies but also forced these companies
(D) not only has captured customers from other phone companies but also these companies have been forced
(E) not only captured customers from other phone companies, but it also has forced them

264. After suffering $2 billion in losses and 25,000 layoffs, the nation's semiconductor industry, which makes chips that run everything from computers and spy satellites to dishwashers, appears to have made a long-awaited recovery.

(A) computers and spy satellites to dishwashers, appears to have
(B) computers, spy satellites, and dishwashers, appears having
(C) computers, spy satellites, and dishwashers, appears that it has
(D) computers and spy satellites to dishwashers, appears that it has
(E) computers and spy satellites as well as dishwashers, appears to have

265. Over a range of frequencies from 100 to 5,000 hertz, monkeys and marmosets have a hearing sensitivity remarkably similar to humans, above which the sensitivity begins to differ.

(A) Over a range of frequencies from 100 to 5,000 hertz, monkeys and marmosets have a hearing sensitivity remarkably similar to humans
(B) Compared to humans, the hearing sensitivity of monkeys and marmosets are remarkably similar over a range of frequencies from 100 to 5,000 hertz
(C) Compared to humans over a range of frequencies from 100 to 5,000 hertz, the hearing sensitivity of monkeys and marmosets is remarkably similar
(D) The hearing sensitivity of monkeys and marmosets, when compared to humans over a range of frequencies from 100 to 5,000 hertz, is remarkably similar
(E) The hearing sensitivity of monkeys, marmosets, and humans is remarkably similar over a range of frequencies from 100 to 5,000 hertz

266. The computer company has announced that it will purchase the color-printing division of a rival company for $950 million, which is part of a deal that will make it the largest manufacturer in the office color-printing market.

(A) million, which is part of a deal that will make
(B) million, a part of a deal that makes
(C) million, a part of a deal making
(D) million as a part of a deal to make
(E) million as part of a deal that will make

267. Kudzu, an Asian vine that has grown rampantly in the southern United States since introducing it in the 1920s to thwart soil erosion, has overrun many houses and countless acres of roadside.

(A) that has grown rampantly in the southern United States since introducing it in the 1920s to thwart
(B) that has grown rampantly in the southern United States, since it was introduced in the 1920s for thwarting
(C) that has grown rampant in the southern United States since it was introduced in the 1920s to thwart
(D) growing rampant in the southern United States since introducing it in the 1920s for thwarting
(E) growing rampantly in the southern United States, since it was introduced in the 1920s to thwart

268. Unable to build nests or care for their young, a female cowbird lays up to 40 eggs a year in the nests of other birds, including warblers, vireos, flycatchers, and thrushes.

(A) a female cowbird lays up to 40 eggs a year in the nests of other birds, including
(B) a female cowbird will use the nests of other birds to lay up to 40 eggs a year, including those of
(C) female cowbirds use the nests of other birds to lay up to 40 eggs a year, including those of
(D) female cowbirds lay up to 40 eggs a year in the nests of other birds, including
(E) up to 40 eggs a year are laid by female cowbirds in the nests of other birds, including

269. Bluegrass musician Bill Monroe, whose repertory, views on musical collaboration, and vocal style were influential on generations of bluegrass artists, was also an inspiration to many musicians, that included Elvis Presley and Jerry Garcia, whose music differed significantly from his own.

(A) were influential on generations of bluegrass artists, was also an inspiration to many musicians, that included Elvis Presley and Jerry Garcia, whose music differed significantly from

(B) influenced generations of bluegrass artists, also inspired many musicians, including Elvis Presley and Jerry Garcia, whose music differed significantly from

(C) was influential to generations of bluegrass artists, was also inspirational to many musicians, that included Elvis Presley and Jerry Garcia, whose music was different significantly in comparison to

(D) was influential to generations of bluegrass artists, also inspired many musicians, who included Elvis Presley and Jerry Garcia, the music of whom differed significantly when compared to

(E) were an influence on generations of bluegrass artists, was also an inspiration to many musicians, including Elvis Presley and Jerry Garcia, whose music was significantly different from that of

270. In many of the world's regions, increasing pressure on water resources has resulted both from expanding development, changes in climate, and from pollution, so that the future supply in some of the more arid areas is a concern going forward.

(A) both from expanding development, changes in climate, and from pollution, so that the future supply in some of the more arid areas is a concern going forward

(B) both from expanding development or changes in climate, and pollution, so that future supplies in some of the more arid areas are a concern

(C) from expanding development, changes in climate, and also from pollution, so that the future supply in some of the more arid areas is a matter of concern going forward

(D) from expanding development, changes in climate, and pollution, so that future supplies in some of the more arid areas are a concern

(E) from expansion of development, changes in climate, and from pollution, so that supplies in some of the more arid areas are a future concern

271. The computer company's present troubles are a result of technological stagnation, marketing missteps, and managerial blunders so that several attempts to revise corporate strategies have failed to correct it.

(A) so that several attempts to revise corporate strategies have failed to correct it

(B) so that several attempts at revising corporate strategies have failed to correct

(C) in that several attempts at revising corporate strategies have failed to correct them

(D) that several attempts to revise corporate strategies have failed to correct

(E) that several attempts at revising corporate strategies have failed to correct them

272. The root systems of most flowering perennials either become too crowded, which results in loss in vigor, and spread too far outward, producing a bare center.

(A) which results in loss in vigor, and spread
(B) resulting in loss in vigor, or spreading
(C) with the result of loss of vigor, or spreading
(D) resulting in loss of vigor, or spread
(E) with a resulting loss of vigor, and spread

273. In theory, international civil servants at the United Nations are prohibited from continuing to draw salaries from their own governments; in practice, however, some governments merely substitute living allowances for their employees' paychecks, assigned by them to the United Nations.

(A) for their employees' paychecks, assigned by them
(B) for the paychecks of their employees who have been assigned
(C) for the paychecks of their employees, having been assigned
(D) in place of their employees' paychecks, for those of them assigned
(E) in place of the paychecks of their employees to have been assigned by them

274. Industry analysts said that the recent rise in fuel prices may be an early signal of the possibility of gasoline and heating oil prices staying higher than usually through the end of the year.

(A) of the possibility of gasoline and heating oil prices staying higher than usually through
(B) of the possibility that gasoline and heating oil prices could stay higher than usual throughout
(C) of prices of gasoline and heating oil possibly staying higher than usually through
(D) that prices of gasoline and heating oil could stay higher than they usually are throughout
(E) that prices of gasoline and heating oil will stay higher than usual through

275. The Anasazi settlements at Chaco Canyon were built on a spectacular scale, with more than 75 carefully engineered structures, of up to 600 rooms each, were connected by a complex regional system of roads.

(A) scale, with more than 75 carefully engineered structures, of up to 600 rooms each, were
(B) scale, with more than 75 carefully engineered structures, of up to 600 rooms each,
(C) scale of more than 75 carefully engineered structures of up to 600 rooms, each that had been
(D) scale of more than 75 carefully engineered structures of up to 600 rooms and with each
(E) scale of more than 75 carefully engineered structures of up to 600 rooms, each had been

276. Even though the overall consumer price index did not change in April, indicating the absence of any general inflation or deflation, prices in several categories of merchandise have fallen over the last several months.

(A) April, indicating the absence of any general inflation or deflation, prices in several categories of merchandise have fallen
(B) April, indicating that any general inflation or deflation were absent, prices in several categories of merchandise fell
(C) April and indicated that absence of any general inflation or deflation, prices in several categories of merchandise fell
(D) April, having indicated the absence of any general inflation or deflation, prices in several categories of merchandise fell
(E) April, which indicated that any general inflation or deflation were absent, prices in several categories of merchandise have fallen

277. Despite Japan's relative isolation from world trade at the time, the prolonged peace during the Tokugawa shogunate produced an almost explosive expansion of commerce.

(A) Japan's relative isolation from world trade at the time, the prolonged peace during the Tokugawa shogunate
(B) the relative isolation of Japan from world trade at the time and the Tokugawa shogunate's prolonged peace, it
(C) being relatively isolated from world trade at the time, the prolonged peace during Japan's Tokugawa shogunate
(D) Japan's relative isolation from world trade at the time during the Tokugawa shogunate, prolonged peace
(E) its relative isolation from world trade then, prolonged peace in Japan during the Tokugawa shogunate

278. Government officials announced that restrictions on the use of water would continue because no appreciative increase in the level of the river resulted from the intermittent showers that had fallen throughout the area the day before.

(A) restrictions on the use of water would continue because no appreciative increase in the level of the river
(B) restricting the use of water would continue because there had not been any appreciative increase in the river's level that
(C) the use of water would continue to be restricted because not any appreciable increase in the river's level had
(D) restrictions on the use of water would continue because no appreciable increase in the level of the river had
(E) using water would continue being restricted because not any appreciable increase in the level of the river

279. According to United States census data, while there was about one-third of mothers with young children working outside the home in 1975, in 2000, almost two-thirds of those mothers were employed outside the home.

(A) while there was about one-third of mothers with young children working outside the home in 1975, in 2000, almost two-thirds of those mothers were employed outside the home
(B) there were about one-third of mothers with young children who worked outside the home in 1975; in 2000, almost two-thirds of those mothers were employed outside the home
(C) in 1975 about one-third of mothers with young children worked outside the home; in 2000, almost two-thirds of such mothers were employed outside the home
(D) even though in 1975 there were about one-third of mothers with young children who worked outside the home, almost two-thirds of such mothers were employed outside the home in 2000
(E) with about one-third of mothers with young children working outside the home in 1975, almost two-thirds of such mothers were employed outside the home in 2000

280. Clouds are formed from the evaporation of the oceans' water that is warmed by the sun and rises high into the atmosphere, condensing in tiny droplets on minute particles of dust.

(A) Clouds are formed from the evaporation of the oceans' water that is warmed by the sun and rises high into the atmosphere, condensing in tiny droplets on minute particles of dust.
(B) Clouds form by the sun's warmth evaporating the water in the oceans, which rises high into the atmosphere, condensing in tiny droplets on minute particles of dust.
(C) Warmed by the sun, ocean water evaporates, rises high into the atmosphere, and condenses in tiny droplets on minute particles of dust to form clouds.
(D) The water in the oceans evaporates, warmed by the sun, rises high into the atmosphere, and condenses in tiny droplets on minute particles of dust, which forms clouds.
(E) Ocean water, warmed by the sun, evaporates and rises high into the atmosphere, which then condenses in tiny droplets on minute particles of dust to form as clouds.

281. Schistosomiasis, a disease caused by a parasitic worm, is prevalent in hot, humid climates, and it has become more widespread as irrigation projects have enlarged the habitat of the freshwater snails that are the parasite's hosts for part of its life cycle.

(A) the freshwater snails that are the parasite's hosts for part of its life cycle
(B) the freshwater snails that are the parasite's hosts in part of their life cycle
(C) freshwater snails which become the parasite's hosts for part of its life cycles
(D) freshwater snails which become the hosts of the parasite during the parasite's life cycles
(E) parasite's hosts, freshwater snails which become their hosts during their life cycles

282. Sor Juana Inés de la Cruz was making the case for women's equality long before the cause had a name: Born in the mid-seventeenth century in San Miguel Nepantla, Mexico, the convent was the perfect environment for Sor Juana to pursue intellectual pursuits, achieving renown as a mathematician, poet, philosopher, and playwright.

(A) the convent was the perfect environment for Sor Juana to pursue intellectual pursuits, achieving
(B) Sor Juana found the convent provided the perfect environment for intellectual pursuits, and she went on to achieve
(C) the convent provided the perfect environment for intellectual pursuits for Sor Juana; going on to achieve
(D) Sor Juana found the convent provided the perfect environment for intellectual pursuits; achieving
(E) the convent was, Sor Juana found, the perfect environment for intellectual pursuits, and she went on to achieve

283. By devising an instrument made from a rod, wire, and lead balls, and employing uncommonly precise measurements, in 1797–1798 Henry Cavendish's apparatus enabled him to arrive at an astonishingly accurate figure for the weight of the earth.

(A) By devising an instrument made from a rod, wire, and lead balls, and employing uncommonly precise measurements, in 1797–1798 Henry Cavendish's apparatus enabled him
(B) In 1797–1798, by devising an instrument made from a rod, wire, and lead balls, and employing uncommonly precise measurements, Henry Cavendish's apparatus enabled him
(C) Henry Cavendish devised an instrument made from a rod, wire, and lead balls, and employed uncommonly precise measurements, and in 1797–1798 was able
(D) Having devised an instrument from a rod, wire, and lead balls, and employment of uncommonly precise measurements, Henry Cavendish in 1797–1798 was able
(E) By devising an instrument made from a rod, wire, and lead balls, and employing uncommonly precise measurements, Henry Cavendish was able in 1797–1798

284. The growth projected for these storms in different computerized weather models varies widely.

(A) projected for these storms in different computerized weather models varies widely
(B) for these storms is projected in different computerized models of weather to vary widely
(C) of these storms, projected in different computerized weather models, vary widely
(D) projected for these storms, which vary widely in different computerized weather models
(E) that varies widely for these storms are projected in different computerized weather models

285. By using a process called echolocation to analyze the echoes of the high-pitched sounds they produce, bats can determine not only the distance to an object, but they also can determine its shape and size and the direction in which it is moving.

(A) can determine not only the distance to an object, but they also can determine
(B) not only can determine the distance to an object but also
(C) can determine not only the distance to an object but also
(D) not only can determine its distance from an object but also
(E) can determine not only their distance from an object, but they can also determine

286. Carbon dioxide, which traps heat in the atmosphere and helps regulate the planet's surface temperature, is constantly being exchanged between the atmosphere on the one hand and the oceans and terrestrial plants on the other.

(A) exchanged between the atmosphere on the one hand and the oceans and terrestrial plants on the other
(B) exchanged, on the one hand, between the atmosphere and the oceans and terrestrial plants, on the other
(C) exchanged between, on the one hand, the atmosphere, with the oceans and terrestrial plants, on the other
(D) exchanged, on the one hand, among the oceans and terrestrial plants, and the atmosphere, on the other
(E) exchanged among the oceans and terrestrial plants on the one hand and the atmosphere on the other

287. Floating in the waters of the equatorial Pacific, an array of buoys collects and transmits data on long-term interactions between the ocean and the atmosphere, interactions that affect global climate.

(A) atmosphere, interactions that affect
(B) atmosphere, with interactions affecting
(C) atmosphere that affects
(D) atmosphere that is affecting
(E) atmosphere as affects

288. Sixty-five million years ago, according to some scientists, an asteroid bigger than Mount Everest slammed into North America, which, causing plant and animal extinctions, marks the end of the geologic era known as the Cretaceous Period.

(A) which, causing plant and animal extinctions, marks
(B) which caused the plant and animal extinctions and marks
(C) and causing plant and animal extinctions that mark
(D) an event that caused plant and animal extinctions, which marks
(E) an event that caused the plant and animal extinctions that mark

289. Although the first pulsar, or rapidly spinning collapsed star, to be sighted was in the summer of 1967 by graduate student Jocelyn Bell, it had not been announced until February 1968.

(A) Although the first pulsar, or rapidly spinning collapsed star, to be sighted was in the summer of 1967 by graduate student Jocelyn Bell, it had not been announced until February 1968.
(B) Although not announced until February 1968, in the summer of 1967 graduate student Jocelyn Bell observed the first pulsar, or rapidly spinning collapsed star, to be sighted.
(C) Although observed by graduate student Jocelyn Bell in the summer of 1967, the discovery of the first sighted pulsar, or rapidly spinning collapsed star, had not been announced before February 1968.
(D) The first pulsar, or rapidly spinning collapsed star, to be sighted was observed in the summer of 1967 by graduate student Jocelyn Bell, but the discovery was not announced until February 1968.
(E) The first sighted pulsar, or rapidly spinning collapsed star, was not announced until February 1968, while it was observed in the summer of 1967 by graduate student Jocelyn Bell.

290. Sound can travel through water for enormous distances, prevented from dissipating its acoustic energy as a result of boundaries in the ocean created by water layers of different temperatures and densities.

(A) prevented from dissipating its acoustic energy as a result of
(B) prevented from having its acoustic energy dissipated by
(C) its acoustic energy prevented from dissipating by
(D) its acoustic energy prevented from being dissipated as a result of
(E) preventing its acoustic energy from dissipating by

291. Last year, land values in most parts of the pinelands rose almost so fast, and in some parts even faster than what they did outside the pinelands.

(A) so fast, and in some parts even faster than what they did
(B) so fast, and in some parts even faster than, those
(C) as fast, and in some parts even faster than, those
(D) as fast as, and in some parts even faster than, those
(E) as fast as, and in some parts even faster than what they did

292. The North American moose's long legs enable it to move quickly through the woods, stepping easily over downed trees, but predators pursuing it must leap or go around them.

(A) moose's long legs enable it to move quickly through the woods, stepping easily over downed trees, but predators pursuing it must leap or go around them
(B) moose's long legs enable it to move quickly through the woods, stepping easily over downed trees while predators pursuing them must leap or go around
(C) moose's long legs enable it to move quickly through the woods and to step easily over downed trees, but predators pursuing them must leap over or go around them
(D) moose has long legs, enabling it to move quickly through the woods and to step easily over downed trees while predators pursuing them must leap or go around
(E) moose has long legs that enable it to move quickly through the woods, stepping easily over downed trees while predators pursuing it must leap over or go around them

293. Early administrative decisions in China's Ming Dynasty eventually caused a drastic fall in tax revenues, a reduction in military preparedness, the collapse of the currency system, and failed to make sufficient investment in vital transportation infrastructure.

(A) the collapse of the currency system, and failed
(B) the collapse of the currency system, and failing
(C) and the collapse of the currency system, also failed
(D) the collapse of the currency system, as well as failing
(E) and the collapse of the currency system, as well as a failure

294. Seismologists studying the earthquake that struck northern California in October 1989 are still investigating some of its mysteries: the unexpected power of the seismic waves, the upward thrust that threw one man straight into the air, and the strange electromagnetic signals detected hours before the temblor.

(A) the upward thrust that threw one man straight into the air, and the strange electromagnetic signals detected hours before the temblor

(B) the upward thrust that threw one man straight into the air, and strange electromagnetic signals were detected hours before the temblor

(C) the upward thrust threw one man straight into the air, and hours before the temblor strange electromagnetic signals were detected

(D) one man was thrown straight into the air by the upward thrust, and hours before the temblor strange electromagnetic signals were detected

(E) one man who was thrown straight into the air by the upward thrust, and strange electromagnetic signals that were detected hours before the temblor

295. The type of behavior exhibited when an animal recognizes itself in a mirror comes within the domain of "theory of mind," thus is best studied as part of the field of animal cognition.

(A) of "theory of mind," thus is best

(B) "theory of mind," and so is best to be

(C) of a "theory of mind," thus it is best

(D) of "theory of mind" and thus is best

(E) of the "theory of mind," and so it is best to be

296. Unlike the United States, where farmers can usually depend on rain or snow all year long, the rains in most parts of Sri Lanka are concentrated in the monsoon months, June to September, and the skies are generally clear for the rest of the year.

(A) Unlike the United States, where farmers can usually depend on rain or snow all year long, the rains in most parts of Sri Lanka

(B) Unlike the United States farmers who can usually depend on rain or snow all year long, the rains in most parts of Sri Lanka

(C) Unlike those of the United States, where farmers can usually depend on rain or snow all year long, most parts of Sri Lanka's rains

(D) In comparison with the United States, whose farmers can usually depend on rain or snow all year long, the rains in most parts of Sri Lanka

(E) In the United States, farmers can usually depend on rain or snow all year long, but in most parts of Sri Lanka, the rains

297. In preparation for the prediction of a major earthquake that will hit the state, a satellite-based computer network is being built by the California Office of Emergency Services for identifying earthquake damage and to pinpoint the most affected areas within two hours of the event.

(A) In preparation for the prediction of a major earthquake that will hit the state, a satellite-based computer network is being built by the California Office of Emergency Services for identifying

(B) In preparing for the prediction that a major earthquake will hit the state, the California Office of Emergency Services is building a satellite-based computer network that will identify

(C) In preparing for a major earthquake that is predicted to hit the state, the California Office of Emergency Services is building a satellite-based computer network to identify

(D) To prepare for the prediction of a major earthquake hitting the state, a satellite-based computer network is being built by the California Office of Emergency Services to identify

(E) To prepare for a major earthquake that is predicted to hit the state, the California Office of Emergency Services is building a satellite-based computer network that will identify

298. Once numbering in the millions worldwide, it is estimated that the wolf has declined to 200,000 in 57 countries, some 11,000 of them to be found in the lower 48 United States and Alaska.

(A) it is estimated that the wolf has declined to 200,000 in 57 countries, some

(B) the wolf is estimated to have declined to 200,000 in 57 countries, with approximately

(C) the wolf has declined to an estimate of 200,000 in 57 countries, some

(D) wolves have declined to an estimate of 200,000 in 57 countries, with approximately

(E) wolves have declined to an estimated 200,000 in 57 countries, some

299. As business grows more complex, students majoring in specialized areas like those of finance and marketing have been becoming increasingly successful in the job market.

(A) majoring in specialized areas like those of finance and marketing have been becoming increasingly

(B) who major in such specialized areas as finance and marketing are becoming more and more

(C) who majored in specialized areas such as those of finance and marketing are being increasingly

(D) who major in specialized areas like those of finance and marketing have been becoming more and more

(E) having majored in such specialized areas as finance and marketing are being increasingly

300. Created in 1945 to reduce poverty and stabilize foreign currency markets, the World Bank and the International Monetary Fund have, according to some critics, continually struggled to meet the expectations of their major shareholders—a group comprising many of the world's rich nations—but neglected their intended beneficiaries in the developing world.

(A) continually struggled to meet the expectations of their major shareholders—a group comprising many of the world's rich nations—but neglected

(B) continually struggled as they try to meet the expectations of their major shareholders—a group comprising many of the world's rich nations—while neglecting that of

(C) continually struggled to meet their major shareholders' expectations—a group comprising many of the world's rich nations—but neglected that of

(D) had to struggle continually in trying to meet the expectations of their major shareholders—a group comprising many of the world's rich nations—while neglecting that of

(E) struggled continually in trying to meet their major shareholders' expectations—a group comprising many of the world's rich nations—and neglecting

301. Unlike auto insurance, the frequency of claims does not affect the premiums for personal property coverage, but if the insurance company is able to prove excessive loss due to owner negligence, it may decline to renew the policy.

(A) Unlike auto insurance, the frequency of claims does not affect the premiums for personal property coverage,

(B) Unlike with auto insurance, the frequency of claims do not affect the premiums for personal property coverage,

(C) Unlike the frequency of claims for auto insurance, the premiums for personal property coverage are not affected by the frequency of claims,

(D) Unlike the premiums for auto insurance, the premiums for personal property coverage are not affected by the frequency of claims,

(E) Unlike with the premiums for auto insurance, the premiums for personal property coverage is not affected by the frequency of claims,

5.7 Answer Key

189. A
190. C
191. E
192. E
193. C
194. E
195. C
196. D
197. C
198. E
199. C
200. A
201. B
202. E
203. D
204. C
205. C
206. B
207. A
208. A
209. E
210. C
211. D
212. B
213. A
214. C
215. B
216. A
217. A
218. B
219. B
220. C
221. A
222. D
223. C
224. C
225. E
226. D
227. A
228. B
229. C
230. D
231. E
232. C
233. B
234. A
235. B
236. D
237. C
238. D
239. B
240. A
241. B
242. E
243. E
244. B
245. C
246. B
247. E
248. E
249. A
250. C
251. E
252. B
253. C
254. A
255. A
256. D
257. D
258. A
259. B
260. A
261. D
262. B
263. C
264. A
265. E
266. E
267. C
268. D
269. B
270. D
271. D
272. D
273. B
274. E
275. B
276. A
277. A
278. D
279. C
280. C
281. A
282. B
283. E
284. A
285. C
286. A
287. A
288. E
289. D
290. C
291. D
292. E
293. E
294. A
295. D
296. E
297. C
298. E
299. B
300. A
301. D

5.8 Answer Explanations

The following discussion of sentence correction is intended to familiarize you with the most efficient and effective approaches to these kinds of questions. The particular questions in this chapter are generally representative of the kinds of sentence correction questions you will encounter on the GMAT.

189. Using digital enhancements of skull fragments from five prehistoric hominids dating to more than 350,000 years ago, anthropologists argue that these human ancestors probably had hearing similar to that of people today.

(A) anthropologists argue that these human ancestors
(B) anthropologists argue, so these human ancestors
(C) anthropologists argue, these human ancestors
(D) these human ancestors, anthropologists argue,
(E) these human ancestors are argued by anthropologists to have

Logical predication; Diction

The verb *argue* here, because it expresses the idea of arguing for a position or theory, should be followed directly by a clause introduced by *that*, without a pause. Verb forms ending with *-ing* with understood subjects, like the one beginning this sentence, must have their subject supplied elsewhere—preferably by the subject of the main clause.

A **Correct.** *Argue* is followed immediately by a *that* clause, and the subject of *using* is supplied by *anthropologists.*

B *Argue* is not directly followed by a *that* clause; moreover, by continuing with *so . . . ,* the sentence does not coherently express the intended idea.

C *Argue* is not directly followed by a *that* clause.

D The subject of the main clause, *these human ancestors*, will illogically be taken as the subject of *using.*

E The subject of the main clause, *these human ancestors*, will illogically be taken as the subject of *using.*

The correct answer is A.

190. The interior minister explained that one of the village planning proposal's best characteristics was their not detracting from the project's overall benefit by being a burden on the development budget.

(A) one of the village planning proposal's best characteristics was their not detracting
(B) one of the village's planning proposal's best characteristics were its not taking
(C) one of the best characteristics of the village's planning proposal was that it did not detract
(D) a best characteristic of the village planning proposal was, it did not take
(E) among the village planning proposal's best characteristics, one was, it did not detract

Agreement; Rhetorical construction

The noun phrase beginning with *one* is singular, as is one of its constituent parts, *the village planning proposal*, so any pronouns for which it is the antecedent should be singular; furthermore, any verb for which the noun phrase beginning with *one* . . . is the subject should be in the singular. The verb *detract* is more appropriate to the thought being expressed than *take.*

A The plural pronoun *their* has a singular noun phrase as its antecedent, namely, *the village planning proposal.* (It is illogical to take the antecedent of *their* to be *best characteristics.*)

B The plural verb *were* does not agree with the singular subject. Also, the verb *taking* should be replaced by the verb *detracting.*

C **Correct.** The verb is correctly in the singular form.

D *A best characteristic* is awkward; the idea is better phrased as *one of the best characteristics*. Also the verb *take* should be replaced by the verb *detract*.

E Instead of the awkward sequence *one was, it did not,* a better choice would be *was that it did not.*

The correct answer is C.

191. Like ants, termites have an elaborate social structure in which a few individuals reproduce and the rest are serving the colony by tending juveniles, gathering food, building the nest, or they battle intruders.

(A) are serving the colony by tending juveniles, gathering food, building the nest, or they battle

(B) are serving the colony in that they tend juveniles, gather food, build the nest, or battle

(C) serve the colony, tending juveniles, gathering food, building the nest, or by battling

(D) serve the colony by tending juveniles, gathering food, by building the nest, or by battling

(E) serve the colony by tending juveniles, gathering food, building the nest, or battling

Parallelism; Rhetorical construction

The sentence most effectively uses parallel structure to contrast two types of termites in the social structure of termite colonies: those who reproduce, and those who serve the colony in a number of ways. The progressive verb form *are serving* should be changed to simple present tense *serve* to parallel *reproduce.* In the final list of responsibilities, parallelism demands that all assume the gerund form as objects of the preposition: *by tending . . . gathering . . . building . . . or battling.*

A The progressive verb form *are serving* is inappropriate for this general claim about termite behavior. It should parallel the previous verb *reproduce.* It is unnecessary to introduce a new clause *or they battle intruders*, because *battling* is another way some termites serve the colony and should therefore be expressed as another object of the preposition *by.*

B *In that they* is an awkward and wordy construction—a poor substitute for *by* in this context.

C The preposition *by* clarifies *how* the termites serve their colony and should govern all of the task descriptions, not just the final one.

D There is no need to repeat the preposition *by*, because all tasks can be described in a series of parallel objects of the same preposition. To violate parallel structure by omitting the preposition before one gerund but repeating it for the rest confuses the reader.

E **Correct.** The sentence uses proper parallel structure and is clear and concise.

The correct answer is E.

192. Global warming is said to be responsible for extreme weather changes, which, like the heavy rains that caused more than $2 billion in damages and led to flooding throughout the state of California, and the heat wave in the northeastern and midwestern United States, which was also the cause of a great amount of damage and destruction.

(A) which, like the heavy rains that caused more than $2 billion in damages and led to flooding throughout the state of California,

(B) which, like the heavy rains that throughout the state of California caused more than $2 billion in damages and led to flooding,

(C) like the heavy flooding that, because of rains throughout the state of California, caused more than $2 billion in damages,

(D) such as the heavy flooding that led to rains throughout the state of California causing more than $2 billion in damages,

(E) such as the heavy rains that led to flooding throughout the state of California, causing more than $2 billion in damages,

Grammatical construction: Logical predication

This sentence introduces the claim that global warming is considered to be the cause of extreme weather changes and then illustrates these changes with two examples introduced by the phrase *such as.* The correct causal sequence of events in the first example is heavy rain, which caused *significant damage and flooding*. The relative pronoun *which*, referring to *changes*, is lacking a verb to complete the relative clause.

A The relative pronoun, *which*, is without a verb. The phrase *which, like the heavy rains* incorrectly suggests that the *extreme weather* is something different from the *heavy rains* and the *heat wave*, and that each of these three phenomena separately caused damage and destruction.

B As in (A), the relative pronoun has no verb to complete the phrase, and the sequence of events in the first example positions costly destruction and flooding as two separate or unrelated results of the rain.

C The causal sequence in the first example is confusing, suggesting, somewhat implausibly, that heavy flooding occurred on its own but caused damage only because of the rain.

D The sequential logic of the first example is confused—indicating, implausibly, that flooding caused heavy rain and that the rain, but not the flooding, caused more than $2 billion in damages.

E Correct. This version of the sentence correctly uses the phrase *such as* to introduce the two examples of extreme weather changes, and it correctly identifies the sequence of events in the first example.

The correct answer is E.

193. The voluminous personal papers of Thomas Alva Edison reveal that his inventions typically sprang to life not in a flash of inspiration but evolved slowly from previous works.

(A) sprang to life not in a flash of inspiration but evolved slowly

(B) sprang to life not in a flash of inspiration but were slowly evolved

(C) did not spring to life in a flash of inspiration but evolved slowly

(D) did not spring to life in a flash of inspiration but had slowly evolved

(E) did not spring to life in a flash of inspiration but they were slowly evolved

Parallelism; Idiom

The construction *not . . . but* shows a contrast. The words following *not* must be parallel in construction to the words following *but*. In the original sentence *not* is followed by a prepositional phrase (*in a flash of inspiration*), while *but* is followed by a verb (*evolved*). To make the two contrasting elements parallel, *not* should be followed by a verb rather than a phrase.

A The construction following *not* is not parallel to the construction following *but*.

B The construction following *not* is not parallel to the construction following *but*.

C Correct. In this sentence, *not* is followed by the verb *spring* just as *but* is followed by the verb *evolved*.

D *Had . . . evolved* introduces an incorrect verb tense.

E The construction following *not* is not parallel to the construction following *but*.

The correct answer is C.

194. Hundreds of species of fish generate and discharge electric currents, in bursts or as steady electric fields around their bodies, using their power either to find and attack prey, to defend themselves, or also for communicating and navigating.

(A) either to find and attack prey, to defend themselves, or also for communicating and navigating

(B) either for finding and attacking prey, defend themselves, or for communication and navigation

(C) to find and attack prey, for defense, or communication and navigation

(D) for finding and attacking prey, to defend themselves, or also for communication and navigation

(E) to find and attack prey, to defend themselves, or to communicate and navigate

Idiom; Verb form

The sentence explains that fish discharge electric currents for several purposes, which are most efficiently and effectively described in a parallel structure: *to find and attack*, *to defend*, *or to communicate and navigate*. The use of *either* is inappropriate in this sentence because more than two uses of electric currents are listed; idiomatic usage requires *either* to be followed by *or* to identify alternatives, not by *also*.

A *Either* inappropriately introduces a list of more than two alternatives, and it should not be followed by *or also*; parallelism requires that *for communicating and navigating* be changed to *to communicate and navigate*.

B *Defend* is not parallel with the list of gerunds, leaving the reader to wonder how to make sense of *defend themselves*.

C The lack of parallelism obscures the relationships among the items in the series; it is especially confusing to list an infinitive phrase (*to find . . .*), an object of a preposition (*for defense*), and nouns with no grammatical connection to the verb phrase (*communication and navigation*).

D This answer choice also violates parallelism by mixing an infinitive with objects of the preposition *for*. *Or also* is an unidiomatic, contradictory expression.

E **Correct.** The different ways in which the various species of fish use their electric power are correctly expressed in a series of parallel infinitives.

The correct answer is E.

195. Native to South America, when peanuts were introduced to Africa by Portuguese explorers early in the sixteenth century they were quickly adopted into Africa's agriculture, probably because of being so similar to the Bambarra groundnut, a popular indigenous plant.

(A) when peanuts were introduced to Africa by Portuguese explorers early in the sixteenth century they were quickly adopted into Africa's agriculture, probably because of being

(B) peanuts having been introduced to Africa by Portuguese explorers early in the sixteenth century and quickly adopted into Africa's agriculture, probably because of being

(C) peanuts were introduced to Africa by Portuguese explorers early in the sixteenth century and were quickly adopted into Africa's agriculture, probably because they were

(D) peanuts, introduced to Africa by Portuguese explorers early in the sixteenth century and quickly adopted into Africa's agriculture, probably because they were

(E) peanuts, introduced to Africa by Portuguese explorers early in the sixteenth century and having been quickly adopted into Africa's agriculture, probably because they were

Grammatical construction; Logical predication

The opening adjectival phrase *Native to South America* must be followed immediately by the noun it modifies: *peanuts*. The sentence makes two main points about peanuts—they were introduced to Africa and they were quickly adopted there. The most efficient way to make these points is to make *peanuts* the subject of two main verbs: *were introduced* and *were . . . adopted*.

A *When* incorrectly intervenes between the opening adjectival phrase and the noun it modifies, and it is also unnecessary because *early in the sixteenth century* explains when. *Because of being* is wordy and indirect.

B This version of the sentence has no main verb, since *having been introduced* and *quickly adopted* both introduce adjectival phrases.

C **Correct.** The sentence is properly structured and grammatically correct.

D This version of the sentence has no main verb because *introduced* and *adopted* both function as adjectives.

E This version of the sentence has no main verb because *introduced* and *having been . . . adopted* function as adjectives.

The correct answer is C.

196. It stood twelve feet tall, weighed nine thousand pounds, and wielded seven-inch claws, and *Megatherium americanum*, a giant ground sloth, may have been the largest hunting mammal ever to walk the Earth.

(A) It stood twelve feet tall, weighed nine thousand pounds, and wielded seven-inch claws, and *Megatherium americanum*, a giant ground sloth,

(B) It stood twelve feet tall, weighing nine thousand pounds, and wielding seven-inch claws, *Megatherium americanum* was a giant ground sloth and

(C) The giant ground sloth *Megatherium americanum*, having stood twelve feet tall, weighing nine thousand pounds, and wielding seven-inch claws, it

(D) Standing twelve feet tall, weighing nine thousand pounds, and wielding seven-inch claws, *Megatherium americanum*, a giant ground sloth,

(E) Standing twelve feet tall, weighing nine thousand pounds, it wielded seven-inch claws, and the giant ground sloth *Megatherium americanum*

Grammatical construction; Parallelism

The point of the sentence is to describe several features of *Megatherium americanum*, to identify this creature as a giant ground sloth, and to speculate about its status as the largest hunting mammal in Earth's history. *Megatherium americanum* is therefore the sole subject of the sentence. When its features are presented as parallel adjective phrases and its common identification is presented as an appositive, a single main verb *may have been* is all that is required to complete the sentence. When the conjunction *and* constructs a compound sentence, the subjects *it* and *ground sloth* or *Megatherium americanum* appear to name separate entities.

A The compound sentence structure suggests that *it* and *Megatherium americanum* are two separate entities, making it unclear what, if anything, the pronoun refers to.

B As in (A), *it* and *Megatherium americanum* appear to name different entities. This a run-on sentence; the comma after *claws* is not sufficient to join the two main clauses in a single sentence. The series describing the sloth is also nonparallel.

C The present-perfect tense of the first participial phrase in the series (*having stood*) is not parallel with the (timeless) present tense of the other two participials. The introduction of the main subject *it* leaves *ground sloth* without a verb.

D Correct. The series of present-tense participial phrases describes the main subject, *Megatherium americanum*, which is clarified by the common name expressed as an appositive.

E The identity of *it* is ambiguous, and the second subject of the compound sentence *giant ground sloth* appears to name something other than *it*. This makes the sentence ungrammatical.

The correct answer is D.

197. Delighted by the reported earnings for the first quarter of the fiscal year, it was decided by the company manager to give her staff a raise.

(A) it was decided by the company manager to give her staff a raise

(B) the decision of the company manager was to give her staff a raise

(C) the company manager decided to give her staff a raise

(D) the staff was given a raise by the company manager

(E) a raise was given to the staff by the company manager

Logical predication; Verb form

Who was *delighted*? The *company manager* was *delighted*. The long modifying phrase that introduces the sentence describes a person, not *it*, so the delighted person must be the subject of the sentence. Correcting the modification error also changes the construction from the wordy passive voice, *it was decided by x*, to the more concise active voice, *x decided*; the active voice is generally preferred.

A The modifier illogically describes *it*, not the *company manager*. The passive voice is wordy.

B The modifier illogically describes *the decision*. The construction *decision of the . . . was . . .* is wordy.

C Correct. The modifying phrase correctly modifies the *company manager*; using the active voice creates a more concise sentence.

D The modifier describes *the staff* rather than *the company manager*; the passive voice is wordy.

E The modifier illogically describes *a raise*; the passive voice is wordy.

The correct answer is C.

198. Studying skeletons unearthed near Rome, DNA evidence was recovered by scientists, who were able to deduce from this that an epidemic of malaria struck in the empire's waning days.

(A) Studying skeletons unearthed near Rome, DNA evidence was recovered by scientists, who were able to deduce from this

(B) In studying skeletons unearthed near Rome, DNA evidence was recovered by scientists, who were able to deduce from this

(C) Scientists recovered DNA evidence from studying skeletons unearthed near Rome, being able to deduce from this

(D) Skeletons unearthed near Rome allowed scientists to recover DNA evidence, and they were able to deduce from it

(E) Scientists studying skeletons unearthed near Rome recovered DNA evidence from which they were able to deduce

Logical predication; Rhetorical construction

The sentence explains that scientists recovered DNA evidence from skeletons, revealing evidence of malaria. As the sentence is written, the participial phrase *studying skeletons* is misplaced; grammatically it modifies the subject of the main clause, thus illogically indicating that the *evidence* studied the skeletons.

A The participial phrase *studying skeletons* illogically modifies *evidence*.

B The participial phrase *studying skeletons* illogically modifies *evidence*.

C The sentence incorrectly states that DNA evidence was recovered from *studying skeletons* rather than from the skeletons; the phrase *being able to deduce from this* is awkward and wordy.

D The construction *skeletons . . . allowed scientists* gives the action of the sentence to the skeletons rather than the scientists; the antecedent of the pronoun *they* is ambiguous, possibly referring either to *scientists* or to *skeletons*.

E **Correct.** *Scientists* is the subject of the main clause, and *studying skeletons* correctly modifies *scientists*.

The correct answer is E.

199. Coffee prices rose sharply Monday, posting their biggest one-day gain in almost three years, after a weekend cold snap in Brazil raised concern that there could be damage to the world's largest crop when at a time with supplies already tight.

(A) that there could be damage to the world's largest crop when at a time with supplies

(B) that the world's largest crop could be damaged at a time such as when supplies are

(C) that the world's largest crop could be damaged at a time when supplies are

(D) of the world's largest crop possibly being damaged at a time with supplies

(E) of possibly damaging the world's largest crop at a time that supplies were

Idiom; Rhetorical construction

This sentence describes concern about a potential problem, which is appropriately expressed in subjunctive mood (*could be damaged*). It uses the idiom *at a time when . . .* to explain the current conditions that make the possible future event a reason for concern. The pseudo-subject *there* introduces unnecessary wordiness. In this sentence, a passive verb emphasizes the speculative nature of the damage caused by the cold snap in Brazil.

A The phrase *when at a time with* is confusingly redundant and incorrectly uses the idiom *at a time when*; the pseudo-subject *there* introduces unnecessary wordiness.

B The phrase *at a time such as when* is wordy and an incorrect idiom.

C **Correct.** This sentence correctly uses the subjunctive mood to express a potential problem, and the idiom *at a time when* is correct.

D The preposition *of* after *concern* is an incorrect construction, as is *at a time with.*

E The agency behind *damaging* is ambiguous; the verb has no clear subject. The phrase *at a time that* is an incorrect idiom. As in D, the preposition *of* after *concern* is incorrect.

The correct answer is C.

200. Growing competitive pressures may be encouraging auditors to bend the rules in favor of clients; auditors may, for instance, allow a questionable loan to remain on the books in order to maintain a bank's profits on paper.

(A) clients; auditors may, for instance, allow

(B) clients, as an instance, to allow

(C) clients, like to allow

(D) clients, such as to be allowing

(E) clients; which might, as an instance, be the allowing of

Grammatical construction; Rhetorical construction

This sentence correctly joins two independent clauses with a semicolon. The first clause makes a generalization; the second clause gives a particular example that supports the generalization.

A **Correct.** This sentence correctly has two independent clauses with linked ideas joined with a semicolon.

B In trying to condense two main clauses into one, this construction produces an ungrammatical sequence of words with no clear meaning.

C The preposition *like* should not be used to introduce the infinitive phrase *to allow . . .*; the comparative preposition *like* is properly used to draw a comparison between two nouns.

D *Such as to be allowing* is not a correct idiomatic expression.

E The semicolon is followed by a wordy, incorrect construction rather than an independent clause.

The correct answer is A.

201. A March 2000 Census Bureau survey showed that Mexico accounted for more than a quarter of all foreign-born residents of the United States, the largest share for any country to contribute since 1890, when about 30 percent of the country's foreign-born population was from Germany.

(A) the largest share for any country to contribute

(B) the largest share that any country has contributed

(C) which makes it the largest share for any country to contribute

(D) having the largest share to be contributed by any country

(E) having the largest share to have been contributed by any country

Logical predication; Rhetorical construction

This sentence claims that the 2000 Census showed that at the time Mexico's contribution to the foreign-born population of United States residents exceeded that of any other country since 1890. It makes the comparison in an appositive that modifies *more than a quarter of all foreign-born residents of the United States.*

A The phrase *for any country to contribute* makes the sentence wordy and indirect.

B **Correct.** This form of the appositive is the most efficient way to express the comparison. Depending on when the sentence was written and what the writer intended to express, the verb form could be either *had contributed* or *has contributed.* The use of *has contributed* implies that, from the perspective of the sentence, the comparison between German-born U.S. residents and those from other countries still holds true.

C The antecedents of the relative pronoun *which* and the pronoun *it* are ambiguous. Along with the prepositional phrase, the pronouns contribute wordiness and indirection.

D This construction is awkward, wordy, and indirect, and the use of the present tense of the infinitive is inappropriate.

E This construction is awkward, wordy, and indirect.

The correct answer is B.

202. Recently declassified information from military satellites in orbit thousands of miles above the Earth show the planet continually bombarded by large meteoroids that explode with the power of atomic bomb blasts.

(A) show the planet continually bombarded by
(B) show continual bombarding of the planet by
(C) show a continual bombardment of the planet from
(D) shows continually that the planet is bombarded from
(E) shows that the planet is continually bombarded by

Agreement; Idiom

The sentence indicates that information shows the planet to be continually bombarded by meteors. However, the plural verb *show* incorrectly corresponds to the word *satellites* in the prepositional phrase *from military satellites*, rather than to the singular subject *information*. The correct combination of subject and verb is *information shows*.

A The singular subject *information* does not agree with the plural verb *show*.

B The singular subject *information* does not agree with the plural verb *show*. The verbal noun *bombarding* (rather than *bombardment*) is awkward and unnecessary.

C The singular subject *information* does not agree with the plural verb *show*. *Bombardment from* is an unidiomatic way of expressing the intended relationship. This construction appears to indicate, illogically, that someone or something located on the large, exploding meteoroids is sending the bombardment to Earth.

D *Continually* should modify *bombarded*, not *shows*. *Bombardment from* is an unidiomatic way of expressing the intended relationship. This construction appears to indicate, illogically, that someone or something located on the large, exploding meteoroids is sending the bombardment to Earth.

E **Correct.** The singular subject *information* agrees with the singular verb *shows*.

The correct answer is E.

203. The themes that Rita Dove explores in her poetry is universal, encompassing much of the human condition while occasionally she deals with racial issues.

(A) is universal, encompassing much of the human condition while occasionally she deals
(B) is universal, encompassing much of the human condition, also occasionally it deals
(C) are universal, they encompass much of the human condition and occasionally deals
(D) are universal, encompassing much of the human condition while occasionally dealing
(E) are universal, they encompass much of the human condition, also occasionally are dealing

Agreement; Grammatical construction

The plural subject of the sentence, *themes*, requires the plural verb *are* in place of *is*. Because the *themes* of Dove's poetry *encompass* the human condition and *deal* with racial issues, there is no need to make this a compound sentence by introducing a new grammatical subject, *she*, in a final clause. A single subject with two parallel verbs is the clearest and most efficient form for this sentence.

A The plural subject disagrees with the singular verb. The sentence should retain the focus on the single subject *themes* rather than introduce a new subject and clause at the end.

B The plural subject disagrees with the singular verb. Because *also occasionally it deals with …* introduces a new main clause, the comma between *condition* and *also* is an insufficient connector (creating a comma splice).

C The comma between *universal* and *they* is an insufficient connector, creating a comma splice; the singular verb *deals* does not agree with the plural subject *they*.

D **Correct.** The plural verb *are* agrees with the plural subject. The sentence is effectively worded and grammatically correct.

E The comma between *universal* and *they* creates a comma splice. There is no subject for the verb *are dealing*.

The correct answer is D.

204. Child development specialists believe that, in confining babies much of the time to strollers, high chairs, playpens, and walkers, muscle development can be inhibited.

(A) that, in confining babies much of the time to strollers, high chairs, playpens, and walkers, muscle development can be inhibited

(B) that, in their confinement much of the time to strollers, high chairs, playpens, and walkers, muscle development can be inhibited in babies

(C) that confining babies much of the time to strollers, high chairs, playpens, and walkers can inhibit muscle development

(D) that babies, if confined much of the time to strollers, high chairs, playpens, and walkers can inhibit muscle development

(E) that strollers, high chairs, playpens, and walkers can, if babies are confined to them much of the time, result in muscle development being inhibited

Logical predication; Rhetorical construction

The point of the sentence is that confining babies can inhibit muscle development. As it is written, however, *muscle development* is the subject of the sentence, and the sentence appears to be saying that muscle development confines babies much of the time. Furthermore, the passive construction *can be inhibited* could even be seen as illogically suggesting that inhibiting development is the purpose of confinement. The sentence can be expressed more clearly and concisely by making *confining* the subject of the verb *can inhibit*: *confining babies . . . can inhibit muscle development*.

A The intended meaning of the sentence is obscured. The sentence appears to indicate that muscle development confines babies much of the time, which surely is not what is intended.

B The antecedent of *their* should be *babies*, but given that *babies* comes far after the pronoun, the reader is liable to take the antecedent of *their* to be *child development specialists*.

C **Correct.** The sentence clearly and concisely indicates that *confining babies . . . can inhibit muscle development*.

D The word *babies* is the subject of the verb *can inhibit*, suggesting incorrectly that babies inhibit their own or someone else's muscle development.

E This sentence uses an awkward and wordy construction to indicate that the sites of confinement *can result in muscle development being inhibited*, when in fact the confinement itself is the cause.

The correct answer is C.

205. Travelers to Mars would have to endure low levels of gravity for long periods of time, avoid large doses of radiation, contend with the chemically reactive Martian soil, and perhaps even having to ward off contamination by Martian life-forms.

(A) contend with the chemically reactive Martian soil, and perhaps even having to ward

(B) contend with the chemically reactive Martian soil, and perhaps even warding

(C) contend with the chemically reactive Martian soil, and perhaps even ward

(D) contending with the chemically reactive Martian soil, and perhaps even to ward

(E) contending with the chemically reactive Martian soil, and perhaps even warding

Parallelism; Grammatical construction

This sentence provides a list of three conditions Mars travelers would certainly have to contend with, along with one additional thing they might have to do—*ward off contamination by Martian life-forms*. The items in the list are most clearly and effectively structured in parallel—as phrases beginning with infinitive verb forms—*to endure*, (*to*) *avoid*, (*to*) *contend*, (*to*) *ward off*. Because the sentence introduces all these actions as something travelers *would have to* do, repeating the *hav*[*ing*] *to* construction in the final item of the list is redundant.

A The phrase *having to* is not parallel with the other items in the list, and it unnecessarily repeats the sense of the introductory phrase, which identifies all items in the list as things travelers *would have to* do.

B The verb form *warding* is not parallel with the other items in the list.

C **Correct.** The sentence uses proper grammar and parallel construction.

D The participial form *contending* violates the parallel structure of the list of infinitive phrases. The reader is misled into thinking that *contending with chemically reactive Martian soil* describes what travelers would have to do to avoid radiation doses.

E The participial phrases *contending with* and *warding off* violate the parallel structure established by the list of infinitive phrases.

The correct answer is C.

206. The personal income tax did not become permanent in the United States until the First World War; before that time the federal government was dependent on tariffs to be their main source of revenue.

(A) the federal government was dependent on tariffs to be their main source of revenue

(B) the federal government had depended on tariffs as its main source of revenue

(C) tariffs were what the federal government was dependent on to be its main source of revenue

(D) the main source of revenue for the federal government was dependent on tariffs

(E) for their main source of revenue, tariffs were depended on by the federal government

Agreement; Logical predication

The First World War is designated as past tense in the opening clause of this sentence. The relationship between that time and whatever happened earlier can be most clearly indicated by using the past-perfect tense for the earlier events. [*T*]*he federal government* is a singular subject of the second clause, so a singular pronoun, *its* rather than *their*, must refer to it. The phrase *was dependent on* causes unnecessary wordiness, as does the passive construction in E.

A The plural pronoun *their* inappropriately refers to the singular noun *government*.

B **Correct.** The pronoun *its* agrees with the singular subject *government*, and the past perfect, active verb *had depended* refers clearly to government activity prior to the First World War.

C This version of the sentence is wordy because of the inverted word order that makes the subject of the second clause an object of the preposition *on*.

D This version of the sentence nonsensically makes *source* the subject of the verb *was* [dependent on].

E The plural possessive pronoun *their* does not agree with its singular antecedent *government*. In fact, because of the placement of *tariffs* immediately after the opening prepositional phrase, *their* seems at first to refer to *tariffs*, which is illogical. The passive verb form *were depended on* is wordy and indirect.

The correct answer is B.

207. In 1776 Adam Smith wrote that it is young people who have "the contempt of risk and the presumptuous hope of success" needed to found new businesses.

(A) who have

(B) with

(C) having

(D) who are those with

(E) who are the ones to have

Grammatical construction; Rhetorical construction

This sentence identifies which people have the attitudes needed to be successful entrepreneurs, according to the economist Adam Smith. The main clause *it is young people* is followed by a relative clause that modifies *young people* and defines the attributes important to their ability to found businesses: caring little about risk and being extremely optimistic about succeeding. The use of the idiomatic construction *it is . . . who* is a way of placing primary emphasis on the question that Smith addressed with the quoted words.

A **Correct.** The relative clause beginning *who have* grammatically and concisely identifies the relevant attitudes that *young people* have.

B In this version, the relative clause modifying *young people* is replaced with a prepositional phrase, introduced by *with*. This clause appears to modify *young people* restrictively. Thus, the sentence simply identifies a subcategory of young people (those with *the contempt of risk* . . .) and does not clearly explain which *people* have the attitudes that Smith identifies.

C Replacing the relative clause with a participial phrase introduced by *having* makes the sentence incomplete, since the point of the sentence is to explain which people *have* the attitudes that Smith identifies.

D Inserting the phrase *are those with* makes the sentence awkward and wordy.

E The word group *are the ones to have* is less concise than the simple verb *have* and fails to convey the meaning that is clearly intended.

The correct answer is A.

208. The gyrfalcon, an Arctic bird of prey, has survived a close brush with extinction; its numbers are now five times greater than when the use of DDT was sharply restricted in the early 1970's.

(A) extinction; its numbers are now five times greater than

(B) extinction; its numbers are now five times more than

(C) extinction, their numbers now fivefold what they were

(D) extinction, now with fivefold the numbers they had

(E) extinction, now with numbers five times greater than

Agreement; Diction; Logical predication

The original sentence contains no errors. The semicolon correctly connects the closely related ideas in the two independent clauses. *The gyrfalcon* is the antecedent for *its* in the second phrase.

A **Correct.** The original sentence correctly uses a singular pronoun, *its*, to refer to the singular antecedent *gyrfalcon*, and it properly uses the construction *its numbers are . . . greater than.*

B The use of *more* instead of *greater* inappropriately implies that there are now more numbers, rather than more gyrfalcons.

C The pronoun *their* is plural, and thus incorrect, since the antecedent *gyrfalcon* is singular. *Fivefold what they were* is awkward and nonstandard and implies that there are now more numbers, rather than more gyrfalcons.

D The pronoun *they* is plural, and thus incorrect, since the antecedent *gyrfalcon* is singular. The comma introduces a confusing phrase seeming to modify *extinction. Fivefold the numbers they had* is awkward and nonstandard and implies that there are now more numbers, rather than more gyrfalcons.

E The comma introduces a confusing phrase seeming to modify *extinction.*

The correct answer is A.

209. In his *Uses of Enchantment* (1976), it was psychologist Bruno Bettelheim's assertion that the apparently cruel and arbitrary nature of many fairy tales actually are an instructive reflection of a child's natural and necessary "killing off" of successive phases in his or her own development.

(A) it was psychologist Bruno Bettelheim's assertion that the apparently cruel and arbitrary nature of many fairy tales actually are

(B) it was the assertion of psychologist Bruno Bettelheim that what is apparently the cruel and arbitrary nature of many fairy tales actually is

(C) psychologist Bruno Bettelheim's assertion that what is apparently the cruel and arbitrary nature of many fairy tales actually is

(D) psychologist Bruno Bettelheim asserted that the apparently cruel and arbitrary nature of many fairy tales actually are

(E) psychologist Bruno Bettelheim asserted that the apparently cruel and arbitrary nature of many fairy tales is actually

Agreement; Rhetorical construction

The sentence attributes to psychologist Bruno Bettelheim a particular view regarding the nature of fairy tales. The construction *it was psychologist Bruno Bettelheim's assertion that* lacks the clarity and directness of the more active construction *Bruno Bettelheim asserted that.* The subject of the subordinate clause containing *nature of many fairy tales actually are* is the singular noun *nature*, not the plural noun in the prepositional phrase *of fairy tales.* Thus, the verb of that clause should be *is*, not *are.*

A *It was psychologist Bruno Bettelheim's assertion that* is wordy and awkward. Presumably this phrase is intended to be equivalent to *Bettelheim asserted that* (just as *it is my opinion that* is another way of saying *I believe that*). However, given the surrounding structure of the sentence, *it* appears to refer to some unnamed entity or condition that occurs in Bettelheim's book, and the entire sequence *was . . . development* appears to be predicated of the subject *it.* The plural verb *are* does not agree with the singular subject *nature.*

B *It was psychologist Bruno Bettelheim's assertion that* is wordy and awkward. Presumably this phrase is intended to be equivalent to *Bettelheim asserted that* (just as *it is my opinion that* is another way of saying *I believe that*). However, given the surrounding structure of the sentence, *it* appears to refer to some unnamed entity or condition that occurs in Bettelheim's book, and the entire sequence *was . . . development* appears to be predicated of the subject *it.* The plural verb *are* does not agree with the singular subject *nature.*

C According to the most plausible parsing of the sentence, everything that follows *asserted that* is intended to express Bettelheim's assertion. On that interpretation, though, the sentence is ungrammatical; the subject of the main clause, *assertion*, is not paired with a verb. If the verb *is* were paired with the subject *assertion*, the sentence would be nonsensical.

D The plural verb *are* does not agree with the singular subject *nature.*

E **Correct.** The construction *Bruno Bettelheim asserted* gives vigor to the main clause, and the singular verb *is* agrees with the subject *nature* in the subordinate clause.

The correct answer is E.

210. After weeks of uncertainty about the course the country would pursue to stabilize its troubled economy, officials reached a revised agreement with the International Monetary Fund, pledging the enforcement of substantially greater budget discipline as that which was originally promised and to keep inflation below ten percent.

(A) the enforcement of substantially greater budget discipline as that which was originally promised and to keep inflation below ten percent

(B) the enforcement of substantially greater budget discipline than originally promised and keeping inflation below the ten percent figure

(C) to enforce substantially greater budget discipline than originally promised and to keep inflation below ten percent

(D) to enforce substantially greater budget discipline than that which was originally promised and keeping inflation less than the ten percent figure

(E) to enforce substantially greater budget discipline as that which was originally promised and to keep inflation less than ten percent

Logical predication; Parallelism

This sentence explains the two-part strategy an unnamed country agreed to pursue in order to stabilize its economy. Nominalization (*the enforcement of* . . .) and an incorrect form of comparison (*as that which was* . . .) in the account of the first strategy causes excessive wordiness and indirection and makes the account of the first strategy nonparallel with the account of the second strategy. To reduce wordiness and achieve parallelism, both strategies pledged by the country should be presented in infinitive form (*to enforce . . . and to keep* . . .). The sentence also needs to employ the correct comparative form *greater discipline than. . . .*

A The two strategies (*the enforcement of* and *keeping*) are not presented in parallel form; the nominalized presentation of the first strategy is wordy and indirect, and the comparative form is incorrect.

B The two strategies (*the enforcement of* and *keeping*) are not presented in parallel form.

C **Correct.** The comparative form is correct, and the two strategies are presented in parallel form, as infinitives completing the verb *pledged.*

D The two strategies are not presented in parallel form, and the comparative form is unnecessarily wordy.

E The comparative form is incorrect and wordy.

The correct answer is C.

211. A new satellite sweeping over the poles at altitudes of up to 32,000 miles is called POLAR, giving scientists their best look yet at the magnetosphere, the region of space under the invisible influence of Earth's magnetic field.

(A) A new satellite sweeping over the poles at altitudes of up to 32,000 miles is called POLAR, giving scientists their best look yet at the magnetosphere, the region of space under the invisible influence of Earth's magnetic field.

(B) A new satellite called POLAR that is giving scientists their best look yet at the magnetosphere, the region of space under the invisible influence of Earth's magnetic field, sweeping over the poles at altitudes of up to 32,000 miles.

(C) Scientists are getting their best look yet at the magnetosphere, the region of space under the invisible influence of Earth's magnetic field, from a new satellite sweeping over the poles at altitudes of up to 32,000 miles called POLAR.

(D) Sweeping over the poles at altitudes of up to 32,000 miles, a new satellite called POLAR is giving scientists their best look yet at the magnetosphere, the region of space under the invisible influence of Earth's magnetic field.

(E) Sweeping over the poles at altitudes of up to 32,000 miles, scientists' best look yet at the magnetosphere, the region of space under the invisible influence of Earth's magnetic field, is coming from a new satellite called POLAR.

Logical predication; Grammatical construction

The point of the sentence is that a *new satellite* is *giving scientists their best look yet at the magnetosphere.* As the sentence is written, the participial phrase *giving scientists . . . magnetosphere* illogically modifies the preceding clause *A new . . . is called POLAR*, suggesting illogically that the naming of the satellite is what provides scientists with a look at the magnetosphere. The sentence can be constructed more clearly with *satellite* as the subject of the main clause and *is giving* as its verb.

A The participial phrase *giving scientists . . . magnetosphere* illogically modifies the whole preceding clause, rather than *satellite.*

B The subject *satellite* has no corresponding verb that would create an independent clause; the word *that* introduces a subordinate clause, and the overall result is merely a sentence fragment.

C The modifier *called POLAR* is awkwardly placed too far away from the word *satellite,* which it is intended to modify; in its current incorrect position, it appears to modify *altitudes.*

D Correct. The sentence is constructed clearly with *satellite* and *is giving* as the subject and verb of the main clause, and the modifiers are placed appropriately near the words they are meant to modify.

E *Sweeping* incorrectly modifies *look,* and the main subject *look* is awkwardly paired with the verb *is coming from.*

The correct answer is D.

212. The treasury market dropped in response to a decrease in the value of the dollar and to continued concern that the economy might be growing as fast as to accelerate inflation and drive interest rates higher.

(A) that the economy might be growing as fast as
(B) that the economy might be growing fast enough
(C) with the economy's possibly growing so fast as
(D) with the possibility of the economy growing fast enough so as
(E) with the possibility of the economy possibly growing fast enough

Idiom; Rhetorical construction

This sentence expresses a possible condition related to the relative speed of the economy's growth. The possible condition is expressed succinctly through the modal verb *might* in the subordinate clause *that the economy might be growing.* However, the correct idiom for expressing the relative speed is *fast enough to* precipitate negative economic consequences—not *as fast as.*

A *As fast as* is not the correct idiom.

B Correct. The possible condition is expressed succinctly using the modal verb *might,* and idioms are used correctly.

C *Concern with* is not the correct idiom; the phrases *economy's possibly growing* and *so fast as to* are wordy and awkward.

D *Concern with* is not the correct idiom; the phrase *possibility of the economy growing fast enough so as to* is wordy and awkward.

E *Concern with* is not the correct idiom; *possibility* and *possibly* are unnecessarily and awkwardly repetitive.

The correct answer is B.

213. Like Rousseau, Tolstoi rebelled against the unnatural complexity of human relations in modern society.

(A) Like Rousseau, Tolstoi rebelled
(B) Like Rousseau, Tolstoi's rebellion was
(C) As Rousseau, Tolstoi rebelled
(D) As did Rousseau, Tolstoi's rebellion was
(E) Tolstoi's rebellion, as Rousseau's, was

Logical predication; Rhetorical construction

The preposition *like* correctly compares two equal nouns, in this case, two writers. The comparison must be between two equal elements; it cannot be between a person and an event. The original sentence is direct, clear, and concise.

A Correct. The two writers are compared clearly and succinctly in this sentence.

B *Tolstoi's rebellion* rather than *Tolstoi* is compared to *Rousseau.*

C When used as a conjunction, *as* should introduce clauses, not phrases or nouns.

D *Tolstoi's rebellion* is compared to *Rousseau.* To be correct, this construction would have to be *as did Rousseau, Tolstoi rebelled,* but this is a wordy alternative.

E *Tolstoi's rebellion . . . was against* is awkward and wordy; *Tolstoi rebelled against* is more direct.

The correct answer is A.

214. Japanese researchers are producing a series of robots that can identify human facial expressions, to which they will then respond; their goal is primarily creating a robot that will empathize with us.

(A) expressions, to which they will then respond; their goal is primarily creating
(B) expressions, then responding to them; primarily to create
(C) expressions and then respond to them; the researchers' primary goal is to create
(D) expressions as well as giving a response to them; their primary goal is creation of
(E) expressions and responding to them; primarily, the researchers' goal is creating

Logical predication; Rhetorical construction

This sentence uses two complete clauses to present two main topics—the capabilities of robots designed by Japanese researchers and the goal that motivates this design. The first clause most effectively uses a succession of parallel verbs to describe what the robots can do: *identify* expressions and *respond* to them. Beginning the second clause with the possessive pronoun *their* creates ambiguity, because it is not clear whether the pronoun refers to the robots or the researchers.

A The pronouns *they* and *their* in this version of the sentence are ambiguous, possibly referring to both researchers and robots.

B The phrase *then responding to them* should be converted to a main verb to parallel *identify* and to make clear that the robots can do these two things. The semicolon should be followed by a complete clause, but in this version of the sentence it is followed by an adverbial phrase.

C **Correct.** The wording is concise and unambiguous.

D The phrase *as well as giving a response to them* is wordy; the pronoun *their* is ambiguous.

E *Responding* is the wrong verb form—it should be an infinitive to parallel *identify*.

The correct answer is C.

215. Despite a growing population, in 1998 the United States used 38 billion fewer gallons of water a day when comparing it to the period of all-time highest consumption almost 20 years earlier.

(A) day when comparing it to the period of all-time highest consumption almost 20 years earlier
(B) day than it did during the period of all-time highest consumption almost 20 years earlier
(C) day than were used almost 20 years earlier, which had been the all-time high consumption
(D) day, compared to almost 20 years earlier, that having been the all-time high consumption
(E) day, which is in comparison to the period of all-time highest consumption almost 20 years earlier

Rhetorical construction; Logical predication

When making a direct comparison (in this case, with *fewer*), the standard way to express the object of comparison is with *than*. Here, the sentence uses *fewer . . . when comparing it to*, which not only is unidiomatic, but also creates an illogical predication: *United States* is the only possible subject for the verb *comparing* (surely the sentence doesn't mean to say the United States used 38 billion fewer gallons at the time it was making some comparison!). Also, what is the antecedent of *it* here? Grammatically, there is no clear candidate.

A Instead of using *fewer . . . than*, this version uses the unidiomatic *fewer . . . when comparing it to*, which also introduces a logical predication problem.

B **Correct.** *Fewer than* is correct, and this version of the sentence has no logical predication problems.

C This has a logical predication problem: because the relative clause beginning with *which* immediately follows *almost 20 years earlier*, it seems that the time period is being described as having been *the all-time high consumption*.

D *Fewer than* is preferable to *fewer . . . compared to*; also, there is a logical predication problem: because the phrase beginning with *that* immediately follows *almost 20 years earlier*, it seems that the time period is being described as having been *the all-time high consumption*.

E This is awkwardly and confusingly worded. Rather than comparing the United States' water usage in 1998 to its water usage nearly 20 years earlier, this appears illogically to compare the United States' water usage in 1998 to a period of time, namely *the period of all-time highest consumption almost 20 years earlier*.

The correct answer is B.

216. Analysts believe that whereas bad decisions by elected leaders can certainly hurt the economy, no administration can really be said to control or manage all of the complex and interrelated forces that determine the nation's economic strength.

(A) no administration can really be said to control

(B) no administration can be said that it really controls

(C) that no administration can really be said to control

(D) that no administration can really be said that it controls

(E) that it cannot be said that any administration really controls

Grammatical construction; Verb form

The point of this sentence is to explain analysts' common two-part belief about the limited power of elected officials to control a national economy. It presents this belief as the direct object in the main clause, [*a*]*nalysts believe*, and introduces it with the subordinating conjunction *that*, which governs both the positive dependent clause (*decisions . . . can hurt*) introduced by *whereas*, and the subsequent negative independent clause (*no administration can . . . be said to control . . .*). The additional appearances of *that* in some of the versions of the sentence are ungrammatical.

A **Correct.** Introduced by the subordinating conjunction *that*, the complex clause succinctly contrasts leaders' powers to hurt the economy with their inability to control all economic forces.

B The idiom *can be said to* would be appropriate, but *no administration can be said that it* is ungrammatical.

C The repetition of *that* is ungrammatical, since both clauses are governed by the initial appearance of *that* after [*a*]*nalysts believe*.

D This version of the sentence combines the mistakes described in (B) with those described in (C).

E The repetition of *that* is ungrammatical, since both clauses are governed by the first appearance of *that*. The appearance of *it* makes the sentence unnecessarily wordy and convoluted.

The correct answer is A.

217. Except for a concert performance that the composer himself staged in 1911, Scott Joplin's ragtime opera *Treemonisha* was not produced until 1972, sixty-one years after its completion.

(A) Except for a concert performance that the composer himself staged

(B) Except for a concert performance with the composer himself staging it

(C) Besides a concert performance being staged by the composer himself

(D) Excepting a concert performance that the composer himself staged

(E) With the exception of a concert performance with the staging done by the composer himself

Idiom; Rhetorical construction

This sentence requires attention to idiom and to conciseness. *Except for* is correctly followed by a noun, *concert performance*; *that the composer himself staged* is a clause that clearly and concisely describes the performance.

A **Correct.** In this sentence, the correct idiom is used in a clear and concise expression.

B *With . . . it* is an awkward and wordy construction, and *staging* suggests ongoing action rather than action completed in 1911.

C *Being staged* suggests ongoing rather than completed action.

D *Excepting* usually appears in negative constructions; it is not the correct idiom in this sentence.

E This sentence is awkward and wordy.

The correct answer is A.

218. Nearly unrivaled in their biological diversity, coral reefs provide a host of benefits that includes the supply of protein for people, protecting shorelines, and they contain biochemical sources for new life-saving medicines.

(A) coral reefs provide a host of benefits that includes the supply of protein for people, protecting shorelines,

(B) coral reefs provide a host of benefits: they supply people with protein, they protect the shorelines,

(C) coral reefs provide a host of benefits that include supplying protein for people, as well as shoreline protection,

(D) a coral reef provides a host of benefits; they supply protein for people, the protecting of shorelines,

(E) a coral reef provides a host of benefits, including protein for people, protecting shorelines,

Parallelism; Agreement

When listing several items (here, benefits of coral reefs), they should be expressed in a parallel way, such as by using all noun phrases or all full clauses. Also, pronoun subjects in one clause that refer to the subject of a preceding clause should agree in number.

A The three items after *includes* are not parallel *(the supply; protecting shorelines; they contain).*

B **Correct.** The three items after *benefits* are parallel *(they supply; they protect; they contain).* The subject of the next clause *(they)* is correctly plural given that its antecedent is *coral reefs.*

C The three items after *include* are not parallel: *supplying, shoreline protection, they contain.*

D The three items after *benefits* are not parallel *(they supply; the protecting of; they contain),* and in the next clause they is the incorrect pronoun given that the antecedent here is the singular *a coral reef.*

E The three items after *benefits* are not parallel *(protein; protecting; they contain),* and in the next clause *they* is the incorrect pronoun given that the antecedent here is the singular *a coral reef.*

The correct answer is B.

219. Literacy opened up entire realms of verifiable knowledge to ordinary men and women having been previously considered incapable of discerning truth for themselves.

(A) having been previously considered incapable of discerning truth for themselves

(B) who had previously been considered incapable of discerning truth for themselves

(C) previously considered incapable of discerning truth for himself or herself

(D) of whom it had previously been considered they were incapable of discerning truth for themselves

(E) who had previously been considered incapable of discerning truth for himself or herself

Rhetorical construction; Agreement

The phrase beginning with *having been* modifies the noun phrase *ordinary men and women.* In cases like this, it is best to use a full relative clause, starting with *that* or a relative pronoun such as *which* or *who,* instead of a clause with the *-ing* form of the verb. Also, *themselves* is the correct form of a reflexive pronoun to refer back to the plural noun phrase *ordinary men and women.*

A A phrase starting with the *-ing* verb form, instead of with *that* or *who,* is awkward in this context.

B **Correct.** A relative clause correctly beginning with *who* is used, and *themselves* is the correct form for the reflexive pronoun.

C *Himself or herself* is not the correct form for the plural reflexive pronoun.

D Though the relative and reflexive pronouns are grammatically correct, the relative clause (the clause that starts with *of whom*) is unnecessarily long and complex.

E *Himself or herself* is not the correct form for the plural reflexive pronoun.

The correct answer is B.

220. In early Mesopotamian civilization, castor oil served not only as a laxative, but also a skin-softening lotion and it was a construction lubricant for sliding giant stone blocks over wooden rollers.

(A) not only as a laxative, but also a skin-softening lotion and it was a construction

(B) as not only a laxative, but also a skin-softening lotion, and it was a construction

(C) not only as a laxative but also as a skin-softening lotion and as a construction

(D) as not only a laxative but as a skin-softening lotion and in construction, as a

(E) not only as a laxative, but a skin-softening lotion and in construction, a

Parallelism; Rhetorical construction

The sentence indicates three uses for castor oil. The first two are correctly joined using the correlative conjunction *not only, but also.* However, the three uses are not listed in parallel grammatical form. The sentence would be better with three adverb phrases beginning with *as*: *as a laxative*, *as a skin-softening lotion*, and *as a construction lubricant.*

A The three uses for castor oil are not listed in parallel grammatical form since the first is an adverb phrase, the second is a noun phrase, and the third is an independent clause, which is ungrammatically conjoined to the preceding part of the sentence without an intervening comma.

B The three uses for castor oil are not listed in parallel grammatical form since the first two are noun phrases and the third is an independent clause.

C **Correct.** The three uses for castor oil are listed as parallel adverb phrases, and the correlative conjunction *not only, but also* is constructed correctly.

D The three uses for castor oil are not listed in parallel grammatical form. The placing of *not only* after *as* is incorrect; the phrase *in construction* is also incorrectly placed.

E The word *as* is missing from the second and third elements of the correlative conjunction, so the three uses for castor oil are not listed correctly in parallel grammatical form.

The correct answer is C.

221. An analysis of tree bark all over the globe shows that chemical insecticides have often spread thousands of miles from where they were originally used.

(A) that chemical insecticides have often spread thousands of miles from where they were originally used

(B) that chemical insecticides have spread, often thousands of miles from their original use

(C) chemical insecticides, having often spread thousands of miles from where they were used originally

(D) chemical insecticides, often spreading thousands of miles from where their original use

(E) chemical insecticides, often spreading thousands of miles from where they were originally used

Grammatical construction; Diction

To express the intended meaning, *shows* can be followed by a clause beginning with *that*. Another option would be to use the special clause type *show* + noun phrase + *ing* verb form, such as *show chemical insecticides spreading many miles*—but there should be no pause in the middle of a construction of this latter type. If there is such a pause, then *chemical insecticides* becomes the direct object of *show*, and the following verb-*ing* phrase is an awkward attempt at a modifier of this object. Note also that if something spreads, it spreads from a place or an entity; other ways of expressing this idea in the answer choices are awkward or illogical. Verbs without overt subjects (such as *spreading* here) normally are to be understood as having the same subject as the main clause.

A **Correct.** *Show* is correctly followed by a *that* clause, and a place is correctly identified (*from where*) as the source of the spread.

B *Show* is followed by a *that* clause, but insecticides are illogically said to have spread from a use, rather than from a place.

C *Show* can sometimes take a direct object (here, *chemical insecticides*). However, the construction used here makes *analysis* the subject of *having*. Thus it appears to say, illogically, that the analysis shows that the analysis itself has spread from where the insecticides were used.

D *Show* can sometimes take a direct object (here, *chemical insecticides*). However, the construction used here makes *analysis* the subject of *spreading*. Thus, it appears to say, illogically, that the analysis shows that the analysis itself often spreads from where the insecticides were used. Also, *where their original use* is grammatically incorrect (*where they were originally used* is a correct alternative).

E *Show* can sometimes take a direct object (here, *chemical insecticides*). However, the construction used here makes *analysis* the subject of *spreading*. Thus, it appears to say, illogically, that the analysis shows that the analysis itself often spreads from where the insecticides were used.

The correct answer is A.

222. Consumers may not think of household cleaning products to be hazardous substances, but many of them can be harmful to health, especially if they are used improperly.

(A) Consumers may not think of household cleaning products to be

(B) Consumers may not think of household cleaning products being

(C) A consumer may not think of their household cleaning products being

(D) A consumer may not think of household cleaning products as

(E) Household cleaning products may not be thought of, by consumers, as

Idiom; Agreement

The sentence uses an idiom that is correctly expressed as *think of x as y*. The use of *to be* is incorrect.

A *To be* is incorrect in the idiom *to think of x as y*.

B *Being* is incorrect in the idiom *to think of x as y*.

C *Being* is incorrect in the idiom *to think of x as y*. *Their* does not agree with *a consumer*.

D **Correct.** This sentence uses the idiom correctly: *think of household products as*.

E The passive-voice construction is awkward and wordy.

The correct answer is D.

223. According to the Economic Development Corporation of Los Angeles County, if one were to count the Los Angeles metropolitan area as a separate nation, it would have the world's eleventh largest gross national product, that is bigger than that of Australia, Mexico, or the Netherlands.

(A) if one were to count the Los Angeles metropolitan area as a separate nation, it would have the world's eleventh largest gross national product, that is

(B) if the Los Angeles metropolitan area is counted as a separate nation, it has the world's eleventh largest gross national product, that being

(C) if the Los Angeles metropolitan area were a separate nation, it would have the world's eleventh largest gross national product,

(D) were the Los Angeles metropolitan area a separate nation, it will have the world's eleventh largest gross national product, which is

(E) when the Los Angeles metropolitan area is counted as a separate nation, it has the world's eleventh largest gross national product, thus

Diction; Verb form

The point of this sentence is to explain the implications of a contrary-to-fact state of affairs (Los Angeles metropolitan area as a nation). The subjunctive verb form is needed (*were . . . would have*). To attribute this proposed state of affairs to the calculations of an anonymous agent (*one*) causes unnecessary wordiness. The implication of the hypothetical situation is that the Los Angeles area would have the eleventh-largest gross national product (GNP) in the world, a GNP that is further described as larger than the GNP of any of three nations named. This descriptive information is most efficiently presented as a terminal adjective phrase.

A By introducing the subject *one*, the opening clause becomes unnecessarily wordy and indirect. The relative clause at the end of the sentence causes additional wordiness. The present indicative verb form *is* in the phrase *that is bigger than* . . . is inconsistent with the conditional context established earlier in the sentence (*were* . . . *would*). Since Los Angeles is not a nation, its *national* product is purely hypothetical and contrary to fact.

B Because the *if* clause introduces a situation that is contrary to fact, the verbs *is counted* and *has* should be subjunctive and conditional, respectively (*were counted* and *would have*). The relative pronoun phrase *that being* is awkward, wordy, and repetitive.

C **Correct.** The subjunctive mood of the verbs is appropriate to the contrary-to-fact situation being described, and the terminal adjective phrase without an introductory relative pronoun is an appropriate way of making the comparison among GNPs.

D Although the opening subjunctive verb is appropriate, it must be followed by a conditional verb in the main clause; the relative clause at the end of the sentence, beginning with *which is*, is indirect and wordy. As in (A), *is* is not the most appropriate verb form to express a counterfactual condition.

E The verbs *is counted* . . . *has* are incorrect for describing a contrary-to-fact situation. Beginning the final adjective phrase with the word *thus* makes the relationship of the phrase to the rest of the sentence unclear.

The correct answer is C.

224. Initiated five centuries after Europeans arrived in the New World on Columbus Day 1992, Project SETI pledged a $100 million investment in the search for extraterrestrial intelligence.

(A) Initiated five centuries after Europeans arrived in the New World on Columbus Day 1992, Project SETI pledged a $100 million investment in the search for extraterrestrial intelligence.

(B) Initiated on Columbus Day 1992, five centuries after Europeans arrived in the New World, a $100 million investment in the search for extraterrestrial intelligence was pledged by Project SETI.

(C) Initiated on Columbus Day 1992, five centuries after Europeans arrived in the New World, Project SETI pledged a $100 million investment in the search for extraterrestrial intelligence.

(D) Pledging a $100 million investment in the search for extraterrestrial intelligence, the initiation of Project SETI five centuries after Europeans arrived in the New World on Columbus Day 1992.

(E) Pledging a $100 million investment in the search for extraterrestrial intelligence five centuries after Europeans arrived in the New World, on Columbus Day 1992, the initiation of Project SETI took place.

Logical predication; Grammatical construction

The original sentence becomes illogical when phrases do not modify what they are intended to modify. This sentence mistakenly says that *Europeans arrived in the New World on Columbus Day 1992.* It also says that Project SETI was *initiated five centuries after* . . . *Columbus Day 1992.* To make the modifiers grammatically and logically correct, the sentence may be revised: *Initiated on Columbus Day 1992, five centuries after Europeans arrived in the New World, Project SETI*. . . .

A Project SETI cannot have been *initiated five centuries after* . . . *1992*, nor did Europeans first arrive in 1992.

B *Initiated* . . . modifies *$100 million investment* instead of *Project SETI.*

C **Correct.** The modifiers are grammatically and logically correct in this sentence.

D *Pledging* . . . incorrectly modifies *the initiation*. This is a sentence fragment.

E *Pledging* . . . incorrectly modifies *the initiation*. Europeans appear to have arrived on Columbus Day 1992. The construction is awkward, unbalanced, and imprecise.

The correct answer is C.

225. According to some economists, the July decrease in unemployment so that it was the lowest in two years suggests that the gradual improvement in the job market is continuing.

(A) so that it was the lowest in two years
(B) so that it was the lowest two-year rate
(C) to what would be the lowest in two years
(D) to a two-year low level
(E) to the lowest level in two years

Idiom; Rhetorical construction

In this sentence, *decrease* is used as a noun and cannot grammatically be modified by the adverbial *so that*. The simple prepositional phrase *to the lowest level in two years* is a precise, concise alternative.

A The use of *so that it was* to modify a noun is ungrammatical, and *it* could refer to either *decrease* or *unemployment*.

B The use of *so that it was* to modify a noun is ungrammatical. *It* could refer to either *decrease* or *unemployment*, and the word *rate* is unclear.

C Use of the conditional *would* to state a fact is nonstandard; *lowest* should refer to a noun such as *level*.

D The meaning of *to a two-year low level* is unclear, and the phrase is unidiomatic.

E **Correct.** This sentence uses a clear, simple phrase that conveys an unambiguous meaning.

The correct answer is E.

226. Developed by Pennsylvania's Palatine Germans about 1750, Conestoga wagons, with high wheels capable of crossing rutted roads, muddy flats, and the nonroads of the prairie and they had a floor curved upward on either end so as to prevent cargo from shifting on steep grades.

(A) wagons, with high wheels capable of crossing rutted roads, muddy flats, and the nonroads of the prairie and they had a floor curved upward on either end so as to prevent
(B) wagons, with high wheels capable of crossing rutted roads, muddy flats, and the nonroads of the prairie, and with a floor that was curved upward at both ends to prevent
(C) wagons, which had high wheels capable of crossing rutted roads, muddy flats, and the nonroads of the prairie, and floors curved upward on their ends so that they prevented
(D) wagons had high wheels capable of crossing rutted roads, muddy flats, and the nonroads of the prairie, and a floor that was curved upward at both ends to prevent
(E) wagons had high wheels capable of crossing rutted roads, muddy flats, and the nonroads of the prairie and floors curving upward at their ends so that it prevented

Logical predication; Parallelism; Grammatical construction

The main subject of this sentence is *Conestoga wagons* and the main verb is *had*. The opening participial phrase describes the origin of the wagons, and the rest of the sentence describes the features they possessed. These features must be presented in parallel form as objects of the verb *had*. The sentence first presented is a fragment; the prepositional phrase *with* . . . leaves the subject *Conestoga wagons* without a verb. When the verb *had* finally appears, a new subject *they* has been unnecessarily introduced.

A The subject *wagons* is without a verb. The introduction of a new subject *they* is unnecessary. Given the absence of *had* after *wagons* and of a comma after *prairie*, it is also ungrammatical.

B This version of the sentence has no main verb for the subject *wagons*.

C As in (A) and (B), this version of the sentence fails to provide a main verb for the subject *wagons*.

D Correct. The main verb *had* completes the subject *wagons* and accommodates the two direct objects, *wheels* and *a floor*. The comma after *prairie* helps to clarify that *floors* is a direct object of *had*, parallel with *high wheels*.

E The referent for *it* is ambiguous.

The correct answer is D.

227. The Baldrick Manufacturing Company has for several years followed a policy aimed at decreasing operating costs and improving the efficiency of its distribution system.

(A) aimed at decreasing operating costs and improving

(B) aimed at the decreasing of operating costs and to improve

(C) aiming at the decreasing of operating costs and improving

(D) the aim of which is the decreasing of operating costs and improving

(E) with the aim to decrease operating costs and to improve

Parallelism; Rhetorical construction

This correct sentence uses the grammatically parallel elements *decreasing* and *improving* to describe the two aims of the company's policy.

A Correct. *Decreasing* and *improving* are grammatically parallel; *aimed at* is a correct and concise expression.

B *The decreasing* and *to improve* are not parallel.

C Using *the* before *decreasing* creates a gerund, which is not parallel to the participle *improving*.

D *The aim of which* is awkward and wordy; *the decreasing* is not parallel to *improving*.

E *With the aim to* is not the correct idiom; the correct idiom is *with the aim of* followed by an *ing* verb form such as *decreasing*.

The correct answer is A.

228. Some buildings that were destroyed and heavily damaged in the earthquake last year were constructed in violation of the city's building code.

(A) Some buildings that were destroyed and heavily damaged in the earthquake last year were

(B) Some buildings that were destroyed or heavily damaged in the earthquake last year had been

(C) Some buildings that the earthquake destroyed and heavily damaged last year have been

(D) Last year the earthquake destroyed or heavily damaged some buildings that have been

(E) Last year some of the buildings that were destroyed or heavily damaged in the earthquake had been

Diction; Verb form

The buildings cannot be both *destroyed* and *heavily damaged* at the same time; they must be one *or* the other. The ideas of this sentence are most clearly expressed using two verb tenses: the simple past, *were*, for the earthquake occurring last year; and the past perfect, *had been*, for the time prior to that when the buildings were constructed.

A The buildings are illogically said to be both *destroyed* and *damaged*.

B Correct. This sentence properly states that the buildings were either destroyed *or* damaged and clarifies that they *had been constructed* before the earthquake struck.

C Buildings cannot be both destroyed *and* damaged. The verb tense makes it seem that they were constructed after the earthquake.

D The verb tense illogically indicates that the buildings *have been constructed* since the earthquake.

E This structure indicates that construction of the buildings, rather than the earthquake, occurred *last year*.

The correct answer is B.

229. Because the collagen fibers in skin line up in the direction of tension, surgical cuts made along these so-called Langer's lines sever fewer fibers and is less likely to leave an unsightly scar.

(A) Because the collagen fibers in skin line up in the direction of tension, surgical cuts made along these so-called Langer's lines sever fewer

(B) Because the collagen fibers in skin line up in the direction of tension, a surgical cut having been made along these so-called Langer's lines severs less

(C) Because the collagen fibers in skin line up in the direction of tension, a surgical cut made along these so-called Langer's lines severs fewer

(D) With the collagen fibers in skin lining up in the direction of tension, surgical cuts made along these so-called Langer's lines sever less

(E) With the collagen fibers in skin lining up in the direction of tension, a surgical cut made along these so-called Langer's lines sever fewer

Agreement; Diction

This sentence explains a causal connection between the alignment of collagen fibers and the impact of a particular type of surgical cut. *Because* is appropriate to express that causal relationship. The singular verb in the phrase *is less likely to leave* requires a singular subject (*cut*) and must be coordinated with another singular verb (*severs*). Because *fibers* are countable, the correct modifier is *fewer* rather than *less.*

A The plural subject *cuts* does not agree with the singular verb *is.*

B The verb form *having been made* is inconsistent with the present tense verb *severs*; *less* inappropriately modifies countable *fibers.*

C **Correct.** The adverbial conjunction *because* accurately captures the causal relationship expressed by the sentence. The singular subject *cut* agrees with the singular verbs *severs* and *is*, and *fewer* appropriately modifies countable *fibers.*

D The preposition *with* does not capture the causal relationship expressed by the sentence; the plural subject *cuts* does not agree with the singular verbs (*severs* and *is*); and *less* is an inappropriate modifier for countable *fibers.*

E As in (D), the preposition *with* fails to capture the causal relationship between alignment of fibers and scarring. The plural verb *sever* does not agree with the singular subject *cut* and the subsequent singular verb *is.*

The correct answer is C.

230. In A.D. 391, resulting from the destruction of the largest library of the ancient world at Alexandria, later generations lost all but the *Iliad* and *Odyssey* among Greek epics, most of the poetry of Pindar and Sappho, and dozens of plays by Aeschylus and Euripides.

(A) resulting from the destruction of the largest library of the ancient world at Alexandria,

(B) the destroying of the largest library of the ancient world at Alexandria resulted and

(C) because of the result of the destruction of the library at Alexandria, the largest of the ancient world,

(D) as a result of the destruction of the library at Alexandria, the largest of the ancient world,

(E) Alexandria's largest library of the ancient world was destroyed, and the result was

Logical predication; Rhetorical construction; Grammatical construction

Because it is introduced by a participle, the phrase that begins *resulting from* illogically modifies *later generations.* Substituting the idiom *as a result of* for *resulting from* corrects this error. *The largest library of the ancient world at Alexandria* is both cumbersome and ambiguous because it suggests that the *ancient world* was located *at* (and only at) *Alexandria.* This problem is best corrected by breaking the series of phrases into two distinct parts: *the library at Alexandria, the largest of the ancient world.* Here, the second phrase clearly modifies the first.

A *Resulting from* illogically modifies *later generations*. The series of prepositional phrases is confusing and ambiguous.

B *The destroying of* is wordy and awkward. *And* creates a second main clause, which would need to be appropriately punctuated with a comma before *and*.

C *Because of the result of* is redundant.

D **Correct.** *As a result of* begins the phrase clearly and correctly in this sentence; the *library* rather than the *ancient world* is properly located *at Alexandria*; *the largest of the ancient world* correctly modifies *library*.

E *Alexandria's largest library of the ancient world* is an illogical reference. *The result was* must be followed by *that*.

The correct answer is D.

231. The nephew of Pliny the Elder wrote the only eyewitness account of the great eruption of Vesuvius in two letters to the historian Tacitus.

(A) The nephew of Pliny the Elder wrote the only eyewitness account of the great eruption of Vesuvius in two letters to the historian Tacitus.

(B) To the historian Tacitus, the nephew of Pliny the Elder wrote two letters, being the only eyewitness accounts of the great eruption of Vesuvius.

(C) The only eyewitness account is in two letters by the nephew of Pliny the Elder writing to the historian Tacitus an account of the great eruption of Vesuvius.

(D) Writing the only eyewitness account, Pliny the Elder's nephew accounted for the great eruption of Vesuvius in two letters to the historian Tacitus.

(E) In two letters to the historian Tacitus, the nephew of Pliny the Elder wrote the only eyewitness account of the great eruption of Vesuvius.

Logical predication; Rhetorical construction

The challenge in this sentence lies in the correct placement of a prepositional phrase. In the original version, the placement of *in two letters to the historian Tacitus* appears to suggest that Vesuvius erupted in the letters themselves. Placing the phrase at the beginning of the sentence solves the problem.

A The sentence suggests that the eruption of Vesuvius took place in the letters themselves.

B Beginning the sentence with *to the historian Tacitus* is clumsy and unclear. The verb phrase *being* . . . seems illogically to modify *the nephew*, creating the awkward suggestion that *the nephew* was *the eyewitness accounts*.

C The sentence's meaning is unclear due to an extended sequence of prepositional phrases.

D *An account* is a narrative record; *to account for* means to be the cause of. Using both in the same sentence is confusing and here suggests that the nephew caused the eruption. The sentence also suggests that the eruption of Vesuvius took place in the letters themselves.

E **Correct.** The placement of the prepositional phrase at the beginning of the sentence clarifies the meaning of the sentence; the construction of the rest of the sentence is straightforward.

The correct answer is E.

232. Nearly two tons of nuclear-reactor fuel have already been put into orbit around the Earth, and the chances of a collision involving such material increase greatly as the amount of both space debris and satellites continue to rise.

(A) as the amount of both space debris and satellites continue to rise

(B) as the rise continues in both the amount of satellites and space debris

(C) as the amount of space debris and the number of satellites continue to rise

(D) with the continually increasing amount of space debris and the number of satellites

(E) with the amount of space debris continuing to increase along with the number of satellites

Diction; Rhetorical construction

This sentence opens with a main clause stating a condition (two tons of nuclear-reactor fuel orbiting the Earth) and follows this with a second main clause stating possible consequences of combining this condition (amount of space debris) with a second condition (rising number of satellites). Because debris is not a countable noun, it must be described as an *amount*; satellites are countable, so they must be referred to as a number, not an amount.

A *Amount* is an inappropriate descriptor for satellites.

B *Amount* is an inappropriate descriptor for satellites. *Both* should be followed by two nouns, but here it is followed by only one, so the comparison is grammatically incorrect.

C **Correct.** The sentence is unambiguous and grammatically correct and uses *amount* and *number* correctly.

D By attaching the adjective *increasing* only to *amount of space debris*, the sentence fails to indicate that the number of satellites is also growing. This leaves the function of *and the number of satellites* uncertain and confusing.

E This version of the sentence is indirect, wordy, and confusing.

The correct answer is C.

233. Though being tiny, blind, and translucent, a recently discovered species of catfish lessens their vulnerability with thickened bones and armor plates on their sides.

(A) Though being tiny, blind, and translucent, a recently discovered species of catfish lessens their vulnerability with thickened bones and armor plates on their sides.

(B) Though tiny, blind, and translucent, a recently discovered species of catfish has thickened bones and armor plates on its sides that lessen its vulnerability.

(C) A recently discovered species of catfish has thickened bones and armor plates on its sides that lessen their vulnerability, though tiny, blind, and translucent.

(D) Thickened bones and armor plates on their sides lessen the vulnerability of a recently discovered species of catfish that is tiny, blind, and translucent.

(E) Tiny, blind, and translucent, thickened bones and armor plates on its sides lessen the vulnerability of a recently discovered species of catfish.

Logical predication; Agreement

The point of the sentence is to explain two sets of features of a catfish species, one that makes the species seem vulnerable, and the other that reduces its vulnerability. The sentence as written introduces the unnecessary participial *being* and incorrectly refers to the singular *species* with the plural possessive pronoun *their*.

A The participial *being* makes the sentence unnecessarily wordy. The plural pronoun *their* has no clear antecedent; it cannot refer to *species*, because the sentence has already established, with the singular verb *lessens*, that it is using *species* as a singular noun. Also, the sentence illogically says that the species (not its physical characteristics) lessens their vulnerability.

B **Correct.** The opening set of adjectives introduced by the contrastive term *though* is efficient and sets up a contrast between the features that make the species vulnerable and those that make it less vulnerable. The singular pronoun *its* correctly refers to the singular noun *species*.

C The referent for the plural possessive pronoun *their* is unclear; it is also unclear what the set of adjectives introduced by *though* is supposed to modify. The sentence structure suggests, nonsensically, that they modify *armor plates*.

D This version of the sentence confusingly refers to species as both plural (*their sides*) and singular (*that is*).

E The opening set of adjectives (*tiny, blind, and translucent*) nonsensically describes bones and plates.

The correct answer is B.

234. A recent court decision has qualified a 1998 ruling that workers cannot be laid off if they have been given reason to believe that their jobs will be safe, provided that their performance remains satisfactory.

(A) if they have been given reason to believe that their jobs will

(B) if they are given reason for believing that their jobs would still

(C) having been given reason for believing that their jobs would

(D) having been given reason to believe their jobs to

(E) given reason to believe that their jobs will still

Verb form; Idiom

This sentence asserts that a court decision has qualified a 1998 ruling. It then goes on to explain the series of conditions stipulated by that ruling: workers cannot be laid off if they have been given (prior) reason to believe that continued satisfactory job performance will (always) ensure that their jobs are safe. To express these complicated temporal relationships, the present tense passive verb *cannot be laid off* describes the assurance provided by the ruling; the present-perfect, passive verb describes the prior condition *have been given* . . . , and the future tense verb *will be* describes the outcome the workers can expect. The idiom *reason to believe* succinctly describes the assurance given to workers.

A **Correct.** The sequence of conditions makes sense, and the idiom is correct.

B The present tense *are given* fails to clarify that the assurance of job security must precede the workers' confidence that they cannot be laid off. The phrase *reason for believing* (singular, with no article) is unidiomatic and in this context is inappropriate.

C This version appears to be presenting *having been given reason* . . . as a restrictive modifier of *laid off*. This makes the sentence very awkward and hard to make sense of, and it obscures the requisite nature of the condition (that workers had been given prior reason to think their jobs were safe). *Reason for believing* is unidiomatic.

D Without a comma after *off*, it is unclear what *having been given reason* . . . modifies; the string of infinitive phrases is awkward and confusing.

E As in (D), it is unclear what the participial phrase (in this case, *given reason to believe*) is supposed to modify.

The correct answer is A.

235. Thomas Eakins' powerful style and his choices of subject—the advances in modern surgery, the discipline of sport, the strains of individuals in tension with society or even with themselves—was as disturbing to his own time as it is compelling for ours.

(A) was as disturbing to his own time as it is

(B) were as disturbing to his own time as they are

(C) has been as disturbing in his own time as they are

(D) had been as disturbing in his own time as it was

(E) have been as disturbing in his own time as

Agreement; Verb form

The compound subject of this sentence, *style* and *choices*, is followed by singular verbs, *was* and *is*, and a singular pronoun, *it*. The compound subject requires the plural verbs *were* and *are* and the plural pronoun *they*.

A The verbs and pronoun are singular, but the subject is plural.

B **Correct.** Verbs (*were, are*) and pronoun (*they*) agree with the plural subject in this sentence.

C *Has been* is singular and illogically indicates that Eakins' time continues today.

D *Had been* indicates a time anterior to some other past time; *it was* is singular and the wrong tense.

E *Have been* illogically indicates that Eakins' time continues into the present day.

The correct answer is B.

236. As well as heat and light, the sun is the source of a continuous stream of atomic particles known as the solar wind.

(A) As well as heat and light, the sun is the source of a continuous stream
(B) Besides heat and light, also the sun is the source of a continuous stream
(C) Besides heat and light, the sun is also the source of a continuous streaming
(D) The sun is the source not only of heat and light, but also of a continuous stream
(E) The sun is the source of not only heat and light but, as well, of a continuous streaming

Idiom; Logical predication; Rhetorical construction

The underlined section must be revised to eliminate modification errors and to clarify meaning by using parallel construction. *As well as heat and light* cannot logically modify the sun, as grammar requires; the sentence seems to suggest that heat, light, and the sun are the source of the solar wind. The sentence can be improved by employing the construction *not only x . . . but also y*; *x* and *y* should be parallel.

A *As well as heat and light* is misplaced and potentially confusing.
B *Besides heat and light* is confusing. The word order of *also the sun* is awkward.
C *Besides heat and light* is unclear. *Streaming* should be the more straightforward *stream*.
D **Correct.** This sentence uses the *not only . . . but also* construction to solve the modification error; *of heat and light* is parallel to *of a continuous stream*.
E *As well* is incorrect in the *not only . . . but also* construction. *Heat and light* is not parallel to *of a continuous streaming*. *Streaming* should be the more straightforward *stream*.

The correct answer is D.

237. The psychologist William James believed that facial expressions not only provide a visible sign of an emotion, actually contributing to the feeling itself.

(A) emotion, actually contributing to the feeling itself
(B) emotion but also actually contributing to the feeling itself
(C) emotion but also actually contribute to the feeling itself
(D) emotion; they also actually contribute to the feeling of it
(E) emotion; the feeling itself is also actually contributed to by them

Idiom; Grammatical construction

This sentence should depend on the correlative construction *not only x . . . but also y*, where *x* and *y* are parallel. However, the faulty construction in the original sentence does not properly include the second element, *but also*, and so produces a sentence fragment. James says that facial expressions have two effects: they provide a sign of emotion and they contribute to emotion. Thus, in this sentence, *not only* should be followed by (*x*) *provide a visible sign of an emotion*, and *but also* should be followed by (*y*) *actually contribute to the feeling itself*.

A The *not only . . . but also* construction is violated, creating a sentence fragment.
B *But also actually contributing* is not parallel to *not only provide*; because *contributing* is a participle and not a verb, the result is a sentence fragment.
C **Correct.** The *not only . . . but also* construction is parallel, resulting in a complete sentence.
D The *not only* construction needs to be completed with *but also* and should not be interrupted by a semicolon. *The feeling of it* is awkward and wordy.
E Use of the semicolon in the *not only . . . but also* construction is not correct; the passive voice *is also actually contributed to* is awkward and not parallel to *provide*.

The correct answer is C.

238. Inspired by the Helsinki Accords and outraged by the harsh sentences meted out to a group of Czech rock musicians called the Plastic People of the Universe, Charter 77 was established by dissident writers, philosophers, and other professionals to be a human rights group.

(A) Charter 77 was established by dissident writers, philosophers, and other professionals to be

(B) Charter 77 had been established by dissident writers, philosophers, and other professionals as

(C) Charter 77, established by dissident writers, philosophers, and other professionals, was

(D) dissident writers, philosophers, and other professionals established Charter 77 as

(E) dissident writers, philosophers, and other professionals had established Charter 77 to be

Logical predication; Verb form

This sentence explains what inspired a group of people to establish a human rights group called Charter 77. The passive construction in the main clause illogically makes the opening phrase (*inspired . . . and outraged*) describe Charter 77. The sentence says that Charter 77 was *established* by a group of people. Thus, *Charter 77* refers in this context to the organization as an abstract entity, not to its founders or members. The intended meaning presumably is that the dissident writers, philosophers, and other professionals were both inspired and outraged and were thus prompted to start Charter 77.

A The opening adjectival phrase inappropriately describes Charter 77 instead of the people who started it. The idiomatic expression *established . . . as* is preferable to the nonstandard and somewhat unclear *established . . . to be. . . .*

B The past-perfect verb form *had been established* is confusing after the past tense phrase *meted out to a group. . . .* Additionally, like (A), this version of the sentence creates an opening that somewhat illogically modifies Charter 77.

C As in (A) and (B), the opening phrase illogically describes Charter 77 instead of the people who were inspired and outraged and thus prompted to start Charter 77.

D **Correct.** The opening phrase correctly describes the subject *dissident writers, philosophers, and other professionals*, and the active verb *established* prevents unnecessary wordiness.

E Although the opening phrase describes the people who started Charter 77, the past-perfect tense of the main clause is confusing, making the temporal relationships among the events unclear. The idiomatic expression *established . . . as* is preferable to the nonstandard and somewhat unclear *established . . . to be.*

Th e correct answer is D.

239. According to research covering the last decade, the average number of rooms added by high-end hotel chains was lower than what the hotel industry average did for this period, but their occupancy and room rates grew faster than the average hotel.

(A) than what the hotel industry average did for this period, but their occupancy and room rates grew faster than

(B) than the hotel industry average for this period, but occupancy and room rates grew faster for these chains than for

(C) as compared to the hotel industry average for this period, but occupancy and room rates for them grew faster than with

(D) as compared to what the hotel industry average had been for this period, but occupancy and room rates for these chains grew faster than did

(E) as compared to the hotel industry average for this period, but their occupancy and room rates grew faster than they did for

Logical predication; Agreement; Idiom

This sentence compares one average, *number of rooms added by high-end hotel chains*, with another, *hotel industry average [number of rooms added]*, and then it makes another comparison: rate of growth in *occupancy and room rates* for high-end chains with these same measures in the average hotel. In the sentence as originally presented, the referent of *their* is unclear. The pronoun appears as if it might refer, nonsensically, to *rooms*.

A The phrase *than what the hotel industry average did* is wordy and imprecise. The sentence attempts to compare unlike clauses: *number . . . was lower* with *industry average did*. It also illogically compares the growth in *occupancy and room rates* with growth of the average hotel. The referent for the plural possessive pronoun *their* is unclear.

B **Correct.** The sentence correctly compares one average number with another and growth in *occupancy and room rates* for these chains and for the average hotel.

C The comparative phrase *as compared to . . .* is an incorrect idiom. The referent for *them* is ambiguous. The comparison between the speed of growth *for them*, on the one hand, and *with the average hotel*, on the other hand, does not make sense.

D Like (C), this version of the sentence uses an incorrect idiom (*as compared to*) to make the initial comparison. In the second comparison, as in (A), this sentence nonsensically compares the growth in *occupancy and room rates* with growth of the average hotel.

E Like (C) and (D), this version of the sentence opens with an incorrect idiom (*as compared to*); the second comparison is wordy, and the referent for *they* is ambiguous.

The correct answer is B.

240. Of all the record companies involved in early jazz, the three most prominent were Columbia, Victor, and OKeh.

(A) Of all the record companies involved in early jazz, the three most prominent were Columbia, Victor, and OKeh.

(B) Three most prominent record companies of all the ones that were involved in early jazz were Columbia, Victor, and OKeh.

(C) Columbia, Victor, and OKeh were, of all the record companies involved in early jazz, the three of them that were most prominent.

(D) Columbia, Victor, and OKeh were three most prominent of all the record companies involved in early jazz.

(E) Out of all the record companies that were involved in early jazz, three of them that were the most prominent were Columbia, Victor, and OKeh.

Diction; Rhetorical construction

This sentence aims to emphasize the special prominence of just three specific companies, as opposed to all other companies. Where *three most prominent companies* is not preceded by a definite article, it is unidiomatic. To indicate that these three were more prominent than any others, it should say *the three most prominent companies.* If the intention were, instead, to indicate that these companies were merely among a number of highly prominent ones, it should say *three of the most prominent companies.* Also, in general, one should avoid relative clause constructions when simple adjectives can express the same idea more simply.

A **Correct.** *The three . . .* is used, and *prominent* modifies the understood *companies* in a concise way.

B *The* is omitted before *three*, and *of all the ones that were involved* is inferior to a simpler expression such as *of all the ones involved.*

C *The three of them that were most prominent* is long and awkward; *the three most prominent* is shorter and simpler.

D *The* is omitted before *three.*

E Not only is *the* omitted, but *three of them that were the most prominent* is too long and complex, compared to *the three most prominent.*

The correct answer is A.

241. Analysts blamed May's sluggish retail sales on unexciting merchandise as well as the weather, colder and wetter than was usual in some regions, which slowed sales of barbecue grills and lawn furniture.

(A) colder and wetter than was usual in some regions, which slowed

(B) which was colder and wetter than usual in some regions, slowing

(C) since it was colder and wetter than usually in some regions, which slowed

(D) being colder and wetter than usually in some regions, slowing

(E) having been colder and wetter than was usual in some regions and slowed

Logical predication; Diction

The sentence must clearly indicate that the inclement weather had slowed retail sales. Relative pronouns, such as *which*, should follow as closely as possible the nouns to which they refer. The adjective *usual*, rather than the adverb *usually*, is required when modifying a noun. The phrase *wetter than usual* is correct and concise.

A The insertion of *was* is unnecessary and misleading. The referent of *which* is unclear, because *regions*, not *weather*, is the nearest noun.

B Correct. This sentence is concise, correct, and idiomatic, and *which* has a clear referent, *the weather*.

C With the linking verb *was*, the adjective *usual* is needed in place of the adverb *usually*. The referent of *which* is unclear because *regions*, not *weather*, is the nearest noun.

D This construction is unclear and can be seen as unintentionally indicating that the analysts were colder and wetter. The adjective *usual* should be used instead of the adverb *usually* to modify the noun *weather*.

E This construction is unclear and can be seen as unintentionally indicating that the analysts were colder and wetter. The insertion of *was* is unnecessary and misleading.

The correct answer is B.

242. Twenty-two feet long and 10 feet in diameter, the AM-1 is one of the many new satellites that is a part of 15 years effort of subjecting the interactions of Earth's atmosphere, oceans, and land surfaces to detailed scrutiny from space.

(A) satellites that is a part of 15 years effort of subjecting the interactions of Earth's atmosphere, oceans, and land surfaces

(B) satellites, which is a part of a 15-year effort to subject how Earth's atmosphere, oceans, and land surfaces interact

(C) satellites, part of 15 years effort of subjecting how Earth's atmosphere, oceans, and land surfaces are interacting

(D) satellites that are part of an effort for 15 years that has subjected the interactions of Earth's atmosphere, oceans, and land surfaces

(E) satellites that are part of a 15-year effort to subject the interactions of Earth's atmosphere, oceans, and land surfaces

Rhetorical construction; Logical predication

This sentence describes one satellite and identifies it as part of a larger space project designed to scrutinize Earth's ocean, land, and atmospheric interactions. The relative pronoun *that* refers to satellites, so it should be followed by a plural verb. The idiomatic expression is *effort to* rather than *effort of*. The correct adjectival term is *15-year* rather than *15 years*.

A The relative pronoun *that* refers to satellites, so it should be followed by the plural verb *are*; *effort to* is the correct idiomatic expression; as an adjective, *15 years* becomes *15-year*.

B In this version of the sentence, it is unclear what the relative pronoun *which* refers to—if it refers to *satellites*, it should be followed by a plural verb. Presenting the object of the verb *subject* as a phrase beginning with *how* and ending with the verb *interact* produces a sentence that seems to be about how various conditions react to detailed scrutiny from space.

C This sentence too seems to be making a nonsensical statement about how conditions are interacting to detailed scrutiny. It is not clear whether *part* refers to *satellites* or the *AM-1*.

D This version is wordy and confusing because of the sequence of relative clauses beginning with *that*.

E Correct. The sentence is clearly worded and logically coherent.

The correct answer is E.

243. On the tournament roster are listed several tennis students, most all of which play as good as their instructors.

(A) most all of which play as good
(B) most all of whom play as good
(C) almost all of which play as well
(D) almost all of whom play as good
(E) almost all of whom play as well

Idiom; Diction

The standard formal, written word to express a quantity just short of everything is *almost*, not *most*. With animate entities such as people, *who(m)* is preferred over *which*. For all but a few exceptional verbs, adverbial modifiers (*well*) are correct as opposed to adjectival ones (*good*).

A None of *most*, *which*, or *good* are the preferred forms.
B *Most* and *good* are not the correct standard forms.
C Although *almost* and *well* are fine, *which* is not.
D Although *almost* and *whom* are fine, *good* is not.
E Correct. All of *almost, whom*, and *well* are correct.

The correct answer is E.

244. Recently discovered fossil remains strongly suggest that the Australian egg-laying mammals of today are a branch of the main stem of mammalian evolution rather than developing independently from a common ancestor of mammals more than 220 million years ago.

(A) rather than developing independently from
(B) rather than a type that developed independently from
(C) rather than a type whose development was independent of
(D) instead of developing independently from
(E) instead of a development that was independent of

Idiom; Parallelism

The original point is that the mammals mentioned are thought to be an offshoot of *the main stem of mammalian evolution* and not a descendent of *a common ancestor of* [all] *mammals*. This sentence makes a contrast using the construction *x rather than y* or *x instead of y*; *x* and *y* must be parallel in either case. The mammals are (*x*) *a branch* rather than (*y*); here *y* should consist of an article and a noun to match *a branch*. The second half of the contrast may be rewritten *a type that developed independently from* to complete the parallel construction. The idiom *independently from* is different in meaning from the idiom *independent of*; the logic of this sentence requires the use of *independently from*.

A *Developing independently from* is not parallel to *a branch*.
B Correct. This idiomatically correct sentence properly uses *a type* in parallel to *a branch*.
C The verb *developed* is preferable to the awkward and wordy relative clause using the noun *development; independent of* distorts the original meaning.
D *Developing independently from* is not parallel to *a branch*.
E While a *development* may appear to parallel a branch, *a development that was independent of*. . . expresses a meaning contrary to that expressed in the original sentence. The verb *developed* is preferable to the noun *development*.

The correct answer is B.

245. In 1974 a large area of the surface of Mercury was photographed from varying distances, which revealed a degree of cratering similar to that of the Moon's.

(A) which revealed a degree of cratering similar to that of the Moon's
(B) to reveal a degree of cratering similar to the Moon
(C) revealing a degree of cratering similar to that of the Moon
(D) and revealed cratering similar in degree to the Moon
(E) that revealed cratering similar in degree to that of the Moon

Logical predication; Parallelism

This sentence's second clause, expressing what the imaging of Mercury showed, must be linked to the first clause in a grammatically correct way. This is best done either by an appositive relative clause (requiring the relative marker *which*), or by a clause starting with a nonfinite verb (*to reveal* or *revealing*). Also, whatever is said to be similar to a degree of cratering (on Mercury) should also be a degree of cratering (on the Moon); this must be expressed clearly.

A The use of *which* is correct, but *that of the Moon's* is inferior to *that of the Moon*, because the possessive *'s* and *that of the* redundantly express the same idea. *That of the Moon's* appears to refer, illogically, to cratering of some unspecified thing that belongs to the Moon, not cratering of the Moon itself.

B *To reveal* is acceptable, but *to the Moon* incorrectly compares a physical entity (the Moon) to a degree of cratering.

C **Correct.** *Revealing* is a good way to start the second clause, and *to that of the Moon* properly contrasts two degrees of cratering.

D *And* is incorrect as a way to introduce the second clause; *to the Moon* makes the wrong sort of comparison.

E *That* is not the correct way to introduce an appositive relative clause. *That* is typically used restrictively, whereas the comma preceding it makes the ensuing clause nonrestrictive. This leaves the meaning unclear.

The correct answer is C.

246. The energy source on *Voyager 2* is not a nuclear reactor, in which atoms are actively broken apart; rather a kind of nuclear battery that uses natural radioactive decay to produce power.

(A) apart; rather

(B) apart, but rather

(C) apart, but rather that of

(D) apart, but that of

(E) apart; it is that of

Grammatical construction; Logical predication

The correct version of this sentence focuses on a contrast by using the construction *not x, but rather y*. A comma, not a semicolon, should separate the two parallel parts of the contrast; using a semicolon results in a sentence fragment unless a subject and verb are provided in the construction that follows the semicolon.

A Using a semicolon results in a sentence fragment.

B **Correct.** This sentence is grammatical and logically coherent. The contrast is clearly drawn in the construction *not a nuclear reactor . . . , but rather a kind of nuclear battery*.

C *That of* has no referent and results in an illogical construction.

D *That of* has no referent.

E No word is used to indicate contrast; *that of* has no referent.

The correct answer is B.

247. Many kitchens today are equipped with high-speed electrical gadgets, such as blenders and food processors, which are able to inflict as serious injuries as those caused by an industrial wood-planing machine.

(A) which are able to inflict as serious injuries as those

(B) which can inflict serious injuries such as those

(C) inflicting injuries as serious as that having been

(D) capable to inflict injuries as serious as that

(E) capable of inflicting injuries as serious as those

Idiom; Agreement

The point of this sentence is the claim that common kitchen appliances can be as dangerous as an industrial wood-planing machine. It makes this point by comparing the injuries (plural) caused by blenders and food processors with those (also plural) caused by the wood-planing machine. An efficient way to make this comparison is to use the idiom *capable of*, an adjective phrase rather than a relative clause, after *blenders and food processors*.

A The term *able* suggests agency, which kitchen gadgets do not have. The phrase *as serious injuries as those* is non-idiomatic, apparently comparing injuries rather than the degree of seriousness of injuries. The relative clause makes the sentence unnecessarily wordy.

B Like (A), this sentence introduces wordiness with a relative clause; the comparative phrase *such as* nonsensically suggests that injuries caused by a shop machine are examples of those caused by kitchen gadgets.

C It is not clear what the participial *inflicting* modifies. The sentence suggests that kitchen gadgets inevitably inflict injuries; the singular relative pronoun *that* either incorrectly refers to a plural noun, *injuries*, or implausibly indicates that industrial wood-planing machines have only ever caused a single injury.

D As in (C), the singular pronoun *that* either disagrees with the plural noun *injuries* or implausibly indicates that industrial wood-planing machines have only ever caused a single injury. The phrase *capable to* is not idiomatic.

E **Correct.** This version of the sentence correctly compares the seriousness of one type of injury with the seriousness of another (*as serious as those*), and the phrase *capable of* is a correct idiom.

The correct answer is E.

248. Under high pressure and intense heat, graphite, the most stable form of pure carbon, changes into the substance commonly referred to as diamond and remaining this way whether or not the heat and pressure are removed.

(A) remaining this way whether or not
(B) remaining like that even as
(C) remaining as such whether or not
(D) remains in this way although
(E) remains thus even when

Parallelism; Rhetorical construction

This sentence tells of two things that happen to graphite under intense heat and pressure, and these are best presented as parallel predicates—*changes* and *remains*. *Thus* is the most economical way to say *this way*, *like that*, *as such*, or *in this way*.

A *Remaining* should be a main verb, parallel with *changes*.

B *Remaining* should be parallel with the other main verb, *changes*; *even as* suggests the meaning of *while*, which is not the intent of the sentence.

C *Remaining* should be parallel with *changes*; *whether or not* is unnecessarily wordy.

D *In this way* is unnecessarily wordy; *although* indicates that the heat and pressure are always or definitely removed, but this makes little sense in relation to the rest of the sentence.

E **Correct.** The sentence coherently refers to the possibility of heat and pressure being removed. The sentence is clear and concise and properly uses parallel verb forms.

The correct answer is E.

249. The computer company reported strong second-quarter earnings that surpassed Wall Street's estimates and announced the first in a series of price cuts intended to increase sales further.

(A) The computer company reported strong second-quarter earnings that surpassed Wall Street's estimates and announced the first in a series of price cuts intended to increase sales further.
(B) The report of the computer company showed strong second-quarter earnings, surpassing Wall Street's estimates, and they announced the first in a series of price cuts that they intend to increase sales further.
(C) Surpassing Wall Street's estimates, the report of the computer company showed strong second-quarter earnings, and, for the purpose of increasing sales further, they announced the first in a series of price cuts.

(D) The computer company reported strong second-quarter earnings, surpassing Wall Street's estimates, and announcing the first in a series of price cuts for the purpose of further increasing sales.

(E) The computer company, surpassing Wall Street's estimates, reported strong second-quarter earnings, while announcing that to increase sales further there would be the first in a series of price cuts.

Logical predication; Idiom

The point of the sentence is to describe two actions of the computer company: its earnings report and its announcement of a price cut. To present this information most efficiently, the sentence requires a singular subject "the computer company" and compound verbs (*reported* and *announced*). To indicate that it is the company's earnings and not the report that surpassed Wall Street's estimates, the relative clause *that surpassed* . . . must immediately follow *earnings*.

A **Correct.** The sentence makes clear that the company is responsible for reporting its earnings and announcing its sales plan; the placement of the relative clause *that surpassed* . . . makes it clear that the company's earnings, not the report, surpassed Wall Street's estimate.

B Because this compound sentence opens the first clause with the subject *the report*, and relegates the computer company to the position of object of a preposition, the referent of the subject of the second clause *they* is obscured—particularly since *they* is plural and the intended referent *company* is singular. The function of *that* in the final clause is ambiguous and confusing.

C The placement of the opening modifier *surpassing* . . . makes it modify *report* rather than *estimate*. The plural pronoun *they* does not agree with its intended antecedent, *company*.

D *Surpassing* . . . and the parallel phrase *announcing* . . . both appear to modify the entire opening clause, representing parallel functions of the company's report of its earnings.

E The placement of *surpassing* . . . makes that phrase modify *reported*. . . . The conjunction *while* indicates that the announcement and the report occurred simultaneously. The phrase *there would be* . . . introduces unnecessary wordiness and indirection.

The correct answer is A.

250. Being a United States citizen since 1988 and born in Calcutta in 1940, author Bharati Mukherjee has lived in England and Canada, and first came to the United States in 1961 to study at the Iowa Writers' Workshop.

(A) Being a United States citizen since 1988 and born in Calcutta in 1940, author Bharati Mukherjee has

(B) Having been a United States citizen since 1988, she was born in Calcutta in 1940; author Bharati Mukherjee

(C) Born in Calcutta in 1940, author Bharati Mukherjee became a United States citizen in 1988; she has

(D) Being born in Calcutta in 1940 and having been a United States citizen since 1988, author Bharati Mukherjee

(E) Having been born in Calcutta in 1940 and being a United States citizen since 1988, author Bharati Mukherjee

Verb form; Rhetorical construction

Being . . . since 1988 and born in Calcutta in 1940 is an awkward, wordy construction, which presents an unclear and potentially confusing chronological order. Since in the correct version of the sentence the original phrase (*being* . . .) has been made into a main clause, a semicolon should separate it from the second main clause beginning *she has lived*.

A The phrases are expressed in an illogical and potentially confusing sequence.

B *Having been* suggests that the citizenship came chronologically before the birth. The pronoun *she* is the subject of the first clause; since the author's name is mentioned only after the semicolon, *she* has no clear referent.

C **Correct.** In this sentence, the sequence of events is expressed logically, grammatically, and concisely in each independent clause.

D The progressive verb forms *being born* and *having been* illogically suggest continuous action and fail to establish a logical time sequence. The sentence is wordy and awkward.

E The progressive verb forms *having been born* and *being* illogically suggest continuous action and fail to establish a logical time sequence. The sentence is wordy and awkward.

The correct answer is C.

251. As a result of record low temperatures, the water pipes on the third floor froze, which caused the heads of the sprinkler system to burst, which released torrents of water into offices on the second floor.

(A) which caused the heads of the sprinkler system to burst, which released torrents of water

(B) which caused the heads of the sprinkler system to burst and which released torrents of water

(C) which caused the heads of the sprinkler system to burst, torrents of water were then released

(D) causing the heads of the sprinkler system to burst, then releasing torrents of water

(E) causing the heads of the sprinkler system to burst and release torrents of water

Logical predication; Grammatical construction

This sentence describes a causal sequence of events leading to flooded second-floor offices. One of the steps, sprinkler heads bursting, was presumably simultaneous with the release of torrents of water, so it is best to present these events as actions attached to the same subject (*heads of the sprinkler system*). The sentence as given attempts to explain the sequence in a chain of relative clauses, using the pronoun *which* to introduce successive steps. The precise referent of this relative pronoun is somewhat obscure—it appears to refer to the entire preceding clause—and the sequence separates the simultaneous bursting of heads and releasing of water into two temporally separate events.

A The referent of the second *which* is obscure, and the sentence implausibly separates bursting heads and releasing of torrents into two temporally separate events.

B Joining the relative pronouns with the conjunction *and* makes the freezing of the water pipes the subject of both *caused* . . . and *released*. . . . Thus, it seems to indicate, somewhat implausibly, that the freezing of the pipes directly released torrents of water independently of its causing the sprinkler heads to burst.

C The passive verb *were* . . . *released* obscures the causal sequence behind the releasing of torrents of water. The introduction of a new independent clause without a conjunction is ungrammatical and makes this version a run-on sentence.

D As in (B), the structure of this version makes the freezing of the pipes the subject of both *causing* . . . and *releasing*. . . . The introduction of the sequential marker *then* divides the bursting of heads and releasing of torrents of water into two separate events in the sequence. It indicates, implausibly, that the pipes' freezing directly released torrents of water after it had also caused the sprinkler heads to burst.

E **Correct.** The elimination of the relative pronouns clarifies the causal sequence of events, and the double infinitives *to burst* and (*to*) *release* underscores the simultaneity of these events.

The correct answer is E.

252. Archaeologists in Ireland believe that a recently discovered chalice, which dates from the eighth century, was probably buried to keep from being stolen by invaders.

(A) to keep from

(B) to keep it from

(C) to avoid

(D) in order that it would avoid

(E) in order to keep from

Grammatical construction; Logical predication

The phrase *to keep from being stolen* is incomplete and does not indicate what might be stolen. Inserting a pronoun makes it clear that it is the chalice that might be stolen.

A The pronoun *it* is needed for clarity.

B Correct. The sentence is clarified by inserting the word *it*, which refers back to *chalice*.

C This suggests that the chalice acts to prevent its own theft. The pronoun *it* is needed for clarity.

D This suggests that the chalice acts to prevent its own theft. The pronoun *it* is needed for clarity. *In order that it would* is wordy.

E The pronoun *it* is needed for clarity.

The correct answer is B.

253. The bank holds $3 billion in loans that are seriously delinquent or in such trouble that <u>they do not expect payments when</u> due.

(A) they do not expect payments when
(B) it does not expect payments when it is
(C) it does not expect payments to be made when they are
(D) payments are not to be expected to be paid when
(E) payments are not expected to be paid when they will be

Agreement; Logical predication; Verb form

The plural pronoun *they* cannot be used to refer to the singular noun *bank*. The structure of *they do not expect payments when due* is awkward and unclear.

A *Bank* requires the singular pronoun *it*, not the plural pronoun *they*. The structure of *when due* creates ambiguity in meaning.

B *Payments* is a plural noun, so the singular *it is* is incorrect.

C Correct. In this correct sentence, pronouns and their referents agree, as do subjects and their verbs. The addition of the modifying phrase *to be made* clarifies the meaning of the sentence.

D The active voice is preferable here, since the passive voice leaves it unclear who does not expect the payments to be made. *Payments . . . to be paid* is redundant. *Are not to be* incorrectly suggests that the writer is prescribing that the payments not be expected.

E The active voice is preferable here, since the passive voice leaves it unclear who does not expect the payments to be made. *Payments . . . to be paid* is redundant. *Will be* is not the correct verb form.

The correct answer is C.

254. Faced with an estimated $2 billion budget gap, the city's mayor <u>proposed a nearly 17 percent reduction in the amount allocated the previous year to maintain the city's major cultural institutions and to subsidize</u> hundreds of local arts groups.

(A) proposed a nearly 17 percent reduction in the amount allocated the previous year to maintain the city's major cultural institutions and to subsidize
(B) proposed a reduction from the previous year of nearly 17 percent in the amount it was allocating to maintain the city's major cultural institutions and for subsidizing
(C) proposed to reduce, by nearly 17 percent, the amount from the previous year that was allocated for the maintenance of the city's major cultural institutions and to subsidize
(D) has proposed a reduction from the previous year of nearly 17 percent of the amount it was allocating for maintaining the city's major cultural institutions, and to subsidize
(E) was proposing that the amount they were allocating be reduced by nearly 17 percent from the previous year for maintaining the city's major cultural institutions and for the subsidization

Rhetorical construction; Parallelism

The original sentence contains no errors. It uses the parallel construction *to maintain* and *to subsidize* to show clearly the two areas where the *17 percent reduction* in funds will be applied. In addition, the *17 percent reduction* is closely followed by *the amount allocated the previous year,* making it clear what is being reduced by 17 percent.

A **Correct.** The sentence uses parallel construction and a well-placed modifier.

B *To maintain* and *for subsidizing* are not parallel. The sentence is imprecise, and *it* does not have a clear antecedent.

C *For the maintenance* and *to subsidize* are not parallel, and the sentence is wordy.

D *For maintaining* and *to subsidize* are not parallel, *it* does not have a clear antecedent, and the sentence structure makes it unclear just what the writer is claiming.

E *Maintaining* and *the subsidization* are not parallel, *they* does not have a clear antecedent, and the sentence structure makes it unclear just what the writer is claiming.

The correct answer is A.

255. In the textbook publishing business, the second quarter is historically weak, because revenues are low and marketing expenses are high as companies prepare for the coming school year.

(A) low and marketing expenses are high as companies prepare

(B) low and their marketing expenses are high as they prepare

(C) low with higher marketing expenses in preparation

(D) low, while marketing expenses are higher to prepare

(E) low, while their marketing expenses are higher in preparation

Parallelism; Logical predication

This sentence is correctly written. It uses parallel structure to give two reasons why textbook publishers have weak second quarters: *revenues are low* and *expenses are high.* The construction *as companies prepare for the coming school year* is clear, as opposed to the awkward constructions using the ambiguous plural pronouns *they* and *their.*

A **Correct.** This sentence uses the parallel forms *are low . . . are high* and employs the unambiguous *companies* as the subject of *prepare.*

B *Their* seems illogically to refer to *revenues.* The subject of *prepare* is the ambiguous *they.*

C *Higher* is not parallel to *low,* and it gives no indication of what the comparison is supposed to be (Higher than what?). This construction makes it appear, illogically, that the low revenues have higher marketing expenses.

D *Higher* is not parallel to *low* and is illogical. The infinitive construction *to prepare . . .* is awkward.

E *Higher* is not parallel to *low* and is illogical since no comparison is being made; *their* has no clear referent.

The correct answer is A.

256. Ms. Chambers is among the forecasters who predict that the rate of addition to arable lands will drop while those of loss rise.

(A) those of loss rise

(B) it rises for loss

(C) those of losses rise

(D) the rate of loss rises

(E) there are rises for the rate of loss

Logical predication; Parallelism

The forecaster is making predictions about two different rates. The forecast changes in the rates can be compared using the construction *the rate of x will drop while the rate of y rises*; *x* and *y* should be parallel.

A There is no referent for *those.*

B *It* refers *to the rate of addition,* creating a nonsensical statement.

C There is no referent for *those. Of losses* should be singular to parallel *of addition.*

D **Correct.** This sentence uses a construction that clearly states the predicted changes in the rates; the rates are expressed in parallel ways.

E *There are rises for* is wordy and unidiomatic.

The correct answer is D.

257. Less than 400 Sumatran rhinos survive on the Malay peninsula and on the islands of Sumatra and Borneo, and they occupy a small fraction of the species' former range.

(A) Less than 400 Sumatran rhinos survive on the Malay peninsula and on the islands of Sumatra and Borneo, and they occupy a small fraction of the species' former range.

(B) Less than 400 Sumatran rhinos, surviving on the Malay peninsula and on the islands of Sumatra and Borneo, occupy a small fraction of the species' former range.

(C) Occupying a small fraction of the species' former range, the Malay peninsula and the islands of Sumatra and Borneo are where fewer than 400 Sumatran rhinos survive.

(D) Occupying a small fraction of the species' former range, fewer than 400 Sumatran rhinos survive on the Malay peninsula and on the islands of Sumatra and Borneo.

(E) Surviving on the Malay peninsula and on the islands of Sumatra and Borneo, less than 400 Sumatran rhinos occupy a small fraction of the species' former range.

Diction; Logical Predication

Because the number of Sumatran rhinos has been given, the comparative term *fewer* rather than *less* should be used to account for their numbers. In order to clarify that habitat currently occupied by the rhinos is but a small fraction of their former range, the information about their dwindling habitat is most efficiently presented in an opening participial phrase describing the rhinos, followed by a main clause in which the number of surviving rhinos is the subject, with the predicate explaining where the rhinos currently live. By presenting the information about the population and range of rhinos in two separate independent clauses, the sentence as written does not clarify that the former range of the rhinos once extended beyond the peninsula and the islands.

A *Less* is inappropriate for describing the specific number of surviving Sumatran rhinos. The separate independent clauses obscure the fact that the rhinos' range used to extend beyond the peninsula and the two islands. The referent of *they* is unclear.

B *Less* is inappropriate for describing the specific number of surviving Sumatran rhinos. By using a nonrestrictive phrase *surviving . . .* , the sentence suggests that fewer than 400 rhinos—perhaps only a portion of the total number—occupy a small fraction of the species' former range.

C The opening participial phrase somewhat illogically modifies *peninsula and . . . islands* rather than the rhinos.

D **Correct.** The opening participial phrase correctly modifies *fewer than 400 . . . rhinos,* a phrase that uses the correct comparative term.

E The comparative term *less* is inappropriate for describing the number of rhinos.

The correct answer is D.

258. Certain pesticides can become ineffective if used repeatedly in the same place; one reason is suggested by the finding that there are much larger populations of pesticide-degrading microbes in soils with a relatively long history of pesticide use than in soils that are free of such chemicals.

(A) Certain pesticides can become ineffective if used repeatedly in the same place; one reason is suggested by the finding that there are much larger populations of pesticide-degrading microbes in soils with a relatively long history of pesticide use than in soils that are free of such chemicals.

(B) If used repeatedly in the same place, one reason that certain pesticides can become ineffective is suggested by the finding that there are much larger populations of pesticide-degrading microbes in soils with a relatively long history of pesticide use than in soils that are free of such chemicals.

(C) If used repeatedly in the same place, one reason certain pesticides can become ineffective is suggested by the finding that much larger populations of pesticide-degrading microbes are found in soils with a relatively long history of pesticide use than those that are free of such chemicals.

(D) The finding that there are much larger populations of pesticide-degrading microbes in soils with a relatively long history of pesticide use than in soils that are free of such chemicals is suggestive of one reason, if used repeatedly in the same place, certain pesticides can become ineffective.

(E) The finding of much larger populations of pesticide-degrading microbes in soils with a relatively long history of pesticide use than in those that are free of such chemicals suggests one reason certain pesticides can become ineffective if used repeatedly in the same place.

Logical predication; Rhetorical construction

The sentence is correctly constructed; it has two independent clauses connected by a semicolon. *If used repeatedly in the same place* clearly and correctly modifies *certain pesticides.*

A **Correct.** The sentence is correctly constructed; the modifier *if used repeatedly in the same place* is correctly placed.

B *If used repeatedly in the same place* modifies *one reason* when it should modify *certain pesticides.*

C *If used repeatedly in the same place* modifies *one reason* when it should modify *certain pesticides.* The absence of *in* in the phrase *than those* . . . makes the comparison unclear.

D *If used repeatedly in the same place* ambiguously modifies *one reason* when it should clearly modify *certain pesticides.*

E The comparison *the finding of much larger populations* . . . *than in those that* . . . is improperly constructed in a way that makes *the finding* appear to refer awkwardly to a discovery of larger populations rather than to a research conclusion about the presence of such populations.

The correct answer is A.

259. While some academicians believe that business ethics should be integrated into every business course, others say that students will take ethics seriously <u>only if it would be taught as a separately required course.</u>

(A) only if it would be taught as a separately required course

(B) only if it is taught as a separate, required course

(C) if it is taught only as a course required separately

(D) if it was taught only as a separate and required course

(E) if it would only be taught as a required course, separately

Rhetorical construction; Verb form; Diction

Conditional constructions require specific verb tenses. For a present condition, like this debate between academicians, the subordinate clause introduced by *if* uses the present indicative, and the main clause uses the future tense: *y will happen* (main clause) *only if x happens* (subordinate clause). Logically, the *course* is to be both *separate* and *required,* so the two adjectives should equally modify the noun and thus be separated by a comma: *separate, required course.*

A The verb tense in the *if* clause is incorrect. The adverb *separately* should be the adjective *separate.*

B **Correct.** This sentence has the correct verb tense, and the two adjectives equally modify the noun.

C The placement of *only* distorts the meaning; it should precede *if. A course required separately* is unclear.

D The verb tense in the *if* clause is incorrect. The placement of *only* distorts the meaning.

E The verb tense in the *if* clause is incorrect. The placement of *only* distorts the meaning. The adjective *separate* should be used instead of the adverb *separately* and should precede the noun.

The correct answer is B.

260. Whether they will scale back their orders to pre-2003 levels or stop doing business with us altogether depends on whether the changes that their management has proposed will be fully implemented.

(A) Whether they will scale back their orders to pre-2003 levels or stop doing business with us altogether depends on whether the changes that their management has proposed will be fully implemented.

(B) Whether they scale back their orders to pre-2003 levels or whether they discontinue their business with us altogether depends on the changes their management has proposed, if fully implemented or not.

(C) Their either scaling back their orders in the future to pre-2003 levels, or their outright termination of business with us, depends on their management's proposed changes being fully implemented or not.

(D) Whether they will scale back their orders to pre-2003 levels or stop doing business with us altogether depends if the changes that their management has proposed become fully implemented.

(E) They will either scale back their orders to pre-2003 levels, or they will stop doing business with us altogether dependent on whether the changes their management has proposed will be fully implemented, or not.

Rhetorical construction; Diction

This sentence expresses a dependency between two sets of options: the first is scaling back orders versus stopping all business, and the second is fully implementing changes versus not fully implementing changes. In each case, the most succinct way to express the two options is the *whether X (or Y)* construction, which immediately and clearly signals the presence of two opposed options. In linking the two sets of options, *depend* or *dependent* requires the preposition *on*.

A **Correct.** Each set of options is expressed concisely with a single *whether*, and *depend* is followed by *on*.

B The first set of options is expressed by means of a second, redundant and illogical *whether*; the second set is expressed in an unclear way, unnecessarily delaying the identification of the two options until the very end. *Depends on the changes . . . if fully implemented or not* makes the meaning unclear. This could be an awkward way of trying to say that the outcome depends on whether the changes will be made, but it could just as plausibly be an attempt to say that the outcome depends on the changes, regardless of whether the changes will be fully implemented.

C Both sets of options are expressed without *whether*, and the first set does not even explicitly say that there is such an option. As a result, the existence of two dependent sets of options is unclear until the end of the sentence.

D The first set of options is correctly expressed with *whether*, but the second is not; also, *depend* lacks a following preposition *on*.

E Both sets of options are expressed without *whether*, and the first set does not even explicitly signal the existence of options, so the existence of two dependent sets of options is unclear until the end of the sentence.

The correct answer is A.

261. Until 1868 and Disraeli, Great Britain had no prime ministers not coming from a landed family.

(A) Until 1868 and Disraeli, Great Britain had no prime ministers not coming

(B) Until 1868 and Disraeli, Great Britain had had no prime ministers who have not come

(C) Until Disraeli in 1868, there were no prime ministers in Great Britain who have not come

(D) It was not until 1868 that Great Britain had a prime minister—Disraeli—who did not come

(E) It was only in 1868 and Disraeli that Great Britain had one of its prime ministers not coming

Verb form; Idiom

This sentence explains how Disraeli marked a turning point in British history: he was the first prime minister who did not come from the landed gentry. The placement of the double negative is crucial. While *no prime ministers not coming from . . .* is hard to untangle, *[n]ot until . . . that Great Britain had a prime minister who did not come . . .* separates the negatives into separate clauses, making them easier to decode. An appropriate way to express the temporal relationship is to use the idiomatic phrase *not until . . . that.*

A The phrase *no prime ministers not coming* is unnecessarily confusing. It is also confusing to follow the preposition *until* with two very different types of objects—a date and a person.

B As in (A), the double negative and unlike objects of the prepositional phrase starting with *until* are confusing. Additionally, the verb form *have not come*, which is the present-perfect tense, is inappropriate following the past perfect *had had* in this context.

C The present-perfect tense (*have not come*) is inappropriate after the past tense *were* in this context. *Until Disraeli* is imprecise and incomplete. *Before Disraeli's term in 1868 . . .* or *Until Disraeli became prime minster in 1868* would work.

D Correct. This version correctly uses the idiomatic construction *not until . . . that*, and it correctly uses past tense throughout.

E While it makes sense to say that a historical change occurred *in 1868*, it does not make sense to say that it occurred *in Disraeli*. It is unidiomatic to say *had one of its prime ministers not coming*.

The correct answer is D.

262. Around 1900, fishermen in the Chesapeake Bay area landed more than seventeen million pounds of shad in a single year, but by 1920, overfishing and the proliferation of milldams and culverts <u>that have blocked shad migrations up their spawning streams had reduced landings to less</u> than four million pounds.

(A) that have blocked shad migrations up their spawning streams had reduced landings to less

(B) that blocked shad from migrating up their spawning streams had reduced landings to less

(C) that blocked shad from migrating up their spawning streams reduced landings to a lower amount

(D) having blocked shad from migrating up their spawning streams reduced landings to less

(E) having blocked shad migrations up their spawning streams had reduced landings to an amount lower

Diction; Verb form

The point of this sentence is to explain how overfishing and interference with shad spawning streams affected the size of shad landings. The sentence makes this point by comparing the sizes of annual landings before and after 1920. The sentence most efficiently compares the poundage of pre- and post-1920 landings with the comparative form [*from*] *more than . . . to less than. . . .*

A The present-perfect tense of *have blocked* inappropriately describes an event that caused something to happen before 1920. In addition, *migrations up their spawning streams* is incorrect.

B Correct. The comparison of poundage is efficiently explained, and the sequence of tenses makes sense. Despite a possible superficial appearance of a comparison between countable things (pounds), *less* is more appropriate than *fewer* for the comparison. The fishermen landed different amounts of fish; they did not land the number of pounds in terms of which those amounts are measured.

C The comparative expression *to a lower amount* is unnecessarily wordy. The past-perfect form *had reduced* would make the temporal relationships somewhat clearer than does the past tense *reduced.*

D The present-perfect participial phrase, *having blocked . . . streams*, should be set off in commas; as it stands, it does not make sense. The past-perfect form *had reduced* would make the temporal relationships somewhat clearer than does the past tense *reduced.*

E The present-perfect participial phrase must be set off with commas; the pronoun *their*, which is also in (A), nonsensically refers to *migrations*, and the comparative expression *to an amount lower* is unnecessarily wordy.

The correct answer is B.

263. By offering lower prices and a menu of personal communications options, such as caller identification and voice mail, the new telecommunications company has not only captured customers from other phone companies but also forced them to offer competitive prices.

(A) has not only captured customers from other phone companies but also forced them

(B) has not only captured customers from other phone companies, but it also forced them

(C) has not only captured customers from other phone companies but also forced these companies

(D) not only has captured customers from other phone companies but also these companies have been forced

(E) not only captured customers from other phone companies, but it also has forced them

Parallelism, Verb form

The sentence intends to show the effect of the new telecommunications company on the other phone companies. In the original sentence, however, the antecedent of the pronoun *them* is unclear; it may refer to *companies* or to *customers*. If it refers to *customers*, the sentence structure illogically has the new company forcing customers to offer competitive prices.

A The referent of *them* is unclear.

B The referent of *them* is unclear, and the use of *it* is redundant.

C **Correct.** The verbs are parallel in this sentence, and *these companies* is clearly the object of the verb *forced*.

D The sentence does not maintain parallelism, unnecessarily changing from active voice (*has captured*) to passive voice (*have been forced*).

E The referent of *them* is unclear. *Captured* and *has forced* are not parallel in verb tense, and the use of *it* is redundant.

The correct answer is C.

264. After suffering $2 billion in losses and 25,000 layoffs, the nation's semiconductor industry, which makes chips that run everything from computers and spy satellites to dishwashers, appears to have made a long-awaited recovery.

(A) computers and spy satellites to dishwashers, appears to have

(B) computers, spy satellites, and dishwashers, appears having

(C) computers, spy satellites, and dishwashers, appears that it has

(D) computers and spy satellites to dishwashers, appears that it has

(E) computers and spy satellites as well as dishwashers, appears to have

Idiom; Grammatical construction; Verb form

This sentence correctly makes use of the idiomatic expression *from . . . to . . .* to describe the range of products made by the semiconductor industry. The main verb *appears* is intransitive and is most efficiently followed by the infinitive form *to have made*, which introduces a description of the subject, *the semiconductor industry*.

A **Correct.** The sentence is grammatically correct and uses the idiomatic expression correctly.

B The phrase *everything from* anticipates idiomatic completion with the second preposition *to*; without the *to* it could refer to components coming from the listed items, but this reading is unlikely; *appears having* is an incorrect verb form and makes the clause ungrammatical.

C This version is unidiomatic because *from* is not completed by *to*; *appears that it has* is an awkward and incorrect verb form.

D *Appears that it has* is an incorrect verb form.

E *As well as* is awkward and imprecise here; it is the wrong completion for the idiomatic expression *from . . . to. . . .*

The correct answer is A.

265. Over a range of frequencies from 100 to 5,000 hertz, monkeys and marmosets have a hearing sensitivity remarkably similar to humans, above which the sensitivity begins to differ.

(A) Over a range of frequencies from 100 to 5,000 hertz, monkeys and marmosets have a hearing sensitivity remarkably similar to humans

(B) Compared to humans, the hearing sensitivity of monkeys and marmosets are remarkably similar over a range of frequencies from 100 to 5,000 hertz

(C) Compared to humans over a range of frequencies from 100 to 5,000 hertz, the hearing sensitivity of monkeys and marmosets is remarkably similar

(D) The hearing sensitivity of monkeys and marmosets, when compared to humans over a range of frequencies from 100 to 5,000 hertz, is remarkably similar

(E) The hearing sensitivity of monkeys, marmosets, and humans is remarkably similar over a range of frequencies from 100 to 5,000 hertz

Logical predication; Agreement

This sentence expresses two ideas: the similarity in monkey, marmoset, and human hearing in the stated frequency range, and the divergence in hearing sensitivity above that range. The second idea is introduced by *above which. Above which* should be immediately preceded by the antecedent of *which*, that is, the 100–5,000 Hz range. Also, the subject and verb must agree in number.

A In this construction, *above which . . .* illogically modifies either *humans* or *a hearing sensitivity remarkably similar to humans*, rather than the frequency range.

B The singular subject in this version, *the hearing sensitivity . . .* , is not accompanied by the correct singular verb form (*is*).

C *Above which* is incorrectly preceded by *similar*, rather than by the expression of the frequency range. The sentence appears, illogically, to compare *humans over a range of frequencies* with monkeys' and marmosets' hearing sensitivity.

D *Above which* is incorrectly preceded by *similar*, rather than by the expression of the frequency range. The sentence appears, illogically, to compare *humans over a range of frequencies* with monkeys' and marmosets' hearing sensitivity.

E **Correct.** *Above which* is correctly preceded by *a range of frequencies . . .* , and the verb *is* is in its proper singular form.

The correct answer is E.

266. The computer company has announced that it will purchase the color-printing division of a rival company for $950 million, which is part of a deal that will make it the largest manufacturer in the office color-printing market.

(A) million, which is part of a deal that will make

(B) million, a part of a deal that makes

(C) million, a part of a deal making

(D) million as a part of a deal to make

(E) million as part of a deal that will make

Rhetorical construction; Verb form

The relative pronoun *which* requires a clear antecedent, but none appears in the original version of the sentence. The company's announcement is entirely geared to the future—it *will* purchase the division as part of a deal that *will* make it the largest manufacturer.

A There is no antecedent for the relative pronoun *which*.

B Like a relative pronoun, the appositive phrase (*a part . . .*) must have a noun or noun phrase as a clear antecedent; the verb *makes* should be future tense.

C The appositive phrase requires a clear antecedent; *making* does not indicate future tense.

D This sentence is a little awkward (the article *a* in *a part* is unnecessary) and says something rather different; *as a part of a deal to make* suggests that the deal itself includes making the company the *largest manufacturer* rather than its being the outcome of the deal.

E **Correct.** The future tense is used throughout and the sentence structure is clear.

The correct answer is E.

267. Kudzu, an Asian vine that has grown rampantly in the southern United States since introducing it in the 1920s to thwart soil erosion, has overrun many houses and countless acres of roadside.

(A) that has grown rampantly in the southern United States since introducing it in the 1920s to thwart

(B) that has grown rampantly in the southern United States, since it was introduced in the 1920s for thwarting

(C) that has grown rampant in the southern United States since it was introduced in the 1920s to thwart

(D) growing rampant in the southern United States since introducing it in the 1920s for thwarting

(E) growing rampantly in the southern United States, since it was introduced in the 1920s to thwart

Idiom; Logical predication

The sentence describes the destructive, out-of-control growth of the invasive vine kudzu in the southern United States. Because the sentence does not indicate who introduced the vine to that region, the passive construction *it was introduced* should be used instead of *introducing it.*

A There is no clear subject for the verb *introducing*. This construction appears to indicate that kudzu introduced itself or some other, unspecified thing.

B The adverbial clause *since it was introduced in the 1920s* should not be set off from *has grown rampantly*, which it modifies. Also, *introduced . . . for thwarting* is not idiomatic. *Introduced . . . to thwart* is the correct idiom.

C **Correct.** The sentence correctly uses the passive construction *it was introduced* and the idiom *was introduced . . . to thwart.*

D *Since introducing it* illogically indicates that the vine introduced itself. *Introducing . . . for thwarting* is unidiomatic.

E The adverbial clause *since it was introduced in the 1920s* should not be set off from *has grown rampantly*, which it modifies.

The correct answer is C.

268. Unable to build nests or care for their young, a female cowbird lays up to 40 eggs a year in the nests of other birds, including warblers, vireos, flycatchers, and thrushes.

(A) a female cowbird lays up to 40 eggs a year in the nests of other birds, including

(B) a female cowbird will use the nests of other birds to lay up to 40 eggs a year, including those of

(C) female cowbirds use the nests of other birds to lay up to 40 eggs a year, including those of

(D) female cowbirds lay up to 40 eggs a year in the nests of other birds, including

(E) up to 40 eggs a year are laid by female cowbirds in the nests of other birds, including

Agreement; Logical predication

This sentence describes the behavior of female cowbirds, but it begins by referring to the birds in plural (*their young*) and then shifts unexpectedly to singular (*a female cowbird*). The best construction refers to the birds consistently in plural and places modifiers near the words they modify.

A The sentence shifts unexpectedly from the plural *their young* to the singular *a female cowbird.*

B The sentence shifts unexpectedly from the plural *their young* to the singular *a female cowbird.* The participial phrase *including those of* incorrectly modifies *eggs*, illogically indicating that cowbirds lay the eggs of other birds.

C The participial phrase *including those of* incorrectly modifies *eggs*, illogically indicating that cowbirds lay the eggs of other birds.

D **Correct.** The sentence consistently refers to *cowbirds* in the plural and places modifiers in the correct location.

E The modifier *Unable . . . young* incorrectly modifies *eggs.*

The correct answer is D.

269. Bluegrass musician Bill Monroe, whose repertory, views on musical collaboration, and vocal style were influential on generations of bluegrass artists, was also an inspiration to many musicians, that included Elvis Presley and Jerry Garcia, whose music differed significantly from his own.

(A) were influential on generations of bluegrass artists, was also an inspiration to many musicians, that included Elvis Presley and Jerry Garcia, whose music differed significantly from

(B) influenced generations of bluegrass artists, also inspired many musicians, including Elvis Presley and Jerry Garcia, whose music differed significantly from

(C) was influential to generations of bluegrass artists, was also inspirational to many musicians, that included Elvis Presley and Jerry Garcia, whose music was different significantly in comparison to

(D) was influential to generations of bluegrass artists, also inspired many musicians, who included Elvis Presley and Jerry Garcia, the music of whom differed significantly when compared to

(E) were an influence on generations of bluegrass artists, was also an inspiration to many musicians, including Elvis Presley and Jerry Garcia, whose music was significantly different from that of

Agreement; Rhetorical construction; Grammatical construction

The original sentence logically intends to explain that Monroe's work influenced generations of artists in his own musical field and that he inspired many musicians in other musical fields. Who or what influenced or inspired whom must be more clearly stated. Additionally, the original sentence lacks precision, being overly wordy and using phrases that are not idiomatic. Concise and consistent verb forms, as well as the use of subordinate phrases rather than clauses, improve the precision of the sentence.

A The phrase *were influential on* is wordy and is not idiomatic; the use of verb forms *were* (the predicate of *repertory*, *views*, and *style*) and *was* (the predicate of *Monroe*) is confusing.

B **Correct.** The use of the concise verb forms of *influenced* and *inspired* simplifies and clarifies the sentence. The concise use of *including* avoids the pronoun error and unnecessary wordiness.

C The subject and verb do not agree in *repertory*, *views*, and *style . . . was* (compound subject with singular verb). *Was influential to* and *different . . . in comparison to* are unnecessarily wordy.

D There is incorrect subject-verb agreement in *repertory*, *views*, and *style . . . was* (compound subject with singular verb). *Was influential to* and in *when compared to* are unnecessarily wordy. *The music of whom* is cumbersome and stilted.

E The phrase *were an influence on* is wordy and not idiomatic. The phrases *was also an inspiration to* and *was significantly different* are unnecessarily wordy. The phrase *from that of* is unclear and confusing.

The correct answer is B.

270. In many of the world's regions, increasing pressure on water resources has resulted both from expanding development, changes in climate, and from pollution, so that the future supply in some of the more arid areas is a concern going forward.

(A) both from expanding development, changes in climate, and from pollution, so that the future supply in some of the more arid areas is a concern going forward

(B) both from expanding development or changes in climate, and pollution, so that future supplies in some of the more arid areas are a concern

(C) from expanding development, changes in climate, and also from pollution, so that the future supply in some of the more arid areas is a matter of concern going forward

(D) from expanding development, changes in climate, and pollution, so that future supplies in some of the more arid areas are a concern

(E) from expansion of development, changes in climate, and from pollution, so that supplies in some of the more arid areas are a future concern

Parallelism; Rhetorical construction

The sentence lists three factors that have increased pressure on water resources and expresses concern for future water supplies in arid regions. The preposition *both* creates confusion since it indicates two factors, when the sentence actually lists three. If *expanding development* and *changes in climate* are supposed to be grouped together—implausibly—as a single factor, they should be conjoined by *and*, not separated by commas. The sentence could be constructed most clearly by listing all three factors in parallel form as objects of the preposition *from*: *from expanding development, changes in climate, and pollution.*

A The preposition *both* creates confusion since it indicates two factors, when the sentence actually lists three.

B *Both* indicates that there are two factors. If the entire disjunction *expanding development or changes in climate* is intended—somewhat implausibly—to be the first of the two factors, the comma before *and pollution* makes its relationship to the preceding portion of the sentence unclear.

C Repetition of the preposition *from* disrupts the parallelism of the list and makes the meaning unclear.

D Correct. The three factors are listed in parallel form as objects of the preposition *from.*

E Repetition of the preposition *from* disrupts the parallelism of the list and makes the meaning unclear. *Future* somewhat implausibly modifies *concern* rather than *supplies.*

The correct answer is D.

271. The computer company's present troubles are a result of technological stagnation, marketing missteps, and managerial blunders so that several attempts to revise corporate strategies have failed to correct it.

(A) so that several attempts to revise corporate strategies have failed to correct it

(B) so that several attempts at revising corporate strategies have failed to correct

(C) in that several attempts at revising corporate strategies have failed to correct them

(D) that several attempts to revise corporate strategies have failed to correct

(E) that several attempts at revising corporate strategies have failed to correct them

Agreement; Rhetorical construction

This sentence lists three causes of the company's troubles and asserts that strategies to correct the causes of the problems have failed. The clearest, most efficient way to explain this is to refer to the causes with the relative pronoun *that*, positioning it as an object of the verb *failed to correct*.

A The singular pronoun *it* has no clear antecedent; the conjunction *so* typically indicates that a consequence will follow, but this is not the case.

B The conjunction *so* is inappropriate because no consequences are given; the verb *correct* has no object.

C *In that* is an inappropriate connector because it is not followed by an indication of how the company's troubles result from the three problems listed in the first part of the sentence.

D Correct. The sentence is clearly and efficiently worded, and the referent of the pronoun *that* is clear.

E Because *attempts* is the subject of the final clause, and *that* is the object of its verb (*have failed to correct*), the pronoun *them* has no function.

The correct answer is D.

272. The root systems of most flowering perennials either become too crowded, which results in loss in vigor, and spread too far outward, producing a bare center.

(A) which results in loss in vigor, and spread

(B) resulting in loss in vigor, or spreading

(C) with the result of loss of vigor, or spreading

(D) resulting in loss of vigor, or spread

(E) with a resulting loss of vigor, and spread

Idiom; Parallelism

This sentence uses the construction *either x or y*; *x* and *y* must be grammatically parallel. In this case, *and spread* must be *or spread.* The antecedent of *which* is unclear; replacing *which results* with *resulting* clarifies the meaning.

A *Either* is incorrectly followed by *and*; *which* has no clear referent.

B *Or spreading* is not parallel to *either become.*

C *With the result of* is wordy and awkward. *Or spreading* is not parallel to *either become.*

D Correct. The phrase *resulting in loss of vigor* concisely modifies the first clause; the either/or construction is correct and parallel in this sentence.

E *Either* is incorrectly followed by *and*; *with a resulting loss* is wordy.

The correct answer is D.

273. In theory, international civil servants at the United Nations are prohibited from continuing to draw salaries from their own governments; in practice, however, some governments merely substitute living allowances <u>for their employees' paychecks, assigned by them</u> to the United Nations.

(A) for their employees' paychecks, assigned by them

(B) for the paychecks of their employees who have been assigned

(C) for the paychecks of their employees, having been assigned

(D) in place of their employees' paychecks, for those of them assigned

(E) in place of the paychecks of their employees to have been assigned by them

Logical predication; Rhetorical construction

It is difficult to tell which parts of this sentence go together because of errors and confusion in the underlined portion. *Living allowances* is the counterpart of *paychecks*, so it is better to say *governments . . . substitute living allowances for the paychecks of their employees* because it makes the substitution clearer. This change also makes it easier to correct the modification error that appears in the phrase *assigned by them*, which incorrectly modifies *paychecks* rather than *employees.* The modifying clause *who have been assigned* clearly describes *employees* and fits into the remaining part of the sentence, *to the United Nations.*

A *Assigned by them* incorrectly and illogically modifies *paychecks.*

B Correct. In this sentence, the meaning is clearer, because *paychecks* is separated from *employees.* The relative clause clearly modifies *employees.*

C *Having been assigned* illogically modifies *governments.*

D The correct construction is *substitutes x for y*, not *substitutes x in place of y.* The construction following *paychecks* is wordy and awkward.

E The correct construction is *substitutes x for y*, not *substitutes x in place of y.* The construction following *employees* is wordy and awkward.

The correct answer is B.

274. Industry analysts said that the recent rise in fuel prices may be an early signal <u>of the possibility of gasoline and heating oil prices staying higher than usually through</u> the end of the year.

(A) of the possibility of gasoline and heating oil prices staying higher than usually through

(B) of the possibility that gasoline and heating oil prices could stay higher than usual throughout

(C) of prices of gasoline and heating oil possibly staying higher than usually through

(D) that prices of gasoline and heating oil could stay higher than they usually are throughout

(E) that prices of gasoline and heating oil will stay higher than usual through

Verb form; Idiom

This sentence describes analysts' prediction about prices for gasoline and heating oil. The speculative nature of the analysts' comments is communicated through the modal verb *may be*, so there is no need to reiterate that idea with the wordy phrase *of the possibility of.* The correct idiom to contrast prices with the norm is *higher than usual*—not *usually*, as written. The correct idiom to indicate the span of time from the present to the end of the year is *through the end of the year.* A simple future tense verb would concisely communicate the analysts' prediction: prices *will stay higher than usual through the end of the year.*

A The unnecessary phrase *of the possibility of* makes the sentence wordy; *higher than usually* is not a proper idiom.

B The unnecessary phrase *of the possibility that* makes the sentence wordy; *throughout the end of the year* is not a proper idiom.

C *Possibly* is redundant with *may* and is not needed to indicate the speculative nature of the prediction; *higher than usually* is not a proper idiom.

D The conditional verb tense *could stay* is incorrect since the modal verb *may* has already introduced the concept of possibility; *throughout the end of the year* is not a proper idiom.

E **Correct.** The simple future tense verb *will stay* expresses the analysts' prediction, and idioms are used correctly.

The correct answer is E.

275. The Anasazi settlements at Chaco Canyon were built on a spectacular scale, with more than 75 carefully engineered structures, of up to 600 rooms each, were connected by a complex regional system of roads.

(A) scale, with more than 75 carefully engineered structures, of up to 600 rooms each, were

(B) scale, with more than 75 carefully engineered structures, of up to 600 rooms each,

(C) scale of more than 75 carefully engineered structures of up to 600 rooms, each that had been

(D) scale of more than 75 carefully engineered structures of up to 600 rooms and with each

(E) scale of more than 75 carefully engineered structures of up to 600 rooms, each had been

Logical predication; Grammatical construction

This sentence makes a claim about the scale (size, extent) of the Anasazi settlements and then illustrates that claim with a description of the settlements' structures. The second part of the sentence, introduced by the preposition *with*, describes the structures first in terms of their rooms and then in terms of the roads that connect them together. To describe the noun *structures*, the participial form *connected* should be used, turning the verb into an adjective.

A The verb *were connected* has no subject, since *structures* is the object of the preposition *with*.

B **Correct.** The sentence is logically coherent and grammatically correct.

C The comma preceding *each* makes *each* a subject, but it has no verb, since *that* is the subject of *had been connected.*

D This sentence suggests that the scale or size of the settlements is made up of structures, rather than uses the structures as an example of the settlements' grand scale; it also nonsensically indicates that each room is connected by a complex system of roads.

E This run-on sentence suffers from a comma splice, as the phrase following the comma is a main clause; the referent of the pronoun *each* is ambiguous.

The correct answer is B.

276. Even though the overall consumer price index did not change in April, indicating the absence of any general inflation or deflation, prices in several categories of merchandise have fallen over the last several months.

(A) April, indicating the absence of any general inflation or deflation, prices in several categories of merchandise have fallen

(B) April, indicating that any general inflation or deflation were absent, prices in several categories of merchandise fell

(C) April and indicated that absence of any general inflation or deflation, prices in several categories of merchandise fell

(D) April, having indicated the absence of any general inflation or deflation, prices in several categories of merchandise fell

(E) April, which indicated that any general inflation or deflation were absent, prices in several categories of merchandise have fallen

Rhetorical construction; Agreement

Coordinated noun phrases in which singular nouns are linked by *or* are considered singular, so when the phrase *any general inflation or deflation* is a subject, it requires a singular verb. One of the answer choices incorrectly uses the word *that*. Another phrasing problem is with *indicating/indicated*. *Indicating* works well as a verb form in the options where it occurs.

A **Correct.** *Any general inflation or deflation* is not a subject (it functions as the object of the preposition *of*), so there is no potential agreement problem.

B *Were* is incorrect as the agreeing form of *be*; it should be *is*.

C If *that* is taken as a demonstrative adjective modifying *absence*, it is inappropriate (the word *the* is required); if it is meant as a subordinating conjunction, it is incorrect because it is not followed by a clause.

D *Having indicated* is unclear and unnecessarily long. It appears to say, somewhat illogically, that the indication occurred at some unspecified time prior to the lack of change in April. *Indicating* works well alone and would be a preferable verb form here.

E *Were* here could only be meant either as a plural past-tense verb or as a singular subjunctive-mood verb (appropriate only in certain conditional contexts); in either case it is incorrect. Also, *indicating* works well, and the *which*-clause is unnecessary.

The correct answer is A.

277. Despite Japan's relative isolation from world trade at the time, the prolonged peace during the Tokugawa shogunate produced an almost explosive expansion of commerce.

(A) Japan's relative isolation from world trade at the time, the prolonged peace during the Tokugawa shogunate

(B) the relative isolation of Japan from world trade at the time and the Tokugawa shogunate's prolonged peace, it

(C) being relatively isolated from world trade at the time, the prolonged peace during Japan's Tokugawa shogunate

(D) Japan's relative isolation from world trade at the time during the Tokugawa shogunate, prolonged peace

(E) its relative isolation from world trade then, prolonged peace in Japan during the Tokugawa shogunate

Logical predication; Rhetorical construction

All predicates must have a clear subject; in this sentence, the logical subject of the verb *produced* is *the prolonged peace*. *During* is a concise way to introduce the relevant time period of this peace (the period of the Tokugawa shogunate); the phrase *at the time* clearly refers to the same time period.

A **Correct.** The subject of *produced* is clearly and logically identified; *during* succinctly provides the time frame.

B The phrase *at the time* leaves it uncertain what time is being referred to. The subject *it* of *produced* does not clearly identify this verb's logical subject, since it is singular yet seems to be intended to refer to two situations previously mentioned, *isolation* and *prolonged peace*.

C *Being relatively isolated* is most likely meant to refer to Japan's isolation, but since grammatically it must modify *the prolonged peace* (the subject of the main clause), the sentence would have an illogical and unintended meaning.

D If *at the time* is to be used instead of *during*, it should be followed by *of*; the better choice is to simply use *during* by itself.

E The use of *then* after *world trade* is awkward and redundant, because *during* later in the sentence supplies the time frame for both Japan's isolation and the period of peace. The structure of the sentence leaves *it(s)* without a clear referent.

The correct answer is A.

278. Government officials announced that restrictions on the use of water would continue because no appreciative increase in the level of the river resulted from the intermittent showers that had fallen throughout the area the day before.

(A) restrictions on the use of water would continue because no appreciative increase in the level of the river

(B) restricting the use of water would continue because there had not been any appreciative increase in the river's level that

(C) the use of water would continue to be restricted because not any appreciable increase in the river's level had

(D) restrictions on the use of water would continue because no appreciable increase in the level of the river had

(E) using water would continue being restricted because not any appreciable increase in the level of the river

Rhetorical construction; Logical predication; Verb form

This sentence explains the rationale behind a governmental announcement made at some point in the past. The most efficient way to express the meaning of the announcement is to use *restrictions* as the subject of the clause introduced by *that* and to use a negative subject (*no appreciable increase*) and a positive verb in the subordinate clause that follows.

A It makes no sense to say that a hypothetical increase in river level is *appreciative*. The past tense of the verb *resulted* in this context does not as clearly express the temporal relationships between the announcement and the other events as would the past perfect *had resulted*.

B The use of *there* and the negative verb make the dependent clause unnecessarily wordy and indirect; the relative pronoun *that* appears to refer nonsensically to *level*. It makes no sense to say that a hypothetical increase in river level is *appreciative*.

C By making *use of water* instead of *restrictions* the subject of the *that* clause, this version of the sentence necessitates the use of a wordy and indirect passive infinitive phrase *to be restricted*. The sentence becomes even more wordy and convoluted with the introduction of an awkward, unidiomatic negative subject (*not any appreciable increase*) of the dependent clause.

D **Correct.** The sentence is direct and efficient, and the past-perfect verb *had resulted* appropriately expresses the sequence of events.

E The phrase *using water . . . being restricted* is wordy and imprecise, and the unidiomatic negative subject (*not any appreciable increase*) of the dependent clause introduces further indirection and wordiness. The past tense of the verb *resulted* in this context does not as clearly express the temporal relationships between the announcement and the other events as would the past perfect *had resulted*.

The correct answer is D.

279. According to United States census data, while there was about one-third of mothers with young children working outside the home in 1975, in 2000, almost two-thirds of those mothers were employed outside the home.

(A) while there was about one-third of mothers with young children working outside the home in 1975, in 2000, almost two-thirds of those mothers were employed outside the home

(B) there were about one-third of mothers with young children who worked outside the home in 1975; in 2000, almost two-thirds of those mothers were employed outside the home

(C) in 1975 about one-third of mothers with young children worked outside the home; in 2000, almost two-thirds of such mothers were employed outside the home

(D) even though in 1975 there were about one-third of mothers with young children who worked outside the home, almost two-thirds of such mothers were employed outside the home in 2000

(E) with about one-third of mothers with young children working outside the home in 1975, almost two-thirds of such mothers were employed outside the home in 2000

Idiom; Logical predication

The sentence presents two pieces of data, one from the 1975 census and one from the 2000 census. It does not attempt to explain a logical relationship beyond the numerical difference. The incorrect versions of the sentence attempt but fail to make a logical connection between the two data (*while . . .* , *even though . . .* , and *with . . .*) and/or introduce unnecessary wordiness with the phrase *there was* or *there were.* The most efficient way to present the two data for reader comparison is in two parallel independent clauses joined by a semicolon. To avoid the confusion of misplaced or *squinting* modifiers, these clauses are best structured with subjects designating percentage of mothers with children, followed by participial phrases that indicate that these mothers *worked* or *were employed* outside the home.

A The phrase *there was* introduces unnecessary wordiness, and the singular verb *was* does not agree with the plural predicate nominative *one-third of mothers with children.* The placement of the modifier *working outside the home* immediately after children suggests that the children rather than the mothers were externally employed.

B *There were* introduces unnecessary wordiness; because of its placement, the relative clause *who worked outside the home* appears to describe children rather than mothers.

C **Correct.** The two pieces of data are presented in parallel independent clauses, joined by a semicolon, allowing the reader to note the numerical difference.

D The introductory phrase *even though* suggests a relationship between the two pieces of data that the sentence does not support; *there were* introduces unnecessary wordiness; *who worked outside the home* appears to describe *young children.*

E The introductory word *with* nonsensically suggests the simultaneity of the two pieces of data; the placement of the modifier *working outside the home* attaches it to *young children* rather than *mothers.*

The correct answer is C.

280. Clouds are formed from the evaporation of the oceans' water that is warmed by the sun and rises high into the atmosphere, condensing in tiny droplets on minute particles of dust.

(A) Clouds are formed from the evaporation of the oceans' water that is warmed by the sun and rises high into the atmosphere, condensing in tiny droplets on minute particles of dust.

(B) Clouds form by the sun's warmth evaporating the water in the oceans, which rises high into the atmosphere, condensing in tiny droplets on minute particles of dust.

(C) Warmed by the sun, ocean water evaporates, rises high into the atmosphere, and condenses in tiny droplets on minute particles of dust to form clouds.

(D) The water in the oceans evaporates, warmed by the sun, rises high into the atmosphere, and condenses in tiny droplets on minute particles of dust, which forms clouds.

(E) Ocean water, warmed by the sun, evaporates and rises high into the atmosphere, which then condenses in tiny droplets on minute particles of dust to form as clouds.

Rhetorical construction; Logical predication

This sentence describes a multistep process by which ocean water is transformed into clouds. These steps are most clearly presented in chronological order, with *ocean water* as the main subject of the sentence.

A This sentence provides no sense of steps and illogically suggests that the oceans' water evaporates after it rises high into the atmosphere.

B The antecedent for the relative pronoun *which* is ambiguous, again suggesting that oceans rise high.

C **Correct.** The sequence of steps in a cloud's formation is clear.

D The nonchronological order of the steps by which clouds are produced is confusing, suggesting that dust forms clouds.

E The relative pronoun *which* grammatically refers to *atmosphere*, creating a nonsensical claim that the atmosphere, rather than the water, condenses.

The correct answer is C.

281. Schistosomiasis, a disease caused by a parasitic worm, is prevalent in hot, humid climates, and it has become more widespread as irrigation projects have enlarged the habitat of the freshwater snails that are the parasite's hosts for part of its life cycle.

(A) the freshwater snails that are the parasite's hosts for part of its life cycle
(B) the freshwater snails that are the parasite's hosts in part of their life cycle
(C) freshwater snails which become the parasite's hosts for part of its life cycles
(D) freshwater snails which become the hosts of the parasite during the parasite's life cycles
(E) parasite's hosts, freshwater snails which become their hosts during their life cycles

Rhetorical construction; Agreement

This sentence explains the increased incidence of schistosomiasis as a consequence of the enlarged habitat of the kind of freshwater snails that host the parasitic worm responsible for the disease. The definite article is necessary before *freshwater snails* because the sentence identifies a particular type of snail, namely, those that host the parasite. The correct preposition to express duration in combination with *host* is *for*, not *in*. As the parasite is referred to as singular, the possessive pronoun in the final phrase must also be singular.

A **Correct.** The sentence is clear with all pronouns and verbs in agreement.

B The preposition *in* is inappropriate for expressing duration; the plural possessive pronoun *their* does not agree with the singular antecedent *parasite*.

C A definite article should precede *freshwater snails* to identify a particular type of snail; the plural *cycles* is inappropriate because *its* refers to a singular parasite, which only has one life cycle.

D A definite article is needed before *freshwater snails*; repetition of the word *parasite* makes the final phrase unnecessarily wordy; *cycles* should be singular.

E The repetition of *hosts* makes the final phrase unnecessarily wordy; *cycles* should be singular; *their hosts* should be *its hosts*; the referent for the second appearance of *their* is unclear—does it refer to *snails* or the *parasite*?

The correct answer is A.

282. Sor Juana Inés de la Cruz was making the case for women's equality long before the cause had a name: Born in the mid-seventeenth century in San Miguel Nepantla, Mexico, the convent was the perfect environment for Sor Juana to pursue intellectual pursuits, achieving renown as a mathematician, poet, philosopher, and playwright.

(A) the convent was the perfect environment for Sor Juana to pursue intellectual pursuits, achieving
(B) Sor Juana found the convent provided the perfect environment for intellectual pursuits, and she went on to achieve
(C) the convent provided the perfect environment for intellectual pursuits for Sor Juana; going on to achieve
(D) Sor Juana found the convent provided the perfect environment for intellectual pursuits; achieving
(E) the convent was, Sor Juana found, the perfect environment for intellectual pursuits, and she went on to achieve

Logical predication; Grammatical construction

This sentence focuses on Sor Juana Inés de la Cruz, but the subject of its second clause is *the convent*. This causes a problem because the predicates *born* and *achieving*, which have only understood subjects, are grammatically paired with *the convent*, an illogical subject. Also, normally where a semicolon is used to mark the end of an independent clause (as in some of the options), it should be followed by another independent clause.

A *The convent* is the subject of the second clause, so both *born* and *achieving* are illogically forced to take it as their subject.

B Correct. *Sor Juana* provides the correct logical subject for *born* and *went on to achieve*; the second clause is correctly introduced by *and*, and is constructed as a full clause with a subject and tensed verb.

C As *the convent* is the subject of the second clause, *born* is illogically forced to take that phrase as its subject. Also, the clause after the semicolon is not an independent full clause with a subject and a tensed verb; *she went on* is required instead of *going on*.

D The clause after the semicolon is not an independent full clause with a subject and a tensed verb: *she achieved* is required instead of *achieving*.

E Since *the convent* is the subject of the second clause, *born* must illogically take that phrase as its subject.

The correct answer is B.

283. By devising an instrument made from a rod, wire, and lead balls, and employing uncommonly precise measurements, in 1797–1798 Henry Cavendish's apparatus enabled him to arrive at an astonishingly accurate figure for the weight of the earth.

(A) By devising an instrument made from a rod, wire, and lead balls, and employing uncommonly precise measurements, in 1797–1798 Henry Cavendish's apparatus enabled him

(B) In 1797–1798, by devising an instrument made from a rod, wire, and lead balls, and employing uncommonly precise measurements, Henry Cavendish's apparatus enabled him

(C) Henry Cavendish devised an instrument made from a rod, wire, and lead balls, and employed uncommonly precise measurements, and in 1797–1798 was able

(D) Having devised an instrument from a rod, wire, and lead balls, and employment of uncommonly precise measurements, Henry Cavendish in 1797–1798 was able

(E) By devising an instrument made from a rod, wire, and lead balls, and employing uncommonly precise measurements, Henry Cavendish was able in 1797–1798

Logical predication; Rhetorical construction

The core of this sentence's idea is either the verb *enable*, which must have its logically correct subject *Henry Cavendish's apparatus*, or *be able*, with the subject *Henry Cavendish*; these subjects must also be able to supply the correct subjects for any other verbs that have understood subjects. The sentence should also clearly express the two things that enabled Cavendish's accomplishment (devising the instrument and employing precise measurement).

A *Devising* needs a subject supplied from elsewhere in the sentence, but the only available subject is the illogical *Henry Cavendish's apparatus* (an apparatus does not "devise" anything).

B *Devising* needs a subject supplied from elsewhere in the sentence, but the only option is the illogical *Henry Cavendish's apparatus*.

C Connecting the three parts of the sentence with two occurrences of *and* is awkward; the first two parts are best connected by *and*, but the final portion expressing what Cavendish achieved would be better expressed, for example, as a new sentence beginning, *In 1797–1798, he employed*.

D This variant seems to suggest, illogically, that Cavendish devised an instrument from several objects plus employment; using *employed* instead of *employment of* would be one way of correctly pairing his two actions.

E Correct. The verbs *devising, employing,* and *was able* have their correct logical subject (*Henry Cavendish*), and the actions of devising and employing are paired clearly, with *by* understood before *employing*.

The correct answer is E.

284. The growth projected for these storms in different computerized weather models varies widely.

(A) projected for these storms in different computerized weather models varies widely
(B) for these storms is projected in different computerized models of weather to vary widely
(C) of these storms, projected in different computerized weather models, vary widely
(D) projected for these storms, which vary widely in different computerized weather models
(E) that varies widely for these storms are projected in different computerized weather models

Logical predication; Agreement

The point of the sentence is that there is great variation in projections of how the storms that it refers to will grow. The structure of the sentence makes it clear that the variation is in the computer models' projections.

A **Correct.** The sentence explains concisely that *growth projected* in different weather models *varies widely.*

B *Growth for these storms* is unidiomatic and unclear. The construction *growth . . . is projected . . . to vary* makes it unclear whether the models project widely varying growth or vary in how much growth they project.

C The construction *growth . . . vary widely* places the variation in the growth of the storms rather than in the projections. The plural verb *vary* does not agree with the singular subject *growth.*

D If *growth projected for these storms* is taken as the subject of the sentence, the subject is not paired with a verb and the sentence is grammatically incomplete.

E The phrase *growth that varies widely* indicates that the variation is in the growth of the storms rather than in the projections. The plural verb *are projected* does not agree with the singular subject *growth.*

The correct answer is A.

285. By using a process called echolocation to analyze the echoes of the high-pitched sounds they produce, bats can determine not only the distance to an object, but they also can determine its shape and size and the direction in which it is moving.

(A) can determine not only the distance to an object, but they also can determine
(B) not only can determine the distance to an object but also
(C) can determine not only the distance to an object but also
(D) not only can determine its distance from an object but also
(E) can determine not only their distance from an object, but they can also determine

Parallelism; Logical predication

This sentence explains that bats' echolocation allows them to determine both the distance to an object and other pieces of information. The correct way to construct this sentence using a correlative conjunction is to follow *not only* and *but also* with the same parts of speech. Using nouns to indicate all the kinds of information bats gain through echolocation provides parallel grammatical structure and concise wording: *not only distance, but also shape, size, and direction.*

A Introducing the second main clause *they also can determine* makes the sentence wordy and disrupts the correct formation of the correlative conjunction *not only, but also.*

B The correlative conjunction is used incorrectly because *not only* is followed by a verb, while *but also* is followed by a list of nouns.

C **Correct.** This sentence concisely uses *not only, but also* to connect a series of nouns.

D The correlative conjunction is used incorrectly because *not only* is followed by a verb, while *but also* is followed by a list of nouns. *Its* most plausibly refers to bats, but on that interpretation the singular pronoun does not agree with its plural antecedent, and the sentence indicates, somewhat implausibly, that the bats use echolocation to determine their own shape, size, and direction of movement. Alternatively, *its* could refer to some other thing that is not named in the sentence, but it is implausible and confusing to say that the bats determine the distance of that unnamed thing from an unspecified object.

E Introducing the second main clause *they also can determine* makes the sentence wordy and disrupts the correct construction to be used with the correlative conjunction: *not only* is followed by a noun, while *but also* is followed by a verb.

The correct answer is C.

286. Carbon dioxide, which traps heat in the atmosphere and helps regulate the planet's surface temperature, is constantly being exchanged between the atmosphere on the one hand and the oceans and terrestrial plants on the other.

(A) exchanged between the atmosphere on the one hand and the oceans and terrestrial plants on the other

(B) exchanged, on the one hand, between the atmosphere and the oceans and terrestrial plants, on the other

(C) exchanged between, on the one hand, the atmosphere, with the oceans and terrestrial plants, on the other

(D) exchanged, on the one hand, among the oceans and terrestrial plants, and the atmosphere, on the other

(E) exchanged among the oceans and terrestrial plants on the one hand and the atmosphere on the other

Parallelism; Idiom

This sentence describes an exchange between the atmosphere and the Earth's surface using the paired phrases *on the one hand* and *on the other.* Preceding both phrases with nouns creates a parallel grammatical structure: *the atmosphere on the one hand and the oceans and terrestrial plants on the other.* Although three locations are mentioned, *between* is the correct preposition to describe the exchange since *the oceans and terrestrial plants* are treated as a set, both members of which are located on the Earth's surface.

A **Correct.** The exchange between the atmosphere and the Earth's surface is expressed using parallel nouns and the paired phrases *on the one hand* and *on the other.*

B The placement of all three nouns between the paired phrases *on the one hand* and *on the other* obscures the nature of the exchange and makes it unclear whether the exchange is among all three of the locations, between the first one and the last two, or between the first two and the last one. *On the one hand* appears to encompass all three of the locations, leaving *on the other* dangling.

C The preposition *with* disrupts the expression of an exchange *between* two locations; the construction *on the one hand* and *on the other* is not in parallel form.

D The preposition *among*, the placement of *and the atmosphere* between commas, and the lack of parallelism make the meaning of this sentence unclear.

E If the relationship is supposed to be among all three of the locations mentioned, the binary relationship indicator (*on the one hand . . . on the other*) makes no sense. Alternatively, *among* could appear to distribute, implicitly, to both sides of the comparison (*among the oceans and terrestrial plants on the one hand and* (among) *the atmosphere on the other*). On that interpretation, *among the atmosphere* makes no sense, because *among* signals a relationship involving multiple entities, but *atmosphere* is a singular noun and is not normally construed as either plural or collective.

The correct answer is A.

287. Floating in the waters of the equatorial Pacific, an array of buoys collects and transmits data on long-term interactions between the ocean and the atmosphere, interactions that affect global climate.

(A) atmosphere, interactions that affect
(B) atmosphere, with interactions affecting
(C) atmosphere that affects
(D) atmosphere that is affecting
(E) atmosphere as affects

Grammatical construction; Agreement

The underlined portion of the sentence is an appositive, a terminal noun phrase restating the kind of data being collected and providing additional information about it. This is a clear and economical way to provide the extra information.

A **Correct.** The sentence is grammatically correct and logically coherent.
B The prepositional phrase *with* . . . has no clear noun or noun phrase to attach to and is therefore ungrammatical.
C Using the restrictive *that* after *atmosphere* illogically suggests that there are many atmospheres to differentiate from and the one in question in this sentence is the one affecting global climate.
D The restrictive *that* also follows *atmosphere* as in answer C.
E The phrase *as affects global climate* functions as an adverb, but there is no verb for it to modify.

The correct answer is A.

288. Sixty-five million years ago, according to some scientists, an asteroid bigger than Mount Everest slammed into North America, which, causing plant and animal extinctions, marks the end of the geologic era known as the Cretaceous Period.

(A) which, causing plant and animal extinctions, marks
(B) which caused the plant and animal extinctions and marks
(C) and causing plant and animal extinctions that mark
(D) an event that caused plant and animal extinctions, which marks
(E) an event that caused the plant and animal extinctions that mark

Logical predication; Agreement

This sentence describes a two-part sequence of events, the second of which has led to a particular categorization of geological time. In order to clarify that it is not the first event (asteroid strike) that produced the time division (end of the Cretaceous Period), but the first event's consequences (biological extinctions), the sentence needs an appositive form to restate the content of the main clause (*an event*), followed by a two-part chain of relative clauses (*that caused . . . that mark . . .*).

A The antecedent for the relative pronoun *which* is ambiguous; it is therefore unclear what *marks* the end of the Cretaceous Period.
B The antecedent of *which* is unclear; the compound verbs *caused* and *marks* fail to indicate that the extinctions, not the asteroid strike, are significant markers of geological time.
C Following the conjunction *and* with a participial rather than a main verb is grammatically incorrect because it violates parallelism and produces a fragment at the end of the sentence.
D *Which*, referring to *extinctions*, should be followed by a plural verb.
E **Correct.** The sentence is unambiguous, and the verbs agree with their subjects.

The correct answer is E.

289. Although the first pulsar, or rapidly spinning collapsed star, to be sighted was in the summer of 1967 by graduate student Jocelyn Bell, it had not been announced until February 1968.

(A) Although the first pulsar, or rapidly spinning collapsed star, to be sighted was in the summer of 1967 by graduate student Jocelyn Bell, it had not been announced until February 1968.

(B) Although not announced until February 1968, in the summer of 1967 graduate student Jocelyn Bell observed the first pulsar, or rapidly spinning collapsed star, to be sighted.

(C) Although observed by graduate student Jocelyn Bell in the summer of 1967, the discovery of the first sighted pulsar, or rapidly spinning collapsed star, had not been announced before February 1968.

(D) The first pulsar, or rapidly spinning collapsed star, to be sighted was observed in the summer of 1967 by graduate student Jocelyn Bell, but the discovery was not announced until February 1968.

(E) The first sighted pulsar, or rapidly spinning collapsed star, was not announced until February 1968, while it was observed in the summer of 1967 by graduate student Jocelyn Bell.

Verb form; Logical predication; Rhetorical construction

This sentence presents conditions that are followed by an unexpected outcome: a delayed announcement of the discovery of a pulsar. A compound sentence using a coordinating conjunction *but* is an effective way to present the conditions of the first pulsar sighting and then information about the subsequent announcement of the discovery. The sentence must clarify that it is not about *the first pulsar*, but *the first pulsar . . . to be sighted*. The verbs in the sentence must all be in past tense; using a past-perfect verb to present information about the announcement of the discovery indicates that this announcement illogically took place before the pulsar was first sighted.

A The subject of the opening dependent clause is *pulsar*, and the verb is *was*. The clause needs to indicate not just that the pulsar existed but that it was observed by Bell; the past-perfect verb tense is inappropriate in the concluding clause.

B The opening participial phrase functions as an adjective, but it has no logical noun or noun phrase to attach to; Bell herself was not announced in 1968.

C Grammatically, the opening participial phrase describes the first noun that follows, but it makes no sense to say that *the discovery* of the pulsar was *observed*; *discovery of the first sighted pulsar* is also imprecise; one does not discover a first sighting.

D Correct. The sentence presents the sequence of events clearly and in the past tense.

E This sentence presents events in a way that is confusing; as a conjunction, *while* indicates simultaneous events, but this sentence is about events that occurred in a sequence.

The correct answer is D.

290. Sound can travel through water for enormous distances, prevented from dissipating its acoustic energy as a result of boundaries in the ocean created by water layers of different temperatures and densities.

(A) prevented from dissipating its acoustic energy as a result of

(B) prevented from having its acoustic energy dissipated by

(C) its acoustic energy prevented from dissipating by

(D) its acoustic energy prevented from being dissipated as a result of

(E) preventing its acoustic energy from dissipating by

Logical predication; Rhetorical construction

This sentence opens with a statement that sound can travel long distances through water and then explains why that is so: water layers in the ocean prevent acoustic energy from dissipating. Because *dissipating* is an intransitive verb, *acoustic energy* cannot be its object.

A *Dissipating* is not a transitive verb, so *acoustic energy* cannot function as its object.

B This version of the sentence is wordy, awkward, and indirect; *from having . . . by* erroneously suggests that the boundaries in the ocean are attempting to dissipate sound energy.

C Correct. Here, *acoustic energy* is effectively modified by the participial *prevented from dissipating. . . .*

D This version of the sentence is wordy, awkward, and indirect; *being dissipated as a result of* makes it unclear whether the boundaries contribute to energy loss or prevent it.

E This version of the sentence nonsensically explains that sound prevents the dissipation of its own energy.

The correct answer is C.

291. Last year, land values in most parts of the pinelands rose almost so fast, and in some parts even faster than what they did outside the pinelands.

(A) so fast, and in some parts even faster than what they did

(B) so fast, and in some parts even faster than, those

(C) as fast, and in some parts even faster than, those

(D) as fast as, and in some parts even faster than, those

(E) as fast as, and in some parts even faster than what they did

Idiom; Parallelism

This sentence says *x* rose *almost so fast y*, which is not a correct idiomatic construction; *x* rose *almost as fast as y* is the correct idiom for this comparison. The two elements being compared, *x* and *y*, must be parallel, but the noun *land values* (*x*) is not parallel to *what they did* (*y*). *Land values* in the pinelands (*x*) must be compared with *those* (the pronoun correctly replacing *land values*) outside the pinelands (*y*).

A *So fast* is used instead of *as fast. What they did* is not parallel to *land values.*

B *So fast* is not the correct idiom for comparison.

C *As fast* must be followed by *as* in this comparison.

D **Correct.** *As fast as* is the correct comparative conjunction used in this sentence; *those* is parallel to *land values.*

E *What they did* is not parallel to *land values.*

The correct answer is D.

292. The North American moose's long legs enable it to move quickly through the woods, stepping easily over downed trees, but predators pursuing it must leap or go around them.

(A) moose's long legs enable it to move quickly through the woods, stepping easily over downed trees, but predators pursuing it must leap or go around them

(B) moose's long legs enable it to move quickly through the woods, stepping easily over downed trees while predators pursuing them must leap or go around

(C) moose's long legs enable it to move quickly through the woods and to step easily over downed trees, but predators pursuing them must leap over or go around them

(D) moose has long legs, enabling it to move quickly through the woods and to step easily over downed trees while predators pursuing them must leap or go around

(E) moose has long legs that enable it to move quickly through the woods, stepping easily over downed trees while predators pursuing it must leap over or go around them

Logical predication; Agreement

This sentence explains the advantages of long legs to the North American moose. Since the sentence contains multiple relationships among pronouns, nouns, and modifiers, it is important that the various elements be clearly connected. The structure of the sentence makes it unclear whether *stepping easily over downed trees* is intended to modify the main subject, *the North American moose's long legs*, or the pronoun *it*. Although *it* presumably refers to *the North American moose*, it does so only obliquely, because *moose* does not appear in noun form in the sentence. The best way to construct this sentence is to make *moose* the subject of the main clause so that both occurrences of *it* have a clear antecedent. Because *stepping easily over them* is set off by commas from the preceding and ensuing clauses and because the apparently intransitive verb *leap* intervenes between *downed trees* and *them*, it is unclear whether *them* refers to the moose's legs or the downed trees. The phrase *leap or go around them* should say *leap over*, because the point is that the predators must either leap over the downed trees (or go around them), not merely that the predators leap in the air or else go around the trees.

A The function of *stepping easily over downed trees* is unclear in relation to the rest of the sentence. The pronoun *it* refers only obliquely and unclearly to *moose*, because only the possessive form *moose's* appears in the sentence. Furthermore, the final phrase should say *leap over*, not merely *leap*.

B The function of *stepping easily over downed trees* is unclear in relation to the rest of the sentence. The pronoun *it* refers only obliquely and unclearly to *moose*, because only the possessive form *moose's* appears in the sentence. The plural pronoun *them* has no logical plural antecedent (surely the predators are not pursuing the moose's legs, but the moose itself; nor are the predators pursuing the downed trees). Furthermore, the final phrase should say *leap over*, not merely *leap*.

C The plural pronoun *them* in *pursuing them* has no logical plural antecedent.

D The plural pronoun *them* has no logical plural antecedent (*moose* can be used as a plural, but because in this sentence the singular verb *has* is used, *moose* must be construed as being singular here). Furthermore, the final phrase should say *leap over*, not merely *leap*.

E **Correct.** The pronoun *it* refers to *moose*, and the pronoun *them* refers to *trees*. Also, the final phrase correctly says *leap over or go around them*.

The correct answer is E.

293. Early administrative decisions in China's Ming Dynasty eventually caused a drastic fall in tax revenues, a reduction in military preparedness, <u>the collapse of the currency system, and failed</u> to make sufficient investment in vital transportation infrastructure.

(A) the collapse of the currency system, and failed

(B) the collapse of the currency system, and failing

(C) and the collapse of the currency system, also failed

(D) the collapse of the currency system, as well as failing

(E) and the collapse of the currency system, as well as a failure

Parallelism; Grammatical construction; Rhetorical construction

The sentence provides a list of effects stemming from administrative decisions in the Ming Dynasty. To make the meaning clear, all items in the list should be in parallel grammatical form. The first three are noun phrases—*a drastic fall*, *a reduction*, and *the collapse*—but the final item, *failed*, is a verb. To preserve parallel structure, the fourth item should also be a noun phrase: *a failure*. An alternative interpretation might take *failed* as parallel with *caused*, so that *decisions* is the subject of both verbs, but it is illogical to say that the *decisions* failed to make sufficient investments.

A The list of effects is not parallel since the first three items are noun phrases but the fourth is the verb *failed*. An alternative interpretation might take *failed* as parallel with *caused*, so that *decisions* is the subject of both verbs, but it is illogical to say that the *decisions* failed to make sufficient investments.

B The list of effects is not parallel since the first three items are noun phrases but the fourth is the participle *failing*.

C The list of three effects is followed by the verb *failed*, which lacks a subject, thus making the sentence ungrammatical.

D The list of effects is not parallel since the first three items are noun phrases but the fourth is the participle *failing*.

E **Correct.** The list of four effects is expressed in parallel grammatical form using noun phrases, including *a failure*.

The correct answer is E.

294. Seismologists studying the earthquake that struck northern California in October 1989 are still investigating some of its mysteries: the unexpected power of the seismic waves, the upward thrust that threw one man straight into the air, and the strange electromagnetic signals detected hours before the temblor.

(A) the upward thrust that threw one man straight into the air, and the strange electromagnetic signals detected hours before the temblor

(B) the upward thrust that threw one man straight into the air, and strange electromagnetic signals were detected hours before the temblor

(C) the upward thrust threw one man straight into the air, and hours before the temblor strange electromagnetic signals were detected

(D) one man was thrown straight into the air by the upward thrust, and hours before the temblor strange electromagnetic signals were detected

(E) one man who was thrown straight into the air by the upward thrust, and strange electromagnetic signals that were detected hours before the temblor

Parallelism; Grammatical construction

Some of the earthquake's *mysteries* are described in a series of three correctly parallel elements: (1) *the unexpected power* . . . , (2) *the upward thrust* . . . , and (3) *the strange electromagnetic signals*. . . . Each of the three elements begins with an article (*the*), a modifier, and a noun. This parallelism is crucial, but each mystery is allowed the further modification most appropriate to it, whether a prepositional phrase (1), a clause (2), or a participial phrase (3).

A **Correct.** This sentence correctly provides a parallel series of three mysteries.

B *The* is omitted before *strange*. The verb *were detected* makes the last element not parallel to the previous two.

C Because they use complete independent clauses, the last two elements are not parallel to the first, and the sentence is ungrammatical.

D The constructions beginning *one man* and *hours before* are not parallel to the construction beginning *the unexpected power*.

E The grammatical constructions describing the mysteries are not parallel.

The correct answer is A.

295. The type of behavior exhibited when an animal recognizes itself in a mirror comes within the domain of "theory of mind," thus is best studied as part of the field of animal cognition.

(A) of "theory of mind," thus is best

(B) "theory of mind," and so is best to be

(C) of a "theory of mind," thus it is best

(D) of "theory of mind" and thus is best

(E) of the "theory of mind," and so it is best to be

Grammatical construction; Idiom

This sentence links two independent clauses; in such sentences, the clauses must normally be set off from each other (by a semicolon, for example), or else the second clause must be introduced by *and* or some other conjunction, not merely an adverb like *thus*. Also, a noun like *domain* normally is followed by the preposition *of* immediately preceding the noun phrase describing the domain.

A The second clause incorrectly lacks an introducing conjunction.

B The phrasing *is best to be studied* is awkwardly unusual and unidiomatic; *is best studied* is a better choice.

C The second clause incorrectly lacks an introducing conjunction. The phrase *a "theory of mind"* would refer to one particular theory rather than (as intended) to a theoretical domain.

D **Correct.** *And* introduces the second clause, which uses the concise wording *best studied*.

E The beginning of the second clause is redundant and wordy: the word *and* is unnecessary because the conjunction *so* is used, and *best to be studied* is unidiomatic.

The correct answer is D.

296. Unlike the United States, where farmers can usually depend on rain or snow all year long, the rains in most parts of Sri Lanka are concentrated in the monsoon months, June to September, and the skies are generally clear for the rest of the year.

(A) Unlike the United States, where farmers can usually depend on rain or snow all year long, the rains in most parts of Sri Lanka

(B) Unlike the United States farmers who can usually depend on rain or snow all year long, the rains in most parts of Sri Lanka

(C) Unlike those of the United States, where farmers can usually depend on rain or snow all year long, most parts of Sri Lanka's rains

(D) In comparison with the United States, whose farmers can usually depend on rain or snow all year long, the rains in most parts of Sri Lanka

(E) In the United States, farmers can usually depend on rain or snow all year long, but in most parts of Sri Lanka, the rains

Logical predication; Rhetorical construction

The intent of the sentence is to compare seasonal rainfall patterns in the United States and Sri Lanka. There are many ways to set up such comparisons: *unlike x, y*; *in comparison with x, y*; *compared to x, y*; and so on. The *x* and *y* being compared must be grammatically and logically parallel. An alternative way of stating the comparison is the use of two independent clauses connected by *but*. The original sentence compares *the United States* to *the rains in most parts of Sri Lanka*; this illogical comparison cannot convey the writer's intention.

A This sentence illogically compares *the United States* to *the rains in most parts of Sri Lanka.*

B Comparing *United States farmers* to *the rains in most parts of Sri Lanka* is not logical.

C The sentence awkwardly and illogically seems to be comparing most parts of the United States with *most parts of Sri Lanka's rains.*

D This sentence compares *the United States* and *the rains in most parts of Sri Lanka.*

E **Correct.** This sentence uses two independent clauses to make the comparison. The first clause describes conditions in the United States, and the second clause describes conditions in Sri Lanka. The comparison is clear and logical.

The correct answer is E.

297. In preparation for the prediction of a major earthquake that will hit the state, a satellite-based computer network is being built by the California Office of Emergency Services for identifying earthquake damage and to pinpoint the most affected areas within two hours of the event.

(A) In preparation for the prediction of a major earthquake that will hit the state, a satellite-based computer network is being built by the California Office of Emergency Services for identifying

(B) In preparing for the prediction that a major earthquake will hit the state, the California Office of Emergency Services is building a satellite-based computer network that will identify

(C) In preparing for a major earthquake that is predicted to hit the state, the California Office of Emergency Services is building a satellite-based computer network to identify

(D) To prepare for the prediction of a major earthquake hitting the state, a satellite-based computer network is being built by the California Office of Emergency Services to identify

(E) To prepare for a major earthquake that is predicted to hit the state, the California Office of Emergency Services is building a satellite-based computer network that will identify

Logical predication; Parallelism

This sentence explains what the California Office of Emergency Services is doing to prepare for an earthquake that has been predicted for the state, but the sentence appears to claim that the California Office is doing these things to prepare for the prediction. The two purposes of these preparations should be presented in parallel form, but the sentence as written presents one as a prepositional phrase (*for identifying*) and the other as an infinitive (*to pinpoint*).

A In this version of the sentence, the opening phrase illogically claims that the California Office is preparing for a prediction, but later in the sentence it becomes clear that the preparations are targeted to the aftermath of a possible earthquake, not its prediction. The two purposes of the preparations are not presented in parallel form.

B Like (A), this version of the sentence identifies preparations for a prediction rather than an earthquake; the two purposes of the preparations are not presented in parallel form.

C **Correct.** The preparations are correctly presented as being for an earthquake, and the two purposes of the preparations are presented in parallel form (*to identify* and *to pinpoint*).

D As in (A) and (B), the beginning of this sentence is inconsistent with the rest of it. The opening phrase claims to describe preparations for a prediction, whereas the latter part of the sentence indicates that the preparations are for a predicted earthquake.

E Like (A) and (B), this sentence does not present the two purposes of the preparations in parallel form.

The correct answer is C.

298. Once numbering in the millions worldwide, it is estimated that the wolf has declined to 200,000 in 57 countries, some 11,000 of them to be found in the lower 48 United States and Alaska.

(A) it is estimated that the wolf has declined to 200,000 in 57 countries, some

(B) the wolf is estimated to have declined to 200,000 in 57 countries, with approximately

(C) the wolf has declined to an estimate of 200,000 in 57 countries, some

(D) wolves have declined to an estimate of 200,000 in 57 countries, with approximately

(E) wolves have declined to an estimated 200,000 in 57 countries, some

Logical predication; Idiom

The predicate *numbered* must have its logically correct subject, which is *wolves.* Although *the wolf* can be used to refer collectively to wolves as a category, the noun should be plural in this case since the sentence refers to numbers of them and since agreement is needed between the noun and the plural pronoun *them*. Given the plural subject, the verb in the independent clause should be *have declined*. The object of *decline to* should be a word or phrase naming a number or estimated number (e.g., a phrase such as *an estimated 200,000*), not the phrase *an estimate*.

A The subject of the main clause (*it*) seems to supply the subject of *numbering*, so the latter does not have its correct logical subject, which should be a word or phrase referring to wolves.

B *The wolf* cannot correctly be taken as the subject of *numbering*, as it is singular and in disagreement with *them* occurring later in the sentence.

C *The wolf* cannot correctly be taken as the subject of *numbering*, as it is singular and disagrees with the later *them*; also, a decline is strictly speaking to a number, not to *an estimate*.

D Although *wolves* is a correct subject for *numbering*, a decline should be to a number, not to *an estimate*.

E **Correct.** *Wolves* is a proper subject for *numbering* and agrees with the later *them*. The decline is correctly said to be to a number, *an estimated 200,000*.

The correct answer is E.

299. As business grows more complex, students majoring in specialized areas like those of finance and marketing have been becoming increasingly successful in the job market.

(A) majoring in specialized areas like those of finance and marketing have been becoming increasingly

(B) who major in such specialized areas as finance and marketing are becoming more and more

(C) who majored in specialized areas such as those of finance and marketing are being increasingly

(D) who major in specialized areas like those of finance and marketing have been becoming more and more

(E) having majored in such specialized areas as finance and marketing are being increasingly

Verb form; Diction

The subordinate clause *as business grows more complex* uses the present-tense verb *grows* to describe an ongoing situation. The main clause describes an effect of this growing complexity; the verbs in the main clause should also use present-tense verbs. The present perfect progressive *have been becoming* is incorrect. The preferred way to introduce examples is with the phrase *such as*, rather than with the word *like*, which suggests a comparison.

A *Like* should be replaced by *such as*. *Have been becoming* is an incorrect verb tense.

B Correct. In this sentence, *major* and *are becoming* are present-tense verbs; *such . . . as* is the preferred form for introducing examples.

C *Majored* is a past-tense verb; *those of* is unnecessary and awkward. *Becoming* is preferable to *being* for describing an unfolding pattern of events.

D *Like* should be replaced by *such as*. *Those of* is unnecessary and awkward. *Have been becoming* is an incorrect verb tense.

E *Having majored* is an awkward past participle. *Becoming* is preferable to *being* for describing an unfolding pattern of events.

The correct answer is B.

300. Created in 1945 to reduce poverty and stabilize foreign currency markets, the World Bank and the International Monetary Fund have, according to some critics, continually struggled to meet the expectations of their major shareholders—a group comprising many of the world's rich nations—but neglected their intended beneficiaries in the developing world.

(A) continually struggled to meet the expectations of their major shareholders—a group comprising many of the world's rich nations—but neglected

(B) continually struggled as they try to meet the expectations of their major shareholders—a group comprising many of the world's rich nations—while neglecting that of

(C) continually struggled to meet their major shareholders' expectations—a group comprising many of the world's rich nations—but neglected that of

(D) had to struggle continually in trying to meet the expectations of their major shareholders—a group comprising many of the world's rich nations—while neglecting that of

(E) struggled continually in trying to meet their major shareholders' expectations—a group comprising many of the world's rich nations—and neglecting

Idiom; Verb form

This sentence describes a contradiction some critics have ascribed to the actions and policies of both the World Bank and the International Monetary Fund: although they were created to address poverty in the developing world, they struggled to meet their major shareholders' expectations and neglected their intended beneficiaries. The contradiction is best expressed by joining the two past-tense verbs *struggled to meet* . . . and *neglected* . . . with the contrasting conjunction *but*. The appositive phrase set off with dashes must immediately follow the noun it defines (*shareholders*).

A Correct. The conjunction *but* accurately describes the contradiction between what the organizations did for their major shareholders and what they did not do for their intended beneficiaries, and the appositive clearly defines the immediately preceding noun, *shareholders*.

B The present tense of *as they try to meet* is inconsistent with the rest of the verbs in the sentence. The pronoun *that* seems to have no referent in the phrase *while neglecting that of* . . . since the only likely antecedent *expectations* is plural.

C The appositive grammatically but nonsensically describes expectations rather than shareholders; as in (B), the pronoun *that* does not agree in number with its likely antecedent *expectations*.

D Like (B), this version is unnecessarily wordy, and like (C), it introduces the pronoun *that*, which disagrees in number with the antecedent *expectations*.

E As in (C), the appositive seems to define *expectations* rather than *shareholders*, and the conjunction *and* fails to capture the contradictory relationship between the organizations' actions toward their shareholders and their intended beneficiaries.

The correct answer is A.

301. Unlike auto insurance, the frequency of claims does not affect the premiums for personal property coverage, but if the insurance company is able to prove excessive loss due to owner negligence, it may decline to renew the policy.

(A) Unlike auto insurance, the frequency of claims does not affect the premiums for personal property coverage,

(B) Unlike with auto insurance, the frequency of claims do not affect the premiums for personal property coverage,

(C) Unlike the frequency of claims for auto insurance, the premiums for personal property coverage are not affected by the frequency of claims,

(D) Unlike the premiums for auto insurance, the premiums for personal property coverage are not affected by the frequency of claims,

(E) Unlike with the premiums for auto insurance, the premiums for personal property coverage is not affected by the frequency of claims,

Logical predication; Agreement

The sentence has been written so that *auto insurance* is contrasted with *the frequency of claims*. The correct contrast is between *the premiums for auto insurance and the premiums for personal property coverage.*

A *Auto insurance* is illogically contrasted with *the frequency of claims.*

B *Unlike with* is an incorrect idiom; *auto insurance* is contrasted with *the frequency of claims;* the singular subject *frequency* does not agree with the plural verb *do.*

C *The frequency of claims* is contrasted with *the premiums for personal property coverage.*

D **Correct.** The contrast between *the premiums for auto insurance* and *the premiums for personal property coverage* is clearly and correctly stated in this sentence.

E *Unlike with* is an incorrect idiom; the plural subject *premiums* does not agree with the singular verb *is not affected.*

The correct answer is D.

Appendix A Answer Sheets

Reading Comprehension Answer Sheet

1.
2.
3.
4.
5.
6.
7.
8.
9.
10.
11.
12.
13.
14.
15.
16.
17.
18.
19.
20.
21.
22.
23.
24.
25.
26.
27.
28.
29.
30.
31.
32.
33.
34.
35.
36.
37.
38.
39.
40.
41.
42.
43.
44.
45.
46.
47.
48.
49.
50.
51.
52.
53.
54.
55.
56.
57.
58.
59.
60.
61.
62.
63.
64.
65.
66.
67.
68.
69.
70.
71.
72.
73.
74.
75.
76.
77.
78.
79.
80.
81.
82.
83.
84.
85.
86.
87.
88.
89.
90.
91.
92.
93.
94.
95.
96.
97.
98.
99.
100.
101.
102.
103.
104.
105.

Critical Reasoning Answer Sheet

106.
107.
108.
109.
110.
111.
112.
113.
114.
115.
116.
117.
118.
119.
120.
121.
122.
123.
124.
125.
126.
127.
128.
129.
130.
131.
132.
133.
134.
135.
136.
137.
138.
139.
140.
141.
142.
143.
144.
145.
146.
147.
148.
149.
150.
151.
152.
153.
154.
155.
156.
157.
158.
159.
160.
161.
162.
163.
164.
165.
166.
167.
168.
169.
170.
171.
172.
173.
174.
175.
176.
177.
178.
179.
180.
181.
182.
183.
184.
185.
186.
187.
188.

Sentence Correction Answer Sheet

189.
190.
191.
192.
193.
194.
195.
196.
197.
198.
199.
200.
201.
202.
203.
204.
205.
206.
207.
208.
209.
210.
211.
212.
213.
214.
215.
216.
217.
218.
219.
220.
221.
222.
223.
224.
225.
226.
227.
228.
229.
230.
231.
232.
233.
234.
235.
236.
237.
238.
239.
240.
241.
242.
243.
244.
245.
246.
247.
248.
249.
250.
251.
252.
253.
254.
255.
256.
257.
258.
259.
260.
261.
262.
263.
264.
265.
266.
267.
268.
269.
270.
271.
272.
273.
274.
275.
276.
277.
278.
279.
280.
281.
282.
283.
284.
285.
286.
287.
288.
289.
290.
291.
292.
293.
294.
295.
296.
297.
298.
299.
300.
301.

Notes

Notes

Notes

Notes

Notes